MARIA CALLAS

Also by Anne Edwards

Biography
Sonya: The Life of Countess Tolstoy
Vivien Leigh: A Biography
Judy Garland: A Biography
Road to Tara: The Life of Margaret Mitchell
Matriarch: Queen Mary and the House of Windsor
A Remarkable Woman: A Biography of Katharine Hepburn
(UK title *Katharine Hepburn: A Biography*)
Early Reagan: The Rise to Power
Shirley Temple: American Princess
The DeMilles: An American Family
Royal Sisters: Elizabeth and Margaret
The Grimaldis of Monaco: Centuries of Scandal/Years of Grace
Throne of Gold: The Lives of the Aga Khans
Streisand
Ever After: Diana and the Life She Led
(UK title *Diana and the Rise of the House of Spencer*)

Novels
The Survivors
Shadow of a Lion
Haunted Summer
Miklos Alexandrovitch Is Missing
The Hesitant Heart
Child of Night (UK title *Raven Wings*)
La Divina
Wallis: The Novel

Autobiography
The Inn and Us (with Stephen Citron)

Children's Books
P. T. Barnum
The Great Houdini
A Child's Bible

MARIA CALLAS

An Intimate Biography

ANNE EDWARDS

 St. Martin's Griffin ⚜ New York

FOR STEPHEN CITRON
my muse, my love

www.stmartins.com

Library of Congress Cataloging-in-Publication Data

Edwards, Anne, 1927–
   Maria Callas : An intimate biography / Anne Edwards.
     p. cm.
   Includes bibliographical references (pp. 329–331) and index.
   ISBN 0-312-26986-2 (hc)
   ISBN 0-312-31002-1 (pbk)
   1. Callas, Maria, 1923–1977. 2. Sopranos (Singers)—Biography. I. Title.

ML420.C18 E33 2003
782.1'092—dc21
[B]   2002024518

First published in Great Britain under the title *Callas* by Weidenfeld & Nicolson

First St. Martin's Griffin Edition: February 2003

10 9 8 7 6 5 4 3 2 1

Contents

Illustrations

Maria holds a press conference the day of her Greek divorce from
  Meneghini (*Performing Arts Library*)
The two battling divas, Callas and Tibaldi (*Photofest*)
Maria being greeted by Lawrence Kelly in Dallas (*Andrew Hanson*)
Franco Zeffirelli (*Andrew Hanson*)
Onassis with Presidential widow, Jackie Kennedy (*Photofest*)
Maria following Onassis' wedding to Jackie Kennedy (*Camera Press*)
Maria in Greece in 1970 where she met Onassis secretly (*Photofest*)
Maria and Franco Rossellini on the set of *Medea* (*Photofest*)
With Giuseppe de Stefano (*Camera Press*)
A standing ovation from the audience in Dallas (*Photofest*)
Vasso Devitzi with Maria's boxed ashes (*Private Collection*)
On board the boat that would carry her ashes out to sea (*Private
  Collection*)

'Callas's *Tosca* [at the Royal Opera House] is superb. All that we look for – the beauty, the quickness of response, the womanliness, the sudden flares and flickers over her steady love, the anguish, the courage – all are there. And so is something else which cannot be defined – it has to do with bearing and gesture, and timbre, and phrasing, and utterance of the words, all combined – the mysterious qualities which not only make her Callas, but also make every heroine she portrays distinct and indelible.'

Andrew Porter *Financial Times*, 22 January 1964

Acknowledgements

F OR A LARGE part of my university life I was a music major, a daring choice on my part because I had no specific musical talent which was promising enough to pursue a career in that field, although I had some glimmering dreams of becoming a composer. The written word won out: my love for it, and my need to express myself in the fullest way possible turned me on to the path I have fortunately, and most happily, taken. My love of music, of opera, and of the great singers who have brought them alive for me, has remained and often sustained me.

Although I had numerous recordings of Maria Callas, the first time I saw her live on a stage was in 1964 at the Royal Opera House, Covent Garden, London, in the role of Tosca. I was stunned. Here was a singer who deeply understood not only the music she sang but the words, and the person she was portraying. If, perhaps, Callas did not have the greatest voice of the twentieth century, she was opera's greatest bel canto interpreter. She changed opera as it was performed forever. It is tragic that she died so young, amid so much controversy; that no opera was ever written directly for her; and that so few of her performances were captured on film.

Equally tragic was her life – a grand, passionate opera played out in reality. But above all, Callas was a flesh and blood woman: fascinating, bold, a sort of Cinderella who willed herself to be her own fairy godmother. I have tried to bring the real Maria Callas to life on these pages. I would like to express my thanks to all who have helped me in one way or another. A biographer does not work alone. Good, conscientious people have contributed a guiding hand along the way. Many I have noted in the text. But I would be disregardful if I did not repeat my gratitude to the previous works on Maria Callas by the late John Ardoin, to whom any and all music lovers also owe a great debt.

I am especially grateful to Robert Sutherland, Callas's fine accompanist for his assistance, to the more than one hundred friends and members of the families who were her close associates in Athens (and helped me to reconstruct the war years), New York, Verona, Rome, Milan, and Dallas – all of whom contributed so much with their memories and vivid recall, to the knowledgeable staffs of the British Library, The Library of the City of New York, Lincoln Center Library, The Museum of Broadcasting (New York), and the archivists at the Metropolitan Opera and Royal Opera Houses.

My gratitude extends further to my enthusiastic English editor, Ion Trewin, and to Hope Dellon and Sally Richardson in the United States; to the sustained interest of my agent, Mitch Douglas whose vast personal record collection produced some fantastic Maria Callas interviews and performances; and to Terence McCarthy who has aided me in my research with so many of my former biographies and proved indispensable on this one as well.

My husband, Stephen Citron, is a known biographer in his own field – the musical theatre. He is also a fine musician and lifelong devotee of opera with an encyclopedic knowledge of it that was graciously shared with and was invaluable to me. This time, as always, he has been my greatest source of encouragement.

1

New York City: 1923–1937

UNLIKE THE OTHER Greek immigrants on the huge ship taking them from Athens to New York City, George and Evangelia Dimitriadis Kalogeropoulos and their six-year-old daughter, Yacinthy (Jackie) occupied a cabin in the first-class section. Mrs Kalogeropoulos's Persian lamb coat hung in the small wardrobe alongside two formal gowns she had brought with her. Packed in the steamer trunk in the hold of the ship were her silver candlesticks, tableware, icons and lace dinner cloths. Litza, as the five-months-pregnant Mrs Kalogeropoulos was familiarly known, was not going to arrive in a foreign land as a poor, dispossessed refugee. Coming to America had been her husband's idea and he had sold all their assets to finance their move before consulting her. Young and headstrong (only twenty-five at the time), she had fought bitterly in an attempt to get him to reverse his decision. George refused and, if she had not been carrying their child, she would have kept Jackie and remained with her family.

'My family have always been at the front of things,' she would proudly repeat to her young daughter. 'Your grandfather, my father, was a general, God rest him, as was your great-grandfather Dimitrios Dimitriadis. Your great-uncle Kostas Louros was the king's physician and I...' She would sigh, her surprisingly blue, expressive eyes suddenly filled with resentment, 'I married a pharmacist.'

Litza was only seventeen when a cousin introduced her to the rather dashing-looking George Kalogeropoulos who, though nearly twice her age, had just graduated from the School of Pharmacy at the University of Athens. A handsome man with auburn hair, a roguish moustache and a gleam in his well-set dark eyes, George was intrigued by her youth, her energy and her prestigious background. He came from the small town of Meligala in the Peloponnese and his family was poor. For many years he had been employed as a pharmaceutical assistant in a chemist's shop in

Meligala, the only pharmacy in thirteen counties and an exceptionally successful business. The owner, an elderly man, had offered to sell it to him if he could get his degree. This was what George had been working towards and saving penuriously for. Now his dream was about to be realized.

Shortly after Litza and George met, her beloved father, General Petros Dimitriadis, died suddenly of a stroke. George was filled with compassion. The lively, beautiful young girl he had known was in visible distress and unusually vulnerable. Her father had been the most important person in her life. Nothing had been too good, or too difficult to obtain if it was for 'his Litza', the youngest of his eleven children. Litza found George a comforting substitute and on 7 August 1916, two weeks after her father's death, they were married in a small private service in the Greek Orthodox Church, the bridegroom anxious to return to his new position as owner of the chemist's shop and the bride happy to find an escape from the deep mourning in the Dimitriadis household. Her family were horrified that Litza would not wait out a proper mourning period and her brothers warned her that George had a roving eye. Strong-willed as always, and with George's reassurance that she would have a house and a maid when they married, she could not be deterred. She wore a plain, white, unadorned gown out of respect for her father and there was no wedding reception. One brother, who had accused her of being pregnant, was haughtily excluded by her from the ceremony.

The wedding couple spent a week on the small island of Aegina, which was a short ferry ride from Piraeus, before going to Meligala. The home George had promised her was actually two floors over the pharmacy and was connected by a staircase that led from the first floor to the entrance of the shop. Litza was disappointed but there was compensation: not only would she have a maid but she could redecorate the upper two storeys. Doubts of her wisdom in marrying George set in almost immediately. In Athens she had seen only his charming side, how well he looked and carried himself. Now, she realized that they came from unrelated worlds; could she ever be happy living in his more prosaic one?

Although not wealthy, the Dimitriadis family were considered upper-middle-class and were of patrician heritage. They had produced some fine musicians along with army officers and political figures. One brother, who unfortunately had committed suicide over a lost lover, had been a rising poet. The Dimitriadises' claim to culture was of great pride to Litza. She was 'fanatical about anything to do with the stage', liked to display her musical knowledge and to discuss the well-known artists she had met. Meligala had little to offer of either an intellectual or an artistic nature. Litza managed to drag George away from the pharmacy to the coastal city of Kalamata, where there was a theatre visited by touring companies. Secretly, she harboured dreams of one day going on the stage herself. It was not an unusual ambition for a Greek woman. This was at a time when, almost every other profession being exclusively male, the theatre was one of the rare careers a young woman could dream of entering. But Meligala, and the restraints of her marriage, offered little hope that such a fancy could ever be realized.

The town was picturesque – white buildings that caught the strong morning sunlight and cast graceful cool shadows in the heat of summer afternoons, winding roads and several verdant oases. Well-tended olive groves flourished just beyond the town borders and their owners produced a few wealthy residents, none of whom extended any gracious invitations to the newlyweds. Litza's unhappiness was apparent.

On 4 June 1917, ten months after their marriage (proving her brother wrong), their first child, Yacinthy, was born in Athens because Litza did not trust the local physician. Three years later, on 27 June 1920, Litza gave birth, again in Athens, to a much wanted son, named Vasily. By now Litza was certain that her marriage to George had been a mistake. Still dapper-looking and of a sympathetic nature, with the proprietorship of the store and fatherhood he had lost the spirit of fun that had first attracted her and, as he flirted with all the pretty women whom he served in the shop, her brother's warnings left her uneasy. She turned her attention to little Vasily, a handsome child with large, blue, dreamy eyes and a gentle smile who, she believed, was fated to be either a poet or a musician. Jackie was left very much on her own, a situation that did not seem to disturb the little girl who found her mother cold and diffident at some times and volatile at others.

'Then the world was limited to the shady interior of our house, the darkened rooms and the chatter of the servants [the Kalogeropouloses now had a maid, a cook and a handyman who also delivered prescriptions for George],' Jackie would later remember. The staircase was her world for it led to the sweet-smelling room where her father passed his days. To her, it was a 'magic shop full of beautiful jars and bottles, of glass cabinets cluttered with packets and tubes', and she loved to watch her father 'graciously serving the ladies who came to the shop, carefully wrapping their parcels, passing them over with a bow and murmured comment, twirling the end of his black moustache with a little smile'.

The one thing that bound George and Litza was their children; especially Vasily, the son George so prized, who at three was reading well and could pick out a nursery tune on Litza's beloved piano. Then the unspeakable happened. The child contracted typhoid fever. The family was frenzied as the boy's condition quickly deteriorated. Neither the medications that the local doctor prescribed nor George's potions culled from other doctors he contacted helped. Within a week, Vasily was dead. The house was thrown into a darkened cavern of mourning. Litza declined into such a state of depression that she refused to leave her room and the grey days brought by a harsh early winter only intensified the gloom that spread throughout the house.

It was Easter 1923 when Litza found that she was once again pregnant. She harped on incessantly about returning to Athens where this *son* (she was positive that God was sending her a replacement for Vasily) could have the advantages of which the brother he would never know had been deprived. There were fierce rows with George, floods of tears would fall, bitter words were exchanged. The household was a war zone. Litza was in her fifth month when George sat her and Jackie down at the dining-room table and informed them that he had sold the pharmacy and their apartment, for which he had received a very good price, and – believing this would sweeten the shock – had purchased first-class tickets on an ocean liner leaving from Athens for America in three weeks' time. He wanted the three of them and the coming child to have a new life and so he had contacted an old friend from his university days in Athens, Dr Leonidas Lantzounis, an orthopaedic surgeon, who had emigrated to New York the previous year and was at present working to secure his American licence. Dr Lantzounis had arranged a job for George with a pharmacy as a clerk until he was allowed to practise as a pharmacist.

Litza's rage and resentment did not deter George, who was now resolute that his family should emigrate to America. Litza had been outspoken about her discontent at living over a store in a provincial town like Meligala but the idea of leaving her homeland for so distant a country where she did not speak the language seemed too much and too callous of George to expect of her. The suddenness of his decision also made her suspicious of his motives. From what or from whom was he running away? Litza considered the many times she had seen various married women in the town smiling seductively at him when they came into the store. Had he got himself into a situation from which he could not extricate himself if he remained in Meligala, or even Greece? Had she not been pregnant, Litza often declared later, she would have taken Jackie, returned to Athens, and let George go on to America alone. But there was now their son, soon to be born, to consider. A boy needed a father and a Greek man would never give up a son.

'We will not suffer,' George assured her. 'America is the land of opportunity. We have money enough to live well until I get my licence and then we will be rich. You will see.' He also stressed the wonderful things that New York had to offer – the theatre, concert halls, opera house, museums and a large colony of Greeks who were from some of the best families in Athens. Litza was not convinced. To her, there was no city more beautiful or rich in history, heritage and culture than her native Athens.

She cried when she saw so many of her treasured possessions being packed in crates to be sent to her family home where they would be kept, George promised, just until they had a permanent place in New York. Her mood darkened further as their departure date drew closer. And when they boarded the ship that would carry them halfway across the world to their new home on a steaming day in late July 1923, Litza was so distraught that she would not come up on deck to wave goodbye to the members of her family gathered at the dock at Piraeus to see them off.

Too progressed into her pregnancy to wear either of her gowns to dinner, for the first two nights she refused to join George for their evening meal. On the third night, upon learning that there would be a recital by a singer whose name she recognized, she changed her mind, placed a large embroidered shawl over her daytime clothes and, wearing her best earrings and a tortoise and diamond comb (a family heirloom) in her hair, entered the dining salon on George's arm. They made a handsome couple with their dark, good looks and patrician bearing. From then on, when speaking to other passengers, she referred to him as 'the Doctor', spoke rather disparagingly about the poor people travelling in steerage and warned Jackie, a joysome, pretty six-year-old, still unaware that her stumbling was caused by myopic vision, not to go into that section of the ship for fear that she might become infested with lice.

On 2 August 1923, the day of their arrival in America, George awoke his wife and daughter at 4 a.m. so that they could go up on deck and see the Statue of Liberty when the ship sailed into New York harbour. As they were first-class passengers, with papers (perhaps by Litza's inspiration) claiming they were on a three-month visit to New York where George was to attend a medical convention, and carried with them enough currency to cover all their expenses, they avoided being herded with the rest of the émigrés into the crowded halls at Ellis Island.

Dr Lantzounis, a large, kindly, intelligent man, his Greek heritage immediately recognizable in his strong features, met the three of them on the quay. The men threw their arms round each other and Lantzounis picked up Jackie in his arms. Having been in New York a year, he spoke English and had an air of assurance that helped in getting their luggage quickly cleared. George and Litza were dazed, unable to understand a word that was spoken to them and overwhelmed by the throngs of excited people anxiously searching for a familiar face, and by the height and density of the buildings that rose spectrally through the haze of heat that encompassed the city on this broiling August day.

With all their trunks, two taxis had to be hired, George and the doctor going in one, Litza and Jackie in the other. This meant that Litza was being driven to an unknown destination by a man who could not understand her. All during the ride she grasped Jackie tightly to her, terrified. It did not help that lamp-posts were draped in black bunting. The entire city and the country were in mourning for the death of President Warren Harding who only a few days earlier, had died suddenly of a heart attack in San Francisco on returning from a trip to Alaska.

The Kalogeropoulos family's first home was a three-room apartment in Astoria, Queens, with a view across Hell Gate to the awesome skyscrapers of Manhattan. There was a small park a few streets away with a playground for Jackie. At this time the foreign born and their children accounted for three-fourths of the city's residents. Groups generally tended to live in close proximity instead of taking the individual plunge into American life. But these emigrant sections gradually disintegrated, spreading to other sections as the more ambitious members bettered their circumstances, albeit among another enclave of their own extraction. In 1923 there were about 25,000 Greeks in New York City. Less than one-tenth of them lived in this area of Queens (originally home to Italian immigrants),[1] which was a blue-collar workers' community, a level up from the section where Greeks without English skills or steady wages usually made their home upon arrival in America, but not the area where the well-to-do Greeks were by now ensconced. Litza, both arrogant and humiliated, was scornful of her working-class neighbours and Jackie was not allowed to use the playground the area boasted as her mother did not want her to associate with children of 'a lower class'.

Litza had brought her overweening pride across the ocean with her. No matter what her circumstances, she would not allow herself, or Jackie, to forget that she was a Dimitriadis, a family of high reputation in Athens; nor would she ever accept her situation as an immigrant. George

---

[1] In 1924, Konrad Bercovici wrote: 'A map of Europe superimposed upon the map of New York could prove that the different foreign groups...live in the same proximity to one another as in Europe: the Germans near the Austrians, the Russians and the Rumanians near the Hungarians, and the Greeks behind the Italians...If the Italians move further up Harlem, the Greeks follow them, the Spanish join them, with the French always lagging behind and the Germans expanding eastward.'

settled in quite easily. He started his job within days of his arrival and learned English at amazing speed. His hours were long and he had a forty-five-minute subway commute at the beginning and end of each day. When he finally arrived home each evening he was faced with his wife's bitter complaints.

On 2 December, four months to the day after their arrival in New York, early snow lacing a grey sky, Litza went into labour and was taken by Dr Lantzounis to Flower Hospital on Fifth Avenue in lower New York where he was completing his American residency. Litza kept talking about the son she would soon have. For months she had been knitting blue baby sweaters and caps. The child was to be called Petros after her father. 'Ever since Vasily's death, I had prayed for another son to fill the empty place in my heart,' she later wrote. She allowed no talk of the possibility of having a second daughter. Jackie was told she would soon have a little brother. When, undoubtedly after a difficult birth, a rosy-faced ten-pound-four-ounce baby girl was handed to her by a nurse, she is claimed to have said, 'Take her away.'

'She was big for a newborn child,' Jackie recalled, 'and had a wispy corona of jet-black hair so unlike the rest of us…My father was saying something to Mother about…why didn't she try to look at the child but she just went on staring at the snow and taking no notice. Clearly angry, my father gripped my wrist and hurried out [of her hospital room].'

Four days later, Litza finally agreed to give the child a name, Maria. She nursed the baby reluctantly and often cried when she was brought to suckle at her breast. She would always claim that Maria was born on 4 December, and that she had endured two days of torturous labour in delivering her because of her size. However, Dr Lantzounis recalled that the little girl, who was to become his goddaughter, was delivered the same day he brought her mother to the hospital.[2]

Not until three years later was Maria christened Anna Cecilia Sophia Maria Callas in the Holy Trinity Orthodox Greek Church at 31 East 74th Street. George had legally changed their surname which, he claimed, was difficult for his customers to pronounce. His licence finally obtained, he had applied for American citizenship and bought a drugstore on 38th Street and 8th Avenue. Situated in what was then a 'scruffy' neighbourhood, it had been all that George could afford. Most of their savings were now gone and once again, Litza was living with her family above a shop, this time in a run-down neighbourhood albeit one inhabited by a large

[2] As a child and young woman Maria accepted 4 December as her birthdate. Later, she celebrated her birthday on 2 December, quite likely in defiance of her mother. The exact time and date are impossible to ascertain as the hospital records were lost.

Greek population. Although not a slum, it was several rungs beneath Astoria. Despite this, Litza dressed her daughters in clothes of fine fabric with starched bows in their dark, shiny-clean hair. Both spoke English but only had each other for company.

'I was not allowed out after school,' Jackie recalled. 'Mother exercised even greater discrimination than she had in Meligala [or Astoria] – to her, no one came up to what she saw as our social standards.'

Maria was a plump, happy child. She shared a room with Jackie and adored her older sister who read to her in the evenings. By the time she was five, both she and Jackie were fitted for glasses, their visual problems brought to Litza's attention by Dr Lantzounis. George worked twelve hours a day. He not only mixed drugs for medications but also flower essences for perfumes and cosmetics that he sold in the store along with other notions. Now that they were somewhat more affluent, Litza insisted they move their living quarters further uptown, and rented an apartment on Riverside Drive, which George feared would be too expensive for them to maintain, but he was unable to dissuade his wife who also ranted about her fine possessions that remained in Athens. To compensate for the absence of her precious piano, George managed to find the funds, by teaching Greek in the few spare hours he had on Sundays, to buy her a pianola.

Maria was instantly transfixed by the sounds that came from that instrument. Litza only bought piano rolls that had recorded classic pieces of piano versions of operatic arias, mostly Verdi and Bellini. In the evenings, with George still at work, Litza would sit, pumping away with her feet to produce the music from the machine. At other times Maria would crawl underneath it and operate the pedals with her hands. The pianola brought the few light-hearted times into the home of this dysfunctional family.

'We never played with dolls,' Jackie recalled. 'How could we when the only example of motherhood we knew was a woman forever bemoaning the fact that she had married our father?'

Both girls put up with periods when their mother was in deep depression and the sound of the angry fights between their parents. It would have been unbearable if the sisters had not had each other. Litza was not a woman to hold or kiss her children and she was inordinately strict in her decrees of their maintaining their isolation from other youngsters and to be on their best behaviour and immaculately turned out at all times. Increasingly, George remained away all night, claiming that he was sleeping in the store so that he could get an early start. Litza never doubted that there was a woman involved and made sure her children knew how their father had betrayed his family.

'There was no other woman, at least at that time,' a young Greek friend of George's later recalled. 'His home was a battleground. He once said that he could stand it but that it was unhealthy for the girls that he remained away as much as he could to save them. He would work late hours trying to come up with a perfume or cosmetic that would earn him more money. He was something of a dreamer.'

This was the winter of 1929 and the bottom had fallen out of the stock market. America was reeling head first into a financial depression that would hold the country in its grip for almost a decade. George's business suffered serious reverses as the cosmetic and perfume products on which he set so much store sat on his shelves, his customers unable to afford such luxuries. Forced to sell, he did so, as he had back in Meligala, without first informing Litza of his intention.

The day that Litza heard of the sale of the store for less than their debts, she rushed down to confront George 'as if he had been personally responsible for the financial instability of the Western world'. Then, when his back was turned, she grabbed a bottle of pills and swallowed them, and had to be taken by ambulance to hospital where the drugs were pumped out of her.

George was now working as a travelling pharmaceutical salesman, making his trips through New York and New Jersey (which were his territory) by bus and sleeping in cheap hotels en route, to save what he could from his small salary so that he could give it to Litza. At that, he was luckier than most men even to have a job. Soon it became clear that they would have to move to a cheaper accommodation. They found a fourth-floor walk-up apartment at West 157th Street in Washington Heights, on the very edge of what was then called Negro Harlem, where more than a quarter of a million blacks from the southern states, the West Indies and Africa were crowded. Pulmonary tuberculosis was prevalent in this area. Fourteen streets south of their new home, one block (143rd Street) had the highest rate of death from the disease of anywhere in the city.

Litza was even more protective of her daughters and increasingly resentful of George for bringing them down to this level. It made no difference to her that millions of other men like him had lost their businesses and their jobs, and that many of them were in a worse situation than she was, or that George was doing the best he could. He made sure that his family never wanted for food or the necessities, that the girls had new shoes and were always well-dressed. The apartment contained two bedrooms and a kitchen large enough for their white enamelled table and chairs. The pianola, Litza's icons, lace tablecloths and silver candlesticks had also moved with them, as had their old wind-up phonograph on which Puccini's music could be played.

Litza was often desolate, but there were isolated happy times during these hard days: picnics, holiday excursions when George would join them and they would become a real family. On 6 January, Epiphany Day, they would take the bus downtown to watch the Greek-Americans 'march in procession through the streets, led by priests in their sumptuous robes, with icons borne by acolytes'. They never got to go down as far as the Battery to see the priest throw the cross he carried into the chilly waters with a blessing for the sea, which then was retrieved by a believer who plunged in after it. On 25 March, Greek Independence Day, they would don their best clothes and attend the celebrations and the service at Holy Trinity. George had become very Americanized and never spoke anything but English to the girls. Litza learned the language haltingly. She listened to the Greek programmes on the radio and read the Greek newspaper *Keryx*. When she could afford it, she would attend a performance of one of the two Greek theatrical groups in New York. She was determined to hold on to her ethnicity and the more she clung to it the further she drifted away from George who wanted himself and his children to become more integrated into American life.

Unable to win her mother's love and yearning for her mostly absent father who was gentler and kinder, Maria turned to her older sister for love and attention, which Jackie was happy to give. Maria became her shadow, following her wherever she went. One day she ran heedlessly across the street against the lights to meet Jackie as she got off the bus from school and did not see the car that was bearing down on her. The vehicle struck her, dragging her for a short distance down the street. She was taken to St Elizabeth Hospital on Fort Washington Avenue. Miraculously, although bruised and badly shaken up, she was not seriously injured and was back home in a matter of a few days.

Maria was growing up as a lonely child, left by herself for many hours a day while her sister attended school and her mother suffered her bouts of melancholy. As her birthday was in December, she was not permitted to start first grade until the following September when she would be nearly seven years old. At school she felt awkward, her eyesight – even with glasses – troubling. She was also considerably overweight and shy. She made few friends and never knew in what emotional state she would find her mother upon returning from school. Her greatest joy was to sit quietly and listen to the few records they had on the gramophone.

When Maria was only seven, she began singing to the recordings and it dawned on Litza that her daughter had a talent, inherited no doubt from *her* side of the family. Maria had a good voice. Her ear was phenomenal for a child of her age and, more surprising, she sang with some understanding of both the music and the lyrics, even though she did not know the language in which they were being sung. Signorina Santrina, a piano teacher who lived on the first floor of their building, was already giving Jackie, who showed some ability, lessons at fifty cents a session. Litza convinced Signorina Santrina to take both girls at the same time for an additional twenty-five cents.

Her mother's interest in her suddenly was aroused. Perhaps Maria could achieve the thing she had allowed to slip from her hands – a career on the stage. Unable to buy records, every Saturday afternoon she took the girls down to the main library on Fifth Avenue and 42nd Street where there was a music section and records could be played. When they returned home Maria would sing selections from them – songs like 'La Paloma' and 'A Heart that's Free' (which child star of the 1930s, Deanna Durbin, would make her standards). During these difficult Depression times America was in love with child performers and moving pictures were making idols of them. Why not Maria? Litza insisted. But Maria was not an adorable youngster. She was quite plain, unattractive and fat. Also, she had little desire to become a child star even if, by the remotest chance, that were possible. She hated getting up in front of people. She was ashamed of the way she looked, terrified that people would make fun of her and unable to see more than a few feet in front of herself.

One thing, however, was true. She loved to sing.

'I am sorry for any children who grew up in that period [the 1920s–1930s] of infant prodigies,' Maria would later lament,

> when parents were getting such wonderful ideas about becoming rich and famous...I did have this voice and [my mother] pushed me into a career. I, too, was considered a sort of infant prodigy...As things turned out, I can't complain. But to load a child so early with responsibility is something there should be a law against. Infant prodigies are always deprived of genuine childhoods. It's not a special toy – a doll or a favourite game – that I remember but the songs that I was made to rehearse time and time again, sometimes to the point of exhaustion, so that I would shine at the end of a school year. A child should not be taken away from its youth for any reason – it becomes exhausted before its time.

All of Litza's private disappointment and frustration were unleashed in her ambitions for Maria. In the beginning her daughter's light mezzo-soprano voice was sweet but thin. She was, after all, just a child. If she had sung the kind of popular songs that Shirley Temple was becoming famous for, it would have been one thing. But Litza would only permit her to learn pieces of a more classical nature. It was a wonder, during the

hours she spent with her every day at the old, upright piano (which she
had traded in the pianola to obtain), that she did not ruin Maria's vocal
capacities completely by pushing her voice, making her reach coloratura
notes when it should have been carefully guided at so young an age.

Maria's first public appearances were made at the Middle School in
Washington Heights. At ten, a ribbon tied round her bobbed hair, a short
skirt revealing chubby legs, she sang Gounod's 'Ave Maria' and the
Habanera from Bizet's *Carmen*. A Swedish neighbour, John Eriksen, who
sang in the chorus of the Metropolitan Opera Company, heard her
practising through an open window and offered to give her free
singing instruction. He warned Litza that the girl was not using her
voice in the right way and that it could do great damage if it continued.
He worked with her for several months during the summer of 1934,
helping her voice to open up and extending her vocal range appreciably
so that she was comfortable singing the higher notes of the soprano
arias, as well as showing her how to develop the middle register and
its lyricism. It is no doubt that her unpaid and later unrecognized first
coach saved Maria a great many problems that could have harmed her
voice. Litza knew nothing about vocal training. Her only goal had been
to get Maria to sing louder and higher so that she would command
attention.

When she was twelve Maria had a part in the school production of
Gilbert and Sullivan's *Mikado* and at graduation sang Ambroise Thomas's
dazzling coloratura aria with its stratospheric roulades, 'Je suis Titania'
from *Mignon*. Convinced that Maria could be a child virtuoso, Litza
dragged her to radio auditions, finally winning a place for her on the
Major Bowes Amateur Hour, the most popular talent contest in the
country. Several young winners had been given Hollywood and radio
contracts, and Litza felt Maria might just be one of the lucky ones. Litza
gave her daughter the name 'Anita Duval' in her first correspondence
with the radio programme. Then changed it to 'Nina Foresti' (thinking
the Italian name had more interest to it) for her audition, at which she
sang 'Un bel di'. She was accepted to sing on the show. Terrified, dressed
in an outfit that made her look even younger and more awkward than
her eleven years, she exchanged a few nervous words with Major Bowes
before she began to sing 'A Heart That's Free' with Jackie (now seventeen
and graduated from school) at the piano (neither sister had been permitted by Litza to wear her glasses). Despite a few trip-ups caused by the
insecurity and poor eyesight of both girls, Maria came second to an
accordionist, winning a wristwatch and $50 (a fair sum in those days).
There were no calls from either radio or films.

'An accordionist!' Litza had sneered. 'What do Americans know about good music!'

Litza was convinced that what both her daughters needed was the kind of musical education they could only receive in Greece. She begged George to find the money to get them back to Athens. But George did not want to leave America. This only made Litza more determined and in December 1936 she borrowed money from Dr Lantzounis to pay Jackie's boat fare to Athens where she would stay with her grandmother until Maria finished her school year when the two of them would join her. George did everything possible to keep Maria in New York, but nothing could deter Litza. When Maria's school term ended on 28 January 1937, she sold whatever she had of value, including the piano and, with a loan from one of her brothers to make up the difference, bought two cabin-class tickets on the *Saturnia* for Greece, to sail on 14 March, six weeks later. She promised George that they would return at the end of summer, Christmas at the latest, and he agreed to send them $125 a month for their support, which was almost half of what he was earning.

'Stand at the rail and wave to your papa,' George told Maria as Litza hurried them towards the gangplank the afternoon they were to sail.

'Come with us, Papa,' Maria was to remember pleading as she held his hand.

Litza pulled her away and onward, and in a moment she could not see her father for the throngs of people. Immediately upon boarding she ran to the rail. At first she could not find him among the crowds. Then, suddenly, there he was, waving his hat frantically at her and she waved back. He was shouting to her, but she could not hear what he was saying. Then someone pushed in front of her and when she finally made her way back to the rail he was gone. The ship's whistle blew and the *Saturnia* moved slowly through the dimness of the cool afternoon amid the brooding, ghostly calls of foghorns, her passengers unaware of the imminence of the war clouds that hovered over her destination.

2

Athens: Student Years

THE *SATURNIA* WAS an Italian ship. The captain was a jovial man with a love of opera, keen on keeping his passengers well fed and entertained. That was nearly impossible in the first two days of the voyage as rough weather and a turbulent sea left a great number ill in their cabins, Maria among them. Finally, as they entered more southerly waters, she rose from her bed, in the tiny cabin she shared with her mother, and wandered about the liner. Litza was in a state of exhilaration. For the weeks before they embarked she had been altering and revamping her clothes. Pieces of the Persian lamb coat, worn and out of style, were cut to make a collar and cuffs to cover the shiny edges of a five-year-old black wool coat. An old hat was rakishly transformed with the addition of a long feather. The peach satin bed cover she had brought from Greece, and that had been kept wrapped in tissue all these years, was used as fabric for a hand-sewn tea gown.

Litza seemed suddenly to have been reborn. She made friends with several couples on the ship. 'God knows what stories she told them,' Maria would later comment. 'I heard her tell people I was a musical prodigy, that I had had many offers in America, but was coming back to Athens to work with some of the finest vocal coaches in the world.' She pushed Maria to sing in the lounge to her own uneven accompaniment. Maria was mortified, but the captain heard her and asked if she would sing at a party he was giving that was to be attended by a count and countess. Litza was thrilled and wore her peach satin gown, but Maria, a fresh bow in her hair, her black patent leather shoes shined to mirror perfection, complained that they were not really guests and that she was merely an unpaid performer.

She sang the Habanera from *Carmen*, taking a rose from a nearby vase at the end of the aria and tossing it provocatively to the captain who was seated directly in front of her. Shortly afterwards he presented her with a bouquet of red roses and a doll with a lovely porcelain face, long black hair and dressed in an embroidered Italian folk costume. All her childhood playthings had been left behind in New York. She was, after all, thirteen years old and on her way to becoming a young lady. But the doll meant a great deal to Maria and for years it would decorate the top of her bed.

The *Saturnia* anchored in the port of Patros in the northern Peloponnese. This was the first foreign city that she had ever seen and – at least from her vantage point as she and her mother disembarked – it was filthy and run-down. Greek was spoken in a colloquial manner and the words went by so quickly that she could not understand what people were saying. Litza held tightly to her hand as they made their way through Customs, claimed their baggage and boarded one of the rickety-looking wooden carriages of the train that would take them to Athens. All during the voyage her mother had been telling her glorified stories of the beauty of Greece, how much better it was than New York and now, as the train dragged slowly through the grim winter terrain, she saw hovels and signs of poverty that she had never imagined existed.

'We are in Greece,' Litza kept repeating, tears in her eyes as she stared out of the grimy train window. 'See that sky? Wait until the sun shines. You will never see a sky that is bluer.'

The train moved on to lovelier vistas, distant hills and through small but more picturesque towns, where barefoot women wearing shawls moved slowly as they carried baskets of kindling and vegetables on their heads. Ragged men sat patiently on their donkeys, which were pulling carts heavily laden with what looked like some kind of grain. There were stone walls and rounded trees and houses built of clay with uneven roofs. Nothing looked familiar to Maria. It was as though she had fallen into a time warp, one she would recall and describe vividly decades later.

They arrived in Athens late in the afternoon, the day still foreboding. Litza pointed out the stately Parthenon and the Acropolis, and chattered about Demosthenes and Socrates, that the city was the birthplace of Western civilization. To Maria, Athens looked raw and blunt in the grey twilight. No glorious skyscrapers or the excitement one felt riding the subway in New York when it suddenly came above ground and everywhere you looked pulsed with life. For her mother, who had the imprint that memory leaves of sunnier days when the three mountains surrounding Athens were violet-coloured and vivid green, and the sea stretched deep blue, serene and friendly to the south-west, this was a homecoming. For Maria it was a somewhat frightening journey into the unknown and unfamiliar.

Jackie met them at the station with their grandmother, three of Litza's sisters and two cars so that there would be room for the baggage. 'Mother', Jackie recalled, 'was wearing a tailored suit and an elaborate hat with an enormous feather, clearly intended to impress her relations. [Maria] was introduced as a person of consequence embarking on a brilliant career. She looked embarrassed, and downcast.' Litza chattered all the way in the crowded vehicle she shared with Maria and two of her sisters.

She had extraordinary plans. An uncle, Efthemios Dimitriadis, a lawyer by profession, had many friends in the music world and contacts with a conservatory. Litza wanted to speak to him as soon as possible so that he could help get Maria an audition. Then there was the problem of money. George, she told her family, had been a Scrooge (she did not inform them of his current misfortunes) and had refused to contribute more than $125 a month to their care and Maria's education. She had assumed that her family had remained as affluent as she remembered them before leaving for America. But Greece had also suffered through financial depression and a drastic change in the government, which had levied heavy taxes. Two of Litza's sisters had lost their homes and now they were all living in one crowded house with their widowed mother. Litza, Jackie and Maria would have to share one bedroom. It wouldn't be too bad for Litza, her sisters told her. She would have American dollars and Jackie's wages to help them survive.

'Jackie's wages?' Litza exclaimed, horrified upon learning for the first time that her daughter had taken a part-time secretarial job in order to support herself and that she had not practised the piano for months.

Her grandmother's house was not the elegant villa Litza had previously described to Maria. Mrs Dimitriadis had moved from Litza's childhood home years before, unable to afford its upkeep. The house they all crowded into was a modest bungalow with three small-sized bedrooms and one bathroom. In her adversity, Litza's dreams intensified. She was convinced Maria would save them by becoming a child prodigy. She talked incessantly about what they (she and her daughters) must do to implement this. Maria *had* to be accepted into either the Athens or the National Conservatory. That was the springboard to success for a concert and opera singer in Greece, and Litza refused to let Maria think of anything else. There were hurdles for them to overcome, the first being Maria's age.

Entrants to either conservatory had to be sixteen and to have completed their course of school studies. Maria was thirteen. Litza refused to enter her into a regular school, a fact that did not anger Maria, who had found it difficult to communicate with or be accepted by even her own cousins who were her peers and laughed at her American accent, called her a 'Yankee' and pretended not to understand the little Greek she spoke, although it was clear that they did.

The family's financial problems were a more serious obstacle. After only two months, George was taken ill with pneumonia and hospitalized. When he was discharged he was told he no longer had a job. Still weak, and now unemployed, he had stopped the monthly payments and written asking Litza to return to America immediately with the girls. Not until years later would Maria and Jackie know why their father's support had stopped. Whenever letters came from George, Litza destroyed them. His daughters, therefore, thought their father had deserted them.

Supported by Jackie's meagre salary and donations from the family (who had little enough to take care of themselves), the three women moved out of Grandmother Dimitriadis's house into a fairly comfortable furnished apartment. Litza apparently thought she would be able to maintain the expense of her independence with loans from old friends. A few did help out when she assured them that money from George would shortly be forthcoming. She was living by her wits and on dreams, one being that Maria would be hired to sing on the radio. When her brother Efthemios seemed unable to make the proper contacts to help, Litza took over. Every day Maria, a large bow in her hair, dressed younger than her years, was taken by her mother to the offices of people she had known as a young woman who might in any way be able to advance her daughter's career, either by financial assistance or an introduction to someone with music connections. Maria suffered painful embarrassment by the entire process, but nothing deterred Litza.

Maria had not yet proved that she actually had the ability to become a professional singer at this stage. This made little difference to Litza, who was following in the footsteps of stereotypical American movie and stage mothers – Gertrude Temple, Ethel Garland, or stripper Gypsy Rose Lee's indefatigable mother Rose. Maria's love of singing was being compromised by the overbearing pushiness of her mother. Yet she never rebelled, keeping her resentment locked inside her as she allowed Litza to parade her from one office to another and to sing whenever called upon to do so.

Was Maria traumatized by her mother's ambitions for her? Later in her life she claimed this to be so. But she was also energized by her mother's ambition and believed this was a way to win approval. Although she loathed Litza's agenda, she suffered the humiliation because she knew of no other way to achieve her goal. Once that had happened, she vowed to a cousin, 'I will fly away on my own.'

In September 1937, six months after they had arrived in Greece, Litza's brother Dukas mentioned that he had visited a taverna on the coast not far from Athens where customers got up and sang operatic arias and which was quite often frequented by agents and managers scouting for talent. Litza immediately insisted he take them there. What she found on arriving was shocking. Most of the customers were raucous men. The acrid smell of tobacco and ouzo permeated the place. Minors were not allowed in, but Litza fluffed out Maria's hair, applied rouge to her lips and tossed her old Spanish shawl round her daughter's shoulders. Her height and mature body added to the impression that she was a young woman, not a girl. Maria refused at first to sing, but with her mother prodding her and Jackie prepared to act as accompanist, she finally walked nervously to the raised platform at the rear of the taverna.

'I'm going to sing…' she began in trembling Greek.

'Just sing!' the men ordered.

Jackie played the lead-in to 'La Paloma' and Maria started to sing. The taverna grew quieter, finally almost still and when she had finished there were shouts for more. She went on to sing 'A Heart That's Free' in English, which has some extremely high trills in it that she delivered with strength and purity of tone. An enthusiastic ovation was given her as she returned to her table, not knowing what was expected from her at this point. Litza had told her that they couldn't leave just yet – her hopes being that someone of importance had heard Maria sing and would present himself. This was, in fact, the case. A young tenor, Zannis Cambanis, came over to congratulate her. He turned out to be with the Athens Opera (Lyric Stage) and was studying with Madame Maria Trivella, a teacher at the National Conservatory considered to be one of the finest voice coaches in Athens. He said he would mention Maria to her at their next lesson.

There were at this time two leading conservatories in Greece, the Athens and the National. The Athens Conservatory was considered the more prestigious, but the National Conservatory and its teaching staff were also held in high regard. Litza was beside herself with excitement. She called Efthemios. Did he know Madame Maria Trivella? Well, they had a mutual acquaintance, he said. Litza insisted he call this friend to tell her about Maria and to ask her to contact Madame Trivella and enquire about a possible audition, reminding her that his niece, Maria Kalogeropoulou (the feminine form of her Greek name, Callas now abandoned by Litza), was the same young woman whom Zannis Cambanis had spoken about to her. Efthemios did as Litza asked, not expecting much, but Madame Trivella agreed to hear Maria sing.

Accompanied by Litza, Jackie, her uncle Efthemios, her grandmother and two aunts, Maria arrived for her audition dressed and made up by Litza to appear more mature. Litza had also thought that it would help Maria if she had a friendly audience. However, Madame Trivella insisted the family remain in a reception room while she and Maria went privately into her studio.

Many years later Callas was to recall how nervous she was at this audition. Jackie had come along believing she would have to accompany her, but Madame Trivella had a young student pianist and this was not necessary. Asked what she was going to sing, Maria replied 'La Paloma'. This being a rather short folk song, which could not really tell much about Maria's potential, Madame Trivella enquired whether she might have prepared another selection. Maria suggested the Habanera, Carmen's erotic aria from the first act of the Bizet opera.[1] Standing by the piano, her nervousness gone almost as soon as she began the aria, she sang in full voice, her phrasing remarkable.

Madame Trivella was stunned, not so much by Maria's voice (although that was also the case) but by the young woman's dramatic delivery of the aria; her seeming ability to understand Carmen's passion. She immediately saw her potential. Yet this was an entirely untrained voice and Maria – whom she instantly recognized as being younger than her application stated – was singing from the throat, which would destroy her vocal ability before she was fully matured. Besides her extraordinary presence, which made one completely forget her youth, the girl had a good sense of pitch, an open and emotional quality and the proper physical characteristics – large mouth, long neck, sturdy frame – all attributes that were advantageous for a true opera singer. The amazing thing was the way she used her eyes, her hands, the stress on certain words and phrases that brought the aria suddenly to life. This was something innate, truly felt, which the majority of hopefuls never achieved but that a great diva must possess.

Madame Trivella spent about twenty minutes after Maria had sung to explain to her what she needed to develop and the years of dedicated training, hard work, scales, arpeggios and exercises, thinking of nothing but her voice, that this would involve. 'Are you prepared for such a regime?' she asked. Maria said she was.

When they came out of the studio, Madame Trivella is said by Jackie to

[1] 'L'amour est un oiseau rebelle'.

have exclaimed, 'But this is talent!' Years later, recalling the audition, Trivella added, 'I accepted little Maria as my pupil with great pleasure, for I felt, there and then, enthusiastic over the possibilities of her voice.'

Litza was now faced with the financial problems that preparing Maria for a career in music entailed. There was still no money coming from George, who wrote endless letters demanding that Litza and his daughters, or Maria on her own who was still a child in his opinion, return. Maria, he insisted, was an American and should return to the country of her birth. What little money he had was being held secure to pay for their voyage home. Litza ignored his pleas and never answered his letters. The Dimitriadis family were giving her whatever they could to help in her support; there was Jackie's small salary from her new job of translating film titles, and the three of them had moved to a less expensive rear apartment at 61 Terma Patission. As it was, they were merely eking by. Madame Trivella recommended Maria for a scholarship at the National Conservatory where she could then coach her without cost to the family. However, to enter Maria had to provide evidence that she was sixteen. Litza took that in her stride by masterfully changing the date of birth on her daughter's birth certificate. Madame Trivella was aware of the alteration but let it slip by. Maria was thus accepted, her training now begun in earnest with the start, early in September 1937, of the National Conservatory's new term.

Her schedule, the pressures of the classes she attended, and the amount of study and practising she was expected to do outside the National Conservatory were intense. She had daily private coaching in vocal expression with Madame Trivella, acting and operatic history with George Karakantas, piano with Evie Bana, as well as French and Italian diction courses. There was no such thing as a social life, or contact with other girls her own age. Mostly she locked herself into the small, almost bare room that she occupied at home (Jackie shared a bedroom with her mother) and, seldom taking time to sit down for a meal, got into the habit of eating whatever was handy while she was studying.

The flat on Terma Patission was a commodious six rooms, but it had been rented unfurnished. Litza rented out one room for income and furnished the apartment with whatever spare pieces members of her family were able to give her, the boarder receiving the best of what was available. They were left with a kitchen table, chairs and beds but little more. The heating was minimal. Maria's room contained none at all and she would dress in layers, a blanket over her shoulders, gloves on her hands, as she studied. Somewhere, somehow, Litza had obtained an old upright piano, which was in the combination living-dining room, and it was here that Maria would go over her vocal exercises. Her Greek had improved but she still had an American accent rooted strongly in the areas of New York where she had been brought up.

Contact with the Dimitriadis family matriarch was abruptly ended when Litza, after a fight over money, stopped talking to her mother. Both Maria and Jackie were devastated, their grandmother being 'an island of loving calm, of decent good sense in the restless tides of my mother's insatiable ambition', Jackie recalled.

Litza continued to denigrate George, always blaming him for the lack of even the smallest comfort his family might enjoy. 'You must walk to the Conservatory,' Maria claimed her mother once admonished, 'because your father does not send even money for bus fare.' She never showed Maria his letters (which were coming less frequently), which he later said contained his pleas for them to return home. He also claimed he sent them American dollars, not much, but what he could spare, for times were very rough with him and he was still ill and only employed part-time. From Maria's point of view it seemed that her mother might be right and that her father had deserted them. But that did not stop her from yearning to see him. She later recalled crying bitterly on her four-teenth birthday when there was no word from him. George insisted that was not true. He had sent her a letter with a five-dollar bill enclosed. Perhaps it was lost in the mail, or Litza took the money and threw away the letter. But the end result was that Maria suffered feelings of rejection and further immersed herself in her work at the National Conservatory, spending more of her outside time with Madame Trivella who had taken her personally under her wing. This caused an abrasive rift in the relationship between Litza and Madame Trivella.

Litza feared that she was losing control of Maria and turned her attention to using Jackie to better their desperate financial situation. Tall, slim, attractive and an able pianist, Jackie, she felt, was wasting herself in her current job. What she needed was to marry a rich man and therefore elevate Maria and herself as well into a better lifestyle. Jackie was dating Milton Embiricos, whose family were well-known shipbuilders. Milton, the eldest son, was working hard to rebuild the family's fortunes, severely damaged during the hard times of the early thirties, through real estate and with the purchase of a shuttle boat that made frequent trips between the mainland and Corfu. Litza now got it into her head that Milton Embiricos was the answer to their problems. Jackie would have to tell him how bad things really were with them and ask him for a loan.

Jackie tearfully refused. After all, she had not known Milton that long and was not even sure she was in love with him, and there was a wealthy girl whose family was close to his own whom it was expected he would marry. Litza never let go. 'We're going to starve to death,' she would cry. 'We need money now.' Jackie was reduced to a state of near collapse. She had always met Milton outside their home. Litza insisted he come up to collect her daughter from their apartment. 'As soon as he came into the empty apartment [freezing cold in January] the full scale of the problem was brought home to him,' Jackie wrote in her memoir. Litza clearly indicated that if Milton helped them, she would agree to Jackie becoming his mistress. Jackie was horrified. There were tears and tantrums, but a few days later Litza had worked out an agreement with Milton with what would constitute a fair 'settlement'.

'Within a matter of days,' Jackie wrote, 'tradesmen were delivering furniture, a maid had been hired, the larder was full – all at the expense of Milton Embiricos. Maria would have her voice; I had been offered in exchange.' Jackie soon became 'absorbed into Milton's life...I was taught the rules of behavior. First I could not expect to have formal relations with his family,' and as long as they were together she was never to ask him 'where he had been without me and for most of the time he never told me...and the third thing was that I was never to visit his office or to consider taking a job which...would be demeaning to a man in [his] position'. With the small income Milton now contributed to the family's support, Jackie resumed her piano studies and her mother fantasized on how her two daughters would one day soon *both* be famous, one as an opera diva, the other as a concert pianist. She seemed to have no guilt that she had literally sold Jackie into a sexual relationship that could well mark her life forever. When later confronted with this, she replied, 'Nonsense. Jackie was very fond of Milton.' This was true, but the liaison would forever change her chances of his marrying her.

Maria was not informed at this time of the actual source of their sudden affluence. The apartment had furniture, her room heat. The boarder was evicted and her room turned into a separate one for Jackie. There was a maid, plenty of food, enough money for some new clothes, which – as she had outgrown what she had brought with her from America – was much appreciated. She assumed her father had been responsible. About a year later, when she learned the truth, she was 'prudishly shocked', Jackie recalled, 'and was no longer prepared to accept my elder sister role as she had in the past'. She was also unforgiving towards Litza, but by then there were so many reasons for her anger towards her mother that Litza's base immorality and the gross betrayal of her sister were diminished, although she would later admit that she feared the same fate would befall her if she did not fulfil her mother's ambitions.

She had always been a hearty eater. Now, with a full larder to go to, she would pile up a plate and bring it back to her room, lock the door and eat and study, study and eat – sometimes throughout an entire night – refilling her supply while the others slept. She never had meals with the family. Food became a reward, a compensation. Within a year she was vastly overweight.

Her first months at the National Conservatory had been spent under Madame Trivella's instruction working on simple songs, learning how to use her diaphragm before she attempted any operatic arias. Actually, although she had listened to many of the great operas on recordings, she had never seen one. Milton remedied that and one night took Litza and her two daughters to see *La Traviata* at the Lyric Theatre in Athens. Maria was transfixed. She now knew for certain that opera was to be her world. She could see herself at Violetta, the beautiful courtesan who gives up her lover so that he can have a proper marriage and then dies of consumption. Based on the Dumas *fils* autobiographical novel *La Dame aux Camélias*, it is one of the most romantic roles in opera. As the soprano who sang Violetta that evening was extremely hefty, Maria had no problem in identifying with the character.

On Monday, 11 April 1938, she sang four selections in her first student concert at Parnassus Hall in Athens: 'Leise, leise' (*Der Freischütz* by Weber), a standard for advanced students but most difficult to sing well; 'Plus grand, dans son obscurité' (from Gounod's rarely performed *La Reine de Saba*) which gave her an opportunity to display her dramatic ability; 'Two Nights', a pleasing Greek folk song by Psaroudas; and a duet with Zannis Cambanis, the young man whom she had met the previous year at the taverna.[2] Chosen by Madame Trivella, the programme was certainly ambitious for a fourteen-year-old girl with only six months of professional coaching. But Maria had progressed at an extraordinary pace and her teacher seemed confident she could carry it off, which she did.

'Accompanied by Stefanos Valtetsiotis,' Jackie recalled, 'the imposing figure of Cambanis and…fourteen-and-a-half-year-old Maria, took center stage. It was terrifying, and Mother and I could hardly breathe until it was over. But when they had finished and the applause was lapping all round us and Cambanis was gesturing Maria forward to take her bow, I suddenly knew that things would never be the same again.'

'We all thought she was seventeen,' Cambanis later added in

[2] The programme for this concert has long been lost. This duet was said to have been 'O dolci mani' ('Oh, sweet hands') from Puccini's *Tosca*. This seems incorrect because the aria is sung by Tosca's lover Cavaradossi to Tosca, who must react to his words, but has no lines to sing.

remembering that performance. 'But even at that, we knew she was destined for great things. I, myself, had much to learn at that time. Still, I knew a truly good voice when I heard it. She was not yet ready for the vocal colour to sustain an operatic role, but her dramatic delivery was amazing.'

Another member of the audience that night was to say that 'her voice was not really pleasing, but it was commanding. One did not forget hearing it or watching her as she sang.'

Despite her accusations that Litza had pushed her into performing, therefore robbing her of her childhood, by now Maria was totally obsessed with her voice and her ambitions for herself. There was nothing normal about this young woman's life and it is doubtful that she even knew what was normal for a girl of her age. She had not yet given up the idea that she would return to America and rejoin her father. With all her complaints, Litza was happy to be home in Greece and Jackie – although she had left when she was only six – readjusted very quickly to her surroundings. Maria, on the other hand, spent many years feeling she was the outsider, a foreigner. She made few friends at the National Conservatory. Her life revolved around her lessons and her music. She was consumed by them and walked through the rest of her days 'feeling a stranger even to herself'.

She was also blind to the war clouds that were rolling across Europe in their direction. Not so Jackie who listened with growing apprehension to Milton's prophecy of imminent danger from Italy, Germany's co-partner in the Axis; and to daily broadcasts of the BBC. Hitler was on the march. In April 1939, Mussolini invaded Albania. The enemy was now directly on the border of Greece and the country in grave danger of invasion. Jackie had a serious fight with her mother over Maria, who was an American by birth, and who she felt should return to New York before that happened. Her own situation was more complicated. She had never become an American citizen, which might make re-entry difficult. But even if that was overcome, there was Milton. If she left Greece, his help to her mother would end. She saw it as being her duty to remain as long as Litza did. Maria was another matter. She would be safe in the States. Maria had always been their father's favourite, he would look after her and, with her accomplishments at the Conservatory, she could apply for a scholarship to the Juilliard or some other fine American conservatory.

Litza pooh-poohed the idea of war and was adamant that Maria remain to continue her studies in Athens. 'You can't be that blind or that selfish,' Jackie shouted. But Litza believed that Maria's career was of the utmost importance and that nothing should interfere with her current studies. For weeks, Litza and Jackie did not speak. Maria, now more often staying with Madame Trivella at her apartment than at home, was otherwise occupied. On 2, 9 and 16 April she was to sing her first opera role as Santuzza, a young peasant girl betrayed by her lover, in Pietro Mascagni's *Cavalleria Rusticana*. It would be under the auspices of the National Conservatory at the Olympia Theatre in Athens.

Although the opera was only one act, the role was demanding and required both technical and dramatic skill. Santuzza is dishonoured by her lover (Turiddu) and they have a long impassioned duet. After she is rebuffed and thrown to the floor, she betrays him to the husband of his lover. But when he is murdered, she is wildly distraught and finally collapses in grief and guilt. Such melodramatic demands were a tremendous challenge for a girl of fifteen with little more than eighteen months of vocal training. For six weeks before the performance Maria hardly left Madame Trivella's home where her teacher worked with her long into every night. Madame Trivella's faith in her was a constant driving force and Maria dedicated herself to the task at hand.

'Maria sustained the role of Santuzza like a real professional,' George Karakantas, the musical director, recalled later. 'In rehearsals she would listen as in a trance and sometimes she would walk nervously up and down repeating passionately to herself, "I'll get there one day."...She may not have had full control of her voice, but I remember such a dramatic impact on "Voi lo sapete" and the Easter Hymn that one did not notice any vocal imperfections.'

The country was not as oblivious to the situation in Europe as were Litza and Maria. On 1 September 1939 Hitler invaded Poland and Europe was at war. On 9 April 1940 Germany entered Norway, which fought bravely for two months, assisting a large percentage of its Jewish population to escape before the country was occupied by the Nazis. The Germans marched into Paris by the end of June. With the Italians at their border it seemed impossible for Greece not to anticipate the imminent crunch of Mussolini's army.

For twenty years Greek politics had been caught in an angry schism between royalists and republicans. After years of exile in Great Britain, King George of the Hellenes returned to the throne in 1935, only to hand over power in 1938 to General Metaxas, a royalist general with a long record of conspiracy, who immediately created a military dictatorship, which King George believed would be better able to fend off any invaders. Life became considerably more restrained for Litza, her family and the rest of Greece, with curfews installed, taxes raised and political dissenters arrested on a daily basis. King George remained as a puppet of

General Metaxas, allowed to stay because of his close ties to the British royal family (he was a cousin of Princess Marina, the wife of King George VI's younger brother the Duke of Kent). General Metaxas was pro-Ally and anti-Italian, which seemed in the eyes of many to redeem his otherwise strong-arm tactics.

There had always been a fairly large Italian population in Athens. As the war just beyond Greece's borders progressed, these Italians found themselves in a difficult spot, open to be picked up as foreign agents or on any trumped-up charge. Madame Trivella (although she had lived in Greece for years) was suddenly in great danger, as were those who were her confidants. This did not escape Litza's notice (and was perhaps called to her attention by Milton Embiricos). The time seemed opportune to get Maria into the Athens Conservatory where she could study with the prestigious teacher, Elvira de Hidalgo. Very much against Maria's wishes to remain loyal to Madame Trivella, Litza was pulling every contact she knew to make this possible. Finally, in the spring of 1940, an audition was arranged.

3

The War Years: 1939–1945

MARIA GAVE HER last concert under the guidance of Madame Trivella and the National Conservatory on 25 June 1939, knowing that two days later she would be auditioning with the celebrated Spanish soprano, Elvira de Hidalgo, for entrance into the Athens Conservatory. Litza claimed responsibility for this, having written to de Hidalgo and enclosed recommendations from many people at the National Conservatory along with local reviews of her daughter's performances. However, Maria's growing reputation as a young opera singer worthy of watching had also preceded her. Madame Trivella was most gracious in stepping aside, well aware, in view of current events and the growing hostility towards Italians, of her own precarious position and the problems this could cause her students.

At this final concert with the National, Maria sang, with Michales Koronis, the dramatic duet 'Voi lo sapete' from *Cavalleria Rusticana* and, for the first time, saw an audience rise from their seats to cheer her as she sang with passion her second selection, Amelia's moving last aria from Act Three of *Un Ballo in Maschera*. The evening was highly emotional. Her performance appeared to be enhanced by her inner turmoil. Whether she was accepted into the Athens Conservatory or not, Maria was leaving her first mentor's caring auspices for the unknown. Madame Trivella had been more to her than a teacher. In the last year she had come to play a maternal role in her life. This would be sorely missed.

Adolescence had brought with it a plague of acne that she fought with poultices, tears and thick stage make-up. She was only five foot five inches tall but weighed 180 pounds. Beyond the voice, none of the young men at the National Conservatory had taken more than a friendly interest in her. Not only had her eating problem continued, nothing was being done to understand or control it. She would later say that she felt loved only when she was singing for an audience. Her father (she thought) had rejected her, her mother had used her, her grandmother's love had been denied her; her sister was involved with Milton, her peers excluded her from their social lives and now politics was separating her from the one person who had given her warmth and acceptance – Madame Trivella.

Litza accompanied her daughter to the audition at the Athens Conservatory with Elvira de Hidalgo. Maria chose a seat in the corner of the audition room and waited her turn with several other young hopefuls. Litza was not pleased. 'Why hide yourself?' she asked. Maria did not reply.

'I did notice this girl,' de Hidalgo told an interviewer twenty years later. 'She was fat, pimpled and nervously biting her fingernails. The idea of her wanting to be an opera singer seemed ridiculous to me.'

Maria was the last applicant to sing. Her head was bowed as she walked to the piano and handed the accompanist her music: 'Ocean, thou mighty monster!' from Weber's Oberon, which she had sung previously at two concerts at the National. This was an odd, bombastic choice for so young a woman. De Hidalgo's original pessimism about this applicant was nearly confirmed. Before starting, Maria turned her face away. Then, as the accompanist played the opening chords, she pivoted, head high, facing front, eyes wide, hands slowly rising from her sides. There was an electric moment in the room when Maria began to sing. De Hidalgo was caught completely off guard. She sat bolt upright in her chair. This was not that insecure girl nibbling at her fingers. This young woman commanded attention. And the voice... 'Well, of course her vocal technique was by no means perfect,' de Hidalgo remembered, 'but there was innate drama, musicianship and a certain individuality in her voice that moved me deeply. In fact, I shed a tear or two and turned away so that she could not see me. I immediately knew I would be her teacher and when I looked into her most expressive eyes, I also knew that in spite of everything else [her weight, skin condition etc.], she was a beautiful girl.'

De Hidalgo informed Maria that what she had sung was not right for her age or her voice. She also assured her of her acceptance at the Athens Conservatory and that she would be on a total scholarship. Maria was euphoric for the next week and could hardly wait until her first lessons with de Hidalgo would begin (she would not have a full schedule of classes until the end of summer, with the official start of the term). De Hidalgo had sung at the Metropolitan, Covent Garden and La Scala opera houses, and was famous for her interpretation of Rosina in Rossini's *Il Barbiere de Siviglia*. Dark-haired, with flashing eyes, creamy skin and a vibrant personality, she was the woman Maria fantasized she would one day become. Madame Trivella was not forgotten but, as her former teacher very soon left the National Conservatory and Greece, Maria transferred her dogged regard and attention to her new mentor.

As she had with Madame Trivella, Maria spent every hour she could with de Hidalgo, offering to do errands, clean her apartment, anything to remain with her after her lessons. De Hidalgo immediately welcomed her into her life. 'She was an extraordinarily gifted girl,' she was to say,

> but she was more than that to me. I was aware of the child's loneliness, but even though I loved her – and I always will – as a daughter, it would have been wrong for me to take over from her mother. I would not allow her to do housework but instead encouraged her to look after her hands, her fingernails and so forth. A future prima donna was expected to have elegance both in her singing and her appearance.

Thus began de Hidalgo's efforts, along with her intense vocal coaching, to improve Maria's image. Her weight gain had created a clothes problem for Maria. Dresses in her size were designed for older women and made her look formless and dowdy. To counteract this impression, she wore the brightest colours she could find. 'Once,' Maria was to recall, 'when I presented myself to [de Hidalgo] in ridiculously clashing shades of red and a ghastly hat, she nearly hit the roof. Not only did she tear off my absurd hat but she threatened to stop giving me lessons if I did not make a serious effort to improve my appearance.'

This was easier said than done. Shopping for clothes was such a humiliating experience that she would buy things without first trying them on and let Litza make any alterations that were required. Litza and Jackie nagged her incessantly abut her weight and bad sense of style. Jackie thought insults would get her to do something about them, but not until de Hidalgo took over did Maria try to curb her eating and make an attempt to dress tastefully. She also went on a strict diet, which in turn made her feel deprived and she would binge on sweets and fatty foods in private. The end result was that she actually ate more than before and gained weight instead of losing it. These eating patterns caused increased flare-ups of her acne. She did, however, begin to dress more suitably in dark colours that minimized her size, and to comb her hair back from her face in a more becoming manner.

This was not a time when the medical profession (especially in Greece) looked on obesity as an illness, nor did they have any quick cures for acne. Such inflictions were to be privately endured, and home medicine (scrubbing one's face with strong soap was one) and self-deprival of excess food intake were the only suggested remedies. De Hidalgo's answer was to help Maria build up her self-esteem the only way she knew how –

through dedicated attention to her student's progress and a deep-felt, caring attitude.

Once Maria had entered the Athens Conservatory, de Hidalgo began in earnest a series of vocal exercises to develop her student's stamina and endurance. A soprano with a prestigious past, de Hidalgo had lost her top range at a very early age (she was now only forty-one) and had given up performing in favour of teaching. Considering her professional history, it is disturbing that de Hidalgo continued to follow both Litza's and Madame Trivella's lead and push Maria's voice into singing music that could damage her student's vocal powers while she was still young. De Hidalgo, reliving her career through Maria, wanted to show the opera world that she could produce a great diva capable of dazzling arias that challenged the highest soprano range, while Madame Trivella had been convinced that Maria's range was closer to a mezzo. De Hidalgo, certain that her assessment and her aspirations for her pupil were realistic, started Maria on Italian songs of the seventeenth and eighteenth centuries (like 'Caro mio ben') working with her several hours a day to develop a sense of line, legato, breath control and phrasing. At home, Maria practised arpeggios, scales and roulades to extend her range. In September, language and diction lessons, drama classes and piano were added to her heavy schedule. By April of 1940 de Hidalgo decided to cast Maria as Angelica in the Athens Conservatory's June production of Puccini's *Suor Angelica*. This gave her two months to learn a role that contains 'Senza mamma', one of the most impassioned arias in all opera, and another in which she had to go up to a high C and sustain it.

Suor Angelica is a one-act opera, but a dramatic gem. The role of Angelica runs the emotional gamut from young buoyancy to deepest tragedy. The youthful Angelica has taken the veil in expiation after giving birth to a son out of wedlock. The child is adopted by her aunt but Angelica holds the boy's memory close to her heart. As Sister Angelica she is much loved by the other nuns, administering herbs to heal many of their medical problems, and seems to have found her rightful place in life. When her aunt comes to announce the imminent marriage of Angelica's youngest sister and to ask her to forfeit her rights to the family fortune, she does so gladly as she has already taken her vows of poverty. As her aunt is about to leave, Angelica asks her shyly about her son. 'Oh, he died,' the aunt coldly replies. Angelica restrains her grief until the woman's departure and then lets out a piercing cry. 'What happened to my little child? He died without his mother nearby,' she sings with great pathos and in deep agony. Unable to go on after this tragedy, she commits suicide – which in her faith is the ultimate sin.

Maria was just sixteen and, although she often lived in a world of her own fantasy where she was already transformed into the artist and the diva of her aspirations, such dark happenings were foreign to her. Yet she was able to mould herself into the role of the tortured nun with amazing swiftness. De Hidalgo had been sure she could accomplish this. What her teacher wanted from Maria – perhaps was even obsessive in demanding – was a technical agility with her voice that, combined with her performance ability, would one day – sooner rather than later – transform her into the diva they *both* dreamed she would become.

There was no time in her life for the things most girls of her age fill their days and daydreams with. Jackie wrote in her memoir that Maria (whom she always refers to as *Mary*) was jealous of her private life, that she flirted with Milton when he came to the house and even was seductive to the dentist who filled a cavity in one of her teeth. Her sister regards these indications of Maria's frustrated sexuality as proof that she was oversexed. But while all about her the other young women at the Conservatory could be seen laughing and coupling off with male students, attending parties and gossiping about their conquests, Maria was friendless, once again the outsider although, of all her peers, she was the closest to being absorbed in and a part of her art.

'My interest, perhaps my only interest in life, was my music,' Maria would later confess.

> I was before long so fascinated listening to all of [de] Hidalgo's pupils, not only the sopranos but also the mezzos and even the tenors, singing both light and heavy operas, that I used to go to the conservatory at ten in the morning and leave with the last pupil in the evening. [De] Hidalgo... asked me why I stayed so late [when she had to go home and practise for several hours more]. My answer was that I felt that even the least talented pupil could teach me something.

She sang *Suor Angelica* on 16 June 1940. 'It was a stunning performance,' Zannis Cambanis recalled. 'I wept, I actually wept.' De Hidalgo had asked Costis Bastias, the director of the Royal Theatre for Drama, a wing of the Athens Opera, to attend this performance. Bastias was greatly impressed and recommended Maria to the board of the opera company. The following week she was asked to become a member of the chorus at a salary of 1500 drachmas (about $15) a month, while still attending the Conservatory. This was sooner than Litza had envisioned her daughter would begin a professional career in opera, or to earn a wage, however humble, and she was overjoyed.

Maria's apprenticeship won her five performances at the Greek

National Theatre in Athens where from the wings she sang a song of Humperdinck's (written as incidental music), dubbing the voice of Portia in the Royal Theatre's production of *The Merchant of Venice*.

Very few Athenians in the early summer months of 1940 realized how threatened they were by approaching war. Despite Italy's annexation of neighbouring Albania short months before, and the aggressiveness of the Axis forces, many Greeks believed that they would be able to remain neutral and Athenians retained their confidence that their city was impregnable. Maria was not interested in politics or war. She seldom read the newspapers or listened to the BBC news broadcasts, as Milton and Jackie did, and so their warnings made little impression on her as she immersed herself in her studies.

Then, one morning early in October, Litza burst into her room at 61 Terma Patission, shouting hysterically. 'It's war! The Italians have attacked us! Oh, my God!'

'Mama, what are you talking about?' Maria replied, trying to calm the hysterical woman. 'The Italians wouldn't attack us. You must have had a bad dream.'

Litza's face was ghostly pale and there was terror in her eyes. 'Those bastards! It's true!' she insisted. 'They attacked us only moments ago. It said so on the radio. Mussolini, that poisonous snake, sent an ultimatum. In the middle of the night he sent the premier a telegram demanding us to let their troops occupy Greece. Do you know what Metaxas said? *Ochi*! No! And now their army has crossed over the border from Albania and attacked us! Oh, my God! What is Greece to do? What are *we* to do?'

Maria stared at her mother with disbelief as she rocked back and forth sobbing, her hands pulling at her hair, giving her a wild, mad look. It seemed that Litza had lost her sanity. She remembered going past the Italian legation only a few days before, with Greek and Italian flags flapping side by side in the wind. 'Soldiers will come. They'll rape all the women!' Litza cried.

Jackie had joined them by now and the three women went into the sitting room and gathered around the radio. It was as Litza had said. Italy and Greece were at war, but the announcer assured his listening audience that Mussolini's army was a great distance from Athens, that the Greek army was strong and that Metaxas had issued a statement that the Italians would be pushed back in a matter of days, maybe hours.

It tooks several weeks, and a heavy toll of the lives of Greek soldiers, before Mussolini's ill-equipped troops were driven back, surrounded by Greeks at the ports of Durazzo and Volorë, their backs to the sea. Then the Italians returned, razing whole villages as they swept through the mountainous interior and blocked all the supply routes. There was a severe shortage of food. Ration cards were issued for oil, grain and meat. There was little of any of them to be purchased in the stores. Dairy products, vegetables and fresh fruit were also almost non-existent.

Litza had stocked up on what was available as soon as she heard that food would be rationed and Milton was able to supply some things, obtained through the black market that was already beginning to flourish. However, Christmas 1940 was miserable. The apartment was freezing cold and Litza was in a constant state of frenzy. Through the BBC they had learned that a small contingent of British soldiers were on their way to offer assistance. At the same time the Germans were about to come to aid the Italians.

Milton was drafted by the army but was given an office job in Athens. He insisted the three women try to leave. Maria was, after all, an American citizen. If they could get out of Greece and into Egypt, she might be able to get a visa to return to the States and perhaps take her mother and sister with her.

A boat was about to leave Piraeus en route to Egypt. Milton thought they had a chance of boarding it. They hastily gathered a few belongings and drove with Milton to the harbour. Confusion reigned around them. 'Milton went off to bargain for our passage,' Jackie recalled. 'Just as we were about to board, word came that the Greek battleship the *Elli* had been sunk... Mother flatly refused to get on board the passenger ship [proclaiming that they would all be bombed and drowned at sea] ... We made our way home through the darkened city aware that, for better or worse, we were trapped.'

Then, in the brutally cold January that followed, Metaxas died of cancer; within a few weeks his successor committed suicide. 'Do you believe that?' Litza cried. 'I don't. I don't. Not for a moment. They were murdered. But who cares? They were pro-Nazi anyway.'

Life in Athens became a grim regime. There was a 10 p.m. curfew. The streets were dark, black cloth or cardboard blocked out the lights from within. Men in uniform were a common sight. At the Conservatory most of the young men had left to join the forces. Maria continued her studies and her work with the Athens Opera. She had been cast to share with Nausica Ghalanou, a soprano several years her senior, the supporting role of Beatrice in Franz von Suppé's seldom performed opera, *Boccaccio* (which was to be sung at 5 p.m. because of the curfew). The attention Maria received from de Hidalgo and the seeming ease with which she had advanced so quickly from the chorus at so early an age (she was then only seventeen) was resented by the rest of the company. Her position was not helped by the way she appeared stand-offish, although this was caused by her own fear of being rejected, but was misunderstood.

Another member of the same production, Ghalatia Amaxopoulou, in an interview given twenty years later, recalled that several members of the company deeply resented Maria, feeling that her voice was not right for the role, even after her appearance proved to be an unqualified success in terms of the critics. 'As Maria was born and brought up in America,' Amaxopoulou stated, 'she pronounced Greek with a slightly foreign accent [especially noticeable in the few lines of spoken dialogue that she had] and this was used as a pretext against her being given another role.'

More important, during the eight performances of *Boccaccio* that she sang between January and March 1941 at Pallas Hall, Maria developed a slight wobble. De Hidalgo was alarmed. Perhaps realizing now that she had been guilty of pushing her student ahead at too accelerated a pace, she kept Maria off the performance stage for several months while (according to her) she 'endeavoured to improve her technique without narrowing, but rather widening her scope of expression'.

In July, Maria returned to the cast of *Boccaccio* to play the role of Beatrice six more times. This proved to be a grave mistake. The wobble that had been helped during the interim of non-performance returned. It would be a year before Maria would overcome this problem and sing on a stage again. She was hopelessly unhappy. Life at 61 Terma Patission had become almost intolerable. Hitler had joined Mussolini's forces on 7 April. Two weeks later King George, the remaining royal family and the government escaped first to Crete, then to Egypt. Greece steeled itself for the inevitability of German occupation and with good cause. With the mighty power of Hitler's panzer and motorized divisions, his army had steamrollered its way into Athens only days later and raised the swastika on the flagpole atop the Acropolis. The British with their small force had been unable to stop the Germans. Some British soldiers had been stranded in Athens, their lives in severe danger. A Greek officer and friend of the Dimitriadis family, brought two of these soldiers to 61 Terma Patission, where Litza (not too willingly) took them in and hid them in the tiny room where the family kept their three canaries.

'[After many weeks] we felt sorry for them cooped up like that,' Jackie recalled. They then hit upon a scheme. As one young soldier had blond hair, Jackie and Maria dyed it black and, dressed in some old clothes of Milton's, the two Brits strolled through the centre of town with the sisters. 'It was thrilling as we passed enemy soldiers,' Jackie wrote, 'knowing if they would stop us and ask to see our papers...our secret would be unmasked [and all four arrested by the Gestapo].' They returned home undeterred and unharmed, to a frantic Litza.

Two weeks later the soldiers were secreted out of the country by members of the underground. As terror spread throughout the city, Litza often became hysterical. The Nazis were ever vigilant for those who were helping the underground, or the small but long-rooted Jewish population. Food became even scarcer. Quarrels between Litza and Jackie increased. Maria feared she would never see her father or America again. There was no incoming or outgoing mail and she had no way of knowing that George had been contacting anyone he thought could be helpful to get a letter to his family or to the occupation forces in Greece to let them know they were holding an American citizen, not yet of age, surely against her will. That was not entirely true. Maria was torn. On the one hand she yearned to leave Athens; on the other she knew she could not forfeit her studies with de Hidalgo.

Signs of the Nazi occupation were everywhere. German became the street language. Menus were in German. Banners over the streets showed the direction to the *Soldatenheim*, the soldier's quarters, and the *Stadtkommandantur*, the office of the commander. German soldiers directed traffic. Refugees from devastated villages streamed daily into Athens, further draining the fraction of the supplies the city received and that was needed for mere survival. The situation was made worse because the Germans razed almost everything as they advanced and also seized all the stores of sugar, wheat, flour and other foods they found.

The Greek people remained defiant. Despite the danger of arrest or harassment, they cheered passing trucks filled with British soldiers taken as prisoners of war. Bootblacks, summoned to shine the shoes of the occupation armies, 'approached, spat on the shoes and ran'. There was great hostility between the German and the Italian soldiers, and bitter fights broke out on the streets between them. The Nazis had taken over the railways, the telegraph, telephone, water, electricity and gas companies. Except for the BBC, which could be picked up on short wave, they controlled the news media. Sandbags barred the entrances to all the tunnels that led into the captive city and armed guards stood, guns at the ready, on other outgoing roads if anyone dared attempt to enter or leave without proper identification.

Life was hard. Her father, New York, her early life in America now all seemed like a distant dream. Maria never spoke English any more, warned that it might create a problem for her. The winter of 1941 set in, grimmer, more severe than the previous hardship season. Temperatures dropped to lows not experienced in over forty years and there was no coal or wood to burn. Worse, food supplies were almost non-existent. Bakeries and markets were shuttered. Ration cards were worthless. Meat was only a memory. Pets – dogs, cats, even birds – were killed and cooked. Still such drastic measures to ward off death failed. By Christmas, over 300,000 Athenians had died of illness and starvation. Adding to that appalling figure were the thousands more who had been killed in mass executions after being accused without benefit of a trial of conspiracy, of helping the underground, of sabotage. Proper burials were impossible with such staggering figures. Corpses were left out on the streets at night to be hauled away in the morning to mass graves on the outskirts of the city. All night, rounds of gunfire could be heard as the Germans held back the hundreds of hungry, howling dogs, their masters gone, who had taken to the surrounding hills above the city.

Maria developed an exaggerated fear of the dark and of being alone at night that would remain with her throughout her life. She was traumatized. Nonetheless, her small family were saved much of what others experienced. They did not starve. Milton saw to that. There was an active black market, but even a gold wedding band could buy little more than a scrawny squirrel for a stew. In the early months of the occupation Milton (German marks available to him by some means) managed to get food for them by making periodic trips out of Athens (a very dangerous journey for the starving would kill to find food they could steal). He also brought them blankets and warm clothes. How this was done he never revealed, even to Jackie, and no one dared to ask for fear the assistance might end if they did so. The food Milton brought was an eclectic supply, mainly of dried fruits and nuts, salted fish and a dead animal that was not always identifiable. The meat was cooked immediately and eaten just as quickly, the remaining cache locked in a closet as there was no longer any refrigeration.

The in-fighting between the sisters became intense. Jackie accused Maria of constantly robbing their small stock of food. 'My most telling memory of the occupation,' she accused, was of Maria, 'bent double, reaching for handfuls of figs or nuts [from their larder], her fat backside filling the doorframe'.

Maria's memory diverges from Jackie's at this point. 'The occupation of Athens was the most painful period in my life,' she said in 1957.

I remember the winter of 1941 only too well. It was the coldest in Athens within living memory, and it snowed for the first time in twenty years. For the whole summer I ate tomatoes and cabbage which I managed to get after walking miles and begging farmers in the county to spare a few vegetables [Litza also later claimed she was the one to go on these food-foraging treks]. It was extremely dangerous for the farmers to let anybody have even a little bit of their produce; if the implacable Germans had found out the farmers would have faced the firing squad. Nevertheless, I always managed to get something from the poor farmers.

Whether Litza or Maria actually went out on these dangerous food-foraging trips, Maria agreed that it was Milton, 'my sister's wealthy "fiancé"', who supplied them with food once the bitter winter set in. They made it through the long, harsh, cold days and a spring of torrential rain. That summer (perversely one of the hottest Athens had registered in many years), Maria tells of being introduced to the Italian official in charge of distributing provisions to the troops. 'The Italian was willing to sell me ten kilos of meat once a month for a meagre sum of money. So I gladly strapped the rather heavy package to my shoulders and walked for an hour under the hottest sun, as if I were happily carrying flowers.' The meat, she said, became their only capital; 'We resold most of it to our neighbours and friends, and with the proceeds we were able to buy other indispensable things [wood, oil, candles, flour and sugar] and, with God's help we survived.'

A few of her peers at the Conservatory accused her in later years of 'sleeping with the enemy'. There seems little doubt that Maria had found her sexuality by this time and that she yearned for some youthful encounters. But it was easy enough for the occupation army to find a willing playmate for the price of a dinner or some fuel with which to heat her room. With her weight, despite the lack of food in Athens, still too much for her frame and her skin remaining a serious problem, Maria was no great beauty. (In one interview in later years she called herself 'emaciated' during this time. Photographs contradict this.) However, she did sing in German and Italian for members of the occupation armies when asked to do so and chose songs that might remind them of their homes. There might be no more than five or ten men at these small 'concerts' and from her later mention of them it appeared that her audiences were respectful of her talent and her age. Although she never discussed receiving food or other necessities by way of payment for her singing, it is likely that such gestures were made and accepted by Maria.

During these troubled times Maria buried herself in her studies. She had mastered both German and Italian – not merely because of the ability it gave her to converse with occupation forces (although it helped), but to understand the librettos of the operas in their original language. It would not be until the summer of 1942, when the Germans somewhat eased their ban on public performances, that the dream she had been nurturing finally became reality. The Athens Opera was preparing a production of *Tosca* and she was to sing the title role. She was only eighteen and a half years old when she began her intense preparations for the performance to be presented at Teatro Klathmonos Square, surely the youngest Tosca in the history of the opera.

It had been two years since she had sung Beatrice and de Hidalgo felt she was fully capable now of undertaking such a formidable role, one that has tested some of the greatest divas in the world. Her mentor's belief in her drove her forward. With limited funds, costumes and scenery would be spare. Thus the need for an even greater understanding as the beautiful, wilful and dynamic Tosca who could kill the most powerful man in Rome to save Cavaradossi, her lover, and then take her own life when she realizes her bargain was made with the devil himself and she has instead caused his death.

With few Greeks having even the small pittance a ticket cost, the audience would be mainly members of the occupying forces, German and Italian. That was not a consideration. Maria was to sing Puccini's *Tosca*, and with Greece's most famous tenor, Antonis Dhellentas, as Cavaradossi. That was enough for her. But as she got deeper into rehearsals she felt unhappy with the role and with her interpretation of it. She appeared to know better than de Hidalgo that she was not ready for the task before her and she was unsure that her voice was in the right range for Tosca. She therefore concentrated on her dramatic interpretation. Maria's debut appearance in *Tosca* was on 27 August 1942 which, due to the curfew, began at 5 p.m. Both Litza and de Hidalgo remained in the small dressing room with her as she prepared for her first entrance. She had not only been concerned about her voice; her poor vision also had her on edge. Unable to wear her glasses lest the illusion be lost, she was frightened she would trip or, worse, place the candles wrongly near Scarpia's body in the climactic murder scene at the end of Act Two.

Klathmonos Square was an old open-air amphitheatre. The heat that day had been fierce and Maria's costume was weighty. Between acts, Litza ran back and forth from her seat in the theatre to her daughter's dressing room to help her dry off and to reapply her make-up. Maria was fearful that she did not look or sound feminine or mature enough. In the end she was given a standing ovation and numerous curtain calls. Nevertheless she went home that night disconsolate, certain that her performance had been disastrous.

The reviews the next morning told a different story. Sophia Spanoudi (*Athenaika Nea*) wrote glowingly about her debut, but added that 'her magnificent, dramatic, soprano voice had not yet fully formed'. The music critic for *Provia* 'detected a slight hardness that once or twice crept into her voice', but concluded that 'Kalogeropoulou acted her role with her voice as well as with her body – such accomplishment one rarely finds even among the most experienced artists'.

The most favourable review came from *Vradhyni* and was written by the prestigious and powerful music critic Alexandra Lalaouni.

Not only does [Maria Kalogeropoulou] sustain the role comfortably, and sing it correctly but at the same time she is able to live it with insight and convey it to the audience who were often moved. A true miracle. Her voice is rich all through its long register and she knows how to produce it and give meaning to the words. But, however good her training is, it seems to me there is something else about her; the deep natural musicianship, instinct and understanding of theatre are qualities that she could not have learned at school. Not at her age anyway; she was born with them. It was not at all surprising that she electrified her audience.

With a single performance Maria had become a star and recognized as one of Greece's foremost singers. Her small salary with the opera company was doubled and the commander of the Italian occupation army 'arranged' for her and the cast of *Tosca* to give a concert performance of Rossini's music in Salonika in October 1942 (the last of eighteen performances of *Tosca* was given on 30 September). Although it meant singing for Greece's antagonists, the members of the company, including Maria, were pleased to have another venue. Privately, she was yearning for contact, for love more carnal. Her skin was much improved. She was still seriously overweight, but her current success brought her to the attention of young men (and older ones, too) who had never before looked at her in a sexual way.

4

The Nazis Goose-step
Out of Athens

MARIA AND LITZA were now alone in the apartment at 61 Terma Patission; Jackie – unable to live with the acrimony in that household – had moved to a small hotel, her room paid for by Milton. Maria was seeing an Italian intelligence officer, Major di Stasio, a balding man of large stature, in his mid-forties; Maria eighteen. The Major was an opera buff who had once imagined his baritone voice might lead him into an operatic career. He first heard Maria sing when she did the concert for Italian troops in Salonika. Since that time di Stasio had come to the apartment on numerous occasions, bringing food and small luxuries like soap or sweets with him. Somewhere in Italy there were a Signora di Stasio and several children. He was an unlikely suitor for Maria but Litza sanctioned his attention to her daughter because she believed di Stasio could help Maria find venues in which to sing both then and after the war's end. He was, nevertheless, a man of impeccable manners and, of course, generous.

On Maria's part, di Stasio satisfied her great hunger to be loved and brought her comfort – at least for the moment. Although there is enough evidence to substantiate the existence of a physical liaison, he was greatly paternalistic with no connection with the Conservatory nor the opera company where gossip was a prime amusement. His work was, above all else, secretive and he handled his personal life in much the same way. His visits to Maria were always disguised as tributes to a young artist. He would remain in the apartment for several hours, Litza within calling distance, but always discreet enough to leave the two alone, their meetings uninterrupted. Di Stasio told Maria about various operas, composers and the singers he had heard at La Scala, or those who were in his vast record collection back in Italy.

On 22 April 1943 di Stasio arranged for Maria to give a concert at Casa d'Italia under the direction of Giorgio Lykoudis, sharing the stage with the contralto Arda Mandikian. The Casa d'Italia was formerly the Italian Institute of Culture for Greece and was a handsome corner building that before the occupation had been used for exhibitions, as well as performances and lectures in an auditorium that sat about 250 people. This was Easter week and she sang, mainly because it was attended by officers of the occupation army, *Stabat Mater*, an oratorio by Giovanni Pergolesi which is a sequence of the Roman Catholic liturgy. With Maria refusing even de Hidalgo's pleas that she disassociate herself from di Stasio and the occupation forces, this concert not only caused further dissension between herself and Jackie and Milton, who nonetheless continued to support Maria and Litza financially, but alienated many of her peers and became a serious threat to her continuance as a scholarship student at the Athens Conservatory.

On 2 August, under di Stasio's auspices and with Litza as her 'dresser', Maria travelled for a second time to Salonika to give a concert to an audience of Italian and German troops. The train ride was a welcome relief to the claustrophobic life in Athens, giving glimpses of the sea and beyond the many rugged islands, some of them so large that their crags faded into the blue distance. Litza had some cousins in Salonika with whom they stayed, and to whom she said Maria had been commanded to sing before the occupation troops.

The once beautiful town of Salonika had been seriously damaged during the invasion and gaping holes remained. Not far from town, buildings that had once housed a large factory had been turned into a prison camp incarcerating British soldiers and Jews, with Greek Jews being shipped weekly to Germany in alarming numbers. The concerts were held on successive nights, 2 and 3 August 1943, at the Teatro White Tower before predominantly Nazi audiences. Maria sang two programmes – selections from Rossini and the *Stabat Mater* on the first night; Schubert and Brahms Lieder on the second.

Certainly there were other Greek performers entertaining enemy troops, but that does not negate the serious infraction that Maria was committing. She said later that she never was aware of whom she was singing for but what and how she was singing. She was still young and unknown outside Greece and she sang using her Greek name, Maria Kalogeropoulou (the *ou* ending denoting female gender), all factors that would in the future blur the idea that she might have been a collaborationist.

In early September the Allies invaded Italy, suffering heavy losses, but ending Mussolini's dictatorship. Hitler severed his alliance with Italy and the Germans took over total command of Athens. The trucks and trains returning Italian troops and their officers to their homeland left them miles from the border and they were forced to make the rest of the way through country held by rebel guerrilla fighters. Others, presumably those who might have information valuable to the Allies, suddenly disappeared. One day, shortly before this exodus, Maria was entertaining di Stasio in their apartment, the next day there was no sign of him. She never again was to hear from him, nor to learn what his fate had been. Litza would always deny that Maria had any real feelings for di Stasio; Maria remained silent on the subject.

After di Stasio vanished she buried herself in her music. Her weight ballooned. Food was still scarce and what could be bought on the black market was of little variety or nutritional value. Maria was stuffing herself with dried figs, nuts and ersatz sausage.

Neither her weight gain nor her sadness over the loss of di Stasio's companionship affected her singing in a negative way. On the contrary, her voice was stronger than ever and her interpretations had grown in depth and understanding. She gave two benefit concerts at the Conservatory immediately following di Stasio's 'disappearance'. The first was for a student aid programme; the other for tuberculosis victims, a disease that was a fast-growing danger in Athens. But despite these philanthropic gestures, the Board of the Conservatory still decided to deny her scholarship status which, in effect, meant that she could no longer attend classes or continue her study with de Hidalgo under their banner. Maria was angry, bitter, resentful. She cried and she begged de Hidalgo to talk to the Board. Knowing this would be hopeless and might place her own position in jeopardy, de Hidalgo simply assured her that her vocal lessons would continue privately, no stipend expected or desired.

Maria still had her contract with the Athens Opera and it helped that she was cast as Marta in *Tiefland* a seldom performed work by Eugen d'Albert, a German composer (d. 1932) of French descent and British birth. *Tiefland* is a German verismo opera of passion and murder. The company was walking the line. The choice was one that would please the invaders but being independent of German management would give the Athens Opera the opportunity to present their company to a general audience, at least to those who could afford a ticket. The role of Marta, a woman betrayed by one man and the catalyst for his murder by her lover, was a natural showcase for Maria's dramatic soprano. She would be appearing with the tenor Antonis Dhellentas as Pedro, Marta's lover, and the baritone Evangelios Mangliveras as the man who has betrayed her. Both men were famous Greek singers. Maria was in excellent company.

Mangliveras was in his mid-forties and had sung in opera houses around the world before returning to Greece just before the war. An imposing figure with dark expressive eyes, an ebullient personality and a strong acting style, he took immediately to Maria, who responded full-heartedly. One may notice here a pattern that seems to be forming between Maria and men twice her age or more, and could easily come to the conclusion that she was looking, and appeared to find, father replacements. But in her case there was more than instantly meets the eye. She was not attractive to young men, perhaps because of her size but more likely due to her early maturity, her obsessive dedication to her music, to the exclusion of most other things. Her interest in a man was based on his ability to increase her prospects as a singer.

Di Stasio had been someone who could help her find venues in which she could sing challenging music, which in turn would further her career. He had also been able to supply some small luxuries at a bleak time in her life. With di Stasio gone, she needed a substitute. Mangliveras, known for his great acting ability, spent many additional hours beyond their rehearsals working on her dramatic interpretation of Marta. This caused them to be looked upon, at least by the other members of the company, as being romantically involved and open for criticism as Mangliveras was a married man.

The apple had not fallen too far from the tree. Maria was as ambitious as Litza ever had been and would make friendships and decisions based on how they benefited her career. There was no doubt in her mind that she would succeed as a professional singer. More important was to become the best at what she wanted to be – a successful dramatic soprano with emphasis on both the *successful* and the *dramatic*. She must cut her own niche.

Tiefland opened on 22 April 1944 and played eight performances. Maria's Marta, sung in excellent German, was her best dramatic role to date. The critic writing for the German press in Athens extolled her 'dramatic instinct, great intensity and freedom in her acting. There is a powerful metallic quality in her upper register and the quiet passages exhibit the great variety of precious colours that her youthful and innately musical soprano voice possesses.'

Before completing her engagement as Marta, she also stepped into the role of Santuzza in *Cavalleria Rusticana* for three performances ('Kalogeropoulou made a Santuzza of impulsive temperament. She is a dramatic soprano who produces her voice effortlessly and most sensitively; the tears in the voice much in evidence,' wrote one critic). This was followed by a benefit concert for poor artists (actually almost all artists were poor in Greece at this time), in which she sang the powerful aria 'Casta diva' from Act One of Vincenzo Bellini's *Norma*. Richard Wagner had once written that Bellini was a predilection of his 'because his music is strongly felt and intimately bound with the words'. 'Casta diva' is one of the most difficult of all arias Maria herself would say, not 'because a fine legato is essential but because you are so vocally exposed'. Norma, who dominates 'the savage, ferocious people she serves as priestess'. is trying to avoid war with the Romans at all costs. She is also frantically buying time before they turn on her, for she has broken her vows as priestess and borne two children by her Roman lover Pollione. The aria must be sung clean and clear with exact pitch. It demands a great deal of the singer both vocally and dramatically, and is seldom sung so early in a soprano's career. The drama, the raging conflict within Norma that must be tempered by her need to appear calm to her followers, greatly appeal-ed to Maria. She relished challenge, proving how prodigious she could be, how advanced musically for her years.

Maria was just a few months away from her twenty-first birthday. It had been eight years since she had left the United States, almost six years since she had had any word at all about her father. She seldom spoke English and knew no Americans in Athens. Yet she talked frequently about returning to the States 'when the war is over'. Mangliveras once asked her, 'Why the United States?'

'To see my father and to sing at the Metropolitan Opera.'

For now she had to be content with her work with the Athens Opera. With the defeat of the Italians it seemed the end of the war was in sight. No one anticipated that the worst was yet to come.

The Athens Opera had scheduled Ludwig van Beethoven's *Fidelio* to follow *Tiefland*. The role of Leonore was one that Maria had studied and longed to sing. After her tremendous success in *Tiefland*, with the German critics calling her 'Greece's greatest soprano', she was certain she would be cast in the part. To her disappointment she was not. The Board had chosen an older member of the company. Maria complained that politics had been at play, that the Board had purposely passed her by because of her past associations and that she was being 'reprimanded'. All that might have been true, but once they were into rehearsals the chosen Leonore proved to be ill prepared and it seemed unlikely that she could learn the role in the short time before the first scheduled performance. Maria was then asked to fill in. She instantly accepted.

Once again her leading men were Antonis Dhellentas and Evangelios Mangliveras (whom she called 'Gelo'). There were only to be four weeks of rehearsals. She had learned Leonore's arias in German, but the opera company were presenting *Fidelio* in a Greek translation. Maria was obsessed with being 'perfect' in the role. She was demanding of everyone's time, insisting on extra rehearsals, with the cast, alone with the rehearsal pianist and finally with the orchestra. She had to wear a young man's attire, as Leonore disguises herself as Fidelio in order to try to help her husband Florestan escape from prison. She was heavy and the costume did not become her, the heavily padded shoulders impeding her movement, the weight of it made more difficult by the heat of the torrid August weather and the fact that the opera was being performed in the open-air Herodes Atticus amphitheatre.

Midway through rehearsals, her grandmother suffered a heart attack and became gravely ill. The apartment at 61 Terma Patission was in turmoil. Litza had not spoken to her mother in years, had not even seemed to be concerned about her welfare during the war. Jackie had visited the elderly woman secretly, but Maria had become estranged because of Litza, although her warm feelings for her grandmother had obviously never diminished. She insisted, tearfully, with Jackie that the three of them visit her on her deathbed. Finally, Litza gave in and accompanied her daughters.

The matriarch of the proud Dimitriadis family lay pale and weak, propped up by pillows but hardly able to do more than nod her head almost imperceptibly to let the members of her gathered family know she recognized them. Jackie leaned in close to her and gave her frail body a gentle hug. Maria took her cold, limp hand in hers, tears clearly visible on her cheeks. But Litza remained unemotional as she stood by her mother's bedside and made no effort to communicate with her. Whatever had passed between them had been too bitter for her to forget even in the presence of death. But her grandmother's death did affect Maria. She felt she had been deprived by her mother of the old woman's love and her hostility towards Litza became even more intense.

Maria's appearance in *Fidelio* was a huge success. Through her fervent study of the opera and the role of Leonore, she had come to understand the spiritual and psychological themes that Beethoven meant to express. *Fidelio* is about selflessness in the face of the pursuit of freedom. Leonore is ready to die so that her husband may go free. She is a heroine of the highest order, a romantic with a sense of concentrated power, a willing martyr to the cause of liberty. In the end Leonore and Florestan are saved, but only with murderous blood on their hands. It was a brave choice of programming for the Athens Opera to stage *Fidelio* in view of the ruthlessness of the occupying German army. There were wild cheers from the Greeks in the audience when, in the final scene, Leonore frees Florestan from his chains and the other prisoners go free as well. News of the opera's triumph spread quickly and it stirred the populace who had felt chained by their conquerors for so long. Demonstrations followed. Arrests were made, but the opera continued for twelve performances, the Germans now more concerned about the close advance of the American forces and the possibility of civil disobedience and riots that could further complicate their situation as an occupying army than the subject of an opera.

The public suddenly saw Maria in a new light. The image of her as a possible collaborator was nearly banished. As often happens in theatre, the performer was seen as the character that he or she played. The last performance of *Fidelio* was given on 10 September. Much to the surprise, puzzlement, and condemnation of the company and of Mangliveras, Maria gave a concert in Salonika for the low-spirited Germans. Having recently won back some of her critics who believed she had been a collaborator, her motive is difficult to understand. She claimed to hate the Nazis (as she never had the Italians) and she had to be aware of the negative aspects of such an appearance. She quarrelled with Mangliveras over this. Just a few days later he suffered a sudden heart attack and died before reaching the hospital. Maria mourned privately but did not attend his funeral. 'He prayed so hard for Greece's liberation,' she told a close friend, 'and he was denied ever seeing it come to pass.'

British and Greek troops (who had been in Italy with the Free Greek Army) were now practically at the steps of the Acropolis. On 19 October, after three and a half years of oppressive occupation, the Germans goose-stepped out of Athens. That evening, amid joyous singing, people shouted from windows and crowded the streets, dancing, creating wraithlike shadows in the clouded moonlight. They were a bizarre sight, many of them emaciated to the point of looking like ghostly spectres as they hurled torn German signs into a blazing street fire. Stark reminders of the war abounded; the empty stores, burnt-out buildings, the general dilapidation.

During the long, difficult years since coming to Greece, Maria had purposely ignored what was happening around her to concentrate on her music and on the day-to-day business of simply surviving. The war's end nurtured resentment towards her mother who, by bringing them to Greece, had placed her in constant jeopardy. She had been spirited away from her father, robbed of her right to free choice, lost her youth and was held captive by Litza's dream. Yet if not for that, would she have cocooned herself in her music, advanced at the tremendous speed at which she had? Would she have come so far, so soon, so young in her career if she had remained in America?

In exchange for all her hardships she had reached a dedication, a concentration that it is doubtful she would have achieved under less difficult circumstances. But now she wanted to leave Litza and her overbearing possessiveness, leave Athens with its harsh memories and be reunited with her father. She was, after all, an American citizen, and it was in the United States that she felt she would be able to work with a teacher greater than de Hidalgo and an opera company of international reputation like the Metropolitan. She made plans that, as soon as an American embassy attaché was again assigned to the city, she would seek a method of returning to her 'homeland'. She had no money. Of course, there was always Milton, who seemed able to produce whatever currency was necessary at a given time, but she would try first to arrange some financing on her own.

She was full of plans, secretive, exhilarating. She enquired into which ships were available for passenger service, what her fare would cost. She wrote a long, pleading letter of reconciliation to her father and sent it, along with a newspaper clipping with her picture as Leonore in *Fidelio*, signed *Your younger daughter*, to the last address of his that she had. Then she waited anxiously for a reply. She was brimming with hope that soon she would be delivered from her hard life in Athens and on her way to a hoped-for future as an internationally famous singer. She believed nothing could stop her. Then, one morning in early December just a few days before her twenty-first birthday, she awoke to the frightening sound of near gunshots and screams of terror. She ran to her window and, upon seeing men with guns on the roofs of buildings and people scattering in the street below, quickly withdrew, closed the blinds and ran to find Litza, who was shouting to her from another room. The incredible had happened. The guerrilla resistance fighters, mainly members of the communist party, had come down off the mountains, placed the city under siege and were in the process of attempting to take over the government by means of violence, and the section of the city that they now had under attack encircled Terma Patission. On the street below her bedroom window corpses were strewn. Snipers were poised atop nearby buildings shooting at anyone who emerged. Litza was hysterical and Maria could hardly keep her own emotions under control.

Across town, Jackie and Milton were powerless to help as no one could get in or out of the area that had been seized. Maria and Litza were prisoners in the apartment. So that the snipers could not see them, they kept the curtains drawn twenty-four hours a day, no lights day or night except for a candle in the dining room, which had no windows. They had some food, but not much, and the water supply had been cut off. Maria was afraid to play the piano for fear of drawing attention to them. She had three canaries, that had been her pets for many years, and she would close herself into the dining room with them and sing to their high trilling to keep her mind from freezing with the fear she was experiencing.

'Once,' Jackie recalled Maria telling her, 'desperate for air, they had gone down below and edged open the door, only to find a dead American soldier sprawled across the entrance.' On the twentieth night, when Maria had taken the canary cage back to her room, a sniper's bullet came through the closed window and the drawn curtains, and struck one of the golden birds. It was horrifying. Somehow there must have been a slit in the curtain which had allowed a sniper on the adjoining roof to see into the room. The next morning help came. Milton had managed to find a man willing to place his life at risk by stealthily going into the area, making his way to their apartment and then to guide them through the besieged section to the safe sector of the city. At first Litza refused him entry, fearing the worst. Finally, she allowed him in. Then she was adamant that they could not possibly venture outside the apartment. But once again, with Maria's urging, she capitulated.

The two women put on layers of clothing and stuffed the few small valuables they could into their pockets then, terrified, followed the man (who refused to give them his name) out of the basement door of their building, down into the basement of another, making a circuitous journey through alleyways, hiding until it seemed the path was clear and dodging behind buildings until they were finally beyond the captured area. From there they went directly to Jackie's hotel, where a room had been held for them, and ate their first meal in three weeks.

Hopes were raised for a speedy end to the siege when it was announced over the BBC that Winston Churchill was flying to Athens to speak to the surviving members of the reinstated Greek government and offer aid. On Christmas Eve crowds, Maria among them, lined the streets waiting for a glimpse of the great English leader who symbolized strength. She would claim that one of the greatest thrills she had known was getting close enough to see Churchill raise his hand above his head in a V for Victory sign and then get into his car to be whisked away.

A short time later, with the uprising curbed, a small sense of normalcy returned to the badly bruised city. Maria and Litza went home to their apartment. The curtains were opened and the winter sun allowed to shine in.

In March 1945, the letter Maria had written to her father was returned – 'not known at this address'. Her letter had never reached him. She thought she could contact him through her godfather, Dr Lantzounis, asked Litza for his address and revealed her hope to return to the United

States. 'But I don't want to go back there,' Litza exclaimed with some surprise.

'Not you, *me*, Mama,' Maria replied. 'I am going to America on my own.'

Her mother was distraught. She warned her that it would be a grievous mistake. 'Europe is where great opera is performed,' she insisted.

They had a terrible fight about this. Maria left the house in a rage and went directly to see de Hidalgo. 'Your mother is right,' she agreed. 'You must go to Italy first.' For the first time in their long association, Maria and de Hidalgo had a violent argument with the older woman shouting at her that she must go to Italy, not to America, and Maria shouting back that she had decided and that was that.

The address Litza had given Maria for Dr Lantzounis also proved out of date, but she persisted. She went to see the American envoy who promised to see what he could do to locate her father and the doctor. No ships were yet leaving Greece for the United States, but as she was an American citizen he would see what could be done to secure passage for her on one of the very few westward-bound ships taking on passengers to a port where a vessel might be going across the Atlantic. He also offered to apply for American funds to help her pay for her passage to New York on the second wing of the journey.

Money was an important issue and Maria set to work organizing a concert at the Teatro Kotopoulli-Rex for 3 August. Accompanied on the piano by Aliki Lykoudi, she sang arias from *Don Giovanni*, *Semiramide*, *Aida* and *Il Trovatore*, ending her performance with Spanish and Greek folk songs. The performance was well attended and she was able to pocket the equivalent of nearly $100, more money than she had ever seen but still not much of a stake for the journey she intended to make.

The summer was stifling and Athens still on rationing – eggs, meat, fat and sugar hard to come by. Men in uniform, now of the British and Greek armies (and some Americans) were a constant reminder of the war. Maria had no telephone and walked in the blistering heat across town several times a week to the office of the American envoy to see if there was news on her passage 'home'.

Meanwhile, she accepted the role of Laura in the operetta *Der Bettelstudent* (*The Beggar Student*) by Karl Millöcker, which was to be presented by the Athens Opera on 5 September for twelve performances. 'Before departing,' she later said, 'I wanted to give them a last sample of my art to remember me more vividly. They were obliged to entrust this difficult role to me because no one else could sing it.'

The underlying truth was that Maria was extremely nervous as she waited for word that she could leave Athens; at the same time Litza and de Hidalgo were putting daily pressure on her to change her mind. Rehearsals and performances would keep her occupied and able to avoid, at least to some degree, these constant entreaties. De Hidalgo was loath to lose the best student she had ever trained. But she also truly felt that Maria would be making a serious mistake in her career to go to the United States before establishing herself with an internationally known Italian company. 'A singer's career is built on youth,' Maria replied. (In time she would add, 'Wisdom comes later.') 'You need the prestige that an association with an Italian company would give you,' de Hidalgo counselled. 'Yes, you have had much acclaim here. But the Athens Opera is a provincial company and what was produced by them during the war received no notice elsewhere. At present, singers end their career here, not begin it. You must go to Italy where the bel canto style of singing [which is what de Hidalgo taught] will be better developed and appreciated.'

'Bel canto', Maria explained in master classes she would one day give, 'is a method of singing, a sort of strait-jacket you must put on. You learn how to approach a note, how to attack it, how to form a legato, how to create a mood, how to breathe so that there is a feeling of only a beginning and an ending. In between, it must seem as if you have taken only one big breath, though in actuality there will be many phrases with many little breaths.'

She would never deny that de Hidalgo and her bel canto training had formed a solid base from which to work. She was grateful to her. But this was the time when she must move on. Hers had been an interrupted life. She needed to reconnect with her roots in the same way that her mother had once found necessary. Her youth had been spent in Greece, but her roots were in America. Images of her early years in New York haunted her. She recalled with great longing walking down a street in Manhattan with her father, each of them eating an ice-cream cone, and how they could communicate without saying a word, just glancing at each other, eyes locking. Her world was good then and it would not have changed that much for there had been no bombs to destroy all the landmarks that she could recall – the school she had attended, the park where they went to picnic, the New York Public Library where she had spent so many afternoons.

Just before the eighth performance of *Der Bettelstudent* word came from the American envoy that there was a place for her on a boat leaving Piraeus the very next afternoon that would connect in Le Havre with the SS *Stockholm*, en route to New York. A berth had been reserved in her name. She would arrive in New York in ten days' time. This meant leaving the Athens Opera in mid-run without a suitable Laura. That was not a consideration as far as she was concerned. Litza raged through the apartment as Maria packed her few possessions and, most importantly, her many music manuscripts. Jackie, for once, agreed with Litza. It had just been discovered that Milton had cancer. Jackie could now see that she would not only have to contend with his illness, his family's indifference to the years she had given him and the possibility of losing the small income he had supplied, but she would have the sole responsibility of their mother. She was resentful, bitter.

Neither woman accompanied Maria to the boat. Dr Papatesta and his wife, neighbours at 61 Terma Patission, along with Elvira de Hidalgo escorted her to Piraeus, gave a small celebratory lunch (not a send-off by the mayor of Athens as Litza would later claim), after which Maria boarded the small vessel and stood waving to them, as once she had to her father, until she could see them no more.

Maria knew no one on this boat, or the SS *Stockholm*, and had not yet learned where her father or Dr Lantzounis lived. She could think of no one else to contact in New York. In her purse were $100, her entire personal wealth. Yet she felt free for the first time in eight years. She was saying goodbye to Maria Kalogeropoulou. As her American passport stated, she was now Maria Callas.

5

New York: 1945–1947

MARIA CAME UP on deck at dawn to peer through the early morning haze as the SS *Stockholm*, amid the brooding, ghostly calls of foghorns, slowly entered New York harbour. The voyage had been uneventful. She had remained aloof for most of the journey, not wanting to be recognized and asked to sing. Soon she realized that the few Greeks on board would not know her as Maria Callas and that fellow passengers of other nationalities (and the passenger list read like an international convention) had never heard of her. From that point she moved about more freely, although she posed a lonely figure as she still kept much to herself.

Her accommodation in the tourist section (which Litza would have abhorred) was an upper berth in a cabin for four, shared with two women and a young child, all three Portuguese Jews on the first leg of a long sea voyage to Brazil to rejoin members of the family from whom they had been separated for many years. Communication was difficult, yet Maria certainly understood their apprehension at leaving so much behind without knowing what might face them at their final destination. She nurtured her own concerns about what she would do once she was back in New York. With so little money, her immediate options were few.

The American envoy had given her names of several Greek-American organizations that would find her a temporary place to live and might be able to assist her in her search for her father. She would have to find employment of some sort to help support herself until she had achieved a singing contract. Her sights were high. No other opera company would do but the Metropolitan. Just before the war, she had met the well-known bass, Nicola Moscana, who had heard her sing Santuzza in *Cavalleria Rusticana* (one selection from scene two) in 1939. Moscana, a Greek, whose real name was Nicolai Moscanas, was born in Athens and had studied at the Athens Conservatory and sung in Egypt and Italy before making his debut in 1937 as Ramfis in Aida. He had returned to Athens to see his family and had trouble securing passage out of Greece.

Much impressed by the promise of this young soprano, Moscana had told Maria then that she had a bright future and that if she ever needed assistance in her career to call on him. For Moscana, this had been a casual offer. No doubt he recognized her talent. But within six months he had returned to the United States to become the Metropolitan Opera's leading bass, singing over thirty different roles during the war years when the Met had found itself depleted of many of its finest singers. Moscana remained in constant demand, singing a multiplicity of roles during a season. It never occurred to Maria that with his grand success he might not remember her. She had, after all, never forgotten their meeting, so why should he? Therefore her plan was to contact him as soon as she was organized and her audition pieces were well prepared.

So confident was she in her fantasized happy ending of this fictional scenario that she had given careful thought to what terms she would or would not accept when offered a contract. Although insecure in her personal life, Maria was so single-minded and well-focused on her extraordinary singing talent that she never doubted she would be signed by the Metropolitan. Of greater importance was what she would sing in her American debut. It had to be a role in which she could display her best talent as a dramatic soprano, one where she could command the stage: *Tosca, Norma, Turandot.* Yes, she was heavy, although not obese. Divas were seldom thin and Maria thought only in terms of star roles. She had brought with her all her reviews while with the Athens Opera and with them all the youthful dreams of quick fame that her early success in Greece had inculcated in her.

A wild cheer rose on deck as the Statue of Liberty came in view to the passengers on the SS *Stockholm.* Only three weeks earlier, on 2 September, the Japanese had signed surrender terms aboard the battleship *Missouri* after atomic bombs had been dropped on Hiroshima and Nagasaki. VJ-Day now officially declared, the war was over, the Allies victorious, Hitler and Mussolini dead. No one had yet tallied how many had died in the Holocaust, were dead or missing in the collected armies of the world, or the numbers of innocent civilians who had not survived enemy bombings, strafings and the many other horrors of the most devastating war ever. But in the rosy glow of victory, of a supposed peace that would now reign throughout the world, those grisly figures were not yet raised as ghosts of a second world war that no one had believed could ever happen. People on the ship were ecstatically happy to be coming to America and Maria could be numbered among them.

Midday had passed by the time the SS *Stockholm* was finally manoeu-vred into its berth, anchored and those with valid American passports began to descend the lowered gangplank that would bring them once again on to native soil. The fog had lifted and as Maria, struggling with several heavy portfolios containing her music, started her descent, she suddenly realized the immensity of what was before her. She later recalled how frightened and lonely she felt, that the confidence she had carried with her across the ocean seemed, at least momentarily, to slip away. Hundreds of people were crushing towards the new arrivals. She was quite certain no one would be there to greet her, that she would have to make her way to the baggage shed by herself and go to the counter marked 'Travelers' Aid' as she had been advised to do. So she grasped her precious music portfolios close to her and started to barrel her way through the crowds caught up in tearful and joyful reunions, plopping bags and children everywhere, making it impossible to walk a straight path.

Then, unexpectedly, came a cry, 'Maria!' and a dapper man, with a trim moustache, wearing a fedora, a white handkerchief folded 'just so' in the pocket of his chesterfield overcoat, grabbed hold of her hand baggage and then threw his one free arm round her shoulders. 'Maria! Maria!' he continued to cry.

Maria looked straight into the eyes of her father and began to sob with happiness and relief. Eight years had passed since they had seen each other. Time had mellowed his appearance. Grey streaked his hair. She remembered him as being much younger, but otherwise he had changed very little, even the scent of his hair tonic was the same. Maria, on the other hand, was a thirteen-year-old child when George Callas had last seen his younger daughter. Now she was a woman, full-busted, mature, wearing make-up, high heels and a not-too-attractive form-fitting dress. Yet he had recognized her by her walk, the way she carried her head and 'those blazing eyes'. Perhaps it was something instinctive.

He had received no word of her coming. By chance he had read of the ship's imminent arrival the previous day in the newspaper. Mention had been made that it carried many international passengers, among them some Americans who had been caught abroad during the war and were only now returning home. He called the Swedish Line for a list of those passengers and, miracle of miracles, there it was: *Maria Callas*. He accom-panied her to the baggage shed where she claimed the two small suitcases she had brought with her and then he hailed a taxi to his apartment on West 157th Street, near the one they had once shared as a family. She would stay with him, of course? She quickly and gratefully agreed.

They exchanged notes on their most recent history. He asked about Jackie and was disturbed by what she told him 'And your mother?'

'The same,' she replied.

George was working in a drugstore owned by a Greek family. The salary was not grand, but it paid the bills. He would help her with whatever little he had. She told him all about her singing, her triumphs, her hopes for an American career and, when they reached his apartment, she showed him her clippings, overjoyed at the pride he displayed. It seemed to her that everything was turning out as she hoped it would. Washington Heights had changed very little and her father's apartment was in a building that she knew quite well, for her mother's friends, the Papajohns, with whom she had picnicked as a child, had lived in the building. Only a week had passed when she realized that their daughter, Alexandra, still lived upstairs in her parents' old apartment and that she and her father were lovers.

In fact, Alexandra was running George's household and obviously had been doing so for a long while before Maria's return. She did the shopping, prepared their meals and remained for dinner, after which George would escort her upstairs to her apartment and not return for the rest of the evening. Maria should not have been shocked. After all, her father was still in his fifties and had not had the company of his wife for eight years (and probably not for some years before that). A quiet woman of good bearing and manner, Alexandra was unmarried, in her late thirties and, although stolid of build and simple in her dress, not unattractive. The lovers had known each other for years, their friendship had slowly evolved into its current relationship and had George not still been a married man (albeit in name only), they would have married. If she even fleetingly recalled the years of unhappiness her mother had inflicted on her father, Maria should have had some empathy for his situation. But she felt a tremendous possessiveness once she had been reunited with her father. In the perfect scheme of things, where she was concerned, Alexandra was a thorn.

An unpleasant row took place in which Maria told her father it was either her or his mistress. George refused to make such a choice. In a display of Litza-like wilfulness, Maria left the apartment and took a room at the elegant Astor Hotel (its French Renaissance façade a New York landmark since 1904), which she soon realized she could not afford, although she had a small single room. After five days, George paid her bill and she came back to the apartment with the agreement that while she was living there she, not Alexandra, would be in charge. One can only assume Maria's sense of morality had much more to do with her personal pique about having to share her new-found parent with a rival far younger than her mother. George was no more able to stand up to his daughter than he had been to his wife and Alexandra, on her part, was not strong enough to demand equal consideration.

Maria's money was fast disappearing as she strolled through the city, stopping along the way to eat – sometimes as many as three or four times in an afternoon – American food: hot dogs, hamburgers, pancakes with syrup, and all the sweet desserts she loved and had missed for so long. 'I was hungry as you are hungry when you have not had enough to eat for a long, long time. I ate and ate and ate,' she remembered, 'and I put on a great deal of weight.' This meant the few clothes she had no longer fitted her and she had to buy new ones. What little George could give her, apart from money to spend on household needs, was not enough to cover her personal expenses. She gave some thought to obtaining work but quickly dismissed it. She was not qualified to hold a well-paying job. More important, she had to get back to her music and to activating her career in America. This meant having access to a piano, a vocal coach and an agent. Also, she needed to be somewhere mid-town, away from Washington Heights and the life that she now saw as being middle class.

One of the only people she had contacted from her former life had been her godfather, Dr Lantzounis, now married to a young woman, Sally, only a few years older than herself. Dr Lantzounis, an affluent orthopaedic surgeon, was interested in her career, especially as she often came to their apartment, where there was a piano, to practise. By Christmas 1945 she had secured a loan and a small monthly stipend from the good doctor to enable her to concentrate on her future. She could not yet move out of her father's apartment, but she spent more time with Sally and Dr Lantzounis in their Eastside Manhattan duplex than she did with her father and Alexandra.

Her immediate problems solved, Maria next tried to contact Nicola Moscana. She called the office of the Metropolitan Opera House but staff refused to give her his home address or telephone number. Next she wrote a letter to him care of the Metropolitan. With no reply coming after two weeks, she called the Met and asked to speak with his secretary, not actually knowing if he had one. But he did and the woman agreed that she would pass on the message that Maria was the young woman he had heard sing Santuzza in Athens in 1939, that she was now in New York and wanted to take him up on his offer back then to assist her if he could. Again no reply. This back-and-forth, no-end situation went on for several months before Maria came to accept the fact that Moscana either did not remember her, or simply did not wish to extend his help. Still she would not give up and since he would not reply directly or agree to hear her sing, she continued to write him letters turning from her pleas that he see her to a request that he mention her to Edward Johnson, now acting director of the Metropolitan, adding that perhaps he could suggest her name to the great conductor Arturo Toscanini, who she had heard was a good friend of his.

Time was slipping by too quickly without any progress being made with her career. With Litza no longer by her side to push for her, Maria found she could be more aggressive than she had thought. Letters flew back and forth between New York and Athens, but she did not tell her mother about Alexandra and her father. Nonetheless, Litza's missiles were filled with recriminations and complaints. Milton's illness had progressed and with it his generosity to her had decreased. She was having difficult times and what was Maria doing? She was making the rounds of agents and concert managers, seldom able to get past the front desk, finding that no one in the New York opera world regarded her years with the Athens Opera as a serious credential. The very fact that she had sung Santuzza and Leonore at such a youthful age was suspect. Perhaps these were just student performances (Santuzza, of course, had been just that). Her reviews were in Greek, which had not been translated and which no one could therefore read. The time had not yet arrived when an audition tape could be submitted. Auditions were live and meant great blocks of time had to be reserved to hear them. It was suggested that she find or hire a venue where she could give a recital. That, too, proved impossibly expensive.

At Easter's approach, and after almost six months of rejections, her spirits at a low ebb, Maria got her first major audition, not with the Met but with the world-renowned tenor, Giovanni Martinelli, who had recently become Dr Lantzounis's patient, when he injured his wrist during a performance.

Martinelli was a revered singer, a legend, as they say, in his time. At sixty and under contract to the Met, he was still singing, his voice 'sterling silver', his style impeccable, his technique faultless. Engaged by Puccini at the age of twenty-six for the European première of *La Fanciulla del West*, he had been a leading tenor at the Met since 1913, famous for his Otello. He was transformed into an international star when he sang Tristan opposite the legendary Kirsten Flagstad's Isolde in two world-famous Chicago Opera productions. Martinelli's endorsement would carry weight and Maria was certain that if he spoke to Edward Johnson on her behalf she would have her audition with the Met.

Since January Maria had been working with Louise Taylor, a vocal teacher, who had enthusiastically taken her on for a reduced fee (paid for by her godfather), because she was so struck by her talent. Taylor recommended that she sing 'Casta diva' from *Norma* and Maria hired a rehearsal pianist (his name appears to have been lost with time) to accompany her to Martinelli's Manhattan apartment. Once there, they had to wait a long while until the divo emerged from his private suite to greet her in a cool manner. Clearly, this was an interruption in his day, a promise he made to the doctor who had helped him, which he now regretted. Listening to a young, untried singer was always difficult for a professional if you were a feeling individual, which Martinelli was. Seldom did such an audition end with the discovery of a great and polished talent. This meant having to tell a hopeful that he or she had to be a hopeful for a good time longer, or perhaps to give up the idea of a career in opera altogether. From experience Martinelli knew that to be too friendly could intensify the let-down if the latter proved to be the case.

There was no one else in the room but Maria, the accompanist and Martinelli, who sat in a straight chair. Still a good-looking man with strong Mediterranean features, he motioned Maria to begin. She got off to a nervous start and did not seem able to contradict this first impression. Martinelli did not interrupt her. When she had finished he stood up and told her she had a good voice, one that was worth further study with a strong vocal coach. There was an unpleasantness at times in her tone. The coolness had remained. He shook her hand, thanked the pianist and disappeared instantly.

Maria returned to Louise Taylor, devastated. It was the first time she had sung for anyone that famous and she had been dismissed as a rank amateur. Taylor was furious, not able to understand what might have gone wrong during the audition. Her vocal coach was not the only one who believed in Maria. Taylor's two close friends were forty-something Richard 'Eddie' Bagarozy, a lawyer, and his wife Louise Caselotti, a mezzo-soprano who had made a career in Hollywood during the late thirties and early forties, dubbing the voices of several leading actresses who could barely carry a tune but had been cast in musicals. The Bagarozys, both of whom had given up their former careers, were in pursuit of a dream: to organize an opera company of their own. They had unlimited faith in Maria, who often sang in the living room of their grand Manhattan Riverside Drive apartment, its wide, floor-to-ceiling windows offering a dramatic view across the Hudson river to New Jersey.

The Bagarozys were a handsome cosmopolitan couple of Italian-American heritage who had travelled the world and knew many famous people. Maria had been immediately taken with them. Louise looked very much as though she could have been Maria's older sister and indeed, their relationship took on that special aura. Maria trusted Louise's taste and Eddie's entrepreneurial abilities. They quickly buoyed her spirits. Parties were hosted in grand style by the Bagarozys, and attended by opera buffs and a few genuine 'names'. Maria sang, in a sense as entertainment so that guests would not feel they had been subjected to an audition or were expected to invest money in Eddie's neophyte enterprise (which they were).

Word of the Bagarozys' talented protégée made its way back to Edward Johnson, who already – from Maria's many letters to him – had Maria's résumé. Johnson was a gifted Canadian tenor who had come to the Met by way of Broadway, singing for seven years under the name of Eduardo di Giovanni in Italy. (He was the first Parsifal at La Scala.) He had spent several seasons singing with the Chicago Opera, finally making his Metropolitan singing debut in 1922 as Avito in Montemezzi's *L'Amore dei tre re*. Under contract with the Met for the next thirteen years, he was tapped to become the opera's commander-in-chief in 1935 in the midst of the Depression, following a year of furious fund-raising on his part to keep the Met running after stockholders' contributions had fallen dramatically, placing the Met in crisis.

Johnson had inherited a company that faced ruin. He instigated Saturday afternoon radio programmes of operas, an enterprise that brought the Met $90,000 in its first season. It seemed the Met was saved. Then came the war to add more burdensome problems. Suddenly, as so many European artists were caught by the war in their homelands, the Met was faced with a dire shortage of singers. (The war worked in reverse where conductors were involved, many like Bruno Walter, Sir Thomas Beecham and Georg Széll at the outbreak of war, remained in New York with the Met.) Johnson then started a vigorous campaign to sign talented American artists and fostered a whole generation of important ones including Helen Traubel, Risë Stevens, Leonard Warren, Eleanor Steber, Jan Peerce, Astrid Varnay, Regina Resnik, Dorothy Kirsten, Richard Tucker, Robert Merrill and Jerome Hines.

When Maria had first written to him for an audition, Johnson had had no openings and her credentials – the Athens Opera – held no interest for him. His secretary had finally written to her to enter the auditions held each season for young singers, the winners receiving radio contracts and a chance to appear in one opera in a supporting role during the following season. That was not the way that Maria envisioned beginning her career in America and she had quickly decided against such an approach. With all avenues seemingly closed, she still refused to compromise.

But in June 1946 Johnson was faced with a serious scheduling problem. He had included *Fidelio* in the 1946–7 season and at the moment he did not have a dramatic soprano to sing Leonore. It now entered his mind that a résumé he had received came from the same young singer someone had recently spoken to him about and that it had included her having sung the role with the Athens Opera. Although written in Greek, there were reviews. He had these translated and after reading them put in a call for Maria to come to the Met for an audition.

None of this did Maria know. She was thrilled when she got the call from Johnson's office. It seemed to her that, at last, her dream would be realized. Armed once again with the music for 'Casta diva', she dressed carefully in a simple outfit in which she would be comfortable and took a taxi (a great extravagance) down to the 40th Street entrance to the block-long, warehouse-like, yellow-brick structure that was then the home of the country's foremost opera company.

Edward Johnson proved to be a less imposing figure than Giovanni Martinelli, although far more attractive and charming, with even features and hair gracefully touched with grey. At sixty-eight, he remained a handsome, sartorially splendid man, dressed, as was his custom, in a well-tailored dark suit, jewelled cufflinks in his custom-made, French-cuffed shirt, an English Paisley tie and a pristine white handkerchief poking out of the breast pocket of his suit jacket (which reminded her of her father). He welcomed her pleasantly. Spoke to her for a few moments to ease any tension she might have had and then took a front seat in the small rehearsal hall to which she had been directed.

Never had she sung 'Casta diva' better. Johnson rose to his feet and came up to the piano, where she still stood, and congratulated her. 'Come with me to my office,' he said and led the way through the winding halls of the labyrinthine building. Once she was seated across from him at his paper-stacked mahogany desk, he told her he would like to sign her to a contract. Of course, since she was young and untried, he could not pay her much, but she would make her debut in the upcoming season in a starring role. Maria was exultant. 'Which?' she asked.

'Leonore in *Fidelio*. I understand you sang it in German, but it should not be too difficult for you to learn the English translation we will be presenting.' He then added that if she did well there was a good chance she could also sing *Madama Butterfly*. To his surprise, Maria sat bolt upright in her chair and replied that she did not think either of those roles was suited for her debut in America.

She had recently played Leonore and hated the male costume she was forced to wear. She was much heavier now and knew it would look even more ludicrous on her and she would seem to be no more well-suited to sing the fragile Butterfly. Also, *Fidelio* had been a grand success in Athens due to the political climate at the time, but Leonore did not have any aria that Maria felt would make her debut a striking one. This was the big opportunity she had been waiting for. Nevertheless, she did not want to make a fool of herself and perhaps lose any chance she had to become a leading singer with the Met. She asked if there was not an opening in another opera. No, there was not, she was told.

Maria sat back in her chair. There was a long pause before she replied, 'I'm afraid I can't accept your offer, then.'

'She was right in turning it down,' Johnson said much later. 'It was frankly a beginner's contract; she was without experience, without repertory. She was quite overweight but... the young ones are usually too fat.' At the time, he had been very disappointed and surprised that a singer so new to the United States and without having sung any major roles in any great opera house would say no to a contract with the Met. Regina Resnik, who had had some success with the New York City Center before her recent contract with the Met, was really a mezzo-soprano, but agreed to sing Leonore. The opera was not successful and although Resnik received good personal reviews, the role did not much enhance her career as a singer who, like Callas, had a vivid dramatic sense.

Maria returned to the Bagarozys' apartment and told them what had happened. No one could believe she had refused a contract at the Met. Louise Taylor threw up her arms and told her she had ruined any chance she ever had of making a name for herself in the States. 'Nonsense,' she snapped. 'One day the Met will come on their knees to me, begging me to sing.'

Following fast on the heels of the Met offer came a request from the San Francisco Opera Company for her to audition. This company had been founded in 1923 by Gaetano Merola, a conductor with managerial skills and impeccable taste who had raised his company to rank second only to the Met, whose artists often appeared in his productions. Merola came to New York once a year to recruit new talent and Louise Taylor had set up an audition. It did not go well. Maria hated auditions, not because of having to prove herself, for she enjoyed that aspect. But she was more comfortable singing for an audience rather than one person and, if she did not feel any chemistry with that person, her performance could be affected. She took an immediate dislike to Merola who treated her like a schoolgirl from the moment of their first meeting and his warning, 'You must lose weight. You are much too heavy for your age.'

When she had finished singing he viewed her sceptically for a few moments. 'You are young,' she recalled he told her. 'Go make your career in Italy and then I will sign you up.'

'Thank you,' she replied archly, 'but once I have made my career in Italy I will no longer need you!' And she marched past him and out of the room. The exchange was one that Maria was proud to report. Certainly, she had no deficiency of arrogance. The small circle of admirers – the Lantzounises, Bagarozys, Louise Taylor and some of the invited guests to the Bagarozys' musical evenings – had fed her ego and with good cause. Maria was a tremendous talent, but she was also not everyone's cup of tea. If slightly ruffled, her personality could be highly unpleasant. She was indeed grossly overweight and the daytime clothes she wore for auditions were not flattering. More pertinent, her vocal technique at times seemed lacking in training.

Maria had a great dramatic voice, unique to her, but to a man like Merola, who had to think in terms of a company, not an individual performer, one can understand his concern. Maria was not yet ready to sing with ensemble artists, in duet or trio as well as solo, or to be flexible enough to be cast in a variety of roles. It could be argued that Merola was giving her an honestly felt appraisal and, by saying he would engage her after she had more experience, was offering her something to work towards. Maria's snippy reply was outrageously stupid. It might have made a funny bon mot to relate to her admirers, but she had now said no to the Met and lost any chance in the near future of changing Merola's mind about her. The two highest-ranking opera companies in America were thus out of her grasp.

She might not have been so overweening if the Bagarozys had not encouraged such behaviour. Eddie was still involved in creating his own opera company which, of course, would not only include his wife, but Maria and numerous foreign artists whom, through his association with Ottavio Scotti, an Italian agent, he had managed to sign with promises of great freedom in their roles and escalating bonuses if an opera did particularly well. Among these artists were the tenor Galliano Masini, who had sung with the Chicago Opera during one of its failed former resurrections, the bass, Nicola Rossi-Lemeni, fresh from his debut in Venice that year, the soprano Mafalda Favero, a fine Mimì and Manon, and the Wagnerian tenor Max Lorenz.

For most of 1946 Eddie worked to raise capital to establish a new Chicago Civic Opera Company with these artists in the opera house that had been built in 1929 and had, in 1933, fallen victim to the Depression. In the intervening years various attempts to reactivate the company had failed. Eddie was, above all else, a consummate promoter, able to get to the people and the institutions that might be likely to support such an enterprise. But Chicago was now looked upon as being unfriendly to opera, when even in its 1920s heyday with the world-famous Mary Garden at its helm, the opera house had lost over one million dollars in a single year.

Despite these obstacles, Eddie managed to raise enough money to get things going. He needed a good many more investors. Towards the end of 1946 he started rehearsals in his apartment for a production of *Turandot* which would star Maria. Taking a tip from the Broadway theatre, he held money-raising evenings with selections from the opera. Maria was ecstatic. She could envision an opera company that revolved around herself. In such an illusory mood, she worried how she would handle all the burdens of fame on her own and decided that she needed to have someone beside her whom she could trust entirely. Who else could that be but her mother who was barely surviving in Athens and complaining in bitter letters about how Maria had deserted her at her time of greatest need. Maria, without consulting her father, once again went to Dr Lantzounis to seek funds, this time to bring her mother back to the States. Her godfather, being told erroneously that this is what her parents wished, complied.

Litza's imminent arrival created a major crisis for George and Alexandra. Litza would be returning to the apartment on West 157th Street as George's wife. There could be no other answer for Maria's interference in her parents' lives than a total lack of sensitivity as to George's wishes, a need to end his affair with Alexandra and to put his marriage back together even if that was not what he wanted. Alexandra was distraught and George in an acute state of agitation. Maria kept insisting that this was the best for everyone and in the end George agreed to give his marriage a second chance.

The luxurious British ocean liner, *Queen Elizabeth*, with Litza travelling cabin class, arrived in New York on a frigid Christmas Eve in 1946. Both her husband and her daughter were there to greet her. It was easy to see from the moment of this first reunion that George and Litza would not, even under the best of circumstances, have an easy time reconciling their differences. During Christmas Day there was a violent confrontation. Litza had found evidence of Alexandra's relationship with George. She shouted accusations of 'Your whore!' and threw anything that looked as if it belonged to Alexandra out of the window and on to the street below. She then barricaded herself into the bedroom and forbade George to come anywhere near her. She threatened suicide if Alexandra did not leave the building. Fearing Litza might just be crazy enough to kill herself, Alexandra moved in with her elderly mother a few streets away.

'Father shrugged and decided his worst nightmare had enveloped him and his crazy womenfolk were back in control again,' Jackie wrote. A quasi-settlement was reached with Litza and Maria sharing one bedroom and George sleeping in the other. Maria was frantic: furious at having brought such a problem on herself. Her freedom was suddenly in jeopardy as her mother would carry on hysterically when she decided to spend the night at the Bagarozys' apartment.

Then, to heap more coals on this fiery mess, Eddie Bagarozy found himself facing bankruptcy. The American Guild of Musical Artists had demanded a steep bond to guarantee the salaries of the singers in his company. Unable to post it, his investors withdrew and he was left with no money to pay overdue salaries, for costumes that had been ordered and sets that were being designed. There would be no *Turandot*, no star turn for Maria. She could no longer even escape to the Bagarozys' apartment for it had to be put up for sale.

Just when things looked darkest and Litza was suggesting that perhaps her daughter should find a sales job with a weekly salary, hope appeared with the arrival of the famous septuagenarian tenor Giovanni Zenatella, Puccini's original Pinkerton in *Madama Butterfly* and the founder and director of the Arena di Verona summer festival, held in the spectacular open-air Roman arena, which seats some 25,000 people. Zenatella – opera greats Lily Pons's and Nino Martini's former teacher – was looking for a young soprano to sing Gioconda in Amilcare Ponchielli's dramatic four-act opera *La Gioconda*. The bass Rossi-Lemeni, another member of Bagarozy's ill-fated opera company, had been signed as Alvise, a leader of the Inquisition. Rossi-Lemeni suggested that the director listen to Maria before making a decision on the casting of Giocanda and Zenatella agreed.

Maria sang 'Suicidio', a dramatic monologue from the last act of the opera that she had studied with de Hidalgo. In the aria Gioconda, seized by despair – her lover is lost to her, her mother has disappeared – contemplates suicide. Before Maria was finished, Zenatella was on his feet. She had exactly the right voice and dramatic ability that he was searching for. Eddie stepped in to handle the contract arrangements and the following day presented her with an agent's contract giving him exclusive rights of representation for a period of ten years which, though with reluctance, she signed.

Maria's dilemma had been solved. Not only would she make her Italian debut in a starring role, one in which she could display all her best talents, she would do so under the baton of the great Italian conductor Tullio Serafin, who had conducted at the Metropolitan Opera for ten years and had been a motivating force in the career of Rosa Ponselle. She also would be able to escape the intolerable situation she herself had created by reuniting her parents.

Litza was furious that she was to be left behind in New York in what was truly a hostile and difficult situation and only somewhat soothed when Maria gave her most of the money she was paid upon signing the contract. Three months later, considerably thinner, she was seen off by her parents and Eddie Bagarozy on the eight-day voyage to Naples on the Russian ship SS *Rossia*. Louise Caselotti Bagarozy and Rossi-Lemeni travelled with her.

'The ship was filthy,' Maria told her friend Stelios Galatopoulos. 'The attitude of the crew was just as filthy. It was just like a troop ship, and they had the audacity to expect the passengers, at the end of it all, to thank them in writing for the wonderful way they looked after us. Well, I needn't tell you what I did. Let us say I threw their document, which was filthy too, right into their faces.'

But she was not as confident as her actions might lead one to believe. She knew she could sing Gioconda and wrench all the drama from the role. She was not so sure that the Italians would like her interpretation. She fretted and complained about this and, as always when she was in crisis, she was beset with unrelenting hunger pangs. The meals were terrible on the ship, but there was always plenty of good bread and sweets. She stuffed herself, vomited it up, then stuffed herself again. A pattern she had recently formed. But by the time the ship had reached Naples she had regained all the weight she had worked so hard to lose.

Well, divas were often fat so what did it matter? She was, she now realized, about to be inaugurated into the world of opera as a leading lady, a *diva*. She was twenty-three and gloriously on her way.

6

An Italian Debut: Verona 1947

THE SS *ROSSIA* arrived in Naples early on the morning of 29 July, sun blazing in the sky and Maria anxious to start her Italian adventure. Louise Caselotti Bagarozy led Maria and Nicola Rossi-Lemeni off the ship and into the crowded Customs hall where the English language dominated, as it had aboard the Russian ship. This was the first year since the war that tours were being conducted in Italy and, due to the popularity of recent powerful Italian films like Roberto Rossellini's *Open City* and Vittorio de Sica's *Shoeshine*, and the extraordinary rate of liras to dollars, Americans were in the majority. Seemingly few harboured the bitterness towards the Italians that they felt for the Germans. All was not forgiven, but the bargain prices the country offered for services and goods appeared to be both compensation and penance. Also, Italians were, on the whole, such a lusty, happy lot and the food of Italy pleasing to Americans. All this made for happy touring.

Louise was an experienced traveller but she had not been hired as a guide, nor as the two young singers' vocal coach, but as their agency representative. As such, she was receiving ten per cent of each of their contracts with the Verona Festival. It also gave her a reason to be out of the States while Eddie tried to appease their creditors. Although Rossi-Lemeni was of Italian origin and had made his debut at the age of twenty-five in Venice the previous year, he had been born and educated in Istanbul. Italy was only a little less unfamiliar to him than to Maria.

None of the three travellers saw much of Naples that morning as they were scheduled to take the first train to Verona. With time so short, they arranged to have their luggage sent on after them and rushed through Customs to the railway station. The train service in Italy in 1947 left much to be desired in speed, efficiency or comfort. The journey from Naples to Verona would take ten hours and require two connections, in Rome and Modena, many local stops and a schedule that could run hours late.

Despite her exhaustion, Maria's spirits were high. She confessed to Louise that she felt something marvellous was about to happen and that she was ready to accept it. In Modena the train was so crowded that Rossi-Lemeni was forced to give up his seat to a pregnant woman for the remainder of the trip and to sit on the floor in the aisle. Night had encroached by the time they neared Verona. The train crossed a bridge over the Po, still swollen from the heavy late spring rains. Although Maria could not see much further than the curve of the tracks when the train rounded a bend, the farmlands bordering the river were thriving and rich with verdant growth. It seemed incredible that so little time had passed since the war, when the same expanse had been strewn with debris and the bodies of young men, all brave, all too young to die, whatever side they fought for.

At the station in Verona they were met by Gaetano Pomari, a middle-aged, gracious representative of the Verona Arena. It was now nearly 9 p.m. Their train had been due to arrive at half past seven and at the Pedavena Restaurant a dozen officials from the town were waiting to welcome them at dinner. Pomari handed Maria a bouquet of flowers and hustled the trio into a car, definitely pre-war, a noisy, rattling vehicle that bounced its occupants as it made its clamorous way through the rutted streets of the city to the Hotel Accademia where the new arrivals would be staying for the next seven weeks. Maria had her own room, but she shared a bath with Louise. Since their luggage had not arrived, the women simply freshened themselves before returning to the lobby where Pomari had been joined by a city official, Giuseppe Gambato. The restaurant turned out to be across the street.

Pomari, a bachelor, had for the last seven years shared a commodious apartment directly above the Pedavena with another bachelor about his age, fifty-two-year old Giovanni Battista Meneghini, who had inherited his father's business, which manufactured building materials. Meneghini, who was known as Battista, also shared with his friend Pomari a love of opera and as his business was successful, contributed to the Verona Arena, so it was not unnatural that he would be one of the guests who greeted Maria and her two companions at the restaurant.

Battista was not a man who would inspire immediate interest in a woman. Short, paunchy, with owlish eyes, a receding hairline and a double chin, he was one of the most unattractive men at the dinner. Still, Battista did have 'a way with him': not the general interpretation of charm, but a manner that conveyed interest, a certain sophistication and an aura of success. He spoke no English but his Italian hinted at a good education. In fact, Battista had studied in Venice as a young man with the intention of becoming a journalist. His father's death had ended his early expectations and he took over the family business and the responsibility of his younger brothers and his mother, to whom he remained devoted. During the war, his factories had been converted to the manufacture of important army needs. His position had saved him from serving in the forces.

Clearly, though successful at it, his business bored him. He had never married. He displayed little interest in his brothers' families and he was not a sportsman. He found his outlet in Pomari's world – opera, music, and the history of Verona and neighbouring Venice. Therefore he made a natural guide-host and Pomari had come to rely upon him to escort the Arena's guest divas during their stays in Verona.

'My first impression of him when Pomari introduced us', Maria recalled of her meeting with Battista, 'was that he was an honest and sincere person. I liked him. Then I forgot him, because he wasn't seated next to me at the table and without my glasses I could not see him very well. At a certain moment Louise (who was sitting next to me) passed on to me a message from Meneghini, that he wanted to take her, Rossi-Lemeni and me to Venice the next morning. I accepted the invitation at once.'

Upon awakening the following day to find their baggage had not yet arrived, she changed her mind. Rossi-Lemeni finally persuaded her into going with them in the same dress she had worn the previous day and evening, as Louise was doing. When she and Battista met again in the lobby before leaving for Venice, Maria apologized for the confusion and explained what her problem had been. He was sympathetic to her plight but gallantly maintained that she looked 'beautiful as the day', which – as it turned out – was brilliantly sunlit.

Before starting on their day excursion to Venice, he insisted on showing them a small part of Verona. Battista loved the city and never ceased to wonder at its beauty. As far as he was concerned Verona was as great a city as Rome, Florence or Venice, all of which had dominated it politically for many centuries. Due to its strategic position close to the Austrian border, Verona had suffered heavy Allied bombing during the war; there had been even worse desecrations when the Germans withdrew in 1945. Only two years had passed since then, and although the debris and rubble had been cleared, there were still gaps in the streets where buildings had been destroyed. Yet, miraculously, much of Verona's most treasured architectural heritage had survived – ancient churches, Roman walls, courtyards, grand piazzas and historic homes.

The train ride between Verona and Venice was comparatively short. If petrol had not been so rigidly rationed they could have driven there. Maria sat beside Battista as he talked about opera and his love of it, and how much he was looking forward to hearing her sing Gioconda. He seemed not to notice her weight, although she was painfully aware that the dress she wore did not flatter her and that her legs looked particularly thick in her low-heeled walking shoes. She had been informed by Rossi-Lemeni that Meneghini was affluent and as a supporter of opera knew many important artists and conductors in Italy, but more than his position, Maria was drawn to him by the attention he paid to her.

'I felt Maria liked me for myself,' Battista remembered many years later, 'and not because I might be useful to her. This made me happy as I had never been happy before in my "long" fifty-two years. You see, it was such a mutual feeling. I, too, felt affection (I dare not say love) for her before I heard her sing a single note.'

Louise observed that Battista was a very good guide and that everywhere they went people knew him and greeted him with great respect, but that he and Maria would ever become romantically involved seemed ridiculous to her. 'Battista was nearly thirty years older than Maria. I have heard it said that he had liked the ladies and made many conquests in his youth. But I never believed that to be true,' another member of the company later reflected. 'Of course, although he was not a millionaire, he was quite well-to-do, and the years leading up to the war and the war itself impoverished many former rich families and left their daughters in dire need of finding a husband able to support them in acceptable style. From that point of view Meneghini must have seemed a good catch.'

In fact, Battista had never been seriously involved with a woman before he met Maria. But their relationship did not go from attraction to a more intense emotion until he heard her sing for the first time at an early rehearsal of *La Gioconda*. The morning after their arrival, however, he was merely playing the good host as he took his guests on a gondola ride, showed them the dazzling sights of Venice and paused mid-afternoon for a late lunch in a charming restaurant off the Piazza San Marco. During her time in New York, no man had taken an interest in Maria as a woman and Battista's attention made her feel giddily feminine.

She was overwhelmed when she saw the Verona Arena for the first time. The enormity of it was awesome. Battista had told her how this gigantic amphitheatre was famous for the magnificent productions given there of *Aida*, Verdi's Egyptian masterpiece, and she well understood why. No other opera could fill that space so completely, with its massive exotic decor, the pageantry and the tens of dozens of extras needed to wave peacock plumes from the vertiginous heights of Egyptian walls. She feared her *La Gioconda* would seem a small production on such a vast stage and was nervous that her voice would not have the strength to carry to the back rows of the 25,000-seat open-air theatre.

She spoke about her trepidation to Battista who, quite surprisingly, offered personally to pay for a vocal coach, the excellent Ferruccio Cusinati, who was the chorus master at the Arena, to help her through the next few weeks with any problems she felt she had to overcome. The conductor Tullio Serafin would be arriving on 20 July for rehearsals with the orchestra and the opera would be premièred on 3 August. That gave Maria four weeks to prepare the role.

She now understood that her performances in Greece 'were a sort of early preparatory period, the completion, so to speak' of her schooldays. She had learned how far she could go, what her possibilities were. Now, she stood on the brink of true professionalism, of becoming a real musician. 'One of the luckiest things that ever happened to me...no! *the* luckiest,' she would later say, 'was to have Tullio Serafin conduct for my Italian debut.' From the moment they met in a sweaty rehearsal room backstage of the Verona Arena, fans being installed as they first spoke so that they would not expire from the heat, Maria was awestruck and knew Serafin would be the one to guide her to a position of prima donna.

'Remember,' he told her, 'the voice is the first instrument of the orchestra. Prima donna means just that – "first woman", the main instrument of the orchestra.'

'What you got from that man!' Maria praised when remembering Verona. 'He taught me that there must be an expression to everything you do, a justification. I learned that every embellishment must be put in the service of music, and that if you really care for the composer and not just for your own personal success, you will always find the meaning of a trill or a scale that will justify a feeling of happiness, anxiety, sadness. Maestro Serafin taught me, in short, the depth of music.'

To Serafin's surprise, she came to every orchestral rehearsal, something singers seldom did. 'At first she did this secretly,' Serafin told an interviewer, 'but afterwards, whenever I commented on it she [would] say with a smile, "Maestro, am I not expected to be the first instrument of the orchestra?"'

Maria monopolized every moment of Serafin's private time that she could commandeer to work with him on her diction and intonation. 'When one wants to find a gesture or how to move on stage,' he advised her, 'all you have to do is search for it in the score; the composer has already put it into his music.'

Tullio Serafin, 'Maestro' to his musicians and singers, was not a man of imposing stature, yet he commanded a rehearsal room as surely as he did an orchestra and the performers on a stage. There was something dynamic about him, an energy that surrounded him and seemed to extend from his hands and carry his voice across a room. 'He had the most mesmerizing eyes,' one of his contemporaries recalled. 'You know how royalty are trained to look people straight in the eye and make them feel whatever they are saying is a private conversation – even with dozens of others around? Well that was the Maestro. He lived in music and it lived through him. He always wore this rather comical old felt hat during rehearsals and he would take it off and wave it about like a baton to make a point. Maria was mesmerized by him. He believed he had discovered a singer whom he could endow with greatness. Why wouldn't she idolize him and heed every bit of advice that he gave her?'

'When you reach the stage there must be no surprises,' Serafin told her. And Maria listened closely to his words. She had always been the first to arrive at rehearsals and the last to leave. Now the time she worked *during* rehearsals took on a new, deeper intensity.

Tullio Serafin had been born in Rottanova di Cavarzere near Venice in 1878. A child prodigy on the violin, he had known and played for Verdi while still a child, and had made his debut as a conductor at La Scala in 1900. Within a few years he became 'the grand master of operatic conducting'. Richard Strauss's *Der Rosenkavalier* was premièred under his baton in 1911 and Weber's *Oberon* in the same year. He conducted at the Metropolitan from 1924 to 1934. When he returned to Italy it was as chief conductor at the Rome Opera. He had a warm spot for Verona as he had conducted the very first performance at the Arena in 1913. Now one of the most famous conductors in the world who had worked with the greatest voices of his time, he was known for discovering young talents and moulding them into star performers as he had done with the eminent American soprano Rosa Ponselle who had also sung *La Gioconda* under his direction and baton.

'As soon as I heard her sing,' Serafin recalled about the first rehearsal of *La Gioconda* with Maria, 'I recognized the exceptional voice. A few notes were still uncertainly placed but I immediately knew here was a future great singer.'

Whenever she was not rehearsing with Serafin, Maria was with Meneghini. They had dark, rich coffee at the sidewalk cafés on the enormous Piazza Bra outside the Arena. He took her on a walking tour of Verona, which, as he explained, had once been home to Romeo and Juliet. It always surprised him that tourists seemed to think the story had been completely invented by William Shakespeare. Thankfully, the houses of both the Montagues and the Capulets and Juliet's tomb remained in good shape – would she like to see them? Of course she would – and did. They went through winding alleys where once-grand Venetian and Renaissance houses had long since decayed and been split into small working-class apartments. He never seemed in a hurry to reach their destination. He was enjoying her company as much as she was his.

He took Maria for dinner at Pedavena and at another more formal restaurant with luxurious decor, fawning service and extraordinary food. He ordered for her and when she would eye the dish he had selected he unobtrusively instructed the waiter to serve her some on a side plate and she had not been the least bit embarrassed. He was always gracious to Serafin's wife, the soprano Elena Rakowska who had sung at La Scala and at the Met (a woman with shimmering grey hair, pleasant blue eyes, and a generous smile). And when he discussed music and the opera with the Serafins, his knowledge was astonishing.

Maria was falling in love. She wrote Jackie 'dreamy letters', and to her mother, furiously and frustratingly left with an inattentive George in New York, she sent letters filled with descriptions of Battista, his attentiveness and his constant presence. Litza replied in blistering prose. 'Here was this elderly Italian assuming her role and with an intimacy no mother could match,' Jackie reported.

The final dress rehearsal was held on Friday evening, 1 August. 'Are you going to be there?' Maria had asked Battista.

'I thought I might. Would you mind?'

'No, no. Of course, not,' she assured him. 'I'm never aware of who might be watching.'

This was only partially true. Maria's vision was such that she could not see much of the stage, never mind anything beyond the footlights. More important, though, once she was performing her mind had no room for any thoughts but of the character she was portraying and the music she was singing. That evening would be a particularly difficult one for her, as in Italy the dress rehearsal was the performance critics traditionally reviewed.

She arrived backstage before sunset, while technicians were giving a final check to the speakers spaced throughout the huge amphitheatre. A cot had been provided for her to rest on, but she paced up and down her dressing room, more nervous than usual. The day had been scorchingly hot and the intense heat made her feel sick to her stomach. An additional fan was brought in, but it seemed only to stir up the hot air. In the month that she had been in Italy she had gained over ten pounds and her costumes were tight. The wardrobe mistress had to work almost to the last moment, to ease the waistlines of her dresses.

Yet when the curtain rose on the first scene, set at a Venetian festival and, even as she stepped forward from the crowd before singing her first aria, Serafin and the other members of the company were taken aback with the manner in which she suddenly seemed to take command of the stage and to set the tone for the production. She had been very good in rehearsal, her voice growing stronger with the passage of each session with the Maestro. But on stage, in costume, she seemed to have been transformed into the character she was playing. Here was a Gioconda of desperate yet dignified pathos whose blind mother has been accused of being a witch and who was ready to sacrifice her body and her life to save Enzo, the man she loves who has betrayed her for a married woman. It was the depth of Maria's acting ability that surprised everyone, the look of terror or tenderness that seemed so real, the tremor of a hand at just the right moment, the on-the-edge tension with which she played Gioconda as an agitated, driven woman.

She had memorized every inch of the stage and set during each act so that she would not make a mis-step. But at the dramatic close of Act Two (a dark, rocky meeting place near the water), when Enzo sets fire to the boat in which he was to escape (a scene that required some complicated technical props), Maria tripped and fell. Serafin kept the tempo as, to his amazement and relief, Maria rose to her feet by grasping on to the nearest prop rock as though the fall was part of her performance. She then continued without any evidence that injury had occurred.

At the end of the act she insisted she was all right, but during the third act her ankle had swollen so badly and the pain became so intense that a doctor was called. She had suffered a nasty sprain and he suggested the remainder of the performance be cancelled. Maria refused to do so. How she managed to get through Act Four was a miracle. She was in excruciating pain, hardly able to place any weight on her right foot. But she used the pain to her advantage. As Gioconda, seized by desperation, sings 'Suicidio!' she 'rose magnificently to the climax of the drama. She poured forth vast molten and lyrical sounds with fine musicianship – projected from dramatic soprano to opulent contralto', one critic wrote, adding, 'She went through the gamut of emotion: introspective fatalism in "Ultima croce del mio cammin" ("The final cross in my life"), almost ethereal beauty in "E un di leggiadre volavan l'ore" ("Once life flew gaily by") to complete resignation in "Or peombo esausta fra le tenebre" ("I now sink exhausted in the darkness").' Her last scene, where Gioconda stabs herself and shouts at Barnaba, the man to whom she has offered to trade herself for the life of her beloved, 'Demon maledetto! E il corpo ti do!' ('You cursed demon! You now have my corpse!) was played and sung with 'stark realism, devoid of any sentimentality'.

Gratefully, she sank to the floor at the end of the act. Members of the company helped her to her feet to take her bows and finally carried her to her dressing room where Battista was anxiously waiting for her. He took her back to her hotel and sat with her all night, applying cold compresses to her ankle and administering the mild sedative the doctor had given her, but which did not seem to ease her pain. The next morning a stronger dose was prescribed and her ankle and foot were bandaged to give her support without crippling her mobility. On Sunday evening, 3 August, the thermometer at 89 degrees, Maria Callas made her official Italian opera debut in the sold-out amphitheatre, lit before the curtain rose by thousands of candles. Very few in the audience were aware of her disability, as she moved with agility never revealing that she had a problem. Between acts as she rested, ice was applied and her bandage replaced.

The critics noted 'a rather metallic timbre' of voice, but agreed that Maria Callas possessed 'a most moving and individual quality', and that her singing was expressive and her high notes 'vibrant and effortless'. They prophesied that Maria Callas's star was on the ascent.

'What struck me first', Serafin recalled,

> was the way she would sing recitatives. This young singer (she was twenty-three in 1947 when I first heard her), who was not Italian, had never been to Italy before and who obviously was in no way brought up in the Italian tradition, was able to bring so much meaning to Italian recitative. I believe she achieved this entirely through music. She had of course a sound vocal training but the way she spoke through music was something inborn.
>
> Caruso, Titta Ruffo and Ponselle...they indeed were nothing short of a miracle. Of course they perfected their vocal technique...but they did not have Callas's genius, nor did they really throw new light on their art. Callas was no miracle. She too was naturally highly gifted but all God's gifts were given in the raw-material state. Everything had to be achieved by sheer hard work, determination and complete dedication.

Maria knew that by her third performance she had come into her own. A huge decision had to be made. What was she to do now? Although a success, her Gioconda had not created the international media excitement that might have brought opera companies shouting for her services. In her last two performances she was, according to Serafin, 'brilliant, the finest Gioconda' he had seen. But the critics had not attended those performances.

She had a prepaid return ticket to New York, but it was too soon for her to go back, especially without a contract in hand. What would she do if she did? The Bagarozys could not be helpful to her. She had very little money from her present engagement. Certainly, she could not return to live with her quarrelling parents.

Meneghini made the decision for her. He offered generously to finance her prolonged stay in Italy. She would remain in Italy and he would help her obtain further coaching and see what he could do about getting her another engagement. Louise and Rossi-Lemeni departed from Verona on 18 August, the morning following the last performance of *La Gioconda*. There was an angry confrontation between Maria and Louise at the station. Louise did not want her to forget that she and her husband were her legal agents. She warned Maria that Meneghini was not a professional manager and that it was dangerous for an artist to let her heart rule her career. Maria paid no attention to her advice. Battista had, in fact, offered to represent her and she had enthusiastically agreed to such an arrangement.

Now she was not only in love, she had a mentor on whom she could rely and she was ecstatic. Meneghini took her shopping for new clothes. He dined with her every evening and discussed with her whom he had written to and what his plans were for her. He was under tremendous pressure from his mother, who strongly disapproved of his relationship with Maria, and from Pomari, who thought he was neglecting his business and jeopardizing his position in Verona (there was also a degree of jealousy involved). Battista had not yet proposed marriage and was himself unsure if he wished to marry. Whatever he had expected to happen vis-à-vis Maria's career must have been a disappointment. No agent or opera company in Italy displayed even the slightest interest in her despite her success in Verona. What happened next to bolster her career turned out to be a chance encounter.

By mid-October Battista decided, partly to get away from his mother's criticism and angry discussions with Pomari, to take Maria to Milan where a friend, Luduino Bonardi, owned an opera agency. Maria was led to believe that there was some hope of an audition with La Scala. Their meeting with Bonardi turned out to be more social than business. There was no audition. In fact, Bonardi could do nothing at all for Maria. They left his office, both feeling dejected. On the street directly outside, Battista recognized Nino Catozzo, the director of La Fenice, the beautiful old opera house in Venice. Catozzo was on his way up to see Bonardi as he needed an Isolde for *Tristan und Isolde* to open his inaugural season in December.

'How fortunate you are,' Battista told him. 'Maria knows the role well and she is free in December.'

As further luck would have it, Serafin would be conducting and his approval would be required. The Maestro was also in Milan at this time and Maria and Battista went directly over to speak to him. With Serafin accompanying her, Maria, relying on the music, sang an aria from the opera and admitted she had never sung the role. But Serafin had been most impressed with what he had heard. He agreed she should sing Isolde. She would go back to Verona and study the opera with Ferruccio Cusinati, who was still working with her as a vocal coach and, on 28 October, she would come to Rome to study for twelve days with him.

Her joy could hardly be contained as she submerged herself entirely in the difficult task she had undertaken. Not only great singing was demanded, but tremendous endurance. The opera was to be sung in Italian and was five hours long. ('Strong, comfortable shoes are a must,' Serafin had jocularly warned.) Isolde's arias, especially her 'Liebestod', would demand tremendous stamina.

Battista wrote that he watched her with wonderment and fear as she became 'possessed. Something had taken hold of her and even I, who now knew I loved her, was treated as an outsider.'

7

A Diva Is Born:
Europe 1948–1949

THE JEWEL-LIKE Teatro La Fenice may not have been the largest opera house in the world, but it was the most beautiful with its Venetian gold-encrusted boxes rising to the magnificent domed ceiling covered in fanciful murals painted in the seventeenth century against della Robbia blue skies and feathery white clouds. The world's most celebrated singers had appeared at La Fenice, usually in the summer months, Venice's tourist season, which fortuitously coincided with the time when La Scala, the Met and Covent Garden were closed. Maestro Serafin would conduct and the cast of *Tristan und Isolde* that Maria joined was a stellar ensemble including Fiorenzo Tasso as Tristan, Fedora Barbieri as Brangaene and Boris Christoff as King Mark. The winter season at La Fenice drew some of Italy's most discerning and knowledgeable opera-goers and critics. Maria would now find out if she had the ability to become a world-class artist.

Her four weeks in Rome working with Serafin had been gruelling but also tremendously rewarding. Each day included eight to twelve hours of study, practice and rehearsal. She was the guest of the Maestro and his wife, Elena Rakowska, Battista remaining behind in Verona, where both his family and friends were trying to convince him to break off his relationship with Maria. They claimed his attention to her had caused him to neglect the family business and was creating unwelcome gossip. The idea that a wealthy, fifty-two-year-old man could be having an affair with a twenty-three-year-old singer with no means was shocking. Pomari worried about what the Board of the Verona Festival would make of that unseemly news. Battista had his own agenda and turned a deaf ear. Maria would be his passport into a more international world. He could hardly wait for the four weeks to end, when they could meet again in Venice, his hope being that if her Isolde was a grand success, he could tie up his business ends in Verona and become a full-time opera impresario.

Battista had yet to propose and Maria was anxious that he might lose interest with her being at such a distance for a month. Jackie's plight was in her mind. The two sisters corresponded and Jackie's letters were filled with the horrors of Milton's progressive illness and the insulting way she was being treated by his brother and other members of his family who referred to her as 'Milton's whore' and were doing all they could to see that when he died she inherited nothing.

'You cannot imagine how much I miss you,' Maria wrote to Battista from Rome. 'I cannot wait until I am in your arms again.'

Her longing for Battista did not interfere with her dedicated work on her role and her attention to Serafin's instruction. Maria immediately recognized how much Serafin could give her and in these four weeks a close relationship, one might even call it a collaboration, was begun, which would become the greatest influence in the final emergence of Maria as a true artist.

'He opened a new world to me,' Maria said many years later, 'showed me there was a reason for everything, that even fioriture[1] and trills have a reason in a composer's mind...that they are the expression of the...character, that is the way he feels at the moment, the passing emotions that take hold of him. He would coach [me] for every little detail, every movement, every word, every breath...He taught me that pauses are often more important than the music.'

Serafin also insisted Maria have special costumes made for her role. 'Why? Is this necessary?' she asked, concerned about the cost, which she could not afford and would have to ask Battista to pay for.

'The first act of *Tristan* is ninety minutes long,' he replied. 'And no matter how much you fascinate the public with your voice, they still have all that time to look you over and cut your costume to pieces. So your appearance on stage must be harmonious with the music.'

To Battista from Rome, in the same letter in which she thanked him for sending the money required, she wrote: 'The more I sing Isolde the better she develops. It is rather an impetuous role, but I like it...Yesterday I heard Serafin speaking on the telephone so glowingly of me to Catozzo [the vocal coach in Verona] that I was moved to tears...How I would like you Battista to be near me...If I express all my feelings of you through Isolde, I will be marvellous.'

She arrived in Venice in mid-December and was met by Battista. She wept with happiness and he embraced her warmly. Venice looked so different, the buildings that surrounded the Piazza San Marco, its golden

---

[1] Fioriture are agile decorations of an operatic aria often extemporized by singers.

beauty of the previous summer now sepulchral in the grey light of winter. Most of the tourists were gone but there was still a great deal of activity. The next morning she and Battista had breakfast in the same café off the Piazza San Marco where they had lunched in June, listening to the *marangoni* bells that for centuries had proclaimed the beginning and the end of Venice's working day.

She was to have her first rehearsal a few hours later and was nervous, and Battista did what he could to calm her. He had a habit of speaking in a rat-a-tat way, words popping out like small bullets. '*Mia cara, mia cara,* all will be well. I believe in you. The Maestro believes in you. Trust him. Trust me.'

She did, but she also knew that it was she who would be judged. She entered into the rehearsals with fierce intensity, singing full voice at all times while the other cast members saved their voices. As always, she was the first to arrive at rehearsals and the last to leave. Battista seldom left the theatre, sitting in the back row when she was on stage and nearby when she was resting in her dressing room. On the evening of 30 December, the first performance, he stood in the wings watching her as she made her entrance and waited for her there as she came off stage, whispering encouragement: 'Go on, Maria! There's no one like you. You're the greatest in the world!'

Serafin had told her, 'When I am in the pit, I am there to serve you because I have to save my performance.' But whenever she glanced down she felt she had a friend there. 'He was helping you all the way,' she remembered. 'He would mouth all the words...He was breathing with you, living the music with you, loving it with you. It was elastic, growing, living.'

Her Isolde, sung with great sensuousness of tone, was well received. Her tremendous stage presence was praised and her voice lauded for its warmth 'and appropriate lyricism'. But the acclaim she had hoped for was not forthcoming. She had not created a sensation. Her future was not to be as a great Wagnerian soprano. That hardly saddened her. She admired Wagner and enjoyed singing Isolde. But deep down she understood that she had not yet found her niche. She sang four performances of *Tristan und Isolde* and then went into immediate rehearsal for Puccini's *Turandot*, a role she had not expected to sing but agreed to do when the soprano who had been scheduled to appear took ill.

Turandot was the role she had studied in New York and had been planning to sing with the Bagarozys' failed opera company. This current production was not to be under the musical direction of Serafin, who was committed elsewhere, but he advised her to accept the offer although it meant only two weeks of rehearsal. It was important, he stressed, that she be visible and that the critics could recognize her versatility. Also, Turandot is a supremely dramatic role, a perfect showcase for what he considered at that time (for he would soon discover another side to her extraordinary ability) to be some of her most outstanding talents: her acting ability and the range of her voice.

Turandot is Puccini's most exotic opera, set in ancient Peking. Princess Turandot is a powerful, cruel woman who is possessed by both passion and revenge. The costumes were splendid and with their heavily embroidered kimono lines concealed the current heft of her body. Also, her striking make-up for the role called immediate attention to her large, expressive eyes. It was with this opera, and with her portrayal of Puccini's 'dragon lady', that Maria would create and begin to develop the gestures and eye contact that so impacted on her audiences and that would mark all her future performances.

'Callas made an admirable Turandot,' the critic for *Il Gazzettino* wrote. 'Her voice was precise and resounding, especially in the highest register. [She is] an artist endowed with unusual finesse, sensibility and intelligence as well as with an impressive stage presence. Callas tackled the arduous tessitura of the role with energy and confidence.'[2]

Immediately following her five La Fenice performances of *Turandot* (29, 31 January and 3, 8, and 10 February), Maria received offers from opera companies in Udine (*Turandot*), Trieste (*La Forza del Destino*), Genoa (*Tristan und Isolde*) and Rome (*Turandot*). Although none of these was in a major opera house, Serafin and Battista advised her to accept, believing that it was important for her to continue to be widely seen before the public and to work on her craft in a professional venue. All her reviews were good. She was slowly building a reputation, but true fame still eluded her.

In the summer of 1948 she returned to Verona, this time to appear in the Arena in *Turandot*. She was depressed and her eating problem had escalated along with her weight. She had digressed into the pattern she had formed as a young girl in Greece, sneaking food, taking it back to her room, eating it in solitude, hiding it – beneath her bed, in the medicine cabinet and on a high shelf in her wardrobe – to get through the sleepless, anxiety-ridden nights that had begun to plague her.

She was concerned, not only about her career but her future with Battista. He still had not proposed. He was totally committed to helping

---

[2] Tessitura means texture in Italian. As a musical term it indicates the range of the piece of music in relation to the voice for which it is written. Turandot's arias are brutal on the voice and generally lie above normal range.

her with her career and had almost entirely divested himself of the major responsibility of his family business by passing it on to his younger brothers. They slept together and her co-workers knew they were lovers, as did his family, who were no more accepting of her than Milton's had been of Jackie. They had taken a suite in one of the better hotels in Verona and Battista had moved in some of his beloved antiques. There were always fresh flowers in the many vases. He called it 'their home'. But Maria knew that with a change of heart on his part both home and Battista could disappear, and she believed that she was truly in love with him and that he was indispensable to her life.

True success, grand success, remained out of reach, as did marriage with the man she loved. She thought she might be able to push Battista into a proposal with a threat to return to the States. He was distraught and went to see Serafin to discuss the matter, but he still did not offer her marriage. Serafin was deeply upset that Maria might leave Europe and disrupt the growing interest in her voice. She had been signed to sing Aida under his baton in Turin in September, just six weeks after her engagement at the Verona Arena, and was working with him on the role, when Francesco Siciliani, the director of the Teatro Comunale in Florence suddenly appeared on the scene, giving Serafin the opportunity he needed to convince Maria that she must not return to America.

When Maria had sung Isolde at La Fenice, the first-night programme had been broadcast and Siciliani had heard it. At the time he thought she was most promising and filed away her name for future reference. Serafin had learned that his friend had suddenly found himself without a leading lady for his announced production of *Norma* at the Teatro Comunale. Serafin did not know that Siciliani had already decided to substitute *Madama Butterfly* with a suitable soprano and he called him and asked him to come to Rome to listen to his protégée, the young singer Maria Callas. Siciliani recalled having heard Maria on that radio broadcast and he boarded a train the next morning for Rome.

Serafin had long felt that Maria had the ability to sing a bel canto role like *Norma*, which required extreme suppleness of voice and range. However, he thought such arias were not yet in her repertoire. Maria had never ventured the fact that she had studied and sung 'Mira, o Norma' and 'Casta diva' from *Norma* while under de Hidalgo's tutelage and had often used the latter as an audition piece. Although it is difficult to understand why she had not, in view of the present situation. The answer is probably quite straightforward. Maria always followed the Maestro's lead. She was in awe of him, worshipped him, and was unquestioning about his choices for her. Serafin, their rehearsal time limited, decided

Maria would sing what he knew she sang best. So, accompanied by him on the piano, she rendered four selections: 'Suicidio!' (*La Gioconda*), 'O patria mia' (*Aida*), 'In questa reggia' (*Turandot*) and the 'Liebestod' (*Tristan und Isolde*) – an amazing and prodigious programme for an audition.

Siciliani was impressed, although still not sure that – despite Maria's expressive face and intelligent interpretation – she could sing the role of Bellini's Druid priestess, Norma, which required a range and power that 'this tall, fat woman' had not fully displayed in the selections she had sung. Day was already fading into evening. Serafin's servant brought tea and the three of them sat and talked. Siciliani asked her some questions about her training. She told him that she had studied with the Spanish coloratura Elvira de Hidalgo in Greece. With this information, Siciliani asked her if she could sing coloratura, too. She replied that she could. He was suddenly at attention. 'That seems a tremendous feat for a dramatic soprano,' he said.

Serafin made an instant decision and went to the piano, directing her to come to his side. He asked her what coloratura pieces she had studied with de Hidalgo. After a moment's discussion and her assurance that she still knew the aria, he played a short introduction and Maria embarked on 'Qui la voce', the mad scene from Bellini's *I Puritani*, one of the most difficult arias in operatic literature, requiring a superb coloratura voice. Serafin was gambling on instinct. It was daring – and a revelation. Maria – who, indeed, possessed a prodigious memory – remembered it all and, as she sang, all the bel canto instruction she had learned from de Hidalgo came flooding back to her.

'Hearing this music sung with the cabaletta [a coda, or a fast, brilliant ending] at last, in the correct style, I was overwhelmed. This was the kind of singer one read about in books from the nineteenth century – a real dramatic coloratura,' Siciliani recalled. 'I looked over at Serafin. There were tears streaming down his face. I took action immediately, first telling her she was not going to America or anywhere else and then I telephoned Pariso Votto, the general manager of the Comunale. 'Look,' I said to him, 'forget Butterfly. I have found an extraordinary soprano and we shall open the season with *Norma*.'

This was to be the turning point in Maria's career. On 30 November, six weeks after this momentous audition, she sang Norma in Florence with Serafin conducting. After their first rehearsal Serafin took her aside. 'Now you go home, my dear Miss Callas,' he instructed, 'and speak these lines [of the recitatives] to yourself, and let's see what proportions, what rhythms you find. Forget that you are singing. Of course, respect what is written, but try to be freer, try to find a flowing rhythm for these recitatives.'

Maria's voice ranged just short of three octaves, from an F-sharp below the staff to an E above the staff, an enormous range for a dramatic soprano, which she basically was. Sopranos rarely go below middle C. F-sharp below the staff sung in full voice is in a mezzo or contralto voice range and to hold (as she did) high Cs, Ds and Es placed her also in the realm of a coloratura, a remarkable span. She possessed a creamy sound in her middle range, although her top could sound strident and the lower register occasionally 'bottled', so that it was not beautiful in the classic sense. Her voice was unique, startling and, coupled with her powerful dramatic interpretation (alone among singers of her time), a voice and performance that often needed more that one hearing to realize its true beauty and importance.

She did not foresee it then, although Serafin suspected the outcome – opera could never be sung as before once her full talent was recognized. For Maria was the first coloratura (at least in the twentieth century when voices were first recorded) to sing the high notes dramatically, not merely as ornamentation, nor to display her ability to sound like a trilling bird, but to stress the meaning of the words that landed on those notes and so integrate them into the dramatic line of the story.

In the cadenza at the end of 'Casta diva' her voice made the super-human leap from middle F to a forte high C, stunning the audience. Then came the end of the stretta[3] to the trio where 'she held for twelve beats a stupendous free high D'. This was an almost unheard-of feat among dramatic sopranos and those attending bravoed loudly.

'I believe that at the end of her first Norma,' Serafin commented, 'Callas's impact was so great that henceforth the audience, at least in their subconscious, were changing their approach to opera … At the end of the first performance, and I had this on good authority at the theatre, half the audience attended again the second and last performance.'

The critics obviously agreed with Serafin. 'Although her technique is secure and perfectly controlled,' Gualtiero Frangini of La Nazione wrote, 'her schooling is rather different from what we are accustomed to hearing, as indeed her vocal colour is unusual. Nevertheless her merits are undeniable; her highly accomplished portrayal of Norma is rich in subtle and moving accents of femininity – she is the woman in love, the woman betrayed, the mother, the friend and in the end the implacable priestess.'

[3] The stretta is the passage at the end of an aria in which the tempo is accelerated to make a climax.

She went directly from the last performance (5 December 1948) of *Norma* to La Fenice in Venice to rehearse Brünnhilde in Wagner's *Die Walküre* to open the season on 8 January 1949, again under Serafin's musical direction. *Die Walküre* – was translated to *La Walkiria* and sung in Italian (the only way Italian audiences would accept Wagner). 'Serafin was conducting *I Puritani* during the same weeks,' Maria remembered of this all-important period in her life,

> and a great flu epidemic caused his soprano to become ill. Mrs Serafin, hearing me sing 'Qui la voce' [from *I Puritani*], which I used to vocalize [in her last days with the Serafins in Rome after she was signed for *Norma*], begged me to sing it for her husband when he returned to the hotel. 'Of course,' I said, 'if it will give him pleasure.' [And when he came in] I did. He thanked me, sat silently for a few moments and then left. The next morning about ten, after I sang my second performance [the previous night] of *La Walkiria*, the phone rang. It was Maestro Serafin. 'Come at once to my room,' he said.
>
> 'But Maestro I've not washed yet, or dressed; it will take me about half an hour.'
>
> 'Never mind, come as you are.'
>
> Well, you didn't say no to Serafin, we had a real veneration for the maestri then. So, I put on my bathrobe and went down. In his room was the director of the theatre. 'Sing for me the aria you sang for me last night,' Serafin commanded. I did. 'Look, Maria,' he said when I had finished, 'you are going to sing *Puritani* in a week.'
>
> 'I can't,' I said. 'I have more *Walkirias*; it's ridiculous – my voice is too heavy.'
>
> 'I guarantee you that you can,' Serafin said.
>
> Well, I thought if a man like Serafin, who is no child and knows his job, can guarantee this, I would be a fool to say no.

The harsh regime of the next week pushed her to her very limit as she learned the role of Elvira for *I Puritani* during the day and sang Brünnhilde at night, roles that required quite different skills. And the last performance of Brünnhilde was sung directly following the dress rehearsal of *I Puritani*. It had been a terrific gamble for both Serafin and Maria. Yet they both knew her training had been solid, that bel canto was as essential for Wagner as it was for Bellini. In other words, Maria was prepared for this challenge. 'I was ready. There were no surprises,' she would say later.

Three days after *La Walkiria* closed, *I Puritani* opened. The press referred to her performance as 'a miracle...The warmth and expressiveness of her

Elvira cannot be found in the fragile, transparent coldness of all other Elviras,' wrote one influential critic. The character of Elvira was that of an unstable woman torn between fantasy and reality, insanity and reason. It was a difficult character to embody and for that reason was infrequently sung. Maria had single-handedly brought Bellini's opera back before the public, as she had done with *Norma*.

There was now a great demand for her services. Articles about her and 'the miracle' she had pulled off in Venice appeared in newspapers all over Europe and the States. 'It was no miracle,' Serafin was quoted as saying. '...She had the voice, the technique, the intelligence and everything else. I knew she could do it. To me she [is] the kind of artist who, until [now] one only read about in operatic history books. It was not...really so clever or so daring to entrust her with the Bellini role...you see she had already studied and sung *Norma* for me. I would have trusted her with any role. She had proved herself to me. It was no miracle.'

The next two months went by in a rush of new, delicious fame and a killing sequence of engagements in Palermo, Naples, Rome, Turin; but Maria was teetering from high excitement to deep depression – and she was gaining even more weight. Why had she not been asked to sing at La Scala or Covent Garden or the Met? That was where a singer won world acclaim. And why had not Battista even approached the subject of marriage?

At the end of March she went back to Verona to be with Battista for a few weeks before departing on a tour to Buenos Aires, which he had arranged for her. Shortly after her return, Jackie arrived for a pre-arranged visit. Jackie had many things on her mind. There was their mother to be discussed. Litza was stuck in New York where her relationship with their father had disintegrated into one that was so hostile they seldom spoke although they were living in the same small apartment. There was no money to help alleviate this situation, perhaps to bring Litza back to Greece. Then there was her own situation. Milton appeared to be at death's door and she knew she would be penniless when he died. She wanted to go back to lessons and try for a career of her own.

'When I arrived at Verona railway station,' Jackie wrote,

I took a cab, as directed to the hotel where she and Meneghini were living and where I was to have a small room in their suite. The Receptionist told me to go straight up and a porter opened their door and left me inside...There was a long corridor connecting all the rooms and I cautiously made my way down it, peering into the sitting-room and then on to another room until suddenly I was face to face with the two of them in bed. I was appalled and gave out a terrified gasp. Maria looked up from a score spread across her lap and burst out laughing. The bulky form of Meneghini in thick striped pajamas turned on one side with a groan and fell back to sleep. I fled to the sitting-room where I sat on the edge of a sofa trembling with embarrassment.

When Maria joined her she apologized for the odd reunion, but added that she loved to sleep with Battista. 'I love to feel him beside me, to curl up round him.'

After the sisters had talked for a while, Battista appeared. 'He, too, was no oil painting,' Jackie wrote, the reference to Maria's shocking size, 'though for a man of his age he was strong-looking, fresh-faced with white hair. For someone so short and squat he walked like a young man, though side by side, with her height and bulk, they looked most peculiar.'

It was obvious that Jackie still felt a strong resentment to her younger sister (the final memoir she published is filled with denigrating epithets). Nonetheless, there was that family tie that made her feel, as she had in their youth, protective towards Maria, even though her quest for financial aid was not satisfied. Why hadn't this Italian man married her sister? She heard rumours. Maybe his family did not think Maria was good enough for him. Or perhaps he was basically homosexual. That might explain why he was still unmarried although in his mid-fifties. There was also the possibility that he was simply using Maria to further his own ambitions and had no true feelings of love for her.

Taking a maternal role, Jackie decided to intervene and without Maria's knowledge spoke to a member of Battista's family, suggesting that Meneghini was causing her sister to suffer depression, sadness and a loss of reputation. Something had to be done. Perhaps one of his brothers or his one sister Pia could speak to him. His brothers had never been in favour of the match and had refused even to meet Maria. Greed, as in Milton's family, was the culprit. The brothers were afraid of losing their share of the family business if Battista married and had children of his own. Jackie's approach to the Meneghinis was not so dissimilar from Litza's uninvited visit to Milton's family to ask for a similar resolution to what she considered to be a shocking situation. In this case there was to be a happier ending.

The very next day (no one seems to know by what impetus) Battista finally proposed and Maria became Signora Meneghini on 21 April 1949, during Easter week, not an easy matter as under Italian law it was difficult to marry near to the religious holiday and Battista had to obtain permission to be granted a dispensation to be married outside the church. Maria insisted they be wed before they left for South America. Battista paid whatever sum was necessary to assure that she would be his wife before her departure. The ceremony was held at a small church, the Chiesa del Filippini, in Verona. There were very few people at the wedding, only Battista's sister Pia, the Serafins and Pomari of all of Battista's large family and business acquaintances. Jackie had already returned to Athens and neither Litza nor George knew of the nuptials. Maria sent them a cable 'Siamo sposati e felici (We are married and happy)' written in Italian, which neither of her parents understood and which was far from the truth.

The happiness Maria had experienced in the few short weeks preceding the ceremony did not survive the exchange of vows. There had been problems with her about-to-be in-laws, several of whom were openly hostile once they knew she was to become a member of their family. They never let her forget that she was the daughter of a humble Greek. Her talent meant little to them. Battista would constantly apologize for any slight she experienced. He was a man caught in the middle. Protecting and promoting her career became his shield. Money was something he understood and respected. He had negotiated this, her first truly well-paying contract, the South American tour, which was to begin almost immediately after they were married.

Maria saw the South American tour as a chance for a marvellous honeymoon. Only a week before she was to leave did she learn that she would have a maid and a secretary, but that Battista was not to accompany her. Ostensibly, he explained, he would be supervising the construction of a suitable apartment for them over his offices. He would also need to be in Verona seeing to the business side of her tour. They fought. Maria was hysterical and threatened to cancel the tour. In the end he made her see the foolishness of such an action, for this was the opportunity that he and the Maestro, who would be conducting for her, believed would make her a prima diva. Finally she agreed.

There might well have been family pressure as the Meneghini factories were suffering financial reverses, but Battista was never comfortable in a foreign environment. He seemed unable to learn a second language and whereas in Verona he was looked upon with great respect, elsewhere he was viewed as just being part of the diva's entourage. This was not what Battista had fantasized for himself and it was Maria who would suffer the consequence of his disappointment.

And so, Maria Callas Meneghini, a bride of twenty-four hours, departed on 22 April alone on the rebuilt American liner SS *Argentina* for

Buenos Aires. As Serafin was to join her in South America, once again she was on the high seas sailing without a companion, fearful of the troubled waters that might rise before her.

8

Maria Callas Meneghini

ARIA'S SEA JOURNEY took nearly two weeks. The SS *Argentina*, part of the Moore-McCormack Lines which operated over 700 ships for the United States government, had seen heavy duty as a troop carrier during the war and , though revamped, showed its wear. However, Maria occupied a luxurious first-class suite and was treated royally by the captain, Commodore Thomas N. Simpson. She was now a minor celebrity and, if not all the passengers actually knew that she was a rising diva, most learned it from the liner's daily newspaper which had printed a short biographical piece. As on her last crossing, she did not socialize much, spending the large part of the day in a deckchair, wrapped warmly and studying the scores of *Turandot*, *Norma* and *Aïda*, which were the three heroines she would be portraying at the Teatro Colón in Buenos Aires. In the evenings she dined at Commodore Simpson's table.

She was travelling alone as Maestro Serafin and his family were flying and Maria, having never flown, was frightened of the idea. It was comforting for her to know that Serafin would be at her destination to greet her on arrival. She never was happy in big cities, especially when she was alone, and Buenos Aires was a large metropolis, as cosmopolitan in its architecture as it was in population. Architectural styles were a chaos and a confusion: Spanish, Creole, Gothic, Victorian and French of all eras. The people of Buenos Aires identified with the Parisians and so it had become a city of '*belle époque* solidity, sculptured from impermanent material; a city with high plane trees that looked like Paris in the winter rains, but under the bright Argentine sun seemed oddly artificial'.

The day that Maria arrived in Buenos Aires, a million people were packed into the Plaza de Mayo to honour 'Evita' – also known as the 'Lady of Hope' and the 'Mother of Innocents', the wife of Argentina's dictator, Juan Perón. Evita spoke through a microphone to the crowds from a balcony, her voice rising with emotion, her arms flung wide at times, as though in a gesture to bring her audience closer to her.

Maria's rooms overlooked the Plaza de Mayo and the spectacle made a great impression on her. She wanted to learn more about this dynamic woman who had risen from low birth to become the protagonist, loyalist and spiritual support of the Argentinian 'revolution'. Through marriage to Argentinian dictator, Juan Perón, and her own tireless dedication and ambition, Evita had remade herself into the most powerful woman in her country and a world figure. Argentina did not seem like a dictatorship to Maria. There were none of the grim restrictions she had witnessed when the Germans had been in control of Greece. But Argentina surely was under the hard hand of Juan Perón whose blonde wife, beloved by the people who considered her a saint due to her charity work, softened his touch.

'It's love, love, love,' Philip Hamburger wrote just a few months earlier in the *New Yorker*. 'Love makes the Peróns go round. Their whole act is based on it. They are constantly, madly, passionately, nationally in love. They conduct their affair with the people openly. They are the perfect lovers – generous, kind, and forever thoughtful in matters both great and small.' The great crowds of Perónists were under an illusion. But it was a powerful illusion.

Maria had never been too interested in the machinations of power and politics, and would not be until they involved her. But the kind of adulation that Evita received was something that she herself would have enjoyed. 'Ah, and she doesn't even have to sing,' she commented to her old friend Nicola Rossi-Lemeni, who was now Serafin's son-in-law and was to sing the role of Timur in *Turandot*, Oroveso in *Norma* and Ramphis in *Aida*.

May was the start of the winter social season when the wealthy returned from their country mansions and opened their town houses and attended the opera at the Teatro Colón. Since the start of the twentieth century this magnificent opera house, which bore a significant similarity to Garnier's Paris Opéra, had boasted performances by great artists from Caruso to Rosa Ponselle. It was Ponselle for whom the Met had revived *Norma* and *La Gioconda* twenty years earlier,[1] and it was meaningful to Maria that she would be singing, for the first time, on the same stage on

---

[1] Rosa Ponselle had retired in 1937 at the age of forty and still at the height of her powers. Callas had never seen her in performance, but her recordings were among her most treasured possessions. Ponselle had a dark, exciting quality to her voice which the younger singer much admired. In 1949 she was living in Baltimore, Maryland and teaching at the Peabody Conservatory. Callas met her a decade later.

which Ponselle had previously sung. That did not intimidate her, although Buenos Aires did.

The city's fashion setters worshipped style as much as the Parisians. Often the coming autumn fashions were worn by the Buenos Aires *haut monde* in their grand salons, at the Teatro and on the elegant shopping thoroughfares before they had even been shown in Paris. When the directors of the opera house gave a welcome party for the Maestro and the company, Maria was suddenly aware of her lack of chic. The women, resplendent in glittering jewels, were smartly coiffed and gowned. Her weight, which was approaching two hundred pounds, was an obstacle to being *au courant* with fashion. Wartime drab, make-do and tailored clothes had been replaced by dresses that defined the feminine figure; glamour and titillation abounded. The best Maria could do was to wear free-flowing clothes, on and off stage, that disguised her shapeless body.

She was aware that men did not look at her in the same way they did the more svelte women at such affairs as the welcome party. Work was her defence against self-pity. She tried to make it consume her, but there were still those hours when she would close the door to her small hotel suite and find herself alone with the long, dark night before her. Forgotten at such times was her anger that Battista had not accompanied her on the tour.

'Thank you again for becoming my husband before I left,' she wrote to him, a week after her arrival in Buenos Aires. 'You have made me love you even more. No woman is happier than I am...Above all you are the man of my dreams. My sole purpose in life is to make you the happiest and proudest husband in the world.' She ended the letter by telling him that from this tour forth she was to be known as Maria Callas Meneghini and for him to make sure that all her bookings and contracts included that information.

That first week in Buenos Aires was fraught with dissension. Serafin had been assured that the season would open with Maria singing *Turandot*, but the directors of the opera house wanted to start with *Aida* to star Delia Rigal, an Argentinian dramatic soprano better known to Teatro Colón audiences. Serafin insisted that the terms of Maria's contract be honoured. He won the battle but the consequence was that the company drew sides and Maria found herself in the centre of an unpleasant controversy for which she was not in any way to blame.

'I am so upset by the deviousness of some of my colleagues,' Maria wrote to Battista.

[Mario] del Monaco [the Calaf in *Turandot*] has been particularly unpleasant because...he sang with me rather than with that Rigal woman...I, for my part, have never treated any of my colleagues badly but after a very good rehearsal of *Norma*, when even the orchestra players applauded, the singers who were not taking part began to spread false rumors that I was ill and the opera should be substituted with another. I feel sorry for these louses! The just and great God has allowed me to win because I have never tried to cause harm to anyone and, of course, because I have worked very hard.

This was the twenty-eighth time Maria had sung Turandot, but she never allowed herself to feel comfortable in a role, always searching for more meaning in the composer's music and the text, more ways of conveying the emotions of her character. She had found a new depth to Turandot and there was an edge of excitement and brilliance in the opera that 'stop one's breath', one critic noted, adding that 'her wealth of temperament, and the magnificent way in which her voice rides the progressively ascending final phrases of the duet with Calaf, gave her a distinctive stage presence'. Only a very few singers are instantly identifiable – 'a factor of vital importance to holding an audience's attention and establishing a bond between a singer and the public'. Maria had that characteristic.

Her Turandot was a success, the reviews mostly glowing, although they stressed the unpleasant tone her voice could sometimes produce during the more dramatic phrases of an aria. This was something that Maria knew disturbed people – at least at first hearing. But anger, horror, self-revilement could not be sung in dulcet tones and express what the character was feeling. 'It is not enough to have a beautiful voice,' she once said. 'What does that mean? When you interpret a role, you have to have a thousand colours to portray happiness, joy, sorrow, fear. How can you do this with only a beautiful voice? Even if you sing harshly some-times, as I have frequently done, it is a necessity of expression. You have to do it, even if people will not understand. But in the long run they will, because you must persuade them of what you are doing.'

Early in her career Maria had understood this. However insecure she was in her relationship with men, she always had a tight grip on her art and a fearlessness in her approach to it. She believed opera was about people with grand emotions and to bring them alive she must not stifle the deep, and perhaps raw, feelings of love, tenderness, ecstasy, fear, rage and loathing that brought life and honesty to those being portrayed.

Her stay in Buenos Aires was frustrating. Not only was she longing to be with Battista and having to deal with the pettiness and jealousy of members of the company, she never was accepted into the social fold as were Delia Rigal and Mario del Monaco. And although a meeting with

Eva Perón at a charity affair had been arranged, it fell through at the last moment, due to illness on the part of the country's first lady.[2] Then there was the problem of *Aida*. Rigal held fast to her belief that she was to sing the role. Serafin defended Maria's claim to the part. In the end, a compromise was reached and each sang it for one performance.

Serafin conducted a farewell concert on 9 July, the 133rd anniversary of the Argentinian Declaration of Independence from Spain, at which Maria sang duets from *Norma* and *Turandot* with Rossi-Lemeni and del Monaco. With the encouragement and reassurance of Serafin, and with her own impetus to return to Battista as soon as possible, she summoned up her courage and boarded a plane with the Serafins, their daughter and son-in-law and flew back to Rome, 'with my heart in my mouth and sometimes in my feet', she later said.

Battista met her at the airport. He had a new, very glamorous sports car and they drove to Verona where, after the very long drive, he proudly showed her through their new apartment. The front rooms overlooked the Arena and from the balcony a performance could actually be glimpsed (although not heard). The penthouse, which he had purchased months before they were married, was a complete surprise to her. Battista had not shown her the plans and had been secretive about its decoration. There was gilding everywhere – on the mouldings, the ceiling, framing mirrors and paintings. Her bedroom was in a vivid shade of pink. The adjoining bathroom, in the same strong colour, was fitted with striated pink marble tub and floors. The fixtures were gold with the water rushing from the mouths of dolphins. Battista's adjoining bedroom suite was a shade less flamboyant but luxuriously appointed in beige and gold brocade with brown and rust striated marble in the bathroom.

One stepped down into a high-ceilinged living room, which was furnished mainly with antique Venetian pieces (many that had previously adorned his shared apartment with Pomari), and the formal dining room had a huge, ornate Venetian glass chandelier. Later Maria was to comment that it must have been in the worst possible taste. But at the time she thought the apartment was grand and she was very proud of it (although her favourite room was the large kitchen where she and Battista could eat on a simple wood table).

---

[2] Eva Perón died of cancer in 1952 and was already ill at this time. In the summer of 1947, two years before Callas visited Argentina, Eva Perón had toured Europe, and took a holiday villa for several weeks near Monte Carlo, where Aristotle Onassis lived. Onassis was later to have claimed that they made love at her villa, after which she cooked him an omelette and he wrote out a cheque for one of her charities for $10,000. He described the omelette as tasty 'but the most expensive' he had ever had.

Next morning they left for a short, delayed, five-day honeymoon in Venice. Her former anger at him had long disappeared in the comfort of their being together once again. She had no idea how much she had made on the concert tour and assumed Battista had paid for all the work on the apartment. In fact, her earnings had been somewhat modest, but she now had future contracts that would soon inflate her income. All matters relating to finances she left to Battista. She believed – as was the custom in Italian households of that period – that a wife's earnings were her husband's to spend or invest, although she thought of Battista as being wealthy and her earnings as inconsequential.

The new Signora Meneghini had only eight weeks to play the contented housewife. Battista was suddenly in his glory – the manager of a prima donna – and he went to work and booked her into all the leading opera houses in Italy save the one in which she most wanted to make a debut – La Scala. In Perugia, on 18 September, she sang the role of Herod's daughter in *San Giovanni Battista*, an oratorio by Alessandro Stradella.[3] From there, she opened on 20 December in Naples as the revengeful Babylonian Princess Abigaille in Verdi's then infrequently produced opera *Nabucco*, a performance that drew rave notices for her and her superb voice, 'vitality and great insight into the character'. Attention was called to the electrifying two-octave drop on the word *sdegno* (scorn) in the Act Two aria 'Ben io t'invenni, o fatal scritto'.

The last of her three performances of *Nabucco* was on 27 December, so she and Battista spent Christmas 1949 in Naples. They welcomed the New Year in Verona and, as her next engagement was for three performances of *Norma* in January at La Fenice, she was able to commute when her schedule was not too difficult. In February it was *Aida* in Brescia. With the arrival of March came *Tristan und Isolde* at the Opera in Rome, a concert in Turin and, finally, *Norma* in Catania where Maria received the invitation she had dreamed of for years – would she sing three performances of *Aida* at La Scala, the first on 12 April, before Italy's President Eunardi.[4]

Only later did Maria learn to her chagrin that she was to replace Renata Tebaldi who was suddenly taken ill. This was not just a problem

---

[3] Alessandro Stradella (1642–82) was himself the title character in Friedrich von Flotow's nineteenth-century opera, and greatly influenced the Neapolitan composers led by Alessandro Scarlatti in the late seventeenth and early eighteenth centuries. His oratorio is seldom performed but contains some showy passages for a dramatic soprano.

[4] In 1946, following the execution of Mussolini and the demise of the dictatorship, a plebiscite rejected the former monarchy and Italy was proclaimed a republic. Although women did not have the right to vote, divorce was not recognized.

of injured pride: a diva who had not been first choice. Tebaldi was a great favourite at La Scala. She had been chosen by Toscanini in 1946 for its reopening after the war. Tebaldi's voice was one of 'glowing beauty', smoother, more aesthetically pleasing than Maria's – especially in those arias where powerful emotions were demanded. The Milanese audience were attuned to that sound. And Tebaldi, who was a contemporary of Maria's, was also slimmer, more romantic in appearance. Maria, who had waited so desperately for her chance to appear at La Scala, now feared the comparisons and the possible animosity of the generally volatile Milanese opera-goers who had paid to see Tebaldi and were to have a replacement.

Was she thrilled to be making her debut at La Scala? reporters asked at a press gathering on her arrival in Milan at the end of March.

'Yes, I am thrilled, of course I am thrilled. Great theatre. But I am nearsighted you see? For me all theatres are alike,' she snapped back, her true feelings veiled. 'Am I excited? La Scala is La Scala, but I am near-sighted: *ecco tutto.'*

'*What about your voice, Signora Meneghini? They say your voice is uneven?*'

Maria bristled. 'Well, let them say what they want. I sing the way I sing.'

From the very first rehearsal Maria did not feel comfortable with Franco Capuana, the conductor and musical director. At that moment nothing seemed right for Maria – neither with her life nor her career. She was tired of travelling, of living in strange hotels out of trunks when she wanted to be at home with Battista, and she was terribly conscious of her weight and the poor fit of her costumes. This *Aida* was an old production and both sets and costumes had a tired look to them. Serafin had warned Battista that the La Scala production of *Aida* would not show Maria to best advantage and that *just perhaps* Tebaldi's sudden illness had come upon her for those very reasons.

Meneghini played down all the negatives. He was convinced that Maria should make her debut now, not later, at La Scala. To an Italian, singing at that opera house was like entering God's cathedral. Careers had been made with one appearance at La Scala. He wanted Maria to gain fame as quickly as possible and singing at La Scala seemed to him the one certain way to achieve this aim. He did not study or consider what might be the consequence if her appearance was a failure. Giving him due credit, he believed so strongly in Maria that he did not think it was possible.

Maria herself was torn. She wanted to sing at La Scala, of course. But she was now afraid that her timing had been miscalculated. Then, to make matters worse, she had developed a dermatological problem (that the doctors blamed on nerves), which caused red blotches on her face that make-up did not entirely cover. Battista refused to take the Maestro's counsel, which Maria could now see it would have been wise to have done.

As it turned out, the first performance was a fiasco. In order to mask her skin affliction Maria had added veils to her costumes. Aida, once a princess, is now an Abyssinian slave in Egypt, and such veils made no sense. For someone like Maria who believed in verismo, this was a foolish, vain thing to have done. If Battista was unable to stop her, then the director should have stepped in and refused to allow it. Maria would long regret her obstinacy.

'All the Milanese saw', Franco Zeffirelli (who was an admirer and would later direct her in some of her most famous roles) recalled of the evening, 'was this overweight Greek lady, peeping out from behind her trailing chiffon, and heard the unevenness, the changes of register between contralto and soprano which she thought helped reveal the sharpness of the character of the barbarian princess.'

Maria had suffered the ignominy of some booing (something she never before had experienced) at her first performance and Antonio Ghiringhelli, La Scala's general administrator, did not – as custom demanded – come to her dressing room afterwards. This was a terrible insult to her and a blow to Battista who had hoped Ghiringhelli would offer Maria a La Scala contract. The second and third performances went considerably better, but Ghiringhelli seemed to have mysteriously disappeared. Maria was in a state of depression when they departed the day after her last La Scala *Aida* for San Carlo, where she was once again to sing *Aida* (and would do so with much acclaim and wonderment of what went wrong in Milan). This time Serafin was at the helm and, happily, her skin problem was cured. The disastrous engagement at La Scala, however, had seriously injured her self-esteem.

She had little time to nurse her wounds as she was to leave on 6 May, two days after San Carlo, for a Mexican tour. This time she had no choice but to fly as her first appearance was on 23 May in Mexico City, with rehearsals scheduled from 12 May, and she had decided to stop in New York en route. Battista had insisted that he could not go with her but would join her four weeks later. Litza remained in New York, living in open hostility with George (who she claimed had never renounced Alexandra as his mistress), still writing Maria long letters of her unhappiness with her life, her pride in Maria's career and her pain that 'the daughter for whom she had sacrificed so much, encouraged so long, seemed to have forgotten her mother, who was living in near poverty with a man who was unfaithful'.

'She came to New York to see her mother,' a close associate has said, 'not to assuage her guilt or out of compassion. She felt somewhat abandoned by Meneghini and after the difficulties she had encountered on her own in Argentina, she needed someone to "do battle" for her if this happened again. And who else but the mother tiger who had clawed all others in her path to protect her cub in the past?'

Her father, looking rather too dapper for the 'near poverty' Litza claimed, met her at the airport. Her mother, he explained, was in the hospital with acute iritus, a serious irritation of the eye, but was improving nicely. Maria went straight from the airport to see Litza, who was propped up, make-up in place, a patch over one eye. The meeting was tearful, very emotional. The original plan had been for Litza to leave for Mexico with Maria that same night. Litza had envisioned a return to their old relationship in which her 'rightful' position as her daughter's manager would be reinstated. Now she feared that dream would escape her. Maria assured her that as soon as she was well enough, Litza could join her in Mexico City and gave her money for her travel fare and expenses.

Mexico City was a welcoming experience for Maria. She did not have Serafin upon whom to rely, but her relationship with Guido Picco, the conductor for *Norma*, the first of the four operas in which she would appear, started well. It also pleased her to be able to play the diva to Nicola Moscana (the Greek bass who had refused to see her when she had first arrived in New York from Greece right after the war and whom she never forgave, who now was singing the role of her father, the High Priest Oroveso).

As rehearsals on *Norma* progressed, Maria's attitude towards Picco changed. He did not seem to understand what she was trying to do with the role. He was striving for a more conformist, classic portrayal. Maria became highly emotional. There were long daily calls to Battista in Verona. She felt alone, deserted; fearful that what happened in Milan could recur. She tried to get him to change his plans and arrive as soon as possible. Battista assured her that she would be wonderful but that he could not leave early and that she must understand that her job was singing and his job was to take care of the business end of her career.

Litza finally joined her at the Hotel Prince in Mexico City on 21 May, two days before the first of two performances of *Norma*. Maria was genuinely happy to see her mother. This was Litza's moment of glory. A grand suite on the same floor as Maria's was filled with fresh flowers and waiting for her. She accompanied Maria to the dress rehearsal where she was treated by the company with the greatest respect. The next day Maria had her assistant take them both to one of the finest stores in Mexico City to be fitted out for the opening night party to follow the performance.

Norma is a role that defeats most sopranos who are unable to do full justice to its elaborate bel canto vocal lines. But in this, her third time as the Druid priestess, Maria was to make the role her own.

There was a packed house at the colourful Palacio de las Bellas Artes. Litza remained backstage with Maria until it came time for her to dress. Then one of the theatre staff took her out into the grand lobby and settled her in a front-row-centre seat. On the shoulder of her new, stylish gown was an enormous orchid and in her greying hair the tortoise comb that was her only precious possession. That night a sense of excitement pervaded the theatre. The Mexican press had made much of Maria's appearances in Mexico City, and of her 'meteor-like rise as a prima diva within the last year'. Her La Scala debut was noted but without any mention of the fiasco of her first performance there. The audience was primed to expect something startling from the soprano for whom this production had been newly designed.

Maria looked marvellous in her costume and she was impressively heroic in the recitatives, but she was not on her best vocal form at the outset of the first act and did not hit her stride until Act Three.[5] It is the point where Norma considers the terrifying prospect of having to murder her two children. Maria's control was remarkable. Behind the powerful priestess's façade was a vulnerable woman. Norma becomes understood, as she had never been before. But it was in the final act that Maria truly 'worked a minor miracle'.

Her Norma, despite her early mis-steps, was an overwhelming success. The audience in the Palacio de las Bellas Artes were on their feet shouting 'Brava' as she stepped out for her first solo bow and refused to let her leave the stage. She stood there, the whole theatre in pandemonium, an avalanche of applause, roaring cheers. Bouquets soon lined the proscenium and roses fell from the boxes at her feet, but all she could see was an ocean of faces and a tangle of arms outstretched towards her. She placed her hand on her heart and threw a kiss to the audience. It was not a mere gesture; their zealous approval came close to moving her to tears. And as she stepped back behind the curtain, their shouts and applause still thundering, she allowed herself a brief moment alone before coming out for another bow (and another, and another – so many that she lost count).

[5] Originally *Norma* was a two-act opera. However, in the twentieth century it was broken into four acts.

Litza rushed backstage. She was crying. Everyone congratulated her along with Maria and she accepted it as if it was indeed due her.

'She enchanted us,' wrote the critic for *Excelsior*, 'and if at the end of such a superb performance we were somewhat saddened, it was because we felt that perhaps we shall never again hear another comparable Norma in our lifetime.'

Maria's appearances in Mexico City continued with *Aida*, *Tosca*, and Leonora in *Il Trovatore*. Umberto Mugnai replaced Guido Picco as conductor for the first two operas and the collaboration between him and Maria went extremely well. That could not be said for her relationship with some members of the company.

'*Aida* fared marvelously well,' she wrote to Battista.

> The public was ecstatic over [Giulietta] Simionato [the mezzo soprano who sang the role of Amneris] and myself…I am simply furious with the tenor [Kurt] Baum who is very insulting. He is angry with me because I took a high E flat at the end of the ensemble.[6] His jealousy was so great (worse than any woman's) that I thought he would kill me. Anyway when he heard that I would refuse to sing with him again if he didn't apologize, he came to me before the second performance of *Aida* and asked me to forget what he had said. ['I will never sing with you again and I shall see that you never sing at the Metropolitan!'] the skunk!

Maria had gone from triumph to triumph and by the time *Tosca* was premièred, Mexico City and the world of opera were astir with her success. Tosca had been Maria's first leading role with the Athens Opera when she was only eighteen and studying with de Hidalgo, but she had not sung it since. She was nervous, beginning to feel the strain of Battista's absence and of her mother's constant presence. Litza had not been able to restrain herself and after *Norma* began to take an active part in Maria's work, handing out advice, criticizing others in the company. The maternal presence was what Maria thought she wanted, but once Litza began to assert herself, the old anger at her mother's controlling personality enraged her. To add to her troubled state, she no longer felt that Mugnai was in tune with her performance needs.

Her Tosca did not meet with the wild success of *Norma*, but her highly dramatic and beautifully sung scenes with the American singer Robert

---

[6] Deviating from her usual practice of following the composer's instructions impeccably, at the end of the Act Two triumphal scene, Callas soared upwards an octave and sustained a full-voiced high E-flat through to the end of the orchestral postlude – an amazing feat.

Weede as a truly evil Scarpia were brilliantly realized. Maria was now calling Battista twice a day and, with the time change, waking him in the middle of the night. She was frantic over the situation with her mother and desperate for him to put everything aside and fly to Mexico.

He ignored her request and arrived as originally planned on 12 June, two days after her last performance of *Tosca* and as she was beginning rehearsals on *Il Trovatore*.

Litza had begun discussing her wish to divorce George with the idea that she would leave America and return to Europe where she could be 'more helpful' to Maria. Divorce was something that Maria, now married to an Italian Catholic, could not condone. Mother and daughter exchanged harsh words over this. Battista's arrival on the scene did much to smooth matters between them. Litza's talk of divorce ended and as she did not speak Italian and Battista spoke only a few words of English and no Greek at all, no discussion was possible. Also, there was nothing Litza admired more than people with wealth, and from Jackie she had learned that the Meneghinis were a rich and respected family in Verona. She was proud that Maria had married a man with such a background. He appeared affectionate to Maria and polite to her. As they could not communicate, that was all by which she could judge her son-in-law. His age or appearance had little effect on her, but she did back off from her intrusion into Maria's career as soon as Battista was on the scene.

Maria had never sung Leonora in *Il Trovatore* and when she learned that she was to be engaged for the role she had gone to Serafin and asked him to help her with it. He refused, on grounds of professional ethics, saying he could not interfere with what another conductor might want of her performance. She was to say that she 'plunged into the score the only way she knew how – like a sponge'. Guido Picco was once again her conductor, but this time he seemed to be more simpatico to her. Kurt Baum sang Manrico (so much for his threats never to sing with her again) and, although they were not at their best in duets together, they still managed fine performances. Also in the cast was the American baritone Leonard Warren, who sang the role of Count di Luna and matched Maria's voice in their duets brilliantly.

Il Trovatore brought her Mexico City engagement to a glorious close. There would be no going back. Although the Palacio de las Bellas Artes was not in the same category as La Scala and Mexico City did not have the élan of Milan, by appearing there Maria had become an international star and Battista was besieged with new offers for her to sing. The one remaining problem was Litza. She must divest herself of her mother's smothering presence.

Unable to be forthright, Maria suggested that Litza remain a few extra days in Mexico City where she had made friends with the theatre staff. She then gave her several thousand dollars to cover the additional expenses and to pay off her hospital bills in New York. Then, as a final balm for any lingering doubt that her mother might have had as to her daughter's true intention, Battista purchased two mink coats (very much less expensive in Mexico than in Italy), one for Maria and one for his mother-in-law (with a card from – not the two of them – but Maria).

'Mother', Jackie reported, 'wrote to tell me that Maria had given her the most expensive coat imaginable... Only when I worked out that that coat was not a sign of continuing affection but a guilty farewell pay-off did I begin to realize what had happened.' Litza remained in Mexico for several days after Maria's departure. The hotel was pre-paid, the flowers continued to arrive and for a short time she did not have to share the limelight with her famous daughter.

Maria and Battista flew home to Verona where, for the next six weeks, she was able to rest and to play the housewife. 'It was a game for her,' a close friend from Verona recalls. 'She never could have kept it up for long. But Maria equated her having a husband and home with the security and love she had always sought. The problem was that Battista didn't really want her to be a housewife and probably would never have married her if he believed that was her wish. But it wasn't. It was a game. Just a game.'

9

Maria Meneghini Callas

SHORTLY AFTER HER return from Mexico, and little more than a year after her marriage, Maria woke up to the fact that Battista was not as rich as she thought he was. The fur coats, the money she had given her mother had come from her earnings, as had the new car and a considerable amount of the decorating cost of their penthouse apartment. The Meneghinis were a well-to-do family. However, their wealth was split many ways and much of it was not fluid. Their holdings consisted of properties, factories, land and the family home. When Battista had been in charge of the business he had drawn a substantial salary. By becoming his wife's manager, although he remained a consultant and a member of the board, he forfeited a large part of that remuneration.

No sooner had Litza returned to New York than the pleading letters began to arrive again with renewed and bold suggestions that she leave George and come back to Europe. She could not do that without Maria's assistance and, after all, Maria owed her support for all the years she had devoted to her 'survival and success'. The drachma had just been devalued to such a degree that she felt she could live reasonably well in Athens on a modest $100 a month. Maria was now conscious of every cent that was being spent. At first she ignored her mother's pleas and then she stopped replying to her caustic entreaties altogether.

However, the alienation between her parents was of great concern to her; first from a religious point of view, but underlying this was her belief that if her parents were truly reconciled, Litza would accept her life with George and leave her in peace – free from responsibility. Her returning antipathy to her mother came at a time when her relationship with Battista also was going through a change. She now questioned his decisions and asked for an accounting of what she made and what they spent. She was also suspicious of how he occupied his time when she was on tour without him, her father's continuing adultery raising some doubts about her own husband's faithfulness.

What was brewing inside her was a growing sense of independence. An indication of this was her inversion of her theatrical billing from Maria Callas Meneghini to Maria Meneghini Callas – thus making Callas her surname and at the same time placing the emphasis on her Greek heritage. Nonetheless, she still needed the shelter and security of marriage while asserting her prerogative to approve or disapprove of her husband's choices, although she did not often get her way. Battista had received an offer on her behalf to sing at the Municipal in Rio de Janeiro. Maria insisted she would not let him accept unless he was prepared to go with her, which at this time he said was not possible. For nearly a year after their return from Mexico Maria confined her appearances to Italian opera houses.

With Battista by her side for most of her engagements, she went from one Italian city to another, living in the hotels she so hated, adding new roles to her repertoire to build her reputation as a singer who was not afraid to take a chance or a challenge. In October it was Rome and Rossini's *Il Turco in Italia*, a charming opera buffa which had been censored in London in 1822 on grounds of immorality[1] and seldom presented elsewhere since that time. Maria sang the role of Donna Fiorilla, a dissatisfied wife involved with great delight in an intrigue with the eponymous Turk. She had never played a comic role before and was immediately taken by the idea. She proved that she had a natural instinct, inventiveness and wit as a comedienne, and both the opera and Maria were a huge success.

Three weeks after her final performance of *Il Turco in Italia*, she appeared as Kundry in Wagner's *Parsifal* (also in Rome). The two operas were extreme opposites: one light and comedic, a romantic tale of sex and marriage; the other dark and mystical, a legend of spiritual suffering and religious redemption. In each she portrayed a temptress and did so with steamy expertise. *Parsifal* is an opera of inordinate length (four and a half hours of music with only two intermissions). To make the time-span for the opera more palatable, this *Parsifal* was sung on two consecutive nights, 20 November (Act One) and 21 November (Acts Two and Three).

In the audience of the RAI in Rome for both nights was the film and stage director Luchino Visconti, forty-five and determined to try his

---

[1] Theatre posters for *Il Turco in Italia* featured a very flirtatious white lady and a dashing, very dark-skinned Turkish man in exotic turban and embroidered suit.

extraordinary directorial and producing talents in opera, which was his true passion. Born in the Visconti palazzo in Milan, he came from a wealthy aristocratic family (his maternal grandmother was the Countess Brivio). His highly romantic past included his early years as a playboy in Paris, exploits as a Resistance hero in the war and involvement with the Italian Communist Party. He won critical acclaim with his introduction to neo-realism in his first film, *Ossessione*,[2] made in 1942 when the world was still at war and his gritty street scenes and working-class characters struck a startling note of truth and condemnation. He was also a practising homosexual who kept his private life just that.

Visconti possessed aristocratic good looks, well-defined features, mesmerizing dark eyes and a commanding personality. Besides being rich, he was articulate, a striking figure who dressed with élan and possessed a stunning sense of style. His obsession with opera included his fervent admiration for its most talented singers and Maria excited his senses as had few other divas. 'The first time I saw Maria [as Kundry in *Parsifal*],' he recalled,

> was when she was still enormous. She was half naked in the second act, covered with yards and yards of transparent chiffon – a marvellous temptress, like an odalisque. On her head was a little tambourine hat that plopped down on her forehead every time she hit a high note. She would just bat it back in place.
>
> Every night she sang I secured a certain box and shouted like a mad fanatic when she took her bows. I sent her flowers. She was beautiful but fat on stage…commanding – her gestures thrilled you.

After her last performance of *Parsifal*, they met briefly backstage where he told her he would like to direct her in an opera.

'Why?' she asked.

'Because I think you are the greatest soprano of our times,' he replied.

'She sat there [in her dressing room] for a moment, squinting her eyes at me. Then she reached for a pair of glasses that were on her dressing table and put them on. "Well, you don't look either foolish or mad," she said. "When you find the opera we will talk."'

This was the start of a strong friendship, a future artistic alliance, and for Maria a naive flirtation for she did not perceive Visconti's sexual proclivities in the beginning. He was once again in the audience in Florence

---

[2] *Ossessione* was based on James Cain's *The Postman Always Rings Twice* and was an unauthorized version of the book. Visconti transplanted the story to fascist Italy. Because of its legal status the film was not released in the United States until 1975, when a settlement had been made with the author's estate.

on 14 January 1951 for her debut as Violetta in Verdi's *La Traviata*. She took immediately to the role of the romantic and tragic courtesan created by Dumas *fils* in his drama *La Dame aux Camélias*. This was one of those rare moments in opera when the singer and the role became one. Serafin, who was conducting, was aware of it and so was Visconti, and this was despite her enormous size (for she had gained more weight over the Christmas holidays), the stiffness of the tenor who sang the role of Alfredo, Violetta's young lover, and a production in which the sets and costumes were worn and weary.

Visconti was keener than ever to create a new production of an opera especially for Maria. He suggested Bizet's *Carmen*. 'She was afraid to do Carmen because she didn't know how to dance like a gypsy,' Visconti recalled. She rejected his ideas for Richard Strauss's *Salome* as it involved partially disrobing on stage during the Dance of the Seven Veils (she had worn a most revealing costume in *Parsifal* but had felt extremely self-conscious in it). Despite the glorious vocal opportunity, the Marschallin in Strauss's *Der Rosenkavalier* would demand she sang in German. Maria spoke and sang in numerous languages, although with a decided American accent; that included her Italian. But she found the harsh sound of German, which reminded her of the days of the Occupation, the most difficult to overcome.

In public she appeared to be the loving, dutiful wife, but her close friends were beginning to notice a restlessness in Maria coupled with a sharpness of tongue that crept into her exchanges with Battista from time to time. He was not as clever with her contracts as she believed he should be. There was not the demonstrativeness between them which had formerly been so open. Of course, the honeymoon was long over and that could be expected. But it was Maria's attitude towards Battista, her body posture – often cool and detached in his company – that alerted the Meneghinis' more intimate circle (notably the Serafins and the Rossi-Lemenis) that something was wrong.

Much of what was happening to Maria was caused by her new exposure to the world around her, to sophisticated intellectuals such as Visconti, and by her unhappiness over her weight. She had by now learned how to make up her face and coif her hair to point up her extraordinary eyes and striking bone structure. She often looked to Visconti, who had become a confidant, for advice. 'You are a beautiful woman,' he assured her. 'Yes, you are fat. You don't need me to tell you that. It does not mar your beauty. It only stops you from feeling beautiful because today's perception of a woman's beauty is equated with a slim figure. Fifty years ago that was not the case. Quite the opposite.'

She was falling in love with Visconti, although she could hardly admit this even to herself. 'Just a friend.' she told Rossi-Lemeni when he questioned her about Visconti. 'At some point', Visconti mused, 'Maria began to fall in love with me. It was a stupid thing. All in her mind. But like so many Greeks, she had a jealous streak and there were many terrible scenes.'

Her commitments kept her almost constantly away from Verona. *La Traviata* had been followed by *Il Trovatore* in Naples, *Norma* in Palermo, *Aida* in Calabria, a concert in Turin, back to Florence for another performance of La Traviata, a concert in Trieste, her Florence debut as Elena in *I vespri Siciliani*, another debut as Euridice in *Orfeo ed Euridice*, and finally, on 11 June 1951, less than five months after her first *La Traviata*, she ended her marathon round of appearances with another concert in Florence. The Meneghinis then returned to Verona from where, five days later, they left by plane for Mexico City and a return series of performances from 3 through 22 July at the Palacio de las Bellas Artes, where – at her invitation – her father was to meet them as their guest for the full length of their stay.

Battista had finally sold his share of his family's business to his brothers, a transaction that gave him a more fluid financial base and the time to devote himself entirely to Maria as her manager. Maria had pressured him in this matter, no doubt to improve their financial situation, although she was now earning rather large sums from her performances and the many records that she had made. She feared her own emotions and needed Battista to be omnipresent to remind her that she was a married woman, but this new arrangement was mined with difficulties. At this stage in her career, Maria needed a manager who knew how to build upon her success, to find her the right roles, better productions and venues as well as to negotiate a favourable contract. Battista, despite his grand aspirations, simply was not qualified for the job.

Before leaving Verona, La Scala finally capitulated to her talent and offered her a contract for the 1953 season. She was to sing three leading roles – Constanze in Mozart's *Die Entführung aus dem Serail*, the title role in *Norma* and Elisabetta di Valois in *Don Carlos*, for which she would be paid $500 each for thirty performances ($15,000 in total, and equal to the highest-paid singers at La Scala). Battista urged her to sign, but she wanted to sing Violetta in *La Traviata* for which Renata Tebaldi was scheduled. To Battista's chagrin, she refused. He was furious that she had gone against his decision. But it was the smartest thing she could have done because La Scala would finally bow to her demand and agree to a new production of *La Traviata* to be mounted and directed by Visconti.

Not only was she to appear at La Scala, she also agreed to make her first appearance in London, where she would sing *Norma* in 1952 at Covent Garden, a contract signed just two days before her departure to Mexico and her reunion with her father.

She was proud of her accomplishments and anxious for George to see her on stage and for him to get to know his son-in-law (who was only a few years younger). In the struggle between her parents, Maria had aligned herself with her father. But surely she could not have thought that she might be able to engineer a reconciliation. Litza, on money borrowed from Dr Lantzounis, had returned to Athens and was living with Jackie who, their mother now decided, should study singing and also have a career in opera. When her father told her this, Maria was livid. She did not envisage the idea of another Callas as a competitor, even though she did not believe this was a possibility. Jackie might have a basic talent to sing, but she did not possess the ambition or the stamina to sustain a career. What she understood was that her sister was now their mother's marionette; as if Jackie had not been humiliated enough through her forced illicit liaison with Milton.

The reunion with her father had been emotional, but there was now an awkwardness between them. George was faced with a successful daughter who presented herself more as his benefactress than his loving child. She was almost always too busy to spend a consequential span of time with him. For Maria, her father's visit did not match up to her expectations. She had defended him so long against her mother that her remembrance of him (for she had hardly seen him since the start of her professional career) was unrealistic. George was a simple man, a simple pharmacist of simple tastes. He did not mix well with rich and famous or intellectual people. In that, she now saw that her mother had been right. What she missed was George's genuine humanity, and his discomfort at feeling he was out of place in his daughter's world. Maria might have been more aware of her father's situation if her own had not been so fraught with difficulties.

For Battista to have booked her for the month of July, when the thermometer in Mexico could, and often did, soar past ninety degrees for weeks on end, was pure sadism – or stupidity. Few, if any, buildings in the city were fully air-conditioned. Electric fans recirculated the foetid air of the rehearsal rooms and the backstage of the opera house was an oven. Maria had just completed an exhausting season, taken an overnight flight (this was before jet planes) and had trouble adjusting to the eight-hour time change.

Once again she appeared with del Monaco in *Aida* to overwhelmingly enthusiastic audiences. The heat from the footlights was so intense that by the end of the last performance of *Aida* she was suffering from heat exhaustion exacerbated by the weight of her costumes and the intolerable backstage conditions. Her legs and ankles had swollen painfully. She spent two days in bed but then went on to triumph in *La Traviata*.

George returned to New York to find a stack of abusive letters from Litza demanding that he send her a suitable monthly income to cover her needs. The hostilities between them would continue but for the moment Maria would not be personally involved. The Meneghinis' original plan had been to return from Mexico City to Verona for the rest of the summer and then fly to Brazil where, in September, she was to appear in São Paulo and Rio de Janeiro. However, the oedema in her legs was still giving her great pain and the doctors advised against extended air travel. They decided to go directly to Brazil where the weather was many degrees cooler and to remain there until rehearsals began and they would be joined by Maestro Serafin. First, though, she was to sing three operas in São Paulo, *Aida*, *Norma* and *La Traviata*. Still too ill on the scheduled date for *Aida*, the performance had to be cancelled. It was not until she arrived in São Paulo that she learned that Renata Tebaldi, the diva who was the reigning queen of La Scala, had already set the opera world in Brazil abuzz a week earlier with none other than *La Traviata*. Inevitably, Maria's performances in Rio de Janeiro would be compared.

Battista, certain that Maria would not have have signed the Brazilian contract had she known of Tebaldi's presence, had simply left out that piece of information and, in so doing, placed a formidable obstacle between himself and his wife.

'I am not a piece of meat!' she was heard to shout during one of their arguments. It took Serafin's gentle, placating wisdom to calm her down.

Tebaldi might have looked as sweet and mellow as her voice suggested but, as Rudolf Bing, the newly appointed director of the Met, commented, 'She has dimples of iron.' Tebaldi was no less pleased about being in Rio de Janeiro with Maria present than Maria was to find her still there and scheduled to sing, as she was, at a Red Cross Concert on 14 September.

Singing Alfredo to Maria's Violetta in São Paulo on 9 September was the Italian tenor Giuseppe di Stefano. Darkly handsome and a young man who carried himself with some arrogance, di Stefano and Maria did not immediately hit it off, although their voices blended well. With them in the cast was Tito Gobbi (Germont), one of the finest baritones and singing actors of his generation. The reviews of Maria's *La Traviata* were ecstatic and most noted how different was Tebaldi's approach to the role. A feud was in the brewing.

Maria's first role in Rio de Janeiro was *Norma* and she received a standing ovation, which Tebaldi had not, despite the latter's success as Violetta. The Red Cross charity concert brought things to a head. An understanding had been reached that there would be no encores for either diva. Maria sang 'Sempre libera', a showpiece from the first act of *La Traviata* and an aria much associated with Tebaldi. This sent Tebaldi into a simmering rage. Then Tebaldi sang the 'Ave Maria' from *Otello* and followed it with not one but *two* encores, not with simple piano accompaniment but with the full orchestra, which had to mean that she had rehearsed and planned to sing them despite their pre-performance pact.

Tempers flared between the two women at the dinner given at a local restaurant in honour of all the visiting artists. After Tebaldi said something about 'Sempre libera' not being suitable for concerts Maria, always the champion at sharp jibes, replied 'A good singer can extract any aria and make it soar!' and with that she grabbed Battista's arm and left the restaurant.

The concert manager of the Municipal in Rio de Janeiro was Barretto Pinto, a small, pompous man, married to one of the richest women in Brazil, who commanded the opera season with a tyrannical excess. Pinto took an immediate dislike to the Meneghinis on first meeting when Maria complained in a strident voice that he had booked Tebaldi and herself to sing the same role. Pinto was a devoted fan of Tebaldi's and took umbrage at Maria's obvious dislike of the great diva.[3] Battista recalled that when the two divas spoke earlier at the restaurant in Rio de Janeiro, 'Tebaldi kept saying how she had never been in her best form at La Scala and was trying to put Maria off that theatre... It suddenly crossed my mind that it was Maria's brilliant singing from *La Traviata* [earlier at the concert] that worried her. You see Tebaldi had not been very successful at La Scala during the previous season. It would, therefore, not have been in her interests if Maria sang this role at La Scala... Maria answered Tebaldi rather sharply with words to the effect that perhaps it was a good idea for Tebaldi not to sing at La Scala too often: "People get tired of you."'

Barretto Pinto was furious at Maria for what he considered an outrageous insult to Tebaldi. 'That woman shall never sing again in *my* theatre,' he told an associate. Maria's appearance in *Tosca* followed

[3] Callas was to claim that she had believed that Tebaldi admired her and was her friend until they both appeared simultaneously in Rio de Janeiro. Tebaldi denied that they were ever friends. 'There has never been any love between us,' she was quoted as having said, 'so why speak of being enemies when we were never friends.'

almost immediately upon the heels of her unpleasant exchange with
Tebaldi. During the intense murder scene with Scarpia, several people in
the audience shouted distasteful comments. Maria was thrown for a
moment or two but quickly regained her composure and continued with
the aria. At the final curtain she was given a warm and generous reception. The next morning Pinto asked the Meneghinis to come to his office
where he informed them that Maria was not to sing any more subscrip-
tion performances because she was *protestata* (undesirable). Callas was
enraged and, elbowing Battista out of the way, confronted Pinto, who she
now suspected had placed the dissenters in the audience himself.

She harshly reminded him of his contractual obligations and that they
would have to pay her whether she did or did not sing. She threatened a
legal suit even if she was paid and did not sing and warned him that
every singer in Italy would be cautious after that of appearing in Rio de
Janeiro as long as he was concert manager. Pinto contemptuously told
her that she could sing *La Traviata* but 'no one will come to hear you'.

She sang Violetta in two performances to full houses and many curtain
calls. Battista had written into all the Latin American contracts that Maria
be paid in cash or gold coin at the end of her performances. When she
appeared in Pinto's office he pushed the money across to her and with a
sneer said, 'For the awful performances you gave I should pay you
nothing.'

With that Callas picked up a heavy object on his desk (either a paper-
weight or an inkstand, Battista recalled) and was set to hurl it at Pinto.
Battista grabbed her arm just in time. But when Pinto came around the
desk to ask her to leave, Maria struck him in the stomach with her knee.
Pinto stumbled, nearly falling to the floor. Battista, white with fear that
the police might be called, helped the man to his feet and then ushered
Maria out as quickly as he could. The next morning they were on a plane
heading home to Italy, her reputation as a diva of wild temperament now
established.

On 7 December 1951, four years after singing *La Gioconda* in Verona,
Maria made her official debut at La Scala. Ghiringhelli had agreed to all
her terms. She was to open the 1951–2 season in the role of the Duchess
Elena in Verdi's *I vespri Siciliani*[4] in a new production mounted to mark
the fiftieth anniversary of Verdi's death. Costumes had been designed
especially for her and she would sing all seven performances, which

[4] *I vespri Siciliani* is also known as *Les Vêpres Siciliennes* as it was specially
commissioned for the Great Exhibition in Paris of 1855 and is presented in both
French and Italian translations.

meant the role would be hers alone. This was the moment that would make all her gruelling work, the exhausting tours, the indignation she had suffered, worthwhile. She was twenty-eight years old, her fame established – now she must apply every bit of her talent and energy into sustaining it.

From her first rehearsal on the stage of La Scala she established her star status, although when she arrived – in an unflattering wool sweater and skirt, her hair pulled back into a matronly bun, heavy shoes supporting her still-swollen legs – the large cast and the chorus were disappointed. She did not look like the fiery diva of recent newspaper reports, nor did it seem that she could transform herself into the role of the beautiful Duchess Elena. Yet as she strode across the stage, they were struck by her 'dignity of carriage, the air of... innate authority that went with every movement'. At this first introduction to their leading singer, the cast was in awe at her amazing range – going from deep contralto to a high E-flat with tremendous strength.

I vespri Siciliani tells of the occupation of Sicily by the French in the thirteenth century and the efforts of the Sicilians to remove them. The Duchess Elena is the sister of Frederick of Austria and Maria sang her rousing aria in Act One – 'Coraggio del mare audaci figli' ('Courage, brave sons of the sea') in an electrifying rendition. From then to the climax in Act Three, the wedding of Elena to Arrigo, son of Guy de Montfort, the French governor of the island, she held the audience in the palm of her hand. Costumed in a magnificent ivory satin bridal gown, embossed with golden lions, a glittering tiara atop her dark auburn hair, she sang Verdi's glorious bolero thanking her wedding guests for their beautiful flowers, her voice floating to the top of her range. Then comes the vesper bell which signals both the start of the wedding service and the advance of the Sicilian patriots who slaughter the unarmed French attending the wedding. Maria had turned Elena into a complex and human character, caught between her love for her country and her vulnerability as a woman. She had conquered Milan and was now one of La Scala's greatest artists.

La Scala's new production of *La Traviata* starring Maria and directed and produced by Visconti was scheduled for the following season. She was disappointed by the delay but her schedule was filled with exciting and prestigious productions that somewhat eased her chagrin. She sang Violetta in Parma on 29 December, *I Puritani* in Florence (with Rossi-Lemeni and Serafin on board) in early January, then returned to La Scala on 16 January for eight performances of *Norma*, the role with which she would always be most closely identified. The Milanese were once again electrified.

She would sing Norma again in her debut appearance at London's Covent Garden ten months later, on 8 November 1952. This was the year of the young Queen Elizabeth II's accession to the throne and a sense of youth and fresh starts pervaded the English art world. To the British, what appeared to be a meteoric rise to opera fame of this young woman, Maria Meneghini Callas, appealed to the country's press corps and her name appeared daily in stories, mostly invented, that told about her feud with Tebaldi and her temperamental disposition.

To one young woman in the company, the future prima donna Joan Sutherland, who was singing the minor role of Clotilde, being on the same stage with Callas was the thrill of her lifetime. 'The impact of hearing Callas in the flesh was something one cannot forget,' she recalled,

> and when the voices of Norma and Adalgisa [sung by the great mezzo-soprano, Ebe Stignani] blended in their fantastic duets and trio, I doubted if I would ever experience such a thrill again...I didn't dare approach either of them...but they were both very kindly – Maria having quite a few joking asides with me in her Brooklyn vernacular [Sutherland confused Maria's New York accent for that of Brooklynese]. But what a professional she was and, although she knew the role inside out, she was content to rehearse until things were right.
>
> Her eyesight was appalling and contact lenses were not yet the norm, so she would pace out her movements with her thick glasses on, counting the number of steps she could take from point to point, and only removing them when we reached the final Dress Rehearsals. I doubt if she could see the conductor [Vittorio Gui] but they had worked together a great deal and all went well.

For Maria the importance of this performance of *Norma* was that the opera had not been heard at Covent Garden since 1929, when it had been sung by Rosa Ponselle. She need not have worried about many comparisons. The British critics called her 'the Norma of our day' and the public was wildly enthusiastic. She was a sensation, although there was one critic, the doyen Ernest Newman, who raised his umbrella as he exited the opera house into the rainy night and declared 'in a rather high-pitched voice: "But she is not a Ponselle!"'

The year had been exhilarating and exhausting. There had been very few chances to relax at home in Verona and those had been mostly unpleasant stays. The penthouse apartment occupied the top floor of a building owned by the Meneghini family and Battista's brothers had offices on the ground and first floors. She was in essence 'living over the shop', as her mother had done in the early years of her marriage. The animosity between the brothers and Maria was rife. They blamed her for Battista's defection and they showed her no warmth or even courtesy.

'As our apartment in Verona was over the family business,' Battista later wrote, 'if any of my brothers met my wife on the stairs, they would always ignore her... When once Maria, coming down the stairs, lost her footing and fell, one of my brothers who witnessed the accident did nothing about it but merely shouted, "She is so hopeless that she is incapable of even walking down the stairs."'

Battista made no effort to reprimand his brothers or to demand more respect for his wife. Maria grew quickly to despise her own home, to hate the time she spent there, and much of this anger turned itself on to her husband and ultimately it was her self-esteem that suffered. She was saved from utter despondency by Visconti, who travelled wherever she was to appear, fed her encouragement, and helped her to choose clothes that minimized her weight and yet were youthful and flattering.

Then, in 1953, she went to see Audrey Hepburn in the charming film *Roman Holiday*. The sylphlike star, with her great eyes and gamin face, made an immediate impression on her. One day Visconti was visiting her in her dressing room and she widened her eyes and stared into his. 'Luchino, could I be beautiful if I had a body like that of Audrey Hepburn?' she asked.

'You would be too thin.'

'But beautiful?'

'Well, you would be a truer Traviata, who after all is dying of consumption.'

That was all he needed to say. The next day she placed herself on a rigid diet, no pasta, no bread, no alcohol. She ate only one meal at midday, despite her strenuous schedule. In eleven months' time she had lost sixty-eight pounds. Suddenly a new, glamorous Callas emerged. The metamorphosis was so great that magazines and newspapers all over the world published before and after pictures and, for the first time in her entire life, Maria looked into a mirror and saw a woman she liked.

10

Metamorphosis

THROUGHOUT ELEVEN TORTUROUS months of self-disciplined dieting, a regime that bordered on near starvation at times, Maria was also making other changes in her appearance. Due to her high visibility and to the amount of attention being paid to her by the press, some of the world's leading couturiers – Dior, Balmain, Givenchy – offered her gowns and ensembles for public functions where she would be photographed in their creations. Ironically, the humble girl of questionable taste from Washington Heights quite suddenly became the symbol of Parisian and Milanese high chic. As the weight just seemed to melt away, revealing a curvaceous figure, then a lithe, slim outline, her wardrobe became more daring, bold in colour and design; a stunning wasp-waisted, bouffant scarlet taffeta gown for a charity ball in Venice, an ethereal Grecian form-fitting white crêpe-de-Chine for an evening reception during her third visit to Mexico City.

The butterfly had emerged from the formlessness of a dreary cocoon in full view of her public. Not only had she streamlined her figure, she was constantly reinventing the colour and style of her hair, which went from dark auburn to deep red to bright auburn to blonde in the same eleven-month time-span. Her proudest physical assets were now her legs. She had formerly been embarrassed by their shapeless size and thick ankles, and had been particularly devastated when one critic cruelly noted in a review of a performance of *Aida* that 'it was difficult to discern Callas's ankles from those of the elephant in the scene'. She had cried bitterly after reading that and one can just imagine what such a comment had done to her self-image. Midway through her weight-loss ordeal, she began wearing high-heeled shoes where before she had only worn matronly Oxfords. This added at least two inches to her height, which was five feet seven inches, so that she now appeared commandingly tall.

There had always been two Marias – the self-conscious woman in private life and the magnificent performer on stage. The same two women remained, but now the inner Maria had found a shield to defend herself against the world.

Her extreme dieting seemed to energize rather than exhaust her. In 1953 she sang fifty-five performances of seventeen operas (including *La Traviata*, *Lucia di Lammermoor*, *Il Trovatore*, *Norma*, *Medea* and *Aida*), which took her to Venice, Rome, Florence, Milan, Genoa, Catania, London, Verona and Trieste, while maintaining her recording sessions with Cetra and EMI-Angel Records.[1] During her stay in Verona to sing Aida and then Leonora in *Il Trovatore* she had an unpleasant confrontation with Battista's brothers. No longer would she take their humiliation and insults, and she insisted to Battista that they move to Milan. In the end he agreed that she could find an apartment there and see to its decoration, but stated that he would not break the family ties. The Verona penthouse would, therefore, be their second home and a place where he could be with his family whenever he was needed. Maria gladly accepted this compromise for it would mean that she did not have to accompany him to Verona.

Ten days after her thirtieth birthday, on 13 December, she sang *Medea* at La Scala with Leonard Bernstein, a young American still unknown in Italy, conducting. This was Bernstein's first venture into grand opera and he had only five days to learn Cherubini's complex score, which had not been performed at La Scala for over a century. Bernstein was a dramatic personality – handsome, intense, brilliant. Ignoring Maria's rebukes, he smoked incessantly. When he conducted, his dark hair would spill over on to his forehead as he bounced athletically, his face contorted during the dramatic passages, then relaxed 'to an expression of drugged bliss' during the lyric ones. He had the disruptive habit of singing to himself and punctuating the more striking moments in the score with deep-throated growls. At the first rehearsal the company anticipated a violent clash between their diva and their conductor, for both were volatile people. Instead they treated each other with a restraint forged by mutual respect for their individual talent.

Originally, La Scala had scheduled Alessandro Scarlatti's finest opera, the seldom performed *Mitridate Eupatore*, as this, their second opera in the season. Maria had no sooner received the score when their music director, Victor de Sabata, fell seriously ill and there was trepidation about another director's ability to interpret this great classical document.

---

[1] Callas recorded complete versions of *I Puritani*, *Cavalleria Rusticana*, *La Traviata*, *Tosca* and *Lucia di Lammermoor* in 1953.

Maria had sung *Medea* earlier in the year in Florence and so a switch was made to the more familiar opera. Bernstein was in Italy at the time and Ghiringhelli convinced him to take on the task. As rehearsals continued a fractious chemistry ignited the two artists. Bernstein was the first American conductor Maria had worked with, which created a new dynamic. Not only were they both Americans, they were close to the same age and perfectionists.

'I believe *Medea* inspired Maria very deeply,' Margherita Wallmann, the stage director, recalled.

> She identified with the role. She herself was torn between America, Greece and Italy – like Medea, a wanderer without a real home. And like Medea, when it was necessary, she found the strength to cut long-held ties [her family] to go on and survive... She was still a very young woman, and married to a much older man [Battista had recently celebrated his sixty-first birthday]. I am sure that certain sexual frustrations found an outlet in her work – unfulfilled passions were released on her singing and acting.

Bernstein's intensity matched Maria's. When the final curtain fell on the first performance of *Medea*, he was to remember vividly, 'the place was out of its mind. Callas? She was pure electricity.' What he could have added was that he received almost as great an ovation.

Her association with Bernstein caused her to think increasingly about America. He possessed the fervour, the sense of being intoxicated with his art, with life that seemed so American in spirit. She had not yet had a viable offer from the Met, but in the early days of January 1954 she was invited to appear at the Chicago Civic Opera House the following November. Her career had seemed to come full circle. With Rossi-Lemeni in the company she would finally sing in the opera house where she had originally thought she would make her American debut. Two young concert organizers, Carol Fox and Laurence Kelly, had succeeded where the Bagarozys had failed in bringing an opera company to Chicago.

The contract that Maria had signed with the Bagarozys had plagued her for over five years. In 1949, after her success with *I Puritani* in Venice, she had had an unpleasant confrontation with Louise who was in Italy 'scouting talent' for another opera company that Eddie was trying to form. The Bagarozys were still down on their luck but had not given up hope that they could succeed now where they had failed before. They needed funds and among what they included with their few assets were the contracts that Rossi-Lemeni and Maria had signed, making them their sole representatives for the following ten years. Rather than having any future problems, Rossi-Lemeni made a cash settlement with them at this time and he advised Maria to do likewise. Maria, with Battista's counsel, refused to do so, fully believing the law was on her side. The contract had been signed in the United States and had been drawn with a company that went bankrupt shortly after the first and only engagement that they had handled for her, and for which the Bagarozys had received their correct fee. The catch was that Maria had signed with the Bagarozys personally and not with their company.

Through the years Maria had received dunning letters and threats of a lawsuit. The Bagarozys were demanding ten per cent of everything she had earned as a performer since the signing of the contract as well as damages and legal fees. However, they could only sue Maria in the country where the contract was executed and signed. She, therefore, had no impetus to settle with them and had ignored all communications from their lawyers. But now she wished to make her American debut, and she and Battista were concerned that legal complications might arise.

The contract that Carol Fox and Laurence Kelly offered Maria with the Chicago Opera Company was simply too good to turn down: her choice of whatever three operas she wished to sing, $2000 per performance (twice what the Met was then paying most of their top singers), first-class travel arrangements and their hotel, transportation and other living expenses while in Chicago. Maria agreed to sing *Norma*, *La Traviata* and *Lucia di Lammermoor*. Rossi-Lemeni was also to appear with her and he warned her that the Bagarozys could attach her salary or present her with a court summons. 'Let them try!' was Maria's answer.

Maria's first appearance in *Lucia di Lammermoor* had been in Mexico City in 1952 and her audience and the critics greeted it with great fervour. Still, she had not felt satisfied. The production had been an old one, the director, Guido Picco, not a man of dramatic vision. She repeated the role at La Scala on 18 January 1954, having just signed the contract with Fox and Kelly. Her director and conductor was Herbert von Karajan, of Austrian-Greek heritage, who was one of opera's most remarkable conducting talents. Maria liked the man and respected his musical brilliance, but she hated his visual concept of the opera – stark, stylized sets with moody, dim, shadowy lighting that pervaded the scenes with a foreboding sense of doom. The poor lighting created serious problems for her and the original lighting designer quit after a failed struggle with von Karajan to brighten the set. Still the director persisted in his vision.

Von Karajan's artistic idea was to light Lucia in the famous mad scene so that she looked like a lost, wild, white bird flailing its wings against an inky night sky. Falsely believing her lover Edgar is in love with another woman (a lie told to her by her brother, Lord Henry Ashton, who is Edgar's arch enemy), Lucia agrees to marry Lord Arthur Bucklaw, a match engineered by Ashton. During the ceremony Edgar appears and swears that he loves only her. But it is too late. Lucia has already signed the marriage contract. Verging on madness she murders her new husband and then, in the most famous mad scene in all opera, reappears at the wedding festivities (where Lord Arthur's death is not yet known), and accompanied by a flute, executes the most intricate and dazzling coloratura before she collapses and dies. When Edgar hears the bell tolling her death, he stabs himself.

She wore a fantastic, white, flowing costume with wide, pleated sleeves that moved like giant swan wings set for flight when she raised her arms and then lowered them slowly in defeat, as if they were too heavy for her to lift. The effect was extraordinary and her voice supreme as it rose to a thrilling E-flat in alt and she held it there for ten seconds during the cadenza. The audience in La Scala went wild and there was near pandemonium during her solo curtain calls. Von Karajan had turned an effect into one of the most sensational theatrical moments in Maria's career, but the production as a whole remained disappointing and she was willing and eager to make another attempt at Lucia in Chicago.

First, she would sing *Lucia* and *Medea* in Venice, *Tosca* in Genoa, and Elisabetta in *Don Carlos* as well as von Gluck's rarity, *Alceste*, at La Scala. Her greatest disappointment in La Scala's productions during this season was the delay in working with Visconti, who could not come to a satisfactory financial agreement with the management. *Alceste* had never been performed at La Scala. 'For me,' her conductor Carlo Maria Giulini recalled, 'she was *il melodramma* – total rapport between word, music, and action...She had an amazing capacity to sustain attention even when standing motionless. In my entire experience in theatre, I know of no artist like Callas. It is no fabricated legend: she had something that was different.'

With *Alceste* she was playing a great queen with all the strength of inbred majesty. There was, Giulini observed, 'some mystic transformation', Maria *was* Alceste. Her new figure added much to her desire to sing the role. *Alceste* is based on the drama by Euripides and tells how the Ancient Greek queen offers to die in place of her beloved husband, Admetus, and is brought back from Hades by Hercules. She looked marvellous in her Grecian draped costumes. In the Act Two finale, after Alceste gives herself in death to save Admetus, she allowed herself to be borne aloft over the heads of three of the Greek queen's followers into the temple, a feat that would have been incongruous had she not lost all the weight. Margherita Wallman worked hard with her to overcome her fear of being dropped and Maria, finally trusting herself and the men who carried her, totally relaxed to a stunning effect, her head inclined in death, her long red hair flowing down behind her, not a muscle moving, as she was carried to her entombment.

She returned her hair to its darker colour for her role as Elisabetta di Valois, young wife of the ageing Philip II of Spain in Verdi's *Don Carlos*. Milan audiences had become her devout fans, many switching their allegiance from Renata Tebaldi. They were awed by her versatility, the range of her unique voice, her dramatic powers and now – her glamorous appearance. Certainly she looked every inch the opera's beautiful queen in love with her husband's son from an earlier marriage. But the role did not display her great vocal technique, nor was Elisabetta the kind of inwardly dramatic character that she preferred to portray. The production was successful, her reviews excellent, but she would choose never to sing the role again.

The Meneghinis returned in August to Verona for Maria to sing Margherita in Boito's *Mefistofele*. This stay was even more acrimonious than previous ones due to the Meneghini family. It was difficult for Maria to understand what Battista's family had against her. She had tried from the beginning of her relationship with Battista to win them over, always buying presents for their children at Christmas and on other occasions. Yet, she still suffered the worst insults and indignation from them.

What Maria did not comprehend was the power of the family in Italian life. Family is an Italian's stronghold against the world. Among its members the individual receives help, loans, allies and accomplices to assist him in his ambitions. No Italian who has a family is alone, and no family will let a member break away without a struggle and an offence, for his or her defection means a possible chink in the family wall. With Maria's own dysfunctional background she could not understand this. And although she was of Greek origin and had lived in Greece for eight years, her formative early youth had been spent in the United States where women, unlike those in the Mediterranean countries, led independent lives if they chose. In this period in modern Italian history a woman was still considered inferior to the male, placed on earth to amuse and comfort him, and to bear him many children, preferably boys.

Europe now thought of Maria as 'the Greek diva', but the Meneghinis – who were basically anti-American – saw her as their past enemy. She spoke like an American, was born in New York and had just come from there when they first had met her. They saw a great many reasons to dislike and mistrust her, apart from all the cultural dogma. Maria's fame outshone Battista. They were personally humiliated. Look how he ran to do her bidding, how he left the family business because of her. And where were the bambinos? In her company they were cool, distant, disconnected and often rude. Privately, Battista might not have approved of their conduct, but he seldom confronted any member of his family on the issue and when he did so it was a mild rebuke. He, too, did not want to lose the protection of his family.

Maria left Verona vowing never to return and, unless it was to collect some of her belongings, she never did. The city that had seemed so romantic to her once now only reminded her of that awkward, fat girl who would endure much humiliation and disappointment before she became – by her own brilliance and hard, gruelling work – the slim, lionized diva who had changed the face of opera for ever.

In mid-October, Maria and Battista flew to Chicago. This was the first time that Battista had spent time in the United States. His inability to communicate in English (which he had consistently refused to learn) placed additional pressure on her. The city and the people intimidated him. 'They think all Italians are gangsters,' he complained.

Maria had always wanted to make her American debut at the Met and for a time that had seemed a distinct possibility. The current general manager, Rudolf Bing, an Austrian with English citizenship, had sought her services as far back as 1950 when he had written to his friend Erich Engel at the Vienna State Opera (where Maria had recently performed) enquiring whether she was 'vocally really as outstanding as I am led to believe'. Engel replied that Maria's performance as Norma had been astonishing and that if she could fill the immense opera house in Vienna, he felt certain she could sing anywhere.

Battista worked with Liduino Bonardi's opera agency in the matter of her foreign contracts. Bonardi was the agent to whom Battista had taken Maria directly after her first appearance as Gioconda in Verona and they were old friends. Bonardi spoke English, but would hardly have been called fluent. Bing wrote offering Maria, 'an artist unknown in America', $400 per performance with the guarantee that she would have to stay twelve to fourteen weeks in New York during the Met season.

'I have spoken to the artist *Maria Callas Meneghini* [ignoring the fact that, at this time, 1950, Maria had restored her Greek surname], who is very glad to agree with you to stay in New York longer than two months, if necessary. Regarding the conditions is alright 600 Dollars each performance; but I retain to reduce the conditions to 500 Dollars.'[2]

A confused Bing replied with his original offer – $400.

'Maria Callas Meneghini is very anxious to be in the company of this very well known Theatre,' Bonardi cabled back, 'and she agrees to accept 200 Dollars [sic] each performance.'

Bing was even more puzzled but stayed with his larger first offer. And then, not knowing too much about Maria, asked Bonardi her nationality and was surprised to learn that she was American.

In his next letter Bonardi altered the terms. The money was fine, but there had to be travel and expenses paid for her husband, and she wanted to sing, in addition to *Aida* [which Bing had proposed] 'two of the following operas: *Norma, Puritani, Traviata, Trovatore*'.

As none of these operas was on the Met's schedule and Bing did not feel obliged to pay for her husband's expenses, the offer was withdrawn. The following year he was in Florence and attended a performance of *I vespri Siciliani* in which she sang Elena. 'She was monstrously fat and awkward,' Bing told Bonardi, 'and still has a lot to learn before she can be a star at the Met.' He changed his mind in 1953 and offered her *La Traviata* after her sensational tour in Mexico and Brazil, with better terms than previously, although still refusing to obtain a visa for and pick up the expenses of Meneghini. Bonardi wrote that Maria would not consider such 'an insult to her husband'. Thus, this chance to sing at the Met also came to a disappointing end. Maria had, therefore, signed with the Chicago Opera Company who not only were paying her what was then an astronomical performance fee, but would take care of securing a visa for Battista, and pay for his air travel and other expenses.

Carol Fox and Laurence Kelly had agreed to all her demands because it was necessary for their company to begin its career with a stellar production and no star at the moment would bring them the publicity a new opera company needed better than Maria Meneghini Callas. With Maria signed, the new impresarios were able to secure an incredible cast of singers – Tito Gobbi, Giuseppe di Stefano (who had appeared many times before with Maria both at La Scala and on tour) and Giulietta Simionato, the Met mezzo-soprano who had sung so successfully with Maria on her Latin-America tours. The conductor, Nicola Rescigno, would – with this production – become one of Maria's favoured maestros, although Serafin remained her closest musical adviser and much loved friend, conducting a large percentage of her finest recordings and her most famous roles.

[2] Bonardi was suggesting a compromise. He would go down a hundred dollars, if Bing raised his figure equally.

A bank of photographers – press, newsreel and television – greeted her as she and Battista arrived at O'Hare Airport in Chicago. She looked more like a film star than an opera singer: her hair, now blonde and styled smartly, her trim figure shown to its best advantage in a striking red suit by Dior with a tightly nipped-in waist. A suite in the Ambassador West Hotel filled with red roses awaited her and her husband. Fox and Kelly were doing everything possible to make their prima donna happy and comfortable, although the added expenses were a tremendous gamble for them. They were working on a tight budget, financed by the minor success of a production the previous February of *Don Giovanni* with Rossi-Lemeni in the title role and Eleanor Steber as Donna Anna, performed with sets and costumes leased from other companies. With Maria's agreement to appear, donors had come forth with needed funds, but all they could hope for in the first production, *Norma*, was to break even and then, possibly, to achieve a small margin of profit with the following two operas, *La Traviata* and *Lucia di Lammermoor*.

The first-night audience at *Norma*, on 1 November, included some of operas greatest singers from Chicago's earlier operatic history – Rosa Raisa, who had studied with Luisa Tetrazzini (one of opera's greatest Violettas) and had been with Mary Garden's old Chicago Opera from 1913 to 1937; Giovanni Martinelli, who sang the role of Dick Johnson in the European première of Puccini's *La Fanciulla del West* (*The Girl of the Golden West*) in 1911 and Tristan opposite Kirsten Flagstad in the famous 1939 Chicago production of *Tristan und Isolde*; and the celebrated sopranos Edith Mason (who sang extensively in Europe under Toscanini) and Dame Eva Turner (considered the ideal Turandot by Franco Alfano who completed the opera for Puccini after his death).

Maria did not let anyone down. Her Norma, despite the lacklustre quality of the sets, and the problems of cutting the costumes, designed for heftier divas, down to fit her new size 10 figure, was one of the best performances she had yet to give of the role. The tension she created as Norma was 'hell's fire' one moment, 'sweet and tender' the next – so electric it was palpable.

'[Callas] brings to everything, a passion, a profile of character and of youthful beauty that are rare in our lyric theatre,' wrote one leading critic. 'It is possible to find flaws in Miss Callas's technique – an occasional spread tone in the high fortissimi; a troublesome tremolo in pianissimo. But the net effect is what counts, and that is grand opera singing in the grandest manner...It was a great night for Chicago. It may prove to be an even greater night for opera in America.'

Another critic added that Callas in this production of *Norma* was 'something to tell your grandchildren about'.

There was a tumultuous ovation in the theatre when she came out for her first solo bow. Perhaps no one knew how deep her emotion was as she faced that audience, unable to see more than a blur beyond the footlights but hearing their 'Bravas' rise above her in a tidal wave of approval. She had made it in America. It had taken seven punishing years in which she had felt unrecognized for her ability by her own countrymen and the American press who had made more of her flare-ups and her dramatic weight loss than of her ground-breaking performances in Europe's most prestigious opera houses. Battista was in the wings waiting for her as she made her way backstage after her many curtains. Tears rolled down her cheeks. He put his arm round her shoulders and she let herself lean on him as she walked, crying softly, back to her dressing room.

The next morning there was an effusive telegram of congratulation from Bing with the suggestion that they have some conversations about her singing in the Met's 1955–6 season. *Traviata* and *Lucia* both met with as much success as *Norma*. Yet, something seemed to be missing, somehow askew. Despite Battista's constant attendance, when not working she felt a terrible aloneness. She called her father in New York and, to George's delight, insisted he join her in Chicago so that he could see her in *Lucia*. When he boarded the plane to return to New York, pictures were taken of them side by side, Maria taller and overshadowing the ageing, but still dapper, George. This visit, Maria had expressed strong emotion towards her father and promised to keep more closely in touch.

During the Chicago *Traviata* she had lost another five pounds and now weighed only 117 pounds. She was not dieting any more, but an eating problem – the opposite of what she had struggled with all her life – had suddenly arisen. Unable to eat much at all, she kept saying that, if she did, she would once again be fat and ugly. Battista had to coax her to try small amounts several times a day. She drank a fortified protein concoction; and perversely, she appeared more energetic than ever.

Several threatening letters from Eddie Bagarozy had been received while they were in Chicago. Battista made arrangements with Fox and Kelly to pay Maria in cash *before* each performance so that her money could not be attached. They also advised them not to let any stranger come backstage to see her (as fans or visiting artists often did). A bodyguard was hired to protect her against a possible summons being served. Nothing untoward happened and they both thought that perhaps Bagarozy had given up on his threat to sue.

The Meneghinis returned to Milan only days before Maria was to go into rehearsal at La Scala as Giulia in Gasparo Spontini's early nineteenth-century opera, *La Vestale*. Finally, she was to work with Visconti on an opera. She had written him many letters while she was in Chicago and studied the libretto and score of *La Vestale* in whatever free time came to her. Never had she been more excited about a future production. She couldn't wait to see Visconti again. She had missed him these past weeks and would have been happier if he could have seen her tremendous success in Chicago. It was hard to admit, but Maria was more than a little in love with Visconti. Nor could she face the fact that her eating problem (or rather non-eating problem) could well have been caused by sudden attacks of guilt. Battista had never been more comforting or supportive, but her feelings for him were not the same as they once had been. That might have been fine if she were content to accept the change. She was not. She longed for the excitement of a more romantic relationship than her marriage now offered, and Visconti fulfilled all her fantasies. Guilt plagued her. She was a married woman in love with – of all wild notions – a homosexual man.

Maria had found time to be alone with Visconti on those rare occasions when she was in Rome without Battista, either to record with Serafin or to do some shopping. Although Visconti did not encourage Maria, he also did not discourage her. In truth, he enjoyed the titillation of being with a woman who so obviously desired him, a woman whom he admired almost to obsession. There had been women in Visconti's life, but they had been more worldly types, fully aware that any continuing relationship would simply never happen.

Maria was almost as besotted with Visconti's lifestyle as she was with the man himself. Visconti disliked restaurants and seldom dined out. His friends came to see him at his magnificent palazzo, the via Salaria. In the warmer months he and Maria would lunch or have drinks or dinner on the grand terrace overlooking the lush gardens with their ancient statuary, or on the veranda where he kept an exotic aviary of white doves. When the temperature fell it could be in the library, or in any one of the dozens of rooms which all brought to mind the uniqueness of his set designs. The ground floor of via Salaria with its massive entry hall and many drawing rooms was sheer opulence – marble floors, shimmering crystal chandeliers, vibrant brocades. Some ceilings had been painted by seventeenth-century artists when the palazzo had first been built. Rare antiques filled every room. Fireplaces were often large enough for a full-grown adult to stand erect in. He had a passion for dogs – various breeds at various times in his life: in the past Alsatians, basset-hounds, which he bred. Right now it was mastiffs and there were several of them who followed him from room to room, settled before the giant hearth of a fireplace and glanced up through their thick-lidded eyes at him with unquestioning canine devotion.

He always created his own table settings, chose the wines and carried through a dramatic ritual for after-dinner coffee, which was a thick, filtered brew, immensely strong, that wrapped one in its rich aroma. He liked to make this himself, but he taught Maria how it was done and she found this a treasured task when she could do it for him. On occasion they might have coffee in his massive bedroom on the second floor, where he kept his collection of Russian icons and bronze sculptures. Tables were covered with photographs of the famous (including several of Maria) in silver or jewelled frames.

Visconti was a sensual man, an elegant man, a cultured man, and in Italy he was almost a myth. Maria reacted to all this. He was also an intellectual torn by his devotion to the arts and to politics. His circle of close friends – hetero- and homosexual – reflected this. He claimed later that although they did have an affair, he was very clear about his sexuality to Maria, that she knew whatever was between them of that nature would not and could not last, nor did he want it to. Everything about the relationship spelled danger for Maria where in Italy a man could have as many mistresses as he chose and return home to his faithful wife with impunity, but a woman – found out – would be instantly cast out and humiliated.

Rehearsals for *La Vestale* began in mid-November, almost immediately after her return from Chicago. Rosa Ponselle had sung the role of the vestal virgin Giulia, twenty years earlier, but since then it had not been presented. Giulia – who is condemned to death for allowing the holy fire to become extinguished, her life saved in the end as she is reunited with her lover – required the highest art of a dramatic soprano and a Ponselle or a Callas was hard to find. Visconti had great regard for the work ('a neo-classic *Norma* with a happy ending,' he called it).

Singing opposite Maria in the role of Licinio, the Roman general beloved by Giulia, was the thirty-year-old tenor Franco Corelli, who was making his La Scala debut. 'She hated Corelli because he was handsome,' Visconti said. 'It made her nervous – she was wary of beautiful people [especially a man, in this case]. She was always watching to see I didn't give him more attention than I gave her.'

She allowed Visconti to mould her performance. She seemed to want to be dominated by him. Members of the company who had worked with her before and knew her as 'an aggressive woman in total command' were amazed at her changed attitude. '…She did all I asked scrupulously, so precisely, so beautifully,' Visconti recalled. 'What I demanded, she rendered.' When he asked her to improvise she asked, 'What should I do? How am I to place this hand? I don't know where to put it.'

'The simple fact was,' he added, 'because of this crazy infatuation, she wanted me to command her every step.'

She was not aware, or refused to see the truth. Visconti could never love her in the way she fantasized and he very much regretted having allowed their relationship to move on to a physical plane. He would have to back off, make her understand how impossible it was for him to do more than devote his artistic talents to her great genius. She was, he would say, 'something beautiful. Intensity, expression, everything. She was a monstrous phenomenon. Almost a sickness – a kind of actress that had passed for all time.' But this was the diva, not the woman.

Their rigorous rehearsals left them little private time and, when there was a space, he managed to find something that commanded his immediate attention. Battista seldom attended rehearsals. Maria would remain for long hours at the theatre after her work had been done, listening to the orchestral rehearsals, or in her dressing room reading the score over and over. 'Why am I alone so much?' she asked a close friend.

'Why, Maria, you are seldom alone,' her friend answered.

'Ah yes, here – there, it is true. But *here* [she crossed her hands, the long fingers stretching over her newly youthful breasts] – *here* I am alone.'

11

America the Beautiful

MARIA HAD DISCOVERED herself. The awkwardness was gone; the American accent displaced by mid-Atlantic overtones. There was a delicacy about her, a greater femininity. On stage she had always been able to act out her greatest fantasies. Now she sought them in life. The wonder had gone from her relationship with Battista – if, indeed, it had actually ever been there. It was replaced by gratitude. He had offered encouragement when she was dispirited, comfort when she was rejected. But glory, she was to say, *her glory*, had gone to his head. He was no longer the father replacement she had thought she had married. He lived for the power her fame had brought him, was drunk on it. He used the money she had earned to help bolster his family business, which had seen bad times lately, and he had lied to her about it. 'If you can't trust your husband or your mother, to whom do you turn?' she asked her friend, the author and music critic John Ardoin.

She was proud of her accomplishments, proud of the way she now looked. She felt she deserved to be loved for herself and to be accepted fully by the man she loved. She thought this man could be Visconti, earnestly wanted it to be so. She was not naive, however much he might think her so. He was admittedly, and forthrightly, homosexual. She suspected now that Battista might have had, or still did have, homosexual partners. Yet both men were capable of sexual relations with a woman. That confused her. Was Battista more heterosexual than homosexual and was it the opposite with Visconti?

'I think Maria sincerely believed that Luchino could forfeit his former life if she made him love her enough,' a former co-worker said. 'Pure self-destructiveness! Luchino was, above all else, honest with himself and with Maria. His homosexuality was not something he could simply "give up". It was an integral part of his nature and had a great bearing on who he was and what he had achieved and would go on to achieve. Look at

Death in Venice [the film starring Dirk Bogarde that Visconti was later to direct]. This was a theme that was a great part of his art.'

Bellini's haunting bel canto opera *La Sonnambula* (*The Sleepwalker*) would bring Maria and Visconti back together again at La Scala in February 1955. Only eight weeks had elapsed since her last performance of *La Vestale* and she had not had much private time since. In January she had sung Maddalena in *Andrea Chénier* at La Scala and *Medea* in Rome, where she saw Visconti and discussed with him his revisionist conception of the opera and of Amina, the role she would sing.

La Sonnambula's plot is simplistic to the point of ridiculousness. Amina is a Swiss peasant girl with a malady that causes her to sleepwalk. She is about to become engaged to Elvino, a young farmer. While in her somnambulistic state one night, she walks from her bedroom in her home in the small village, to the bedroom of Count Rodolfo, who is out at the time. Amina is discovered asleep in his bed. Elvino is horrified and announces that he will marry Lisa, proprietress of the local inn who has been in love with him for years. Amina is distraught, but the Count comes to her aid and explains to Elvino and the villagers that sleepwalking is a true malady and disclaims any romance with Amina. No one believes him, but at that moment Amina is seen walking in her sleep along the edge of an insecure bridge over a rushing millstream. After much suspense, she reaches the other side and then collapses. Elvino realizes she has not betrayed him and she wakes to find him at her side professing his love for her and his eagerness to marry her.

Visconti took the only track possible with this fairly ludicrous story. He highlighted the opera's balletic feel, making it more like a *Sleeping Beauty* ballet than an opera. He thus approached the production in this manner: Amina was no longer a peasant girl, she was an elegant, gracefully costumed ballerina, bejewelled and wearing a crown of flowers in her moments of wakefulness. She would walk barefoot in the sleepwalking scenes, hair falling loosely over her shoulders, her white nightdress underscoring her innocence. The sets were idealized visions of a Swiss village.

Bernstein, who had remained in Europe for the winter, was the conductor and he and Visconti worked closely together to best realize Visconti's vision. Within two days of rehearsals Maria began to imagine that Visconti and Bernstein were lovers. 'We [Visconti and Bernstein] were together a lot, and Maria spied on us even when we went outside the theatre to have a coffee or take a little walk. Once Lennie and I went to visit her [she had been ill and not attended rehearsal that day]. When the moment came to leave, we said, "Ciao, Maria. Get well!" and headed for the door. "You stay here!" she commanded me. "I don't want you going off again with Lennie!"'

Her strong feelings towards Visconti became clear to most of her co-workers. She created a similar scene when, after one late-night rehearsal Visconti and Bernstein, looking dashing in their dramatic, twin, red-lined evening cloaks, started out of the stage door together and she cried out to Visconti, 'Why are you going with that homosexual again?'

Visconti always carried a perfume-scented handkerchief in his pocket. Maria asked him to let her keep it with her during the scene where she had to sleepwalk to the Count's bed. She would place it beneath the pillow. 'That way I will be able to walk directly to it,' she explained. 'Luckily, no musician in the audience wore the same fragrance or one night she might have walked right off the stage and into the pit,' Visconti ungallantly commented.

She insisted he remain in the wings during the entire performance (as Battista had once done). 'I had to lead her to the stage before each act and prod her to go on,' he recalled. 'Then she would beg me, "Please take me to this point," and we'd go two feet closer to the stage.'

She wore a waist-cincher beneath her costume. Despite unwarranted fears that it might impair her breathing and affect her singing, she had her dresser pull the strings of the garment as tight as possible so that her now slim twenty-two-inch waist was made two inches smaller. Miraculously, it did not. 'The minute she stepped on stage,' the designer Piero Tosi (named for an ancestral forebear, the seventeenth-century castrato) remembered, 'she looked small, ethereally fragile, and moved with incredible grace. Her steps were like those of a ballerina, and when she stood still, she took a dancer's fifth position.'

For the first sleepwalking scene she was lit by the moon and half-hidden by shadow – 'a sylphide tripping on the moonlight...she was enchanting. When the Count touched her shoulder, she fell to the floor, very softly, like a Margot Fonteyn.'

A spectacular illusion in the final act was created as she walked bare-foot across the bridge, a silhouette, the lake and mountains seen in shadowed moonlight behind her. At the point near the end of the bridge, where Amina steps on a broken plank, Maria appeared to fall. She simulated this in such a manner as to amaze everyone backstage (from the audience's view she seemed to have fallen). She did this by standing absolutely still. Then she filled her lungs with air, which gave her the illusion of lifting upwards. Then she quickly exhaled with all her strength. In the shadowy lighting it gave the illusion of falling. 'What can you say?' Tosi asked. 'She was a theatrical wizard and she knew it.'

The critics were equally impressed with her vocal brilliance and grateful that here was a Bellinian who could sing both Norma and Amina, two vastly different roles, dramatically and vocally. 'Callas was just glorious,' Bernstein enthused. She sang, 'as if she were the first instrument of the orchestra – at times she was the violin, the viola, the flute. In fact there were moments I felt I was singing the role myself and was dubbed with her voice. Remember I was the conductor.'

Because of her short-sightedness Maria had a difficult time seeing the conductor in the pit during performance and so, as she did with all her conductors, she worked especially hard with Bernstein during the rehearsals to get everything right, the cadenzas, the embellishments. Every note, phrase, gesture and movement was tirelessly rehearsed. Resentment arose in the company as overtime became a daily occurrence. Costumes had to be refitted if there was the smallest irregularity. She sat in on discussions with the lighting engineer. No detail was too small to escape her attention.

After the successful première of *La Sonnambula* a party was given. Bernstein asked her to sing sections from *Tristan* in Italian while he accompanied her on the piano. They had some unpleasant words. Maria was tired and she never liked to sing at parties, whereas Bernstein was enervated after a performance. She was also in a difficult situation with Battista and Visconti both present. On Visconti's urging, she finally sang, but not well, and the incident greatly disturbed her, spoiling for her what had been an evening of much gratification. Later, after most of the guests had dispersed, she asked Bernstein, who was standing next to Visconti, 'Why must it be that all the attractive men are homosexuals?' When no one replied, she pressed Bernstein, looking him straight in the eye, 'I want to know the truth and all the truth. Are you a homosexual?' Bernstein turned away and within a few minutes left the party with Visconti.

Maria respected Bernstein as the maestro and felt he was in tune with her musically. But she never let herself like him personally, nor does it seem he ever became fond of her.[1]

Within days she was in rehearsal at La Scala in a new production of *Il Turco in Italia* with Rossi-Lemeni as the Turk and with the young Franco Zeffirelli as director and producer. Zeffirelli was a rising star in the Italian theatre and he brought a freshness to the production, which more strongly emphasized its buffo content. The sets were amusing, Maria's

---

[1] In Bernstein's memoir *Findings* he admits to this and in a cruel stroke published a most unflattering photograph of Callas, her face contorted in anger.

costumes charming. 'She was adorable. Really, really funny,' Zeffirelli recalled. 'At one point she even danced a little tarantella and hit her rival Zaida over the head with her shoe.' Laughter, rare at most opera performances, filled La Scala. Critics were amazed at Maria's versatility. Here was a dramatic soprano who could sing, with extraordinary brilliance, both Norma *and* opera buffa.

Maria was now the queen of La Scala, called by many 'the most glamorous opera singer in the world', able to get what she wanted, and what she wanted was to have Visconti mount a production of *La Traviata* with her in mind. Violetta was beautiful and Maria, for the first time in her life, felt beautiful: her new appearance – and Visconti – gave her this confidence. Happy to please his leading diva, Ghiringhelli agreed to Visconti's terms and work began on a new production of *La Traviata*. It was a main concern of Visconti that his Violetta was to feel comfortable in all her surroundings. The exquisite sets must feel so familiar to her as to be real. What he sought from Maria's performance was 'something tender, very interior'. Concentration was placed on Violetta's state of mind, her extremely fragile feminine psyche that evoked the image of Greta Garbo in *Camille*, the memorable 1930s film version of Alexandre Dumas *fils's La Dame aux Camélias*. In the opera the doomed heroine becomes Violetta Valéry, a tragic courtesan who forswears love in a misguided attempt to protect her lover Alfredo's honour.

The drama of the opera evolves in the interaction of its three principals: Violetta, Alfredo and Alfredo's sternly insensitive father, Giorgio Germont, who demands of Violetta a release of his son from their private vows of love. Violetta has led an illicit life and if Alfredo is to inherit his wealth and property, she must give him up. More, if his son's affair with Violetta becomes known, his daughter's prospect of a good marriage will be doomed. Because of her love for Alfredo and her fear that she will destroy his future, Violetta agrees to break off the affair. Soon after, she is diagnosed consumptive – a death sentence in the nineteenth century. With Violetta's poignant death scene, their reunion and Alfredo's forgiveness come too late.

The role of Violetta is demanding. The first act requires coloratura flexibility and a climactic top extension. In the second act,[2] the subtlety and legato of a true lyric soprano and ultimately, in the final act, darker, heavier, tragic accents of a dramatic soprano are called for.

---

[2] The Metropolitan Opera performs *La Traviata* in three acts. With its huge holding stages, the Met is able to segue from the set of the country estate to the gambling club scene in moments. Most European opera companies, however, perform the opera in four acts, as Verdi wrote it.

'[Maria] found new colours in her voice, new values in her musical expression, all through a new understanding of Violetta's innermost being,' the conductor Carlo Maria Giulini noted. 'Everything came into rapport.' This was painstaking work. Maria's obsession with perfection was pushed to the ultimate by Visconti's demanding reach, not only for excellence, but for the realization of his vision.

Violetta's lover, Alfredo, was sung by Giuseppe di Stefano who had sung the role with Maria numerous times before. A discordant note tween di Stefano and Visconti arose from the first rehearsal. Maria would do the same small section of recitative a hundred times without complaint until Visconti thought she had it right. The tenor took exception to such a tedious exercise, and began to show up late or not at all for rehearsals.

'It's a lack of respect for me, and also for *you!*' Maria angrily told Visconti.

'I don't give a damn!' Visconti replied. 'Let the fool come late! We'll act out his scenes together!'

And they did, over an over, giving meticulous attention to the intimate love he wanted her to feel natural with in the love scenes between Violetta and Alfredo.

Visconti had staged it so that during the love duet, 'Un dì felice', Violetta, in an exquisitely simple black satin gown, long white gloves and holding a small bouquet of violets, edges slowly away from Alfredo as he declares his love for her. Violetta knows this is wrong, that she can only bring her young lover unhappiness. They are alone on stage and she stands near the edge of the proscenium lit softly when, with an exquisite motion, Violetta stretches her white-gloved arm behind her and gracefully shifts the train of her dress so that she can turn and retreat. But in the moment that she pauses, Alfredo steps close and draws her into his arms. 'In surrender,' the production's designer Piero Tosi recalled, 'the bouquet fell to the floor. It was unforgettably touching. Theatrical beauty.'

Conductor Giulini remembered being overwhelmed by the beauty of the production that was unveiling itself before his eyes. Unquestionably, Visconti staged the opera to serve Maria. He had changed the period from the early 1800s to *fin de siècle*, because Maria's tall, slender figure would be enhanced by the costumes of that era: gowns with tight bodices, bustles and elegant trains. He claimed he modelled Violetta after the great actress of that period, Eleanora Duse, but there is more than a hint of the great tragedienne, Sarah Bernhardt, in the last two acts.[3] The sets,

---

[3] Violetta's costumes in the second act had admittedly been suggested by those worn by Sarah Bernhardt in the late nineteenth-century French stage version of the story *La Dame aux Camélias*.

by Lila de Nobili (considered the finest designer of that time), crystallized Visconti's vision and gave 'an illusion of truth, but with a quality of painting, a sense of poetic distance'. Visconti wanted the production to have an insinuation of decadence, 'an unforgettable dream of *belle époque*'. Maria had played many death scenes, but never any that could compare with the pathetic beauty given to Violetta's words in the final act 'Se una pudica vergine'. There was, in her entire performance, 'an almost unbearable reality'.

This *Traviata* was most surely Visconti's great gift to Maria, everything and every character in the production underscored Violetta musically and dramatically. Maria was at the peak of her talents, pushed there, no doubt, by Visconti's genius – and his ego. Di Stefano sang the role of Alfredo beautifully, matching Maria in her grasp of their duets. Still, he never quite seemed as impassioned as she, nor as moving in his recitatives. On the first night the audience went mad. They wanted only Maria and refused to allow her to leave the stage. They shouted her name, wept openly, stamped and applauded. Maria drank it all in like air to a suffocating woman. Instantly the proscenium became a thick field of red roses. Still dressed in the simple white nightgown she wore in her death scene, Maria bowed her head as she scooped up a bouquet. Tears streamed down her face. She touched one hand to her lips and stretched her arm in a balletic motion to dispatch a kiss on the tips of her fingers to the unseen audience beyond.

Di Stefano was enraged. He had been deprived of his solo bows. 'Everything for Callas! I shall never sing with her again!' he shouted as he left the theatre that evening.[4] To the company's shock, he did not return the next day and Giacinto Prandelli sang Alfredo in all the remaining performances.

The most amazing thing, Giulini felt, was how Maria managed to bring the same measure of greatness to each performance, no matter who was singing Alfredo. 'There were even moments when it all seemed so real, when Violetta's pain was so deep, that I shed tears in the pit. I had never had such an experience before, nor have I since.' The public obviously shared his emotion and from that time Maria was known as la Divina – the divine – much as Sarah Bernhardt had been called 'The Divine Sarah'.

The Visconti–Callas *La Traviata* would have an impact on opera that would change the face of it for ever. Singers would now have to interpret

---

[4] Di Stefano, in fact, would record *Rigoletto* with her that September, appear opposite her that same month in *Lucia di Lammermoor* and go on to Chicago to join her at the Civic Opera House as well as become closely involved with her later in life.

a role with perceptive acting; staging would become more important; fresh versions of old 'war horses' expected. It also had a strong effect on the relationship between these two dynamic personalities. Maria had become more and more demanding of Visconti, insisting that he remain backstage with her during every performance until the moments when she made her entrances. This reached a point of mania on the final night when during the Act One prelude, Maria grabbed his arm in a vice and began to pull him on stage with her. 'Just until the curtain is ready to rise,' she cried softly.

Visconti drew sharply away and she stumbled and then caught herself. 'No, No,' she begged. 'Stay just a second more!' But Visconti turned away, walked hurriedly into the wings, and disappeared backstage.

Their relationship suddenly changed. Visconti was 'unavailable' when she was in Rome four weeks later for a recording session with Serafin, who told her she must not pursue this impossible cause or she would destroy her marriage and suffer only rejection and pain. Seeing the hopelessness of the situation, Maria withdrew, but it would take two years to heal her wounds sufficiently so she could work with Visconti on a different emotional level. Her sexual passion dissolved into the creative passion they shared. But his effect on her would mark her for ever, both privately and professionally. She had been awakened to her own strong sexual needs, and Visconti had given her the confidence in herself as a prima donna and to find the truth in all her roles.

If Battista was consciously aware of her affair with Visconti and its disintegration, he did not reveal it, continuing in his relationship with his wife, at least publicly and with close friends, as if nothing untoward had occurred. Maria was pleased to have him there by her side and seemed to be closer and kinder to him than she had previously been.

The house she had bought at 44 via Buonarroti, a fashionable section of Milan, was filled with beautiful antiques that Visconti had helped her select. The formal garden contained fine statuary. Air-conditioning units were installed so that the Meneghinis were able to spend July and August, which Maria had free, in relative comfort despite the humidity of the Italian summer. She and Battista occupied separate bedrooms, although he brushed this arrangement off as unimportant.

'No two people were as happy as we were in our Milan home,' Battista wrote later. 'Maria was just happy to be near me. As I always woke up very early she insisted that I would be with her when the maid brought her coffee. After her "Good morning" greetings...we would discuss the plans for the day. I always helped her dress with her greatest mutual pleasure and even did her pedicures.' Visconti had given her a present of a black standard male poodle whom she had named Toy. Maria had never had a dog before and she treated Toy like a beloved child. He was kept meticulously groomed, slept at the foot of her bed and followed her around the house, settling nearby when she sat down. 'I would have been a good mother,' she said ruefully to Battista one day. During their marriage she had suffered the disappointment of one early miscarriage. But her career demands always won over her infrequent longing for motherhood.

More letters made their way back and forth across the Atlantic between Rudolf Bing and Maria's foreign representative, Bonardi. The Met was coming close to agreeing to Maria's terms, but there were still some unsolved issues concerning Battista's expenses and her demands that the Met pay for transporting Toy to America and back to Italy again when the season was over. Bing's exasperation grew. He desperately wanted Maria and was willing to agree to higher terms than those of the Met's other great artists. She could sing the roles of her choice: *Norma*, *Tosca* and *Lucia*. He finally offered a sum towards Battista's expenses, but he 'drew the line when it came to her dog'.

Still, the Met contract was not signed when the Meneghinis (Toy remaining in Milan) left for Maria's second season with the Chicago Opera Company, following a successful Berlin engagement in *Lucia* with a penitent di Stefano as Edgar. No sooner were they settled in their suite at the Ambassador West Hotel than a threatening letter arrived from Eddie Bagarozy, claiming he would sue her and then attach all monies that she made. The Meneghinis demanded that Carol Fox and Laurence Kelly provide protection, as they had done the previous year, and that Maria be paid in cash before her performances, and they agreed. Believing she was now safe from Bagarozy's vindictive wrath, Maria started rehearsals on *I Puritani* with di Stefano and Rossi-Lemeni.

Opening night was a glamorous event: women begowned and bejewelled, their voices raised with the 'Bravas' of the men in the audience. Champagne flowed at the post-performance party given by Fox and Kelly for Maria and the other members of the company. Chicago was at Maria's feet. She was entertained royally, her two performances of the opera were sold out, as were all the performances of her next two operas with the Chicago – *Il Trovatore* and *Madama Butterfly*. Bing flew to Chicago and attended the first night of *Il Trovatore*, which Maria was singing with the great Swedish tenor Jussi Björling. Fox and Kelly were not pleased to see Bing as they suspected (rightly) that Bing had come to Chicago for the express purpose of getting Maria to sign a contract with the Met, which could well mean this might be her last engagement with their company.

'I remember saying that during "Ah sì, ben mio" in the third act it was Callas's quiet listening rather than Björling's voice that made the dramatic impact,' Bing wrote.

> He didn't know what he was singing but she knew. Then we [Bing and his associate, Francis Robinson] went backstage, where I offered my very best version of the kiss-the-hand routine I had learned as a child, and the picture got into all the papers – and, finally, the Metropolitan signed Maria Callas to a contract that had been sweetened by a compromise to pay Battista's air fare, three thousand dollars towards his personal expenses, and an agreement that Maria's fees of twelve hundred dollars would be paid to her in cash *before* each performance and that the Met would offer her protection from Bagarozy's threats (in case process servers were hovering nearby). This last clause proved unnecessary.

After her final performance of *Madama Butterfly*, a role to which she brought a new sense of inner understanding, Chicago's Marshal Stanley Pringle and Deputy Sheriff Dan Smith pushed aside the guard outside her dressing room and marched inside. Maria was seated at her dressing table, still in Cio-Cio-San's Japanese kimono, and about to remove her make-up. Battista jumped up from his seat in the corner of the room and called out for help, claiming later he thought Maria was about to be attacked. Smith thrust a subpoena into her hand as she raised it to protect herself. Then the two men strode out of the room, past the astonished guard and out of the theatre, their work accomplished. But as the door stood open a photographer snapped a picture of Maria, her face twisted in fury, that appeared prominently in newspapers around the world.

Maria was certain that Fox and Kelly, piqued because she had signed with the Met, had allowed the subpoena servers to get into the theatre and by her bodyguards. She vowed never to appear in Chicago again. The Meneghinis left the next morning for home with the knowledge that if Maria were to have any peace in New York the following year, something had to be done about Bagarozy who was suing them for $300,000 plus lawyers' fees. (In the end he was to settle for the amount of $40,000. But before Eddie Bagarozy – always the tragic figure, it seemed – could enjoy his victory, he died in a car crash.)

Maria was jubilant that she would soon make her Met debut, but she no longer needed the approval of the American critics to soothe a ruffled vanity or to build up a lack of confidence. World acclaim was already hers. Certainly she had her detractors, those who still found the metal that could sometimes harden her tone ugly, those who preferred the comfort in opera of less real performances than hers. And she was not fated to be the darling of the press – most especially the American media. Opera stars seldom were front-page news. Maria was different. She was a dramatic personality, highly photogenic, always saying something that was controversial or worth quoting. Her temperament was fiery, her language sometimes harsh. Combining those qualities with her now glamorous looks and her extraordinary success made her a perfect celebrity for the press to feed upon. Many of the stories written about Maria were not true, some were exaggerated, others were fact, but the more sensational stories, real or fiction were the only ones that seemed to get printed.

These were the finest years in Maria's career, her voice at its peak. Visconti had brought her to full flower as an actress and as a woman. Now she was in flux, having achieved so much that she was not sure of what she wanted next. She remained the ultimate perfectionist. No member of any production in which she sang ever worked harder than Maria. She was driven to maintain a high level of originality and excellence, always to attempt to improve on her last performance. Her co-workers found this difficult to match and she had no patience for those who did not try.

She was also becoming less and less patient with Battista, her sexual appetite unsatisfied, her regard for him slipping. The components in their relationship had reversed. Maria was now the more sophisticated, the more knowledgeable about life, art, antiques and the world of opera, and at times he seemed more like a member of her fast-growing legion of fans who came backstage to warm themselves and build their egos from the reflection of her success.

Litza continued to play the martyred mother, deserted by her famous daughter, needy, always stirring trouble. Maria would never forget her mother's complicity in her career, although not in the same light as Litza did. She arranged to have money sent monthly to her mother, but it was always too little in Litza's extremely vocal opinion – for she was now giving interviews to the press, voicing her complaints and feeding their growing profile of Maria as a monster. After all, Litza cried, was not her daughter the most famous opera singer in the world, rich beyond her wildest dreams, and had not she, her loving mother, struggled, starved and dedicated herself to this daughter who was now so ungrateful? Fame was gratifying, but it did not protect Maria from pain in her private life.

Before starting her first season with the Met, Maria returned with Battista to Milan where she sang *Fedora* in Umberto Giordano's Russian verismo opera, presented for the first time at La Scala on 21 May 1956,

after four intense weeks of rehearsals in which Maria worked with director Tatiana Pavlova to get the right Russian quality in her performance.
'Maria had the knack of taking everything she could from an associate,'
Nicola Benois, the designer, said. 'With the help of Pavlova, herself a
great actress in both Russia and Italy, she created a Fedora rich in range,
depth, and authenticity. Being Eastern Orthodox may have given Maria
some special kinship for this role. On the stage, she became Russian 100
per cent.'

Controversy arose as soon as the public had been informed that Maria
was singing *Fedora*. 'Some critics wrote that Maria was unsuited for
verismo declamation,' the conductor Gianandrea Gavazzeni, recalled.
There was also concern that the heavy orchestration and unvocal music
of Giordano's opera would prove disastrous to her. This was not the
case. Maria's Fedora was a haunting portrayal, her vocal colouring extraordinary and never did the orchestra overwhelm her performance.

She and Battista arrived in New York in mid-September, where they
were met at the airport by Francis Robinson and faced with a small army
of photographers and reporters. 'Madame Callas,' a member of the press
said, 'you were born in the United States, brought up in Greece and are
now practically Italian. What language do you think in?'

To which Maria replied, 'I *count* in English.'

12

'Please Save La Scala'

I S NEW YORK anxious to hear me?' Maria wrote to Rudolf Bing shortly before her departure for America.

Bing replied that they were. 'What almost everything written about Miss Callas fails to catch is the girlishness, the innocent dependence on others that was so strong a part of her personality when she did not feel she had to be wary,' he was to say. But Maria *was* wary about her debut with the Met. She feared the New York press, who had never been kind to her, always playing up what they saw as negatives in her personal life and her performances. 'Everything is a game to them,' she complained to Bing, 'and it's about selling newspapers and their coming out the winners.'

The Met had recently expanded its season to twenty-four weeks, which meant the first opera, *Norma*, would be performed in late October with rehearsals starting in mid-September. Opposite her, as Pollione, was Mario del Monaco with whom she had had an obstreperous backstage clash the previous January when they sang *Norma* at La Scala. During her curtain calls, there had been what Maria called 'hissing snakes' emanating from one section of the audience, although the sound had been drowned out by 'prolonged clamorous applause'. Meneghini accused del Monaco of hiring a claque and placing them in the gallery. There were high-decibel Italian insults exchanged between the two men. Del Monaco claimed that on his exit in the final scene of the opera, Maria had kicked him in the calf. He had limped backstage in pain and by the time he could return for his curtain calls 'Callas had usurped all the applause'.

Maria refused to allow any personal grievances she and del Monaco may have had to interfere with her performance. She believed he was perfectly cast as Pollione to her Norma and to her that was the major issue.

Nonetheless, their off-stage attitude to each other presented additional tension. More trying was a cover article published in *Time* magazine. A reporter for the publication had interviewed Litza in Athens. Her mother, portrayed as a woman near poverty, was quoted as saying that when she had written to her 'famous, rich daughter asking for one hundred dollars for my daily bread', Maria had replied, 'Do not come to us with your troubles. I can't give you anything. Money doesn't grow on trees...I have to "scream" for my living, and you are young enough to work. If you can't make enough money to live on, you had better jump in the river and drown yourself.'[1]

When Jackie learned of their mother's interview, she told Litza, 'I hope you were careful.' Litza just smiled. Her hope was that the article would bring Maria 'like a naughty girl back to her mother's side'. The letter that was quoted in *Time* was an altered version of one written by Maria four years earlier in 1952 in response to Litza's threats that it might be better 'to drown myself than to live in such penury when my daughter, for whom I have sacrificed all, and who wouldn't be where she is without me, is living the life of a wealthy woman'. Litza had also given damaging and misleading interviews to the press at the time, followed by several appalling dunning letters, demanding she help finance her sister's singing career and keep Litza in a style that behoved the mother of a famous and rich diva. Despite her mother's mendacity, Maria had made an arrangement for a monthly sum to be sent by her accountants to her, and this order was still being carried out at the time of this current débâcle. Litza, however, was now thinking of coming to New York and she needed a large stipend to do so. The interview was her bizarre way of achieving this.

'When the [*Time*] article appeared,' Jackie recalled, 'it was a bomb-shell...[Mother] portrayed Maria as an ungrateful harridan who had abandoned her poor devoted mother to a life of misery...it made abundantly clear that she was the one who had discovered Maria's talent and who had single-handedly nurtured it. It was Mother's sacrifices during the war that had kept us fed and in music lessons, and it was only when she was no longer needed that she had been so cruelly cast aside.' (It had been, in fact, Jackie's relationship with Milton that had supplied their needs during the war.)

The story was reported on the nightly television news, broadcast

---

[1] Mrs Callas was grossly misquoting her daughter's letter, which said: '...I have to "scream" for my living. If you can't live on what I am sending you each month, you are young enough to work. [Her mother was fifty-two at the time.] And if you expect Jackie to become a great diva one day, you had better jump in the river and drown yourself.'

across the country and, with only two days remaining of rehearsals, the media plagued Maria's every move. To add to her difficulties, New York was experiencing one of its cruellest Indian summer heatwaves in over thirty years and the Met's antiquated cooling system had broken down. Despite all these vexations, Maria remained in control, working as hard and with the same obsessive attention to detail as always. This was not to be her greatest Norma, but she received overwhelming applause and sixteen curtain calls from an audience that had been ready to hate 'this Bronx [sic] girl who had deserted her native land and treated her mother in such an appalling fashion'.

Howard Taubman in the *New York Times* reported: 'Occasionally [Callas's voice] gives the impression of having been formed out of sheer will power rather than natural endowments...Miss Callas may be forgiven a lack of velvet in parts of her range. She is brave to do Norma at all. She brings sufficient dramatic and musical values to her performance to make it an interesting one.'

'I guess it's hardest to be accepted in your home town,' Maria commented.

A gala party hosted by Angel Records was given in her honour at the Hotel Ambassador after the first performance of *Norma*. The Ambassador, on Park Avenue between 51st and 52nd Streets, was the city's *grande dame* of elegant residential hotels, popular in diplomatic circles and called the 'social embassy of two continents'. The Trianon Ballroom, where the party was held, was a vast, magnificent room gleaming with white Italian marble and gilding, and had been the scene of receptions for prime ministers, princes, kings and queens. Maria entered just moments before the stroke of midnight, a proud tuxedoed Battista beaming at her side, two detectives following close on their heels to protect the million dollars' worth of diamonds – a startling necklace, drop earrings and bracelet – loaned to Maria for the evening by the pre-eminent jeweller Harry Winston.

There was applause as – looking every inch as regal as some of the hotel's former honorary guests – she carefully manipulated the unfamiliar red-carpeted staircase that led into the ballroom. She wore a white satin gown that closely followed the lines of her slim but curvaceous body. Her stiletto heels caused her to tower over Battista. Maria had been uneasy about this gala affair. Rudolf Bing and many of the stars of the Met were present, which only called attention to Renata Tebaldi's absence (although invited she had decided not to attend). The guest list was indeed stellar – Manhattan's most glittering society figures, stage and film stars among the 150 guests (Marlene Dietrich for one in a skin-tight,

eye-catching, gold lamé gown), Wally Toscanini (the conductor's daughter), Leonard Bernstein and the gossip columnist, famed party giver,
friend and occasional enemy of the rich and famous, Elsa Maxwell.

Grossly overweight, rumoured to be a lesbian, in her seventies and with
only a small income of her own, Maxwell had, nonetheless, managed to
become a powerful force in the swirl of society. Invitations to her parties
(always paid for by other people) were greedily sought after. She was also
renowned for her match-making abilities, which had brought Rita
Hayworth and Prince Aly Khan together, and her help to Prince Rainier to
lure the rich and famous back to a Monaco of declining popularity during
the early years of his reign before his marriage to Grace Kelly. Maxwell was
a good friend of Tebaldi and she had not written kindly about Maria in
her syndicated column. She was cool to Maria when they were introduced
but she would eventually be won over by Callas's fame and change camps.
'Elsa isn't really evil,' Maria once said. 'She never disguises her motives. If
she had less girth and more charm she probably could have been as
accepted in society as those whose entry she sponsored.'

Five days later, just before she was due to sing the Saturday matinée,
Maria developed a sore throat. During the overture she sent word to Bing
from her dressing room that she would be unable to go on. 'I literally ran
to her room,' Bing recalled. 'and found her genuinely ill with a doctor in
solicitous attendance.' Fearing a riot out front and the return of hundreds
of tickets, Bing begged her to go on against the doctor's advice. Maria
agreed she would try. Her throat was sprayed to numb the pain and she
carried through bravely, her voice at times sounding scratchy but her performance extremely moving. During curtain calls, Bing remembered,
'some idiot threw a bunch of radishes on stage; fortunately Miss Callas
was so short-sighted she thought they were tea-roses'.

On 15 November Maria sang the first of her two Met performances
of *Tosca* with the Canadian bass-baritone, George London, as Scarpia
and Giuseppe Campora as Cavaradossi. The conductor was Dimitri
Mitropoulos, a Greek, born in Athens, whom she had met briefly during
her years at the Athens Conservatory.[2] By now the New York reviewers
were more laudatory to her, especially commenting on her great dramatic skills and the power she exuded in the murder scenes with Scarpia, and
later in the last act when she realizes she has been betrayed and her lover
is dead. Still, they retained certain reservations at the hardness her tone
could sometimes take.

[2] Scenes from this production of *Tosca* were presented on the *Ed Sullivan Show* recorded
in kinescope on 25 November 1956 and preserved.

The press made front-page news of her first night of *Lucia*. In the duet at the end of the second act, Enzo Sordello, the baritone singing the role of Lord Henry Ashton, Lucia's nefarious brother, held a high note beyond the value Donizetti and the conductor Fausto Cleva had given it. The effect of this was to make Maria appear short of breath. Unable to control her reflex action to this, Maria said, *'Basta!'* ('Enough!') sufficiently loudly for the audience close to the stage to hear and misinterpret as 'Bastard!'.

To grandstand at the cost of another singer's performance and in so doing endanger the integrity of the production was unpardonable behaviour in Bing's opinion. 'I ordered the balance of [Sordello's] contract cancelled,' he wrote. 'He got on the front page of the newspapers tearing up her picture, and then booked space on the plane that was taking her back to Italy.' Sordello had also informed the press photographers that he would be on the same flight as the Meneghinis. Cameras flashed as the three of them boarded the plane separated by several other passengers. Maria and Battista changed their seats as soon as they discovered that Sordello was directly across the aisle. They never spoke, but when the plane landed in Rome, Maria and Battista waited several minutes before disembarking. Then, with the airport manager's assistance, they were guided to a private exit, bypassing the gate where many photographers were gathered. 'I don't like this man taking advantage of my publicity,' she wrote to Bing, a mild rebuke but she was never to forget or forgive Sordello's bad behaviour.

Her first season at the Met had not been the success she had wished for herself and for Bing, who nevertheless seemed undaunted by the few quibbles of reviewers. Putting it bluntly, his job was to fill the seats in the opera house and Maria's appearances had been completely sold out. The headlines and scandal had proved as much a lure to see and hear her as had her pre-appearance publicity as being 'the greatest dramatic soprano in the world'. No sooner had she arrived in Milan, than a new contract from Bing arrived for her to sign, at an even higher stipend, for the Met's next season. Before this could take place she would return to Chicago for a concert, then fly to Europe to sing *Norma* again (2, 6 February 1957) at Covent Garden, *La Sonnambula* for six performances at La Scala (2–20 March), followed by two new roles in Visconti productions there: *Anna Bolena* (14 April–5 May), and *Ifigenia in Tauris* (1–10 June).

Maria was most enthusiastic about singing Donizetti's *Anna Bolena*, the tragic story of Henry VIII's second wife, who was beheaded at her husband's command. The opera had fallen out of the repertory within twenty years of its initial production in 1830. But in the autumn of 1956, it was resurrected by a group in the composer's birthplace, Bergamo, to honour their native son. La Scala recognized that 'it would be an ideal vehicle for Maria Callas, both musically and theatrically'. The conductor, Gianandrea Gavazzeni, discussed the possibility with Visconti, who was immediately excited. 'For nearly two weeks,' Gavazzeni said, 'I met with him daily at his home in Rome, playing the score over and over on the piano, and discussing the libretto's tragic qualities. Visconti agreed that it was an ideal role for Maria and she did not hesitate to agree.'

When rehearsals for *Anna Bolena* began on 21 March, Maria and Visconti had not met in eighteen months. Maria's feelings towards him had undergone a dramatic change. Visconti had told numerous people that she was obsessively in love with him, was jealous of his male companions and had made a public display of her feelings that had been highly embarrassing. Maria retreated into denial. It was ridiculous. She had never been in love with Visconti. Her admiration for him was entirely on a creative level. She was later to tell Stelios Galatopoulos that her growing dislike for Visconti the man had to do with his duplicity and his use of 'foul language, the derogatory way he referred to women in general…were totally unacceptable'. And Battista – who would claim that he knew Visconti better than Maria – would say, 'Whereas [Visconti's] admiration and affection for Maria became more intense as they worked together and got to know each other better, her aversion for him increased.'

Maria also blamed Visconti's overt homosexuality for her growing dislike of 'the man' along with, what she called – 'her naivety and youth at that time. If you did not like a person [then] his homosexuality would be a disgusting and unforgivable sin,' she told Galatopoulos. 'On the other hand, if you liked the person you could well consider his homosexuality to be an unfortunate phase, hopefully a passing one…At first Luchino's homosexuality shocked me but…my feelings would have been the same if he were one hundred per cent heterosexual. Fortunately, I did get over my prejudices and not too late in life.' Not soon enough, however, to accept her culpability in the disintegration of their friendship, nor her own futile attempt to get Visconti to abandon his sexual preference.

And what would she have made of Battista's later statement that 'Outside the theatre it was I, not she, who was a friend of [Visconti]'? It seemed by her actions that she accepted their friendship, although it would become one more thing she held against her husband.

Her mixed emotions about Visconti did not diminish her enthusiasm to sing *Anna Bolena*. She remained respectful to him during their collaboration for she held him in high regard as an artist and could see that the production was going to be splendid. The set designer, Nicola Benois, and Visconti worked on every aspect of the sets using black, white, and grey 'like the grey of London'. Enormous royal portraits lined the broad staircase of the castle where Anna makes her first entrance in a regal gown of sombre blue while Henry's new love, Jane Seymour, wore red and the guards scarlet and yellow to contrast with the forbidding backgrounds.

Visconti accompanied Maria to her fittings every day, making sure the smallest detail of her gowns was right, that they were sculpted to her body. 'Her jewels were huge,' he recalled. 'They had to go with everything about her – her eyes, head, features, her stature. And believe me, on stage Callas had stature.'

'How she walked in her gowns!' Benois remembered. 'Like a queen. All her costumes were inspired by Holbein's portraits of Anne Boleyn, but no single detail was authentic...Luchino gave me precise documentation from history, but he did not seek reality...To collaborate with Luchino was like attending an academy. He is not only a director, he is a man of knowledge, culture, and taste.'

With time, Maria would become less enchanted with Visconti's genius. 'The moment we get too big for our boots, we are really finished,' she told Galatopoulos a number of years later. She was, she said, 'not trying to minimize [Visconti's] contribution, but, for heaven's sake let's keep things in logical perspective!'. It did not please Maria that the audience applauded every new set. She admired the effect that had been created but felt that in a drama as tragic as *Anna Bolena* the character being portrayed should remain the focal point of each scene she is in. This notwithstanding, and her own risible feelings now towards Visconti (which he seemed either to ignore or be insensitive to), Maria absorbed all that he said 'like a sponge', then would add her own brilliant interpretation to the role.

The final scene was one of overwhelming power. It is set in the deep, subterranean chamber of the Tower of London where Anna awaits her execution. High up, through barred windows, light entered stealthily into the chamber. Slowly the shadows lifted and 'soldiers could be distinguished, their hats silhouetted in a dim gold light, as if in a painting by Rembrandt....Bit by bit the women of the court who had followed their queen to prison grew visible.' Finally, Callas emerged from the shadows, seated, unmoving. 'The audience did not dare breathe, cough, stir,' Piero Tosi, who had designed the La Scala sets for *Sonnambula*, recalled of this production. 'There was absolute silence except for Callas's voice in a prayerful song....Here Visconti showed his genius, for he never intruded on this sound, so perfect, so expressive. Callas's stillness created incredible tension while her voice, human, yet crystallized, seemed almost an object.'

The La Scala audience were so moved that it took several seconds before the applause came. When it did, it rose in a tremendous crescendo. Everyone stood and in their excitement it seemed that they might rush forward on to the stage. Maria, taking her bows, could see nothing except the glare of the lights beyond the edge of the stage, as the deafening roar of approval thundered over her. Her voice had been at its peak – this she knew. The applause continued for twenty-four minutes, a La Scala record. A beaming Battista was standing in the wings when she finally began to make her way to her dressing room. Visconti came back and kissed her on the cheek. There were tears in her eyes – maybe true emotion, perhaps excitement, exhaustion. She drew away and disappeared into her private quarters, door closed and guarded as she removed her make-up and dressed for the opening-night party.

Such a large crowd had gathered outside the stage entrance to the theatre that the police, guns ready, had been called to hold them back fearing they might rush Maria when she was sighted and that injuries would occur. As each singer left the theatre there was applause, but order was retained. Then Maria, dazzling with diamonds, a guard on each side of her, Battista a few steps behind, emerged wearing a striking black chiffon gown. The crowd cheered and shouted. Maria paused nervously for a moment, her face chalk-white. Then she started forward with her protectors down the long loggia to her parked limousine with the same regal air that Anne Boleyn had assumed as she went to her death. No one ventured to come too close to her by breaking through the police cordon. The moment before she stepped into her car, she turned, smiled. It was a mysterious, enigmatic half-smile, her 'Gioconda' smile that so often shaped itself when she was feeling her way into her true emotions.

She was engulfed by fame. Privacy was no longer a commodity she could claim. She was alone as she had never been alone before. She had been betrayed by her mother and no longer had any real connection with either her father or her sister. Battista might stand by her side, do her bidding, but he lacked judgement and she no longer trusted him. What had brought them together no longer existed. At night she would close the door and be by herself. In Milan she kept Toy in the room. She had a hard time sleeping. She ate peckishly, careful to the point of obsession not to regain any weight. Work was her placebo and her incentive. She could overcome almost anything when she was working, any hurt, discomfort, disappointment but not loneliness.

She remained bitter towards Visconti and never again would visit his house in Rome. On occasion, if Battista insisted, she would join them for dinner at a restaurant. Her own relationship with Visconti was a thing of the past, as were so many things before her present life.

She had only a week between *Anna Bolena* and what would be her fifth and last production under the direction of Visconti, Gluck's *Ifigenia in Tauris*, the story of a Scythian princess fighting to end human sacrifice. Although Visconti was to say that this was the most beautiful opera on which they had worked together, Maria was to find it one of their most difficult and fractious collaborations. She wanted to play the role in a more classic frame than Visconti had designed. Sets and costumes had a Tiepolo fresco appearance, not in keeping with the setting of the story. 'I am a Greek woman and this is a Greek story!' she argued to no avail, for Visconti had decided (successfully as it turned out) to update the story, which gave it a somewhat more relevant and political tone.

Present during a large part of the rehearsals was Elsa Maxwell, newly befriended by Maria, who preferred to have her on her side rather than on Tebaldi's. Maxwell had arrived in Milan in time for the opening night of *Anna Bolena* and had remained as her houseguest. It saved Maria from being alone with Battista, a situation that was becoming difficult. Maxwell – an infamous turncoat – was now Maria's greatest fan. She was belligerently on Maria's side in any battle (as she had been once with Tebaldi).

During rehearsals on *Ifigenia* there had been an unpleasant set-to with the Vienna State Opera – where she had been scheduled to sing *La Traviata* following *Ifigenia* – and its artistic director, conductor Herbert von Karajan. Maria claimed that when her contract with Karajan was finally presented to her (through Battista), it included one additional performance and was not, she insisted, at the pre-agreed salary – which was to be higher than anyone else in the production. Battista interpreted the wording as meaning Karajan himself, who as conductor received $2100. Karajan refused to pay Maria more than $1600 per performance, the largest sum the Vienna State Opera had ever given a singer. Maria stood her ground and refused to sign the contract. The media made a lead story of it, laying the blame on 'a demanding diva'. Maria was demanding, no doubt about it. But the contest was more about the egos of two artists – not one. She sang to constantly sold-out houses, something few opera singers could achieve, and Vienna would have profited even had they paid her the $500 more per performance that was in contention. But Karajan, a man of Germanic obstinacy and pride, would never have agreed to a singer receiving as great a sum as he did.

Elsa Maxwell sent several stories back to her American publisher in defence of Maria who, she wrote, was surrounded by an 'evil web of invective'. Maxwell, whose hard-headed aim was to collect famous people as her friends, was now Maria's devoted fan and supporter. She opened a door into a world of the charmed circle of international society for Maria, who was dazzled by such celebrity, power and wealth. While all this wrangling with the Vienna State Opera and Karajan was taking place, Maria accompanied Maxwell to Paris (Battista remaining in Milan) for three days where she had tea with the Duke and Duchess of Windsor, cocktails with Baron and Baroness Rothschild, and was the guest of Prince Aly Khan at the races. Now divorced from Rita Hayworth, Aly Khan remained the eternal seducer and his charm was not lost on Maria. Like her, he lived his life in the glare of publicity. At forty-six, slim, though balding, he was a vital, attractive man, sun-bronzed from his love of the open air, possessing deep-brown 'bedroom eyes', a devastating smile and well-oiled charm – he was also very rich. With Maxwell as chaperone, Maria dined with him that same evening at Maxims.

Maria did not make as strong an impression upon Aly Khan as he made upon her. She had arrived at a point in her marriage where she knew things could not go on as they were, that she needed more from a man than Battista could offer. He lacked the vitality, the excitement, the ability to satisfy her sexual yearnings – which she had more and more been feeling of late. She was thirty-four and she realized that her biological clock was ticking. The dilemma was great. Battista was a staunch Catholic and they had been married in church. Divorce would be no easy matter. Nor could she see herself as the gay divorcée. Despite her success, her acknowledgement of her own accomplishments and attractiveness, she needed the security – or perhaps it was the mask – of marriage.

Entranced with the new world Maxwell had opened for her, Maria agreed to Elsa hosting a party in her honour in Venice on 3 September, ten weeks hence. On 17 June she departed from Paris to Zurich where, two days later, she gave a concert. Battista rejoined her in Rome on 20 June for rehearsals of *Lucia di Lammermoor* to be presented for one performance at the RAI, with Serafin conducting. From Rome they flew to Cologne for two performances (4 and 6 July) of *La Sonnambula*, then returned to Milan for a short rest before flying to Athens where she had been asked to sing at the Athens Festival being held in the open-air Herodes Atticus Theatre. This was her first trip to Athens since she had boarded the *Stockholm* for New York just after the war and she had only accepted after she learned that Litza and Jackie would be out of the country. However, Elvira de Hidalgo would be there.

Evangelina (Litza) and George Callas and their daughters, baby Maria (the only one born in the United States) and her older sister Jackie circa 1924. The former Kalogeropoulos family were now American citizens.

PS 189 MAN
PRINCIPALS

JAN 1937

Maria (third row centre with glasses) dressed in a scout costume for a school pageant. She was thirteen and would in a few weeks time be torn from her roots and taken to Greece by her mother.

Viewing herself before making her Italian debut in 1953 in *La Giocondo* at the Arena di Verona.

With her conductor, voice coach and lifelong mentor, Tullio Serafin.

LEFT Her weight soared along with her passion for the much older Battista Meneghini who became her husband and manager. RIGHT She lost over seventy pounds and became proud of her body, but many of her childhood insecurities remained.

At home in the appartment in Verona that Meneghini furnished. She now suffered great rudeness on the part of her in-laws who were only too happy to use the money that Meneghini syphoned off her earnings for them, but treated her like a loathed outsider.

LEFT With a new figure came a positive attitude and pride in her appearance. Here she strikes a seductive pose in the apartment in Verona decorated by Battista. RIGHT She made her American debut in Chicago, 1954, in *Norma*, one of her greatest roles.

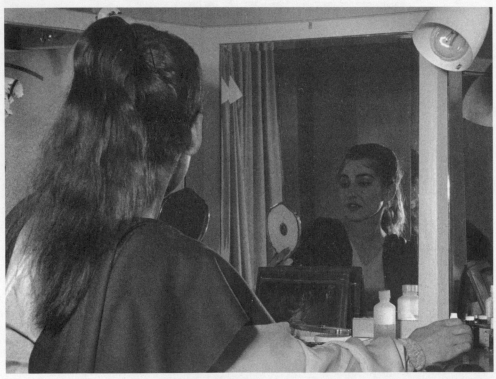

At her dressing room table. Propped up against the mirror is the painting of the Virgin Mary that she took with her everywhere she went.

LEFT One year later, in 1955, she returned to Chicago to sing *Butterfly* and was subpoenaed backstage in a law suit filed by Eddie Bagarozy, an early mentor. She expressed her rage as she walked behind the bailiff. RIGHT (inset cartoon): The media quickly picked up on the news value of Maria's confrontation with the baliff serving her with a subpoena. This cartoon depiction appeared in the *Chicago Tribune*.

'No more,' she signals the reporters the next day.

TOP She fell in love with director Luchino Visconti (seen here second from right) who influenced her career and her personal style. A homosexual, he could not reciprocate her feelings. She was jealous of Leonard Bernstein (seated) who was having an affair with Visconti while they were working on the La Scala production of *La Sonnanbula* starring Maria. 'Don't you dare leave with that homosexual!' she shouted at Visconti. But the two men departed together.

RIGHT With famed party giver Elsa Maxwell who would introduce her to Aristotle Onassis.

RIGHT She discovered that
Meneghini was transferring
her earnings into his private
bank account and sending
large sums to members of his
family. The marriage, already
in difficulty, suffered further.

BELOW Michel Glotz,
seen here with Maria at
the theatre, became her
French representative as
she began distancing
herself from Meneghini.

Onassis enters the scene. The famous moment caught on camera when Maria, in a chinchilla coat – a gift from Onassis – is caught in a bear hug between her husband and her new lover at 3 am after a party hosted by Onassis in her honour.

In Venice, before the lovers first cruise together on *The Christina*, Meneghini eyes Onassis with suspicion.

LEFT Dining out with Onassis and his sister. (Rex Fetures)
RIGHT Caught leaning on the shoulder of the Metropolitan Opera manager
Rudolph Bing after years of animosity between them.

Onassis kisses Princess Grace of Monaco's hand, a gesture that seems to be ignored by her.
At the time her husband, Prince Rainier, and Onassis were battling for power in Monaco.

Maria holds a press conference the day of her Greek divorce from Meneghini. Her greatest hope was that Onassis would now marry her.

The two battling divas, Callas and Tibaldi, make up with a hug that appears genuine.

Maria being greeted by Lawrence Kelly in Dallas. Kelly had been responsible for her early Chicago performances and was now aligned with the Dallas Civic Opera Company. BELOW She would sing *Lucia di Lammermoor* under Zeffirelli's direction.

Onassis turns his attention to Presidential widow, Jackie Kennedy. Maria is distraught and for a long time inconsolable.

Maria dines at Maxim's following Onassis's wedding to Jackie Kennedy – and goes home alone.

Maria in Greece in 1970 where she met Onassis secretly.

Maria and Franco Rossellini on the set of *Medea*.

The final tour made with her former co-star and current lover Giuseppe de Stefano.

A standing ovation from the audience in Dallas.

Vasso Devitzi, once her old friend, but in the end a Machiavellian deceiver, with Maria's boxed ashes.

On board the boat that would carry her ashes out to sea. Front row right end Devetzi, left – Feruccio and Maria's most loyal friend, Bruno. Jackie Callas can be seen several rows behind wearing sun glasses.

Maria's ashes are dispatched to the sea – but a sudden wind sends them back into the faces of those on board.

Maria.

Earlier in the year, George Callas had taken the final steps to secure his freedom from Litza, who received the news via a lawyer's letter. Fearful that she would not be treated fairly unless she was present to fight for a 'fair settlement', Litza decided to take Jackie with her to New York with the idea that Jackie should pursue her career there. She had old friends, Mr and Mrs Zarras, with whom they could stay. The Zarrases were very rich, she promised, investing an ordinary Greek immigrant couple with glamour, wealth and position. She also assured Jackie that with their many contacts she would see to it that her career was launched 'with a big public concert'. Jackie, aware that she was approaching forty and that her only hope would be to trade on her sister's fame, agreed – although with great trepidation – and with the small amount of money she had saved from Milton's ungenerous 'gifts' purchased their tickets.

The Zarrases' 'grand home' turned out to be a humble house in the Greek-American part of Queens (an outlying section of Manhattan). As soon as they were shown by Mr Zarras into the tiny room they were to share and the door was closed, Jackie turned on her mother. 'You told me these people were going to sponsor my career,' she cried. 'Can't you see how poor these people are? They can't afford a thing.'

'If you will sing, I will manage to get the money somewhere,' Litza promised. This time Dr Lantzounis and his wife did not proffer their financial aid. George managed to be away 'on a sales trip' while his wife and older daughter were in New York (although Litza did file a claim of support) and Jackie, realizing the futility of her mother's current dream of her singing a concert and being discovered as a 'second Maria Callas', simply gave up. She never had Maria's fighting spirit or ambition, or even a hint of her sister's great talent, and she knew it and was only too pleased that Litza agreed to cut short their visit in New York, which was threatened with more disappointment when they learned that Maria would be in Athens while they were in New York, meaning they would miss seeing her in either city.

The Athens concert was problematic from the start. Maria had first offered to donate her fee to the promotion of the festival. To her surprise and injured pride, this offer was haughtily refused. Then, when the managers realized the size of her normal fee, they complained bitterly. On her arrival in Athens on 28 July, the temperature a blistering 89 degrees, the press carried a story that she was money hungry and charging an exorbitant fee when the people in her 'homeland' were struggling for the barest essentials.

Revisiting her youth was more traumatic than Maria had expected. Athens had never seemed like home to her. Living there had not been her choice and most of her memories of her years in Greece were unhappy ones. Everywhere she turned her own unattractive image and the horrors of the war came back to haunt her. The carping press made things worse. It had been a huge mistake of judgement for her to have accepted the engagement. Once there, however, she was determined to rise above the problems and to perform at her peak. On the day of the concert she awoke with a sore throat. The doctor was called, her throat sprayed, but her condition grew worse. The day progressed without improvement and by early afternoon she notified the festival managers that they would have to cancel her performance. Thrown into a panic and unable to find a suitable replacement, the managers put off announcing the cancellation until an hour before the concert. The press now accused Maria of collecting her fee despite her non-show, which was not the case – she was not paid when she didn't sing.

A slight breeze had cooled the oven-hot day when she appeared two days later on the evening of 5 August to face an antagonistic audience. She looked beautiful in a flowing chiffon gown, diamonds glittering on her neck and at her ear lobes. She soon won them over with a glorious but difficult programme, which included the 'Liebestod' and the mad scene from *Hamlet*. She sang brilliantly and even performed as an encore the trying second part of Lucia's mad scene when it was requested by Prime Minister Karamanlis. De Hidalgo remained close to Maria following the concert as she was besieged by a crowd of fans, past acquaintances and young hopefuls all trying to get her attention. It was pure mayhem, no bodyguards to protect her and Maria returned to her hotel exhausted, badly jostled and near tears. 'I'll never come back to Athens again,' she vowed to de Hidalgo.

'Ah, but you are Greek. You will see. You will,' her old teacher insisted.

She returned to Milan exhausted with little time to rest in the two days before she was to leave to appear in *La Sonnambula* with the La Scala company at the Edinburgh Festival. Her throat had continued to bother her and she notified Ghiringhelli that she would have to cancel as her doctor had insisted she have thirty days of total rest and non-singing. Ghiringhelli was beside himself. 'He said that it would be better for La Scala not to go at all than to go without me, for the guarantee of my name had been the basis of the contract,' Maria later told an interviewer. 'What gave me strength and made me go against my doctor's and my husband's strenuous advice was [the management's] moving statement, "La Scala will be forever grateful to you, Maria, for all your work and sacrifice, and especially for this latest gesture." Little did I know that this eternal gratitude was not as eternal as all that.'

She sang four performances, as per her contract, and then prepared on 30 August to leave for Milan to rest before departing four days later for Venice and Elsa Maxwell's party. The problem was that La Scala had scheduled *five* not four performances, although – by an oversight it was claimed – the last had not been included in her contractual arrangements. The La Scala management begged her 'to save La Scala', they did all they could to keep her from leaving. But Maria was on the point of nervous collapse, her vocal chords inflamed along with her patience. She could not, *would* not sing the extra performance no matter what La Scala paid her. On this note she left Edinburgh.

When she arrived home she was greeted by a host of front-page stories about her disloyalty to La Scala. Nothing was said about the last performance not being in her contract and insinuations were made that there was nothing wrong with her throat for she was planning to attend Elsa Maxwell's Venetian soirée on 3 September. Maxwell had sent her the prestigious guest list, which included the names of Tina and Aristotle Socrates Onassis, the fabulously rich Greek shipping tycoon and his socialite wife. Onassis was later so say, 'There was a natural curiosity there; after all we are the most famous living Greeks in the world!' But Maria was not feeling warmly towards her ethnic roots at this time and she had little interest in meeting a fifty-six-year-old married man, however rich, with a reputation as a philanderer and a rogue.

13

Onassis Enters

VENICE WAS SUPREMELY beautiful that September. Daytime skies were clear blue; the light luminous and the tender touch of the air warm and friendly. Autumn had not quite arrived and summer not yet relinquished its grip. Maria and Battista were installed in one of the most expensive suites at the Gritti Palace, compliments of the hotel. Elsa Maxwell's impending ball in honour of Maria had already received worldwide publicity. Maxwell was a wonder woman at promotion. The ball was being held at the grand palazzo of the Countess Castelbarco who was only too happy to host the celebrity guests on Maxwell's list. There were to be over a hundred people (including Noël Coward, Marlene Dietrich, Merle Oberon, Princess Marina – widow of the Duke of Kent – Tina and Ari Onassis, two countesses, several counts, a baron and representatives from the world's richest and most restless glitterati). Two orchestras had been hired – one to play in the garden, the other in the ballroom.

Although it was visually evident that Maria had lost a shocking amount of weight and had arrived in Venice looking pale and exhausted, her love for the city renewed her spirit. 'It's beautiful, just beautiful,' she said as she stood, glowing, by the terrace windows in the sitting room of their suite looking out over the Grand Canal. 'I don't want to read a newspaper the whole while we're here,' she told Battista and then promptly got on the telephone to Maxwell to hear all the current gossip, some of which concerned Mr and Mrs Aristotle Socrates Onassis.

They had been married in 1946 when Tina was seventeen and Onassis forty. 'Greek marriages are not infrequently arranged,' Tina had recently said. 'But my marriage to Ari was arranged only by Eros the god of love.' She was the younger daughter of millionaire Greek shipping magnate Stavros Livanos who – since he had married Tina's mother, Arietta, when she was only fifteen and he was forty – could hardly object. Stavros, who was the third generation of one of Greece's most famous shipbuilding families, operated his business out of London. Tina and her sister Eugenie were raised in England, attending Heathfield, a boarding school in Ascot. With the advent of war, in 1940, the sisters were sent for safety to Montreal where they remained at a convent school for two years before rejoining their parents in apartments at New York's Plaza Hotel.

Tina was an elegant blonde beauty. She was fluent in Greek and French, but her first language was English, which she spoke with a clipped, upper-crust British accent. There had been many women in Ari's life but, until he met Tina, no one he wished to marry. She represented all the things – beauty, money, heritage, sophistication – that Onassis wanted to possess. He had clawed his way ruthlessly to his current position of wealth and power. Though his parents were Greek, he and his sisters grew up in Greek-occupied Smyrna, Turkey, where his father prospered in the tobacco business. His mother died when he was only five and his grandmother, a devout Greek Orthodox, raised him. At sixteen his ordered life was thrown into chaos when, on 9 September 1922, the Turkish liberation forces led by Kemal Ataturk advanced on Smyrna. It was a night of hell as thousands of desperate Greeks attempting to escape the revenge of the Turks made their way to the harbour of Smyrna hoping to board a ship that would carry them to safety.

Streets were littered with the dead and dying who had been shot in cold blood by Ataturk's men. The slaughter was horrific. Women and children were not spared. Ari saw his father dragged from the house and several of his relatives and friends brutally murdered. His father's life – for the moment – was saved, but he was imprisoned. Ari – now the only man in the family – was responsible for his grandmother and brood of six sisters. Eventually, after some time in hiding and nearly starving, he managed to get them all on to a packed boat that took the family to Piraeus, concealing from them the knowledge of his father's certain execution following their departure.

He arrived in Greece, his grandmother dying en route, penniless but determined. The grief of the past, the need to survive and his rage to succeed had brewed within Onassis a tremendous lust for life, and had honed him into the charismatic man whom women seemed unable to resist. He was short and swarthy, his manner brusque, the edges rough. But there was a pirate air of adventure about him that women found exciting and men challenging.

Tina and Onassis were a glamorous couple. Both enjoyed nothing but the best. They entertained on a grand scale – film stars, famous writers, society's 400, historic figures like Winston Churchill, the Duke and

Duchess of Windsor, and royalty from many countries. The Onassises' homes were magnificent and their yacht, the *Christina*, considered the most expensive and fabulous in the world. They shared an appetite for adventure: hunting whales off the coast of Peru, flying in their private plane to Saudi Arabia, skiing in the Alps. Their parties on the *Christina* were legendary. Their two children, Alexander and Christina, were raised as though they were the heirs to the world, not simply a shipping fortune.

But as time passed Tina and Ari spent less of it together. For Onassis business deals had become his oxygen, his first passion. 'Ari's idea of home was cafés, restaurants, clubs, or wherever there was a telephone and he could unpack a suitcase. Home was something he could take with him,' one commentator observed. And there were women – dozens of them – wherever he rested to satisfy the sexual needs he accepted as obligatory as his after-dinner brandy and cigar. He was away from home and Tina for weeks, often months, and by the late fifties their marriage remained no more than a façade, each living his or her own private life. 'He had his friends and I started to find mine,' Tina later told the London *Daily Express* columnist William Hickey. Just weeks before the Onassises (reunited on the *Christina* after a two-month unofficial separation) arrived in Venice, several photographs of the glamorous Mrs Onassis and the millionaire Venezuelan oil man Renaldito Herrera had appeared in the tabloids and slick magazines. Gossip columnists boldly referred to them as 'an item'.

Elsa Maxwell rang Maria at the Gritti Palace to tell her that the Greek shipping magnate and his straying wife would be at the ball in Maria's honour. Maria loved gossip (something that she and Visconti had enthusiastically shared), but little else about the couple she was to meet for the first time intrigued her, for Elsa had also informed her that Onassis had often stated how opera bored him and that the 'shrill voices of its divas seriously hurt his ears'.

Onassis's take on their impending introduction was in direct opposition to Maria's. He might not have been an aficionado of opera, but he maintained a passionate interest in all things Greek: ships, history, deposed royalty and the country's most famous people. Therefore he had read a great deal about Maria Callas (whom he considered 'the other most famous living Greek') and what he had absorbed made a deep impression.

What interested Onassis about Maria had nothing to do with opera. Of course, her celebrity intrigued him. He collected the famous as some people do great art – to announce to the world how rich and cultivated he was. But it was the story of 'her early struggles as a poor girl in her teens [who] sailed through unusually rough and merciless waters', that got to him, as well as the story that 'during the German occupation her family was starving, literally starving, and while studying she did not only have to run the house as well but help to find food, which was very hard to come by. [That took] tremendous courage and strength of character that enabled her to overcome these tremendous difficulties... [and for her] as a dedicated performer to assert herself in the tough and competitive world of the stage,' he saw as a 'great achievement'.

His own painful memories of his wartime experiences, the privations he suffered to help his family, his fierce will to succeed against tremendous odds and his Greek heritage seemed to him to make this woman he was about to meet a kindred spirit; someone cut from the same cloth as himself, a woman, who in a way, could be his shadow image.

Coached by Maxwell, Maria arrived at the Palazzo Castelbarco by gondola, fashionably late. The palazzo was brilliantly lit, inside and out. The sound of popular dance music floated on the warm breeze that greeted her as she was helped from the narrow swaying boat and stepped gingerly on to the private landing that led to the entrance of the illuminated building, its massive, carved wood doors agape – a welcoming gesture to arriving guests. She wore a splendid scarlet Balmain gown, a wisp of matching tulle draped about her shoulders, five strands of pearls with a dazzling diamond clasp about her long neck. Her hair was drawn dramatically back from her face, diamond and pearl earrings accenting its magnificent contour. Never had she looked more elegant.

Her entrance into the impressive ballroom, a few steps in front of Battista, drew immediate attention from the gathered guests. With Elsa Maxwell by Maria's side, and the Countess Castelbarco by Battista, the Meneghinis inched their way further into the festively decorated room, pausing for introductions and greetings. Suddenly Maria and Onassis were face to face. Afterwards, her lingering memory of that momentous meeting was of a leonine head bending over her hand, which he held in his as he kissed it in continental fashion. He was not a tall man, perhaps about her own height if she had not been wearing high-heeled sandals. She was at that moment much more interested in the beautiful blonde woman standing next to him, to whom she had just been introduced: Tina Livanos Onassis, who was wearing a spectacular diamond tiara and an ethereal tiered chiffon gown in variegated shades of blue that underscored her amazing sky-blue eyes. The colour of Onassis's eyes could not be discerned as he let go of Maria's hand and smiled broadly at her, for he wore thick-rimmed tinted glasses.

'We are, you know, the two most famous Greeks in the world,' he said, his voice deep, his English mildly accented.

'And what are you most famous for, Mr Onassis?' Maxwell claimed Maria replied, although she never recorded his answer.

The evening was a memorable one for Maria, but not necessarily because of her meeting with Onassis. More and more she was being drawn to the members of the society and celebrity world courted by Elsa Maxwell. The opera world was inbred, choking at times: filled with intense jealousies and petty feuds. One always had to be on one's guard. Seldom were their gatherings either relaxing or fun. But here the sound of laughter filled the massive room and the music that was played was light and meant to entice the celebrants to dance. Maria had one short turn with Onassis around the dance floor. She noted 'his touch seemed somehow magnetized and it set up an alarm in me'. She had heard about his flagrant womanizing from Maxwell and how he thought of every woman he met as a potential mistress. 'There was no place in my life for such a man,' she later asserted.

She drank more than usual, laughed more than usual and even sang a sultry rendition of Hoagy Carmichael's famous blues song, 'Stormy Weather', with Maxwell (who in her youth had earned a living playing piano in silent movie houses) accompanying her. 'Never', Maxwell gloated in her weekly column, 'have I given a better dinner and ball in my life...Even two princesses who hated each other were found exchanging smiles, while another *comtesse* who couldn't remain in the same room with Merle Oberon [they had once shared the same lover] stayed until 5 a.m.'

Maria and Battista departed at the discreet hour of 1 a.m. after an invitation to join Onassis and Tina and their guests for 'breakfast' on the *Christina* at noon that day. Battista immediately agreed. 'Why did you do that?' Maria asked later, early day socializing not her idea of fun.

'He is a powerful man,' Battista replied. 'And he knows everyone.'

At noon one of Onassis's private motorboats, steered by two uniformed members of the *Christina*'s crew, whizzed them through Venice's winding canal waterways to the mouth of the harbour where the yacht was anchored. It was Maria's first time on board the *Christina* and she was duly impressed by its grandeur. An elaborate buffet (a display of exotic fruit, caviar, baby lamb chops, sausages, ham, eggs – a chef standing ready to prepare them as requested, a boggling array of smoked fishes, including kippers cooked especially for his English guests, and breads and sweet rolls freshly baked by the *Christina*'s French pastry chef) had been set out with numerous staff members on hand to serve. Only a few of the yacht's famous passengers were up and about. Onassis spent a lengthy time talking to the Meneghinis, offering them one of his motorboats and pilot during their week's stay in Venice (which Battista accepted) and inviting them to join him and his wife in the near future on the yacht's soon-to-be-taken Mediterranean cruise.

'I have a very full schedule,' Maria said.

'Of course,' he replied, 'but there is always time when it is sought.'

The Meneghinis saw both Onassis and Tina (more often Onassis) several times during their Venice stay. 'He's pursuing you,' Maxwell confided to Maria.

'Don't be ridiculous. He's just been pleased to meet another Greek,' Maxwell claims she shot back.

'Tina's Greek and so are most of the members of his crew and entourage – the secretary, that broad-shouldered bodyguard who shadows him. Just remember, Elsa warned you.'

What Maria had not been alerted to was Maxwell's own oncoming pursuit. She was well aware of the famous party giver's lesbianism (despite Maxwell's insistence in her autobiography that she was asexual and simply could not stand to be kissed by a man). Until this time it did not seem to have anything to do with their friendship, which was based on their mutual need: Maria to have someone pave the way for her into the social world; Elsa to add another celebrity to her list of famous people whom she called friends. Then, directly after the Venice ball, Maria received the first of many impassioned letters from Elsa that both shocked and disgusted her.

Maxwell's sudden daily (sometimes twice daily) letters were hand delivered to her for the length of her stay in Venice. They were, according to Battista, 'passionate love letters...distorted by grotesque remarks which referred to lesbian relationships of other well-known people'. Maria's immediate reaction was to break off from a woman whom both she and Battista now thought to be 'dangerously strange'. But to do so, and so soon after Maxwell's Venice party, would almost certainly trigger her lethal penchant for revenge that could be terribly destructive to Maria's career and image. Maria therefore decided to ignore the letters – in fact at a point not to open any more – and to avoid seeing Elsa when possible. Battista would answer the telephone and if it was Maxwell, would make some excuse for Maria not being able to talk to her. Maxwell, adversely, misinterpreted Maria's silence as indicating a receptive response and that Battista was now 'policing her telephone calls'.

The situation Maria encountered upon her return home to Milan put both Maxwell's unwelcome overtures and the possibility of an eager married suitor like Onassis entirely out of her thoughts. The press had been vicious in their accounts of her recent appearances (and non-appearances) in Athens and in Edinburgh. Unfortunately, the night of the Venice ball, 3 September 1957, occurred on the very same evening as the fifth *La Sonnambula*, the one Maria had refused to sing in Edinburgh citing ill health. Photographs appeared of her dancing at the party and looking particularly radiant. But in fact the week in Venice had only exacerbated her feeling of exhaustion. She could not understand why, but her usual energy appeared to have deserted her. Walking was difficult and, more troubling, she was experiencing a frightening shortage of breath.

Her declining health began in Athens when she realized that she had gained over five pounds and that her clothes were tight on her. This greatly upset her and she went back to the stringent diet she had kept when she had first lost so much weight (small servings of fresh fruit and raw meat). It is not clear if she was taking any form of diet pills or supplements (she did use a good number of vitamins and homeopathic drugs, self-prescribed), but she had lost fourteen pounds during her short stays in Edinburgh and Venice, and was now far below a healthy weight for her height and age. Also, she had worked very hard in Athens and in Edinburgh with little sleep (which wasn't helped by her late hours in Venice).

Immediately upon her return to Milan, she submitted to a thorough examination and was told firmly by her doctors that she must rest for at least thirty days and gain back at least ten pounds. Tests that had been performed had located a tapeworm, believed to have been caused by her consumption of raw meat (she favoured chopped beef steak). The problem was that she was contracted to sing in *Lucia di Lammermoor* and *Macbeth* with the San Francisco Opera Company from 27 September through 10 November. On 12 September she cabled Kurt Herbert Adler, the general manager of the company, that her doctors forbade her to leave Milan, explaining that she was no longer strong enough to travel. She then offered to sing with the San Francisco Opera the second month of the season, which would give her time to recover her physical strength and hopefully purge herself of the tapeworm.

Having seen photographs of her dancing in Venice, Adler did not believe that she was telling him the truth. She then forwarded him her medical reports. He replied that either she appeared as scheduled or her contract would be cancelled. The newspaper coverage of this boldly insinuated that she had faked an illness to get out of a contract.

'What I did wrong was go to that blessed party in Venice though I must emphasize that there was nothing deliberate about it,' Maria later told Stelios Galatopoulos. 'But remember I did not cancel San Francisco. All I asked for was a postponement of two weeks so that I could get myself together. There was also another thing...I relied on my husband who was obviously not a very good agent, to protect me....I am not trying to make excuses for the things I did wrong, but I will not be made a scapegoat either.'

The press refused to drop the story. Her 'early' departure from Edinburgh and her cancellation with the San Francisco Opera Company had been blown up into *le scandale*: Callas – the impossible diva, egocentric, non-professional. She was being pilloried, her integrity attacked, her reputation slandered. Adler's attitude, even after she sent him her doctor's report, had fed the rumour that it had been fabricated. Still suffering from the purges to rid herself of the tapeworm, and truly feeling ill and debilitated, she turned to La Scala and Ghiringhelli to come to her defence.

She believed she had every right to expect this. For the six years she had been with La Scala she had given them full measure of her talent and more, working longer and harder than anyone else, singing whatever role they asked her to sing. Out of 157 performances at La Scala, she had postponed only two because of illness – a record no other La Scala performer could equal. 'Each year Ghiringhelli gave me a present: a silver bowl, a silver mirror, a chandelier, costumes and lots of sugared words and compliments. But now he would not speak up to defend me,' she complained. She and Battista finally succeeded in getting him to agree to issue a statement on her behalf, a promise that was not kept.

Her bitterness hard to contain, Maria departed with Battista for New York on 5 November, her weight still hovering at a dangerous low, her physical condition frail. She had some out-of-court business to settle regarding the long litigation with Bagarozy. Then there were meetings with Rudolf Bing to decide on the roles she would sing the following season (they agreed on *Lucia* and *Tosca*). Laurence Kelly, who had once brought her to Chicago, had now broken off his ties with Carol Fox and started a new opera company in Dallas and she had agreed to appear in concert during the opening festivities for his company under the baton of Kelly's partner in the enterprise, her old friend Nicola Rescigno. Elsa Maxwell had returned to New York and bombarded her with telephone calls and letters. She finally spoke on the telephone with Elsa and asked her to 'please, please leave me alone. I have many problems and don't need *this*.'

Her life with Battista was becoming more difficult. Their marriage was unravelling but he could not see the signs. She felt he was handling her career and their business matters badly. They fought. 'Calm yourself, calm yourself,' he was constantly telling her. 'You are just upset over…' and he would mention some incident that had been unpleasant that day. She visited her father who had aged shockingly, and Leonidas and Sally Lantzounis (to whom she confided her unhappiness), before leaving with Battista, on 17 November, for rehearsals in Dallas. What she did not know was that Elsa Maxwell would follow her there in time to see the concert with the excuse that she was covering it for her column.

On Maria's arrival, the headline in the daily newspaper read 'DALLAS FOR CALLAS'. Not only the operaphiles, but an overwhelming percentage of Big D's expanding population was excited about *The Diva* coming to their booming town. In the past twenty years, Dallas had grown from a cow town into a metropolitan city, but one without the cultural establishments that helped cities that had had fifty to a hundred years (like New York, Philadelphia, Boston, Chicago and San Francisco) to nurture an intellectual society. Kelly and Rescigno had few problems raising funds for this, Dallas's first opera company. Almost everyone knew who Maria Callas was and her celebrity made the gregarious Texans feel 'mighty proud' that she was to inaugurate their 'fine op'ra house'.

With Battista, Maria occupied the grandiose 'Presidential Suite' in the city's oldest and most prestigious Adolphus Hotel (built and named for a beer baron), with its rich wood panelling and imported crystal chandeliers, and were fêted from the moment of their arrival. Huge bouquets of flowers filled their rooms (seven, including a dining room and full kitchen staffed by the hotel if so requested). A gift box from the city's most famous store, Nieman Marcus (which was 'just up the street a stretch') contained a sterling silver flower bowl and matching pair of candlesticks, a present from the hotel management. Dallas was so pleased to have 'the world's most famous soprana', that angry letters were sent to the *Dallas Morning News* chastising the editors for publishing reports about Maria's recent career problems. Maria immediately cheered to this warm, generous and protective welcome but calls from Maxwell, now ensconced in the same hotel, put her back on edge. 'This has to end,' Maria told Battista. He believed she meant Maxwell's harassment, which was probably true, but there was no doubt that Maria was also referring to the difficulties in their marriage.

In the first part of the concert, gowned glamorously in form-fitting red silk, she sang in top form selections from Mozart's *Entführung*, Bellini's *I Puritani*, Verdi's *Macbeth* and *La Traviata*. She returned for the second half to sing the mad scene from Donizetti's *Anna Bolena* in a dramatic black velvet gown that drew gasps as she stepped out on stage. The deep V neck and stark look of the dress emphasized her thinness, but produced a perfect effect for the tragic queen, about to be beheaded, whom she was portraying. When she began to sing 'A dolce guidami', the lighting narrowed to frame her face, shoulders and hands. The silence in the concert hall was almost palpable. Off stage, Maria's face might not have been considered beautiful because her features were too large. Her current extreme gauntness emphasized this in perhaps not so flattering a manner, but on stage the lighting and accentuating make-up transformed her. Her eyes were so large and defined that people sitting in the last row of the balcony could catch their expression, and her wide mouth, heavily rouged, seemed to give birth to the glorious tones and wrenching emotion of her voice. John Ardoin wrote tellingly, 'Oddly enough one noticed Callas's mouth most when she was not singing. Then, it so often shaped itself into a peculiar half-smile, a bemused look as though she sensed an irony which had escaped the rest of us. This look had about it all the enigmatic beauty writers have long ascribed to Leonardo's Gioconda.'

There was also the way she carried herself on stage, her distinctive, graceful, even-stepped walk that could be so regal yet poignant; and her marvellously expressive hands, which she used eloquently, as though they were the silent extension of her emotion. Dallas gave her a vociferous, cheering ovation when the last note of her aria had ended and she stood unmoving before them. She had captivated Dallas and the people there had presented her with the assurance she needed as a performer. But her private life remained in chaos. She left Dallas for New York where she would get a connecting flight to Italy a day before Battista, leaving him to iron out some details on a return appearance with the Dallas Civic Opera during their next season. To her shock upon boarding her plane, Maxwell occupied the seat next to hers. Before many minutes, Maria told Elsa that her harassment was unendurable, that she found her disgusting. 'Say anything you want about me in your filthy column,' she said in a loud voice that could be heard by other passengers in the first-class section. 'It's worth it if it means I'm finally rid of you.' She then moved her seat and ignored Maxwell for the remainder of the flight.

When she arrived home there was another letter from Maxwell:

I feel compelled to write and thank you for being the innocent victim of the highest form of love that a human being can have for another... It brought you no happiness and, except for a few marvellous moments, it brought me only profound misery... You destroyed my love on the flight from Dallas. And yet I believe I almost touched your heart once or twice...I was and always will be your most eloquent defense lawyer – I stood up to your enemies, Maria, of which you have many!

Once home in Milan, Maria almost immediately began rehearsals at La Scala for the Verdi opera, *Un Ballo in Maschera*, in which, for the first time, she would sing the role on stage of Amelia.[1] She was at a juncture in her life where the road behind her was impassable and the road ahead not yet cleared. What she was left with was her 'intense commitment to music, an indifference to compromise.' She knew she often demanded too much of her voice, that she abused it because she so desperately wanted to sing *everything*, every role that was a challenge, even those that she knew were a stretch for her to deliver vocally. Unlike many of her peers in and before her time, Maria could not 'cheat' and drop some of the high notes of an aria. She had to sing the music as written by the composer. For the past eight years her voice had done as she commanded and she had been at her finest vocally. Maintaining this standard was of prime importance to her.

As rehearsals began for *Un Ballo in Maschera* she found herself unusually exhausted at the end of the day. Uneasiness plagued her. What if her voice failed her? Battista told her she was worrying unnecessarily. Hadn't she given one of her finest concerts ever in Dallas? Yes, but that was not an entire opera. Life at home was anything but happy. She kept to herself, slept alone. Battista never complained. He had an invisible wall that surrounded him and kept him from feeling what other people felt. Although living together, they were doing so in two separate worlds.

---

[1] In 1939, when she was only fifteen, Maria Callas had sung Amelia's third act aria 'Morrò, ma prima in grazia', and she had recorded the opera in September 1956 with Giuseppe di Stefano and Tito Gobbi.

14

Crossing Troubled Waters

NOT SINCE HER first Gioconda in Verona had Maria experienced stage fright. She believed it had something to do with her myopia, as she was unable to see past the prompter's box. Audiences therefore remained anonymous to her, faceless and so not to be feared. Another explanation for her self-confidence on stage rested on her intense study of each role she sang and her awesome total commitment during rehearsals, especially when she was learning a new role. Maria's perfectionism demanded that she not only be note and word perfect, but that her footwork and the location of sets and props be firm in her mind so that there would be no chance of her stumbling – or worse, falling.

She had already recorded *Un Ballo in Maschera*, but there was a vast difference between singing a role in a recording studio and on the stage of an opera house. A live performance required a singer to act visually as well as musically, and it was this blend of the two art forms that transformed Maria into the greatest diva of her time. She seemed, literally, to sing with her entire body – a perfect trilogy of voice, movement and emotion. Her recordings were most often exceptional, the listener aware that he or she was hearing a great artist. But to see her live, on stage, was an experience that few people ever forgot. Tickets for her appearances were purchased far in advance and coveted. Audiences came, not necessarily to see a particular opera but to both see and hear Maria Callas. And for these devoted fans, particularly in Italy, there was every chance that they would demand a refund at the box office if the great diva was unable to sing and a replacement – no matter how fine a singer – stood in for her.

A reputation of such magnitude was a great burden for Maria to support. Because of it, any mis-step on her part would be blown up out of proportion and duly reported around the world. Maria Callas, alone among all the great singers of the day – male or female – was news.

Her first appearance at a rehearsal immediately set the mood for the entire company. She was always on time and her punctuality quickly became the rule. There was no nuance, musical or dramatic, that she did not explore, often trying the patience of the other members of the company, who might have to work longer hours than planned. During the tedious rehearsals for *Un Ballo in Maschera* she had a secret to guard – a fear that her voice might fail her. Opera singers are often worried about this possibility, but not until they are far older than Maria was then. But her early abuse of her Voice (a word she capitalized in letters to friends, giving it human distinction) was now beginning, if in a discreet manner, to whisper warnings to her: an occasional twinge in her throat, a note that almost slipped away from her. This only intensified her need to get everything exactly right, so that no glitch, however small, would be allowed to interrupt her performance, nor cause her to be confused on stage.

Her emotional state was not helped by her growing resentment towards Ghiringhelli and the board of La Scala who had not come to her immediate defence during the Edinburgh fiasco and the vicious media attacks that had followed. To avoid a confrontation, Ghiringhelli remained aloof during the rehearsals, not once coming to see Maria – from her point of view an unforgivable breach of gratitude, etiquette and common courtesy.

The conductor of *Un Ballo in Maschera* was Gianandrea Gavazzeni, who had only recently so successfully conducted her La Scala production of *Anna Bolena* (now, to her irritation being referred to as 'Visconti's *Anna Bolena*', due to his brilliant revisionist direction). Maria trusted Gavazzeni's instincts and respected his musicality (although she was to say every one of her roles would have been just that much better under the baton of Serafin, whom she considered 'the master'). Gavazzeni, at forty-nine, was young for a conductor with such a prestigious background. He had composed numerous critically acclaimed works, which he had occasionally conducted in performance, was a well-known music critic, had written a definitive book on Donizetti and had been a maestro for a decade at La Scala.

Maria would be singing once again with Giuseppe di Stefano, this time in the role of Amelia's lover, Riccardo. Their relationship had not always been easy. Di Stefano was a 'natural, instinctive singer who cared little for the niceties of a composer's notation'. Maria, on the other hand, believed almost blindly in being true to the composer's intention. Di Stefano also had little patience for the kind of repetitive rehearsal that Maria demand-ed. Nonetheless, Maria was more than aware that their voices were well paired and that di Stefano's great charm and the intensity of his singing (notable for its unfailingly beautiful tone, a rich, velvety sound and the use of an exquisite pianissimo) brought out the best in her performances.

Only two years older than Maria, di Stefano was a well-built, hand-some man, dark-complexioned, very Italian with a quick, fiery temper – but more often he displayed a warm, spirited side of himself. He possessed a ready wit and was in his element entertaining friends at the flamboyant parties he liked to host. His generosity was legendary. He once took the entire cast of a company with whom he was appearing in San Francisco for a weekend at his own expense to Las Vegas.

'I believe there was always a certain sexual attraction between Callas and di Stefano,' a La Scala staff member recalled.

> But di Stefano was happily married, or so it appeared, for I don't recall any gossip to the contrary (and opera companies thrive on gossip) and Callas (who everyone knew was *unhappily* married) never to my knowledge encouraged familiarity with the other singers [at La Scala]. She was always generous, never bitchy or demeaning. But she was stand-offish. With her director, the creative team, and La Scala's staff, it was a different matter. You might say that she aligned herself with the executive arm.

There were two other *Un Ballo in Maschera*s – in Stockholm and Paris – being produced at approximately the same time as La Scala's. These companies had chosen to use Sweden as the locale for the story, a setting at variance with the libretto most often in use, which was set in Boston in the seventeenth century. Verdi's opera had been controversial since 1858, when he first submitted it to the San Carlo Theatre in Naples. His original libretto was based on *Gustave III ou Le Bal Masqué* written by Daniel Auber in the early eighteenth century, which in turn had been founded on the true story of the murder of Sweden's King Gustav III (1792) at a masked ball. Like Auber, Verdi had used real names and the actual locale – Sweden.

Naples, at that time, was still straining under the domination of Austria and its ruling family, the Habsburgs, who had been given the state in the 1713 peace agreement that followed the War of the Spanish Succession. When Verdi's new opera was seeking production, Garibaldi's armies were on the push to bring Naples back under Italian control and unify Italy into one nation. Insurrection burned in the hearts of the city's patriots and hatred for their Austrian overlords was becoming hard to contain. The Neapolitan censor feared that *Un Ballo in Maschera*, with regicide at its centre, would further fan the flame. They insisted Verdi rewrite the opera. He refused and left Naples.

He soon realized, however, that *Un Ballo in Maschera* would never be performed unless he changed the locale. A Roman impresario finally offered to produce the opera if Verdi would agree to a new setting. King Gustav III of Sweden now became Riccardo, Governor of Boston in the seventeenth century: the improbability of an Italian governor in what was then still the Plymouth Colony, or of the staid pilgrim population attending a masked ball, apparently of no concern. Nonetheless, the story was a good one. Riccardo, the governor of a part-fictional Boston, is in love with Amelia, the wife of Renato who surprises the lovers when they meet for a secret tryst. The injured husband warns Amelia that she must die for her infidelity – although Amelia's life is eventually saved. There are political overtones, signs of tragedy advance in a Shakespearean mode and the climax is reached with the dramatic fatal stabbing of Riccardo at a brilliantly lit, festive masked ball, his costume revealed by his page to Renato, his assassin, whom he forgives with his dying breath.

La Scala's artistic team was in a quandary as to where the locale of their production should be set: Sweden or Boston. Maria tried to convince the others to settle on Verdi's original concept, but finally agreed that if the composer had thought well enough of it to move the story to Boston, then so should La Scala. Verdi's score, however, had been composed with a royal court in mind and it jarred with the on-stage presence of early American Puritans who believed in simplicity, and strictness and gravity of behaviour (which is why Paris and Stockholm had employed the royal court of Sweden as its locale). A royal aura was only partially achieved by using elaborately carved wood for the walls of the governor's office and reinventing Amelia as a great lady from London. This allowed Maria to wear an elegant wardrobe (in contrast to the severe costumes of the pilgrim women), trimmed with luxurious furs. Maria looked spectacular in her wide-brimmed hats, lush white furs, Indian beadwork adding an exotic touch. She sang as though Verdi had created her arias with a prescience that this not-yet-born diva would one day sing them. The première was an unqualified success; the audience caught up in a fervour of enthusiasm as they called Maria out for curtain after curtain. Ghiringhelli suddenly appeared backstage as she was making her way through the tangle of ropes and people to her dressing room. He was all smiles as he kissed her on the cheek. 'Ah, the till must be full!' she cracked, as she disappeared inside.

She sang five performances, the first, a few days after her thirty-fifth birthday, the last on 22 December, her voice in top form and never failing her, La Scala audiences applauding her ardently. She had only five days to relax before she was scheduled to leave for Rome where, on 2 January she would sing *Norma*. It was a very short time between engagements and she had worked herself even harder than usual in the last few weeks losing five pounds, which she blamed on the weight of her costumes and the heat they generated. In contrast, her dressing room had been icy cold, the radiators either clogged or closed to conserve heating costs.

She remained close to home during Christmas. The weather was miserable, with freezing rain. The day before she was to leave for Rome she awoke with a cold, her voice hoarse. The doctor was called. Her throat was medicated, but the doctor advised her to delay her journey. 'No, no, I can't do that,' she insisted. She was the first singer to arrive on the subheated rehearsal stage of the Teatro dell'Opera in Rome. While she waited she sat studying the score – one she had sung more times than any other living soprano – until she was joined by the conductor, grey-haired Gabriele Santini, under whose baton in 1954 she had sung *Medea*, also in Rome. 'I was shocked at how shrunken she seemed,' he recalled. 'It was quite chilly and she was wrapped in a thick fur coat, a fur hat pulled down over her ears. Her eyes looked enormous when she removed her glasses. She bounded up to greet me, full of energy as always, and suggested we might go over the cabaletta of "Casta diva".'

Rome was suffering an acutely bitter winter and the management had the temperature in the theatre, where the cast was rehearsing, down so low that all the singers complained. By the next day, with no added heating, several members developed colds. Maria remained bundled up, fortified by large doses of vitamins. Directly after rehearsals she returned to the Quirinale Hotel and went directly to bed. The dress rehearsal was on the afternoon of 31 December and, according to Santini, Maria sang superbly, lightening the cabaletta of 'Casta diva', which gave it a fresher interpretation. She repeated the aria early that evening on live television with equal adeptness.

A quiet evening alone with Battista at the hotel had been planned, but Visconti was in town and asked them to join a small party he had organized at the chic nightclub, Circolo degli Scacchi. Battista promised that he would get her home early and protested that it would be an insult to Visconti to avoid him so openly by refusing his invitation. Maria rested for a while, then dressed and left with Battista at about 10 p.m. for the club. She was photographed by the paparazzi, who always inhabited such celebrity spots, as she drank a glass of champagne to welcome in the new year. They departed some time between one and one thirty in the morning. When they arrived back at the hotel she had an argument with Battista before going to bed. Elsa Maxwell was in Rome and had been at the club, and Maria claimed Battista knew this and had not told her, fearful she would then refuse to go.

She awoke at about 11 a.m. to the frightening discovery that her voice was no more than a hoarse whisper. A throat specialist was found (this being a holiday, not an easy matter) and he medicated her and told her not to talk for the next twenty-four hours. The following morning, which was the day of the first performance, she awoke with some small improvement, but her voice had not fully returned. At Maria's request, Battista rang Carlo Sanpaoli, the artistic director of the Teatro dell'Opera, informed him of this and warned him that they should have a replacement standing by in the event that Maria's voice did not respond to the treatment she was currently taking. Sanpaoli was beyond reasoning. A replacement could not even be considered. This was a much touted, sold-out gala performance. Italy's President Gronchi and his wife were attending. If Maria Callas did not appear, they would have to cancel and return all the money. People had paid higher than usual prices to hear Callas sing Norma. 'No! No! It is impossible! Maria must appear!' Sanpaoli shouted. Battista hung up, defeated. 'You will have to sing,' he told Maria. Much against her will and her better instincts, Maria agreed.

The doctor gave her shots and swabbed her throat throughout the day. About 5 p.m. she tried vocalizing and found that her voice had returned, but she was afraid to try it full-voice. She left early for the theatre, the doctor still in attendance. Sanpaoli came by the dressing room every fifteen minutes or so. His face was flushed, grim. He was a seriously unsettled man. 'There's no way we can cancel!' he kept repeating to the doctor, who had suggested that it would be best for Maria if she did not sing.

Maria finally insisted that Sanpaoli not be allowed into the dressing room. She had a small Madonna above her make-up mirror and while she sat before it, she silently prayed. An hour before the performance she was able to sing full-voice. The doctor consented, albeit reluctantly, that she could sing but strongly advised her 'to be cautious', a pointless warning for a dramatic soprano about to perform the vocally and emotionally draining role of Norma. Maria was helped into her priestly robes, crossed herself before the Madonna and prepared for her entrance.

'Casta diva', in the early part of the first act, is one of the most difficult arias in a dramatic soprano's repertoire. A fine legato is essential. All the pitches have to be exact. The singer is vocally exposed. Norma must dominate the fierce, savage people she serves as priestess. They are readying themselves for war against the Romans and to save her lover, Pollione, the father of her two children, Norma must turn them back and yet keep them appeased. She is frantically fighting for time. As Maria reached the difficult cabaletta in the final section of the aria, her breath grew uneven and she started to push. Suddenly, her voice began to slip away. She continued on as best she could, going through all the motions and emotions that she knew by rote. The audience bristled, but she continued for a short time, finally coming to the terrifying conclusion that it was hopeless. Her voice was gone. Realizing what had happened, Sanpaoli ordered another singer to cover from the wings as Maria mimed. Sanpaoli rushed backstage to her dressing room as soon as Act One ended with calls from the balcony telling her to go back to Milan: 'You've already cost us a million lire!'

Within moments, almost the entire artistic staff had crowded into her dressing room as Maria stood horrified before the Madonna, her back to them, seeing only their reflections in the mirror. 'You can do it! You must continue!' they insisted.

'I have no voice,' she whispered hoarsely.

'Walk through it, then!' someone wildly suggested.

Maria spun on them. 'Nooooo...' she managed in a shaky whisper, pushed them aside and collapsed on a small cot against the far wall of the room. She knew, now, that she had made the gravest error of her career by allowing them to persuade her to sing in the first place and she was not going to humiliate herself further or do permanent damage to her voice. An announcement had to be made that the remainder of the performance would be cancelled. This was done over a loudspeaker just before the start of Act Two, a disastrous piece of public relations. Sanpaoli should have come on stage to make this announcement himself and mitigate the situation by explaining that Callas had been taken ill and, although she had valiantly tried to carry on, she was now too sick to do so.

The audience left the theatre in belligerent mood. Many had seen the photograph of her drinking champagne in a nightclub on New Year's Eve and been told by an exploitative and highly exaggerating press that she had not left the Circolo degli Scacchi until 4 a.m. the next morning. Maria was helped through a private passage of the theatre to a waiting car and taken back to the Hotel Quirinale, the doctor and Battista holding her up on each side as they rode the service elevator to the Meneghinis' suite. Within ten minutes there were shouts and insults outside her windows.

Maria was in a terrible state. 'It's all over,' she cried weakly as the doctor gave her a shot to calm her down.

Despite the fact that the next day the doctor issued a statement that she was suffering from bronchitis and tracheitis, papers around the world declared that Maria Callas had been attending all-night parties, drinking heavily, and so was unable to sing before an expectant audience and the

President of Italy and his wife. Two days later Sanpaoli managed to find a
replacement (Anita Cerquetti) to sing Norma in the remaining four performances, although within a week – with two performances to go – Maria
had regained her voice and offered to swallow her pride and appear.[1] She
returned to Milan, distraught, not understanding how her good intentions had so backfired, to find a kind letter from Mrs Gronchi saying she
hoped her health was improving and that she and the President knew
that she had been taken ill and could in no way continue. There was also
a huge bouquet of flowers with a card from Aristotle Onassis that said, in
effect, that only another Greek as famous as she could understand the
exorbitant price of such fame – and that he wished her a speedy recovery.

Maria was to do a concert in Chicago on 22 January, then sing
Traviata, *Lucia* and *Tosca* 6 February–5 March, with the Metropolitan
Opera. Despite her frail health and the knowledge that her mother (to
whom she had not spoken or written in several years) was presently in
New York, she was anxious to leave Europe and the battering she had
taken from the opera houses in Rome and Milan behind her. But trouble
brewed ahead as well.

During the 'siege of the tapeworm' (as she called it), she had cancelled
an appearance with the San Francisco Opera and they, in turn not accepting her medical documents, had filed a complaint against her with the
American Guild of Musical Artists (AGMA). This meant that if AGMA
found her in default they would either terminate her membership (disal-
lowing further appearances in the United States), or suspend it for a
period and Bing would have no alternative but to cancel her contract,
something he certainly did not want to be forced to do as Callas was his
greatest draw. 'I need not tell you how upsetting this would be,' Bing
wrote to Maria before she was to start on her travel plans, 'not only to our
whole repertory planning but also personally to me. I was looking
[forward] so much to your return and I felt that your next performances
here would be almost more important than those last year.'

Bing's associate, Francis Robinson, met the Meneghinis on their arrival
in New York on 18 January. Two days later Maria appeared before a
twenty-person jury at AGMA headquarters and for two hours answered
questions and presented (through her lawyer) her medical records as

---

[1] Callas would later sue the Rome Opera for non-payment of fees due her according to
her contract. The Rome Opera replied with a counter-suit for an even larger amount to
compensate them for the losses they incurred due to cancellations. The Roman
Supreme Court took fourteen years to hand down the verdict that Callas was genuinely
ill. The theatre's counter-suit was dismissed and in 1971 she was awarded $1600
in lost fees.

evidence that she had been genuinely ill. The jury listened impassively and she returned to the hotel not knowing whether she could sing in either Chicago or with the Metropolitan. The next day she was informed that the case had been dismissed, that although she had been in breach of contract there were the mitigating circumstances of her ill health. Maria flew to Chicago where she sang a brilliant concert on 22 January, returning the following day to New York and rehearsals for *Traviata*. She had regained her self-confidence, but her problems had not ended.

Due to the Metropolitan's heavy schedule there were to be no on-stage rehearsals until the final dress rehearsal. This meant that Maria did not have the time she required to memorize the set and her movements on stage. Also, the Met's *Traviata* had been premièred by Renata Tebaldi at the start of the season and the production had been greatly influenced by her demands – a refusal to do anything other than what she had always done. Maria's Violetta was a far more dramatic woman, edgier, her tragic end making a greater impact because of this. Then there were the sets which were 'cluttered and awkward to navigate without a compass', she complained.

Her mother's presence in the city did not help her state of mind. Litza called the hotel but Maria refused to speak to her. She could not find forgiveness for her mother's betrayal: the scathing, hurtful, mostly untrue interview she had given *Time* magazine, the gist of which she had repeated publicly several times since then.

Litza and George had finally divorced the previous year and she had come to New York for the proceedings and remained, staying with members of the Greek community in New Jersey where, as the mother of Maria Callas, she enjoyed a certain celebrity. Maria had never discontinued her monthly allowance, but neither had she raised it with her greater earning capacity. Litza had gone to work in the jewellery boutique in Manhattan owned by Jolie Gabor, Zsa Zsa's mother. This had proved too exhausting and she turned to her artistic and sewing skills, and bought bisque dolls, painted their faces to resemble Maria and dressed them in the costumes of her principal roles – as Violetta, Tosca, Lucia, Norma and Turandot – selling them at a nice profit at several local gift shops in the Greek communities.

Litza's friends believed she was on good terms with her daughter. She would talk about watching the operas she was appearing in from a box and spending time backstage and at the hotel with her, although Maria never once saw her during this time. Several friends, concerned at how little Litza had to live on, wrote Maria rather nasty letters, in effect urging her to contribute more to her mother's welfare. She did, in fact, instruct her accountant to increase Litza's allowance by $50 a month, but still refused to see her.

Jackie, who had remained in Athens, was appalled that their mother was now selling 'Maria Callas Dolls'. 'In one letter I received a photograph of Mother and in the background were some of the dolls,' Jackie wrote. 'There was this woman who had rejected all the normal expressions of motherhood as she struggled to turn her youngest daughter into a machine to success, yet she was now surrounded by those symbols of sweetness and caring.' It was bizarre. Litza had refused to allow Maria to play with dolls when she was a child, and now 'here she was actually making them. It was hard to believe.'

Maria did see her father many times and even took George with her for a television interview where he was asked questions about his famous daughter while she beamed beside him. 'He was a most encouraging influence,' she said at one point, smiling. No mention was made of her mother's role in her life.

Her appearances with the Metropolitan were a grand success, notably *Tosca*. 'Never had there been such a *Tosca*', Bing recalled. 'Nearly everything she ever did spoiled that opera for me; I never fully enjoyed any other artist in one of her roles after she did it...A few motions of her hand did more to establish a character and an emotion than whole acts of earnest acting by other singers.'

Yet, with all his admiration, his patience was tried by both her demands and those of Meneghini. She still refused to tour with the company and put off signing a contract for the next season that was offered her unless certain 'whims' (Bing's words) were included. That meant full expenses for her husband, no touring, escorts from rehearsals to protect her from the avid press and a private car among them. 'I could not have yielded to her urgently expressed whims and continued to keep the Metropolitan going as an artistic enterprise,' Bing explained and so there was a constant running battle between them.

On 6 March she flew back to Milan, her spirits high due to her success in the States. A compromise was finally reached between herself and Bing, and she signed a contract that included doing a tour in the following season, while Bing agreed to pay Meneghini's expenses up to a certain degree and to create a new production of *Macbeth* for her. In addition she would sing the operas of her choice: *Macbeth*, *Tosca* and *Lucia*. More and more she was looking beyond Milan and La Scala, who had not forgiven her for what they believed was shockingly bad behaviour and disregard of her responsibility to the opera companies 'she had let down'. Both La Scala and the Teatro dell'Opera in Rome were funded by the same state agency and the management of La Scala had received reprimands regarding Maria's 'behaviour'.

Ghiringhelli felt his position was jeopardized and for this he blamed Maria. An arrogant, self-centred man with a vengeful streak, he refused her calls and walked right by her in the Restaurant Biffi without acknowledging her presence. Furious, Maria swore she would never speak to him again. She was scheduled to sing *Anna Bolena* and *Il Pirata* at La Scala in April and May and, despite her injured pride and the poor treatment she had endured from them in recent months, she honoured her contract, refusing to give La Scala the opportunity to say, 'Callas has walked out – as usual.' She believed she was doing the right thing. Therefore 9 April, the first night of *Anna Bolena*, was a crushing experience.

In the square outside the theatre an angry crowd had gathered protesting against her appearance. She had to be brought into the theatre (accompanied by Battista and her maid Bruna) with the protection of armed police. Nowhere else in the world were the opera and its great singers as revered as in Milan. They were held up as gods and goddesses and when they showed feet of clay, or voices that did not stand the test of time, the Milanese opera-goers could become ferocious in their disappointment. As Maria waited for her entrance she suffered terrible anxiety. Would the Milanese audience shout ugly epithets at her, walk out during one of her arias, throw rotten fruit or dead flowers at her feet? Such things had happened to other singers who had fallen out of favour. Battista reported to her in her dressing room that there was a full house and that police had been stationed at the doors in case of any disturbance. This last bit of information upset Maria even further.

It took great courage for her to make her entrance, fearing there might be a claque waiting for that moment to shout at her. However, the audience was silent, seemingly respectful. She put everything she had into her performance and at the curtain was greeted with applause and called back for several bows. But sections of the audience remained seated while others stood and no flowers or tributes were thrown on to the stage. 'It was the most beautifully sung, moving *Anna Bolena* she had ever done – or would do,' Maestro Gavazzeni, her ardent ally at La Scala during this trauma, later said. 'She *was* Anna Bolena, condemned for something of which she was not guilty, facing those who condemned her with inordinate dignity. I was near tears.'

Deeply hurt by the cold treatment of Milan's opera-goers and the management of La Scala, Maria arrived home on the night of her last performance to find the front door and windows of her home smeared with animal faeces, which had also been used to scrawl obscenities. In a state of near hysteria, she refused to enter the house fearing what or whom she might find. Battista went in and called the police, and with Toy and two suitcases the Meneghinis drove that same night down to the small town of Sirmione on Lake Garda where they had only recently bought a summer cottage, Maria clinging to her beloved pet and sobbing intermittently during the length of the journey.

Battista claimed that by the time they had reached their destination, Maria had gained enough control to discuss the immediate future. She was committed to La Scala for one more opera before the season ended: a new role for her – Imogene in Bellini's obscure early opera, *Il Pirata*, which broke away from the florid style of Rossini then in vogue (1835). Ghiringhelli had given her enough provocation to cancel. 'That's exactly what he wants me to do, but I won't give him that satisfaction,' Maria promised. During the time their home in Milan was being cleaned and repainted, the Meneghinis remained on the shore of Lake Garda while Maria taught herself the new role. Seldom sung, the opera had been especially revived for her and the production set in motion the previous year. Preparing for a new role involved a tremendous amount of work. First there was the memorization, then the breakdown of the score followed by concentrated work with a pianist 'to remind you exactly of the value of notes and not let one slip by you'. This she could do in Sirmione. But then she needed to attend the maestro's readings – Antonino Votto under whom she had frequently sung at La Scala and on tour, which meant returning to Milan. 'Finally,' Maria would recall, 'you build the whole thing together – stage, colleagues, orchestra – and eventually you reach the point of performing the opera straight through, which you must do three or four times to measure your strength and learn where you can rest.' There were costume fittings, wig fittings and finally the dress rehearsal. 'Then you must have no less than three days [of rehearsals] before the first performance... After [which] good, solid work starts because then you fill in the blank spots... There's nothing like stage performances in front of an audience to fill in the details.'

As the intense preparation for *Il Pirata* accelerated, Maria was suffering from stomach pains and an inability to evacuate. Severe haemorrhoids were diagnosed and an operation recommended. 'I have no time,' Maria countered. Despite her discomfort, Maria never missed a fitting or a rehearsal and she kept her physical problem to herself. She was looking frail and Votto was greatly worried that the pressures before her would be too much. The doctor warned her that she could damage her health further if she did not attend to the current crisis. 'Maria Callas is not allowed to miss a performance,' she insisted wistfully.

She was given much support by Votto, Franco Corelli, the pirate of the opera's title and by Ettore Bastianini – who sang the role of Imogene's deceived husband, Ernesto – who did not know how much pain she was suffering but felt she was not well. Her determination drove her on. Battista later wrote that she returned home late each night after rehearsals in an extreme state of exhaustion and discomfort, crawled into bed with Toy stretched out beside her and studied the score for at least an hour more before finally turning off her light. Then, when breakfast was brought to her the next morning, she would be sitting up in bed, going over it once more.

Il Pirata opened on 19 May for five performances. Maria's interpretation of Imogene was gripping. She had an understanding of the woman she was portraying. But not until the opera's final dramatic scene did she gain full control of her voice in a wrenching aria where Imogene anticipates the death of her lover, Gualtiero, the pirate. Then she stunned the audience as she moved commandingly into the searing and vocally difficult cabaletta finale in which Imogene has a vision of the scaffold on which the pirate is to be hung. 'There behold the disastrous scaffold!' she sang in Italian ending on the word *palco*, which ironically means both a scaffold and a theatre box. With fire in her eyes and venom in her voice, she gestured meaningfully at Ghiringhelli's darkened, empty private box. This she did in each performance (her voice gaining strength daily), to the growing cheers, shouts and clamouring of the audience, whom she had won back and who were now anxious that they might never hear her sing at La Scala again.

The next morning she awoke doubled over with pain and was taken to hospital in a private car and operated upon for her rectal condition. On Sunday, 22 May, just two days after surgery, she sang the second performance of *Il Pirata*. That Wednesday and Saturday she sang again. Only her doctor and a few close friends knew she had had surgery so recently. Miraculously, her voice had grown stronger at each performance, which she ended, as she had the first night, with her venomous gesture towards Ghiringhelli's empty box.

Ghiringhelli waited until the final performance on 31 May to get his revenge. The audience rose in tumultuous ovation as Maria came out for her first curtain and called her back repeatedly, their excitement seeming to grow and not diminish, their past hostility to have vanished. Suddenly, as she took her sixth bow, Scala's massive fire curtain was dropped so sharply, separating Maria from the audience, that she stood too startled to move for a few moments and Corelli came rushing to her to make sure she had not been hurt.

When she left the theatre a short time later, flowers were strewn across her path. People were shouting, 'Viva la Divina!' Some were weeping. 'Don't leave Milan!'

'I shall never sing at La Scala again as long as Ghiringhelli is its manager,' Maria vowed as she got into her waiting car with a solicitous Battista at her elbow. She felt she was at the lowest ebb in her career, but she was hardly out of those shallow seas. More trouble and humiliation lay in wait for her before the tides would change and her life steered into uncharted waters by that other 'most famous Greek'.

15

The Other Greek

S ELDOM DID MARIA travel without Battista. She had, however, been invited to sing at Covent Garden's Centenary Gala in the presence of Queen Elizabeth and Prince Philip on 10 June 1958, and Battista was busy in Milan working out her schedule for the coming season. With her maid and confidante, Bruna (who was as close as a member of her family), Maria flew to London where she had a suite at the Savoy Hotel. Battista was to join her in a few days' time. Bruna was only a few years older than Maria, yet she presented a somewhat maternal figure, still able to observe the line between servant and mistress. She asked for no special consideration and, whatever the hour, was at Maria's side when summoned. Maria trusted her as she did no one else.

Maria had numerous friends in London, including Lord and Lady Harewood, whom she visited in their beautiful home in Orme Square. Lord Harewood is the Queen's cousin, George Lascelles. His mother was King George VI's only sister, Mary, the Princess Royal. Harewood is one member of the royal family who has made a career for himself outside 'The Firm' (as Prince Philip described the family's position as Great Britain's public relations representatives at home and abroad). As a young officer in the 3rd Battalion of the Grenadiers in Italy during the Second World War, Harewood was seriously injured, taken prisoner and moved to Colditz (known as 'the punishment camp') as soon as he was released from hospital – in a sense being held as a royal hostage until Germany's collapse. A good-looking man, with strong personal opinions, artistic, intelligent, Harewood had fallen in love with opera from an early age and had founded, with Harold Rosenthal, *Opera* magazine and at Covent Garden was controller of opera planning. His wife Marion (whom he would later divorce) was too 'full of herself' to please Maria, but she was extremely fond of Harewood and trusted his opinions.

Also in London for a brief few days was Aristotle Onassis who kept a

luxurious suite of rooms at Claridge's Hotel. Ari and Tina seldom travelled together any more and, although he adored his two children and
smothered them with expensive gifts, he chose not to be with them most
of the time. He kept hotel suites, apartments, homes all over the world
and would often hop off in his private plane for a day or two, or a month.
But even when his children were with him on the *Christina* (named for
his young daughter), he might not see them for days as he remained in
his office on board, or entertained his adult guests, while his children
were confined mostly to their lavish, toy-filled nursery quarters.

Most of Onassis's life was spent making deals. His transactions sometimes forced him to take on whole countries – as was the situation with
his current relationship to Monaco where he kept the *Christina* docked
and where he had reached the pinnacle of power, a position that created
a corrosive relationship between Onassis and the small principality's
Prince Rainier. Onassis was the head of a massive financial empire that
included, along with his shipbuilding business, vast interests in real
estate, air travel, offshore oil rigs and all they produced, and a long list of
impressive, if less involving, investments. Fidelity was to him a very un-
Greek concept. He was a man of strong appetites and a beautiful, willing
woman was as important to him as insulin to a diabetic. Yet he tried to be
discreet and always prided himself on his respect for women – and his
generosity to them. He was not alone at Claridge's, but when Lord
Harewood invited him to join a small dinner party he and Marion were
hosting at home, he accepted. On learning that Maria Callas was to be
there, he came without his London companion.

Maria and Onassis had not seen each other since the ball and the
buffet aboard the *Christina* in Venice. If Maria was unnerved or affected
by his presence at what was a rather intimate gathering, she gave
no outward sign. But it was clear to others that his interest in her was
quite intense. She had to leave early as the gala concert was the following
night and she had a rehearsal the next day. Onassis insisted on escorting
her back to the Savoy in his car. The next day he left London on
business, without attending the gala, but he did send Maria an extravagant floral tribute of red roses with a card that said simply 'The Other
Greek'.

The gala had stirred up much excitement and received great press
attention. So many stars were appearing that Covent Garden did not
have sufficient appropriate dressing rooms for all of them. Lord
Harewood had solved the crisis by converting his commodious private
office into a changing area for Maria by removing his desk and installing
a dressing table. A French chaise and a Japanese screen were appropriated

from the props department and vases were filled with lush arrangements made by Constance Spry, London's premier florist.

Along with Maria, the dazzling list of performers included ballet stars Dame Margot Fonteyn and Michael Soames, the great Canadian tenor Jon Vickers (who was scheduled to sing opposite Maria in *Medea* in Dallas that autumn), mezzo Blanche Thebom, Joan Sutherland and the leading singers of the Royal Opera. 'As was so often the case [with such star-filled galas],' Sutherland recalled, 'there were too many items on the programme. The result was last-minute cutting, and I remember being rather "miffed", to put it mildly, that the duet from *The Bohemian Girl* which I was to sing with John Lanigan, another Australian stalwart in the company, was drastically cut, including a long cadenza, whilst Maria Callas sang the whole of a very slow Mad Scene from *I Puritani*.' Sutherland had only recently come into her own and was rapidly gaining stature as the soprano who was well on her way to the kind of divahood that Maria (and, to some extent, Renata Tebaldi) enjoyed, which fostered a growing sense of competition between them. It did not help Maria's view that the Royal Opera was mounting a new production for Sutherland of *Lucia di Lammermoor* with her revered maestro, Tullio Serafin, conducting and Franco Zeffirelli doing the sets and costumes.

The gala was a huge success. Maria 'held the audience spellbound in an example of consummate operatic singing and acting', one critic wrote. Afterwards Maria and the rest of the performers lined up for the usual presentation to the royal couple. She looked spectacular in a black, form-fitting sequin gown. 'Prince Philip looked me up and down as though he were undressing me!' she told Lord and Lady Harewood later at a small supper party.

Battista soon joined her in London where, ten days later, she sang Violetta at Covent Garden for five performances of *La Traviata*. Although her voice was not at its best, her Violetta, Peter Heyworth wrote in the *Observer*, 'represents a great interpretation, conceived as an organic whole, such as only comes our way very, very rarely…It was a performance of outstanding distinction and musicality, full of detail that again and again illuminated the part as if for the first time.'

To her delight, Maria had a three-month stretch before her with no engagements. After the summer she would return to the States for an arduous American schedule that included Birmingham, Atlanta and Dallas and then in December, a concert at the Paris Opéra. She had still not fully recovered from the emotional season at La Scala or from her surgery and physical setback. She and Battista went almost directly to Sirmione, first collecting Toy in Milan.

A sun worshipper, Maria claimed its warmth brought out her joy at being alive. If the day wasn't unbearably humid, she could remain stretched out by the pool, greased, as she said, 'like a Greek olive', jumping into the cool water from time to time where she would splash around like a waterwheel, arms whirling, legs kicking, tire herself out and then return to her lounge. Lunches were served alfresco. Bruna, who travelled with her, fed and pampered her well. Toy was never far away and often joined her in the pool, while Battista commuted between Sirmione, Milan and Verona.

Her summer was not as idyllic as she would have wished. Battista, whose English had never improved and who never wrote one letter or sent off a single telegram without a flurry of others quibbling their way across the ocean, had not come to an agreement with Bing and the Met for the following season. When he was in Sirmione there were endless discussions with Maria that were continued in his calls when he was away. More and more, as Maria was faced with Battista's inadequacy as an agent and manager, she insisted on outside representation. Her British scheduling and contractual arrangements had been taken over by Sander Gorlinsky, who had first entered her life in 1952 when she made her debut at Covent Garden in *Norma*. Gorlinsky was the most powerful impresario and manager of opera and ballet artists in Great Britain. His international counterpart, the fabled Sol Hurok, handled all her appearances outside Italy except for the Metropolitan: those Battista refused to relinquish.

At the heart of Battista's running battle with Bing and the Met were the lack of new productions for Maria and their insistence that she tour with the company for seven weeks after the close of the season. Battista was carrying out Maria's own wishes and his stand was perfectly legitimate, and Bing was fully aware of this. 'Miss Callas was an ordinary rather than an extraordinary artist,' he wrote in his autobiography. 'She fought against the tour. It was always difficult for me to get commitments from foreign artists to extend their American stay – or return to the United States through the month of May [when touring ended]...I was often asking artists to take, for the privilege of touring with the Metropolitan, fees lower than they could earn by staying home.' As Birgit Nilsson wrote in 1959 [as she was preparing for her Metropolitan debut], 'I am quite well-informed about your seven weeks' tour...I find that it is impossible to accept your offer...I am afraid it would be too hard a job, and a fee of 1500 dollars does not at all cover what I can get for that time from other companies.'

Bing also had problems obtaining the services of the Metropolitan's top conductors. Nor could he bring the theatrical values of the Met's best productions to regional theatres, which were not equipped to handle solid sets. Therefore special inexpensive 'tour sets', painted drops that could be hung as backdrops, were deployed. 'All we had to offer out of town were singers of Metropolitan caliber,' Bing admitted. Whom the opera-goers in tour cities *most* wanted to see at this time was Maria Callas and they were willing to pay any price even to see her in a pinch-penny production. If Maria would do the tour, the Metropolitan would at least break even. Without her they would suffer a loss. Bing offered her more than any of the Met's other singers, but she did not feel she had an obligation to the Metropolitan to sing in less than good conditions to help them with their financial problems.

When this situation finally reached an impasse, the true picture was never presented to the press who were made to believe that once again Maria Callas was acting the prima donna at the expense of a company who had fostered her career. None of this would have occurred if Battista had not waffled on the issue for over a year, which gave Bing the impression that he could, with some concessions, win Maria to his side. Therefore he falsely led the tour cities to believe that it would all be worked out and they would have Maria Callas. By the time he received her final refusal, replacing her with another singer of at least near-magnitude was an impossibility as these artists all had their schedules laid out far in advance.

Other issues were at stake besides the choice of material and the poor quality of the touring productions. Maria was concerned that unless she could work under optimum conditions with a fine conductor and director, and had time to prepare properly, she would compromise herself and possibly not give her best performance. There were many critics ready to pounce on any mis-step she took, to carp on the lack of beauty her tone might evince, a note she might have had a problem reaching. It was always that way when one was as famous as she. Expectations were high, any wavering from that standard – even momentarily – was not acceptable. And the truth was that Maria's own expectations were as high as her critics'.

However, money also played a major role in the stand-off with the Metropolitan. There had always been fractious relations between Bing and Battista, whose financial greed knew no bounds. With the sky-rocketing success of his wife, Battista had become very rich and no longer dependent on his family's business interests. All the money Maria earned after expenses and taxes was placed in a separate Milan bank account. Maria was then given an allowance for her personal expenses. Battista insisted this separation of monies was for tax purposes and necessary, and she – preferring to concentrate on her art – accepted the situation (a natural one for Italy, where husbands control their wives' money).

For her American tour and her appearance in Dallas, Sol Hurok had negotiated the highest fees Maria had yet to receive and Battista saw the proposed Metropolitan tour as a large loss in fantastic future income. 'It was necessary to exasperate [Bing] to such a degree that he would cancel the contract himself,' he later confessed. 'Bing could not stand the sight of me. He had described me as greedy and grasping and that money was only important to me. You can see how annoyed the "Prussian corporal" [Meneghini's name for Bing] would be if I outwitted him.'[1] He also told Stelios Galotopoulos that it was he, never Maria, who dealt with financial matters or demanded exorbitant fees. He fully admitted doing so 'as this was necessary for her fame as the world's premier opera singer'.

The multi-city tour that Sol Hurok had organized for Maria was of an entirely different calibre from what Bing and the Metropolitan were offering. The Russian-born Hurok was an impresario in the grand style. He believed in giving his stars the best of everything both on stage and off while they were under his auspices. He paid unflinchingly for Maria to be able to travel with Toy (and with Bruna). Battista's expenses were not in contention (although there were limits). She had the use of a car and driver, a comfortable suite (always stocked with champagne and abundant floral displays) and, more important, the best people that could be found to support her. The trade-off was a star who was happy and who would shimmer on stage, so that no one felt cheated at the high price they had paid for their ticket. Maria herself was receiving nearly triple the fee that she would have from the Metropolitan.

Maria was very pleased with the schedule and plans for Hurok's American tour, which would kick off in concert form in Birmingham, Alabama on 11 October and continue on to Atlanta, Montreal and Toronto before she arrived in Dallas to sing *Traviata* on 31 October and 2 November, and *Medea* on 6 and 8 November. From Dallas, she went to Cleveland, Detroit, Washington DC and San Francisco, singing the same concert as in her earlier appearances, then return to Milan.

---

[1] The contest between Bing and Battista over money had been an ongoing one. Battista proudly recounts the following anecdote in his memoir regarding his demand that Bing pay Maria in cash before a performance:

'I heard he was planning to play a trick on me ['the Miser' Bing called him]. When I came to his office before curtain he would hand me a huge stack of one dollar bills. "Fine," I said. "Then I shall make myself comfortable and forbid Maria to begin the performance before I finish counting all that paper twice!"'

Battista made sure that Bing was told this and, at the pre-performance meeting, was paid as usual in large bills.

Just before her 6 November appearance in *Medea*, Bing issued his famous statement that he was firing Maria Callas and that her contract with the Metropolitan was cancelled forthwith. BING FIRES CALLAS! were the banner headlines in the press. 'Madame Callas is constitutionally unable to fit into any organization not tailored to her own personality,' he added.

'When I think of those lousy *Traviatas* he made me sing without rehearsals, without even knowing my partners,' Maria countered to the press. 'Is that Art?...and other times, all those performances with a different tenor or a different baritone every time...Is that Art?'

Back came Bing: 'I do not propose to enter into a public feud with Madame Callas since I am well aware that she has considerably greater competence and experience at that kind of thing than I have.'

Maria did not reply to Bing's waspish words. Her answer was contained in her magnificent performance of *Medea* that evening. To listen to the tape of that performance provides little doubt but that Bing's venom seared through Maria, firing the vitriol in her voice (directed as much towards Bing as to Jason), when Jason, here sung by the great Jon Vickers, deserts Medea. Maria had sung many Medeas, had, in fact, given the Cherubini opera a new lease of life when she sang it at the Florence Festival in 1953. But this, her first Medea in America, was the greatest of her career.

She was instrumental in the choice of the artists working with her. What she wanted was an 'authentic style of classicism' in the production, *Medea* being a classic Greek myth about the sorceress who helps Jason to win the Golden Fleece and, when deserted by him, kills his two children and his new wife. The legend was realized with the brilliant vision of the director Alexis Minotis, the eminent actor-producer from the Greek National Theatre who was married to Greece's leading tragedienne, Katrina Paxinou, and by Yannis Tsarouchis who designed the sets and costumes (the latter made from Greek fabrics). Her old friend and colleague, Nicola Rescigno, wielded the baton and, besides the incomparable Vickers, there was the rich-voiced mezzo-soprano Teresa Berganza (as Neris) in her American debut and the bass Nicola Zacarria (Creon) who had once attended the Athens Conservatory with Maria and with whom she had frequently sung.

Medea requires a wide, emotional range and Maria did not disappoint. From her searing entrance, to her anguish and torment, the restrained pitiableness as she begs Creon for just one more day before her exile, to the stalking lioness she becomes in the second act, Maria was astonishing. Vocally, she had no problem with the many top B-flats and Bs, or with an added high C at the end of that act. There was one moment in the recitative when the words slipped away from her and there followed an instant or two of awkward silence. But she came back quickly without losing her control.

Maria's Medea was a sensation and the remainder of the tour an outstanding success. Bing had won a pyrrhic victory. He had not given in to Maria Callas, but the Metropolitan suffered a great artistic and financial loss with her departure from the company. When she returned to Milan in early December she was faced with a more personal dilemma. She had called one of their accountants and asked for a rather modest sum to be transferred to her private account from their business account as she was having some new gowns made and was told that there were not enough funds to cover. Maria was shocked and puzzled. After some emotional questioning, she unearthed the unsettling fact that Battista had transferred almost all the funds from the Milan account to a private account he kept in Verona, of which she had no previous knowledge and on which she could not draw. There followed a terrible row with Battista who admitted the transfer, investments made in his name and rather large sums dispersed to members of his family.

Maria was devastated. Any trust left in Battista was shattered. She now made calls to several of her foreign agents and insisted that cheques no longer be made payable to Battista, but should be in her name only. Battista did not accept this easily or casually. His Italian pride – and his money flow – had been seriously damaged. The two wore brave faces in public but their relationship had been irreparably compromised. With heavy heart, Maria – joined by a brooding Battista – departed for Paris where, on 19 December, she would make her long-awaited debut at a gala concert at L'Opéra before René Coty, the President of France, the proceeds being donated to the Légion d'honneur. Maria was being paid $10,000, which she was also contributing to the cause. Some of international society's most monied and famous members had paid the highest ticket price ever charged by L'Opéra for the opportunity to hear Maria Callas sing, among them the Duke and Duchess of Windsor, Emile de Rothschild, Prince Aly Khan and the fashion model Bettina (Simone Bodin, his mistress), Charles and Oona O'Neill Chaplin, Jean Cocteau, a long list of foreign royalty, élite members of the American and French film colonies, luminaries from the opera, music and art worlds, business tycoons – and Aristotle and Tina Onassis.

The year 1958 had not been an easy one for Onassis. In June he had been called before a Congressional Committee in Washington who were investigating his shipping record in the United States, which the committee believed was suspect. Their main concern was that Onassis had defaulted on his obligations to the United States government and the shipping industry by manipulating transfers of registered ships through his children's trust funds to a Liberian company, thereby avoiding tax levies and the necessity of hiring American seamen whose wage scale was considerably higher than other countries'. On the evening after the hearing the committee counsel declared, 'Onassis was the best goddam witness we've ever had before this committee.' Onassis had lost the battle but won the war. To ship from and to the United States, his shipbuilding contracts with Bethlehem Steel had to be honoured, but he was also ordered to pay $14 million towards the cost of construction, greatly depreciating his profit.

He had been brilliant in his all-day session on the witness stand, bandying thrusts with Herbert Zelenko, a tough, adversarial liberal Democrat from New York. But Onassis had studied well for this appearance and could not be flustered.

Power was what Onassis sought more of, for he was already one of the richest men in the world. In 1951 he had anchored his old yacht, *Olympic Winner*, in the harbour at Monte Carlo and within seven years had the controlling interest in SBM (Société des Bains der Mer), the financial establishment that held the deeds on most of the principality of Monaco's prime real estate, giving Onassis almost as much power as its monarch, Prince Rainier.[2] During the last few months of 1958, the two men were preparing for a final showdown and it had all the elements of the shoot-out in a Hollywood Western. These were two men who knew they could not coexist in the same town: one a stranger – the dangerous foreigner – the other the 'boss' of the invaded territory. It seemed that Onassis had the upper hand and that he was about to step over the line where Rainier would have to answer to him. All these power moves had taken a great deal of Onassis's energy, which was a good part of the reason he had not pressed his attentions on Maria at an earlier time. He also had been having an affair with an American socialite and old friend of his wife's, the very attractive Jeanne Rhinelander.

[2] The real estate owned by the SBM and controlled by Onassis at this time included the Hôtel de Paris, the Hermitage Hôtel and the Monte Carlo Beach Hôtel (the three largest and most luxurious in Monaco), the two Sporting Clubs, Winter and Summer, the Country Club and the spectacular golf course on the crest of Mont Agel. Then there were the Café de Paris, numerous villas, gardens and tourist attractions. He was now planning to take over the Casino and to expand the harbour to accommodate ocean-going liners on luxury cruises. He also controlled the Olympic Maritime in Monte Carlo where over one hundred of his employees monitored the movements of his ships worldwide.

Simultaneously, Tina's romance with the much younger Renaldito Herrera was common knowledge and they were often photographed together in places where Onassis was not and at parties which he did not attend.

The Onassises' marriage was quickly disintegrating, with separations between himself and Tina of more frequent and long duration. They were staying together mostly for 'the children's sake' and because marriage was a safe harbour for Onassis against any demands for a more permanent arrangement by one of his mistresses.

However, Onassis's interest in women to this juncture was mainly sexual. He held them in high regard and treated them well. But he retained his true friendship and admiration for one man, Sir Winston Churchill. In the summer of 1958, Churchill and his wife Clementine were holidaying in the South of France and accepted an invitation from Onassis to lunch with him at the Hôtel de Paris. This was followed a few days later by a leisurely lunch on the *Christina*, which was anchored in the harbour of Monte Carlo. Thus began a remarkable friendship that lasted until Churchill's death seven years later.

Onassis had a true affection for Churchill. One of his closest colleagues, Costa Gratsos, believed that the key to the relationship was 'Onassis's rooted belief in the hegemony of the Anglo-Saxon races. He thought the system created by the British and the Americans at the end of the war would last for ever – and he revered Winston as the embodiment of that system.' He also basked in the exalted company that generally surrounded the Churchills. 'They are people of *real* class,' he told a friend. By the end of the summer of 1958, the Churchills had cruised with Onassis and Tina on the *Christina*, and 'a constant flow of distinguished visitors passed through to pay their respects'. There had also been a treasured weekend invitation to Chartwell, the Churchills' estate in Kent.

As Christmas approached, Tina announced that she would be spending the holidays with her sister in New York. Before then, on 19 December, they would attend the concert and grand gala at which Maria Callas was to sing. Tina knew Ari had no great love for opera and was expecting that he might back out of going. On the contrary, he was most enthusiastic. She knew her husband very well and suspected his interest in Maria Callas was different from that he had shown in so many other women. This was confirmed as the day of the gala approached, for he displayed unusual interest in all the press coverage. 'She is a remarkable woman,' he told his wife. 'Truly remarkable.' And he wore a smile that she equated with 'the look of a lion about to come face to face with his prey'.

Maria and Battista occupied a magnificent suite at the elegant Hôtel Crillon on the Place de la Concorde. On the morning of the concert, Maria rehearsed on the vast stage of L'Opéra with the Hungarian maestro, George Sebastian, the chief conductor with the Paris Opéra. In the first half of the concert she would sing arias from *Norma*, *Il Trovatore* and *Il Barbiere de Siviglia*, and then be joined for the complete second act of *Tosca* by Tito Gobbi as Scarpia and Albert Lance as Cavaradossi. The day was clouded, rain-threatening, a dampness penetrating the air. Maria returned to the hotel at about 2 p.m. to find the suite, fire going in the sitting-room hearth, filled with massive floral bouquets. The most impressive were two large baskets containing several dozen red roses. 'No card?' she asked Battista.

'No card,' he replied, annoyance creasing his jowly face.

'Is something the matter?' she enquired.

'No card. Perhaps an admirer?'

'Perhaps,' she snapped and went into the bedroom to change her clothes.

Just before they were to leave for the L'Opéra that evening, an identical basket arrived. This time it had a card with a message written in Greek. But again no signature. Maria immediately recognized the handwriting. 'Onassis.' She smiled. 'How romantic he is!' Only later did Battista recall the somewhat wistful tone in her voice as she said those few words.

16

Aboard the *Christina*

To be in the audience when Maria Callas sang overshadowed the impact of hearing her on record, for she simply commanded a stage. On the night of the Paris gala concert the power of her presence was almost overwhelming and this did not go unnoticed by Onassis. Maria held sway over an audience as no one he had ever seen before – even Eva Perón, as he told a close confidant, adding, 'If Madame Callas had chosen the arena of politics instead of the limited stage of opera, she might now be one of the most powerful women in the world.' For Onassis, power was a tremendous aphrodisiac and, as Maria stood centre stage in Garnier's rococo opera house (the painted ceiling backed up by florid frescoes along the walls, and gilded statues of Nubian slaves brandishing massive candelabra), some of international society's most famous faces a blur before her eyes, one could actually feel the aura of regality that she exuded.

On stage, Maria appeared taller than her actual height, a concept that was bolstered by the thick crown of hair that was coiffed back from her dramatic face, the front swept up from her forehead with considerable elevation. The affecting use of her hands and the expressiveness of her huge, kohl-rimmed eyes were mesmerizing. Like Sarah Bernhardt, the tempestuous Frenchwoman considered to be the greatest actress who ever lived and the theatre personality she most resembled in her ability to enthral an audience, Maria also had the uncanny faculty of seeming to become the character she was portraying while retaining her own personality. It was not mere coincidence that Bernhardt had originated many of Callas's most famous roles – Tosca, the Lady of the Camellias (Violetta), Medea and Lady Macbeth, to name just four. (There were even those who claimed that since Bernhardt had died only a few days before Maria's birth, she had been imbued with the divine Sarah's spirit.)

For the occasion of this special gala she wore a magnificent gown in her favourite deep shade of cardinal red. Round her neck was a diamond necklace (valued at $100,000, loaned to her by Van Cleef and Arpel. Diamonds (her own) also glittered on her ear lobes. She sang well in the first part of the concert but it was in the last half, in the staged performance of the second act of *Tosca*, especially in her scene with Scarpia (beautifully sung by Tito Gobbi) that she was at her most compelling.

At the end of the concert the esteemed audience rose to its feet shouting their 'Bravas!'. Onassis looked in wonder about him. He was not fond of opera, but he recognized genius and admired the power such genius had over people. If he was intrigued by Maria before this evening, he was now strongly drawn to her, or perhaps to the seductive idea of possessing someone who also had power and a charismatic personality. Onassis was a user of people and the women who had been important in his life were no exception. He had married Tina to have a hold over her father, Stavros Livanos, one of his chief competitors in the shipbuilding business. Before Tina, there had been his long-time mistress, Ingeborg Dedichen, whose father was among Norway's leading shipowners. But Onassis no longer needed the kind of referred power these liaisons brought him. Now he was working on his image. A 'king' must have a suitable 'queen' and Maria had the look and the magnetism that fitted that requirement. She was also 'news' and as such would draw greater attention to him.

It helped that he found Maria sexually attractive and believed, even in this early stage of their relationship, that her passion could match and kindle his. Her great talent as an opera singer had small effect on him, while her fame aroused him. He was, in fact, later to tell her, 'Opera sounds strange to my ear. But there's something mystic about you when you're on stage. There is no way to explain what you do except to attribute it to some god. You are inimitable, something amazing. No wonder they call you la Divina!' Many rich men collected valuable art or fine antiques. Onassis acquired exceptional people to bolster his image and his self-esteem. Maria was his new obsession.

Following the concert there was a reception and dinner dance for 450 members of the audience who had paid four times the normal ticket price to attend. Onassis commanded his way to Maria's side. As he took her hand to kiss it in his usual continental manner, Maria was later to comment, 'Our hands, the textures of our skin, [were] so pleasing to each other's touch.' (Ingeborg Dedichen once had said of Onassis, 'Ari's skin had a smell, a warmth, a softness that fascinated me.') There is little doubt that Maria and Onassis were strongly attracted to each other. With his prodigious and heated sexual past, Onassis had found that married mistresses (of whom there had been many) were the least troublesome.

Such 'arrangements' were not unusual in the circles in which he socialized and his own marital situation could not be damaged more than it
was at this time (or so it seemed). While for Maria red flags flashed
dangerously.

Her relationship with Visconti had never threatened her marriage, nor
had the paparazzi made anything of it because they were aware of his
sexual proclivities and assumed theirs was no more than a close professional friendship. Yes, her marriage was floundering, her feelings for
Battista had changed. But Maria had a tremendous fear of having to live
alone. Almost always there had been someone on whom to lean – her
mother, then Battista and, for the short time in New York, where she had
been mostly on her own (although her father had been a presence) the
Bagarozys. Despite the indisputable fact that all these 'props' had been
disastrous, she still was not sure she could manage by herself. She also
had to deal with her personal insecurity and the small assurance that
being married gave her, and guilt – for Battista was a Roman Catholic, a
faith she had taken upon marrying him in which divorce was not accepted. With all these hurdles to jump, there was the knowledge that Onassis
himself was married, that they were both 'news' and, with his history of
flagrant womanizing, their alliance could only end up a scandal costing
everyone involved a good deal of unhappiness and, perhaps, her
marriage and career.

So when Battista mentioned (much impressed and with great enthusiasm) that Onassis had suggested they join Tina and himself later in the
year on a cruise, Maria replied with an immediate and decisive, 'No, no,
no!'

'Why?' she was asked. 'It would be a good vacation and he will have
very important people also as his guests.'

'No,' she repeated and Battista shrugged his shoulders, but did not
entirely give up persuading her.

Shortly after the New Year they left for the States, where Maria, under
the auspices of Sol Hurok, sang three concerts – the Academy of Music,
Philadelphia; Carnegie Hall, New York City; ending on 29 January (1959)
at Constitutional Hall, Washington DC – after which they returned to
Milan, where she had a two-month span before her next engagement and
six additional concerts in Madrid, Barcelona, Hamburg, Stuttgart,
Munich and Wiesbaden. What Maria now realized was that it was easier
to live with Battista while on tour where they had very little private time
together than it was in Milan or Sirmione and when they received an
invitation to the Contessa Castelbarco's annual Venice ball, on 29 March,
she did not have to be goaded into accepting. It seems doubtful that she

did not know that Tina and Ari would also be among the Contessa's guests.

The Onassises, after a stormy few months with Ari on protracted business trips, reunited just a short time before the Contessa's gala event. Together, and with a stellar cast of guests of their own, they arrived in Venice on the *Christina*, anchoring the yacht at the mouth of the Grand Canal. Tina appeared happy as she entered the Palazzo Castelbarco on her husband's arm, bedecked with jewels he had presented to her as reconciliation gifts – a diamond and ruby necklace and an antique Russian bracelet in the form of a flexible snake studded with diamonds and rubies that wound in three coils up her forearm.

As soon as Onassis sighted Maria he moved swiftly through the many gathered groups to her side. She was at that moment standing apart from Battista, engaged in conversation with several people. He interrupted, took her hand, kissed it and then, with a cursory apology to the others, led her to a corner of the large room and sat her down on a banquette. Tina, Battista later noted, had been 'acutely aware of her husband's glance tracking the diva around the crowded ballroom' and as soon as she was able made her way to where the couple were huddled, joined almost simultaneously by Battista. There was a short social exchange. Onassis invited the Meneghinis for a proposed cruise in the Mediterranean in June. 'Yes, do join us,' Tina added graciously. Maria explained that she was singing five performances of *Medea* in June at Covent Garden and did not see how she could commit herself to a cruise.

'Medea?' Onassis asked with interest (feigned or otherwise). 'A Greek story, after all! We shall arrange the cruise a little later and that way Tina and I can be at Covent Garden.' Tina did not look overly thrilled at this plan but politely agreed. Battista was most enthusiastic.

'I don't know,' Maria hedged. 'Can I let you know later?'

'Of course.' Tina smiled uncomfortably. Except for the instance when she had found her husband in flagrante delicto with Mrs Rhinelander, she had not taken his womanizing too seriously. Power and money were his dual mistresses, his pursuit of them the two seductresses in his life. But she was genuinely suspicious about Maria. 'He talks about her too much; he never talked about the others,' she confided to a friend.

The morning after the Contessa's ball, the Meneghinis left Venice for Madrid where Maria was to appear at the Teatro del Zarzuela before continuing on to her string of other concerts, for which she was being highly paid. 'If Battista thinks he's getting hold of this money, he has a surprise in store,' she told a confidante, for she had arranged for all her fees from this series of concerts to be paid privately to her. There were red roses from Onassis delivered to her dressing room before all the concerts, each with a note reinforcing his wish that she and her husband accept his invitation for the *Christina* cruise. When the Meneghinis returned to Milan on 25 May, a telegram awaited them. Ari and Tina were hosting a party for 150 people at the Dorchester Hotel after her first performance of *Medea*, which they had learned would be the first time the opera had been presented at Covent Garden in over a hundred years. They hoped she would be the guest of honour – and perhaps could help them to secure some of the many tickets they needed, price being no object.

Battista immediately set to work to oblige. He still did not realize that Aristotle Onassis was on the scent of his wife. Had he done so, he would have agreed with her not to encourage his friendship or accept his hospitality. All Battista could see was the fame, the great wealth, the power that Onassis wielded. 'They say that Sir Winston Churchill is his closest friend!' he told Maria. 'And he has said that if we go on this cruise with them [Tina and Ari], he will see that Churchill and his wife are among the guests!'

Maria still refused to accept the invitation for the cruise but saw no way to decline the Dorchester party without being insulting. A party with 150 people sounded safe enough – a long cruise on the private yacht of a man she found sexually exciting was quite another matter. For Maria had been unsettled by her reaction at seeing Onassis in Venice. She was, she feared, falling in love and she wanted to stop things before they accelerated faster than she could deal with them.

On the day of the first performance of *Medea*, Maria received several opulent baskets of red roses from Onassis, two with his signature and one from 'Tina and Ari'. He arrived at Covent Garden forty-five minutes before curtain (Tina followed a half-hour later) and sat in Covent Garden's Crush Bar dispensing tickets and Dom Perignon to his guests as they filed in. 'He was in a particularly ebullient mood,' one guest recalled. 'For a man who often said that opera bored him, he had the contrary appearance of someone about to attend his own coronation.'

However, what his current acquaintances, business partners and close friends did not know was that Onassis's first grand passion, before Ingeborg Dedichen and at the age of twenty-three, had been the world-acclaimed Italian soprano Claudia Muzio, whom he had met shortly after he arrived in Buenos Aires, one of the thousands of impoverished refugees from the eastern fringe of Europe. Soon he was living a double life – as a switchboard operator on a business exchange and, with the money he made on deals he picked up by listening in to conversations, as something of a man around town, using the few hundred dollars he made in a fast deal to buy smart clothes. His long-time business associate Costa Gratsos has said, '[Onassis] had an instinct for knowing the image best calculated to impress a particular person, a particular group...he invented the multiple personality; it made him a hard fellow to unravel.'

The young Onassis, street-smart and far-sighted about the importance of self-promotion, knew he had to raise his image if he wanted to succeed as an entrepreneur. Muzio was singing Mimì in *La Bohème* at the Teatro Colón and her picture appeared in the newspaper at parties with some of the city's most influential men: bankers and rich, international merchants and financiers who might be inclined to invest in a sharp young man like himself. Muzio, although eleven years his senior, was a striking, robust woman; her dark Mediterranean colouring and her large expressive eyes memorable. For a week Onassis used all the money he had to send her daily baskets of red roses (obviously to become his trademark when courting a woman), with poetic cards attached. Finally, he appeared backstage and introduced himself. The next evening he took her, on borrowed money, to the most expensive restaurant in Buenos Aires, where they were photographed by a press photographer (whom he had alerted) and the picture made it into the pages of not one but two newspapers.

Muzio possessed a beautiful voice and great style. Her father was the stage manager at Covent Garden where she had often appeared. She was renowned for her singing of Violetta and Desdemona, but it was her dramatic private life that often got her the most press coverage. She was a passionate woman and the energy and guile of her young fan coupled with his romantic overtures intrigued her. She knew nothing about his life and did not care to hear about it. They quickly became lovers. She demanded much more of him than the young girls and whores with whom previously he had had sexual relations and – according to his later statements – she taught him about what it took to please a woman. He accompanied her to the Club de Residentes Extranjeros, the smartest club in town where she introduced him to some of her influential friends. She called him by the pet name of 'Stranger', a clue to how she viewed their liaison, and three weeks after their first meeting she continued on her opera tour with no 'goodbye', not even a note.

Onassis had been devastated, but he had also learned a great lesson – a famous woman can be of immeasurable help in bringing important contacts to the door of an ambitious man. It was that way with Claudia Muzio. Onassis found new acceptance. He was no longer a total unknown. There would be many women in his life who formed stepping stones to his public notoriety, nearly all of them older, richer and more experienced than himself. Then one day he realized that he was the lover who was 'older, richer and more experienced'. His vociferous disparagement of opera had more to do with his youthful pain at Claudia Muzio having rejected him than an actual dislike. He seemed to be recreating a situation in which he was in control and could thus write a new ending to this ego-hurting youthful experience. He was even wooing Maria (who resembled Muzio in many ways) in much the same manner he had Muzio – with flowers and flattery and impressive attention to detail. He knew that Maria wanted to move into a new social circle, a more sophisticated world than Battista provided for her. Therefore, the grand gestures, the prestigious guest list for the Dorchester party in her honour, a list larded with British and foreign titles (the Duchess of Kent, Princess Alexandra, Lord Mountbatten, Lord Harewood and Lady Churchill – Sir Winston being indisposed that evening), and a roster of celebrities that included Gary Cooper, Douglas Fairbanks Jr, Noël Coward, Vivien Leigh and Michael Redgrave.[1]

Maria's Medea lacked some of the spirit of the Dallas production and her pace (perhaps caused by Maestro Rescigno's uneven conducting) was unaccountably slow. Nonetheless, with Jon Vickers in splendid support, she remained the consummate actress and the final act was so gripping that one could literally observe a good section of the audience leaning forward in their seats in suspenseful anticipation. She took twelve curtains but personally was not happy with her performance and there was a moment later in her dressing room when she almost changed her mind about attending the Dorchester party. Battista insisted she go and did not seem in the least bit concerned that a huge box, a gift from Onassis, contained a magnificent chinchilla coat, which she wore over a stunning, form-fitting black gown despite the fairly warm air of the June evening – a gesture that seemed to announce a deliberate change in Maria's attitude. She, of course, loved expensive furs and jewels, but despite her fame, her income did not afford too many such luxuries, due in great part to Battista syphoning off large sums for his own use and to his poor money-managing talents. Most of the diamonds and furs Maria wore were borrowed from merchants and designers, and had to be returned. There is no doubt that owning a chinchilla – a high-status fur – appealed to her; it also sent a deliberate message to Onassis. And whereas most men might well have demanded their wives send back such an extravagant gift to an admirer. Battista seemed proud that something so obviously expensive was now hers.

---

[1] Vivien Leigh's husband, Sir Laurence Olivier, was at the time appearing at the Royale Theatre in New York in *The Entertainer*. Neither Coward nor Redgrave had yet been knighted.

Onassis met the Meneghinis in the lobby of the Dorchester when they arrived at about 1 a.m. With him was a press photographer. The other guests could not help but notice how glowing Maria looked as Onassis strode around the room by her side, his hand intimately, and protectively, under her elbow. 'This one's important,' Tina told a friend. 'He never paraded any of the others.' They danced a tango, his hand planted securely on Maria's hip, and when it ended and she said wistfully that she loved the tango and was sorry it wasn't played more often, he paid the orchestra leader a large additional sum to continue with more of the same, to the exasperation of many of his guests.

If Battista was aware that he was being cuckolded publicly, he gave no evidence of it, smiling as the two danced, their bodies seductively close, Maria's high heels causing her to be several inches taller, Ari's lips brushing her bare shoulder. She left with Battista at 3 a.m., Onassis on one side of her, Battista on the other. At the door to the Dorchester a photographer took the soon-to-be-famous picture of both men, their arms clasped round Maria's chinchilla-clad person, Onassis in his dark glasses smiling possessively, Battista looking like the beaten contestant. Ironically, both being shorter than Maria, they are clutching each other's hands, while Maria stares down dreamily at 'the other Greek'.

This was on the evening of 17 June 1959. Maria's next performance of *Medea* was 22 June, five nights later. This gave her some 'time off' and she used it, she told Battista, to shop and to rehearse privately with the Maestro. In fact, Onassis had arranged the use of an elegant Knightsbridge mews house where they rendezvoused several times. (Onassis would later ungallantly brag that Maria was so impatient that on the way to their destination in the back seat of his limousine with its dark-coloured windows she had performed oral sex on him while kneeling on the floor.) Her new lover was now insisting that she and Battista join the planned cruise of the Mediterranean later that summer. Maria, still filled with trepidation, remained hesitant. It is difficult to understand Battista's position. He could not have been blind to what was taking place between his wife and Onassis. But he still wanted to accept the invitation and was pressuring her to agree. It seems he might have realized Onassis's interest in Maria and hers in him – but remained strongly under the impression that Maria would never act upon it and that the powerful Greek would be a helpful ally, both in terms of business and social matters.

The last London performance of *Medea* was on 30 June, after which the Meneghinis returned to Milan for a few days before flying to Amsterdam where Maria sang a concert on 11 July. Three nights later she appeared at the Théâtre de la Monnaie in Brussels. Maria was now free until mid-

September. She had no excuse for refusing to join the *Christina* on its summer voyage and, on 22 July, giving in to her honest feelings, she and Battista flew into Nice where they were met by one of Onassis's several chauffeur-driven limousines and taken to the yacht, which was anchored in the harbour at Monte Carlo.

Maria stood on the deck of Aristotle Onassis's magnificent yacht, the *Christina*, huge dark prescription sunglasses masking her eyes and half her face. Although it was late evening, the lights that encircled Monte Carlo's rich man's harbour were glaringly bright and intensified the problems of her myopic vision. She settled her glance on Prince Rainier and Princess Grace, who had dined on the yacht, as they stepped down the gangplank of the giant white craft and walked the few feet to their crested limousine. When they reached the car they turned and waved a final goodbye to their host, who waved back at them from the top of the gangplank. It was well known, even to Maria who took little interest in matters outside the world of opera, that Onassis and the Prince of this tiny principality of Monaco had a deep dislike of each other. But Onassis now had a controlling interest in Monaco's casino, real estate and hotels. Rainier had to abide 'the Greek', as he privately called him. Onassis was his enemy. He was also a power whom he must cultivate to overthrow – or so his advisers counselled.

The moment the royal car pulled away, the boat's motor was started. The illuminated waters of the harbour swirled out from beneath the bow as the *Christina*, believed to be the most luxurious yacht afloat, headed out to sea where she would cruise the warm waters of the Mediterranean for three weeks.

The night was humid, even for July, and the breeze created by the movement of the boat most welcome. Onassis strode across the deck towards Maria. Battista, a notoriously bad sailor, had gone to their cabin immediately upon Princess Grace's and Prince Rainier's departure to pre-medicate himself with dramamine in hopes of warding off any early sign of motion sickness. He later wrote that he did not know that Maria and Onassis were lovers before the cruise. They say that often the husband or wife is the last to know of his or her mate's adultery which, if Battista was writing the truth, would be the case, for almost everyone on board the *Christina* was aware of the situation and anxiously wondering what was in store for them – stormy fights steered by jealous outbursts or the calm just before a hurricane.

From all future accounts based on stories told to intimates by the two lovers, their physical union had first occurred in London in the charming mews house off Eaton Square that they used for their rendezvous. By the time Maria had left London for Amsterdam she was clearly besotted with Onassis and also told Peter Diamand, who was managing the Amsterdam and Brussels engagements, 'Keep my money until you hear from me. There will be many changes in my life in the next few months. All my instincts tell me so. You'll hear many things...Please stay my friend.'

Perhaps some insight into the intimacy that occurred between Maria and Onassis in London can be gained from the personal memoir that Ingeborg Dedichen wrote about her own affair with Onassis. Granted this was twenty years earlier, but Onassis was thirty-five at the time, long after sexual patterns are usually formed.

> We would undress and sleep in the nude – lying one next to the other...Ari would put two fingers on my shoulder and delicately stroke my back. Won over by his magnetism, I felt a tingling all over and pressed myself to him while he continued his caresses. This simple contact gave me the greatest pleasure, and he could make it last forever. Finally, we could no longer resist, our bodies expecting one another, and we let ourselves be carried away in the swirl of love that united us...
>
> Neither of my two husbands had skin that I liked to stroke as much as his. And neither of them provoked in me such an overwhelming emotion...Often during the course of our amorous rites, he would lick me between the toes, carefully, like a cat cleaning itself. He would embrace every part of my body and cover me with kisses before devoting himself to the feet he adored.

If Dedichen can be trusted (and the rest of her memoir is extremely sound), there seems no doubt but that Onassis had learned well (perhaps from Muzio) how to please a woman and, considering the many unromantic years that Maria had spent with Battista, it is easily understandable that she could become so fascinated and well-seduced by such a man, especially one able to give her all the material things she so dearly coveted.

After a short time on deck, Maria and Onassis joined the rest of their party in the *Christina*'s grand salon where he had entertained royalty in a style which the super-rich Shah of Iran and numerous Saudi princes had found luxurious. There were sixty crew members – including valets, maids, waiters, barmen, beauticians, masseurs, and a French and Greek chef – who, except for parties in port, seldom looked after more than fourteen cruise passengers. Grand art was interspersed with strikingly vulgar touches. Onassis's magnificent suite, which contained his study, two sitting rooms, the bedroom, two dressing rooms and bathrooms, was on the bridge deck. An 'El Greco' of a Madonna and Child hung over the French writing table in the study.[2] A rare, ancient, jade Buddha decorated with diamonds and rubies, its hands and tongue able to move with the motion of the boat (there was only one other like figure in the world and it was owned by Queen Elizabeth), sat nearby on the marble-topped library table. Venetian glass covered the walls and wardrobe doors of his dressing room leading into his bathroom, which was lined with brown Siena marble and had a sunken marble tub and a shower, the door of which was a mirror on the outside and transparent on the reverse.

In the children's suite (Alexander was eleven, Christina nine) the salon was decorated with murals painted by Ludwig Bemelmans, the creator of the famous children's classic *Madeline*.[3] A series of Marcel Vertés frescoes depicting allegorical scenes – Tina ice-skating in a short skirt and his children picnicking on grass – covered the four walls of the dining room. The games room contained balustrades and a fire mantel made entirely of lapis lazuli. Bar stools in the room where the guests gathered for pre-dinner cocktails were covered with white whale foreskin ('Madame,' Onassis had once told Greta Garbo, 'You are now sitting on the largest penis in the world'). The jewel-like mosaic at the bottom of the swimming pool was a replica of the one from the Palace of Knossos and it could be raised to deck level for dancing. On board were forty-two telephones, all on separate private lines, a telex system, air-conditioning plant, radar, a cinema, an operating theatre as well as a fully equipped gym with sauna and steam room, and a library of over 3000 classic and rare books.

There were nine guest suites, all with marble bathrooms and solid-gold fixtures. Each suite consisted of sitting room, bedroom, dressing room and twin baths, and was named after a Greek island. Maria and Battista occupied the largest one, 'Ithaca', that was always reserved for Greta Garbo when she sailed on the *Christina*. In a gesture that expressed his respect for Churchill, Onassis had insisted that he and his wife Clementine take his private suite, the regal 'Chios'. He then moved to one closer to Maria and separate from Tina, who had her own suite. Lady Churchill occupied 'Ithaca', which was across the corridor from 'Chios', and her husband's two male nurses (who also functioned as bodyguards) were put in 'Crete', from which they had direct access to 'Chios.'

[2] There was much controversy over the authenticity of this 'El Greco' titled *Madonna Supported by an Angel*. Onassis also owned another El Greco – *Boy Lighting a Candle* – which hung in the salon and was under suspicion of being of dubious origin. In time, both were believed to have come from El Greco's school but were not painted by the artist himself.
[3] These murals sold in 1999 at Sotheby's in an auction of Ludwig Bemelmans's work for $363,000.

When Maria and Onassis entered the grand salon, Churchill – in an oversized wheelchair – sat in the centre of the room with its Persian rugs and concert Bösendorfer piano. Barely ambulatory and vastly overweight, he held court as the majority of the other guests – Lady Churchill, their daughter Diana Sandys, Churchill's secretary Anthony Montague Browne, Churchill's doctor Lord Moran, Onassis's sister Artemis, her husband Dr Theodore Garofallides and Tina – gathered respectfully around him as he drank his host's hundred-year-old brandy and listened with half-shut eyes to their lively conversation. The man who remained Great Britain's most world-renowned prime minister, though ill and incontinent, loved the sea air and the attention paid him by his host, to whom he was a hero of mythic stature. Churchill was also a worldly man and age had not withered his ability to divide the obvious from the obscure. His host relished undercurrents of jealousy and intrigue – it was part of the excitement that was to be expected of cruises on the *Christina*. This time, however, it had the feeling of the real thing. By the end of the first day out, as the yacht sailed through the Mediterranean on its way to the Aegean, Onassis and Maria strolled the deck hand in hand, or his arm was about her waist. Tina withdrew more and more to her suite or spent time on deck with her sister-in-law and Lady Churchill. Battista, despite his precautions and the relative smoothness of the sea, took to his bed with the motion sickness he had feared.

And Maria? She had never looked so radiantly happy. 'For once,' she told fellow guest Anthony Montague Brown, 'I feel like a woman.'

17

A Cruise To Be Remembered

THE BEAUTIFUL DAYS of the Aegean summer were in full bloom as the *Christina* fanned its leisurely way through its fabled blue waters. If there were any tensions among the yacht's passengers during the early days of the cruise they were kept well concealed. Tina maintained a flow of gay chatter and appeared oblivious to her husband's attentions to Maria. When Battista, briefly subduing his *mal de mer*, did emerge from their suite he was too awed at being in the presence of Sir Winston to do more than sit by silently as the venerable politician held court.

Maria sat at Ari's side, her leg often brushing his, as the two men (both of whom loved the sea and ships) discussed 'politics, history, human affairs, and human nature'. She seemed surprisingly comfortable despite the proximity of her gracious hostess and the knowledge that her lover's two children (and Diana Sandys's young daughter Celia) were never too far away. She knew, as the others did, that currently the Onassises' marriage was an open one for both sides; Ari having to abide Tina's young lover, Renaldito Herrera, on a recent voyage. Nonetheless, Tina was protective of her children and – on past voyages – had practised considerably more discretion than her husband was now using.

Neither Tina nor Ari could be called a good parent. Each had their own agenda. Tina, only twenty-eight, was not content to lose her identity as a forfeit for marriage – or motherhood. Endowed with ravishing good looks, rich in her own right – her father being one of the wealthiest Greek shipowners – Tina carried herself with an air of self-assurance. She had also retained her attraction for and to the opposite sex, was, in fact, a fairly lusty woman. Ari was the first one to admit that the distancing between them was mainly his fault. To his close friend Costa Gratsos he confided that having sex with the mother of his children created a psychological block. The problem had started eleven years earlier, after the birth of Alexander. He had gone for private consultation regarding the situation. When Tina became pregnant again a little more than a year later he had suggested an abortion, but she had refused to comply on religious grounds.

Both Christina and Alexander (Alexi) were old enough to understand what was happening between their father and Maria. A member of the party described Christina as 'a watchful, slightly ominous presence', who had not inherited her mother's beauty, nor her father's charisma. Of stolid build, her features seeming overlarge for her narrow face, she lacked the pre-adolescent charm little girls so often possessed. 'You wouldn't be aware she was there,' the guest recalled,

> then you would notice her sitting off to the side, with her soulful eyes taking in everything that was happening. God knows, Tina was not maternal. Her children were not her pride. They were simply to be endured and well looked after. Both showed great longing for their father's attention [the guest added]. And I must say that Ari often devoted more time to them than did Tina. Christina was not a pretty child, but he would tell her she was. 'Don't you look especially beautiful this morning,' he would say, a wide grin on his face as he hugged her to him. Tina, on the other hand, was never demonstrative – at least in public. Alexi was a talkative boy, his looks more refined than Christina's. He was always reluctant to leave the presence of the adults and, of course, his father.

Christina would later say that the cruise that brought Callas into their lives was the end of Alexi's and her own childhoods. Both had been used to moving from one house to another, one country to another. Except when they were on the *Christina* (which had been named for her, a fact Christina was proud to announce), they were seldom with both parents at one time. The yacht was a constant in their lives and the young girl, shy, withdrawn, feeling awkward always beside her beautiful, graceful mother, instinctively felt that this dramatic woman, of whom their father seemed so enamoured, was a threat to that small bit of stability she enjoyed. She was not a happy child. One thought of the cliché phrase 'poor little rich girl'.

Maria was insensitive to everything but her own feelings. She was to say that she had been determined that nothing and no one would spoil the happiness she felt in her love for Onassis and his apparent strong feelings for her. She indicated that this meant the interference of either Tina or Battista. What harm might be done to the two children, whose lives would be marked forever by her actions, appeared to be of no conscious concern to her.

Cruising with Sir Winston aboard meant that activities on the *Christina* centred greatly upon his pleasures and rigid time schedule. The former prime minister, pushed in his wheelchair and carried by his two strong male nurses when necessary, made a thorough inspection of the installations before the yacht was allowed to move out to sea. Happily, he reported to his host, the *Christina* was seaworthy. Churchill believed in punctuality and meals being served at set times. At the stroke of 9 a.m. each morning Onassis's valet, Louis, took a tray with fresh orange juice and a pot of coffee to the old gentleman's bedside. Exactly twenty minutes later a second tray arrived with a large bowl of cooked cereal, a tall jug of thick cream and well-done toast. This was followed in another twenty minutes by a third tray bearing a snifter filled with his favourite brandy. That consumed, he was ready to start the day. This usually meant dictating letters and catching up on his reading in the morning. At exactly twelve noon he appeared for lunch. ('His appetite was insatiable,' Onassis remembered). If the weather was clement he would be taken up on deck.

About every other day the *Christina* would anchor in a well-known port and whoever chose to would go ashore. Maria, in one of the many gaily flowered dresses she had bought for the cruise, always did. She was joined by Onassis, most often Tina and the other guests, except Battista who remained on board claiming that the only time he enjoyed the cruise was when the yacht was at anchor. Dinner, by Sir Winston's command, was served every evening precisely at 8.15. Gambling was one of Churchill's favourite pastimes and so games of *chemin de fer* and poker were arranged on cloudy days and evenings after dinner. As an alternative there were movies in the grand lounge followed by a sumptuous buffet, the evening often ending with Churchill singing 'rather naughty soldiers' songs' in a raucous voice heavily laced with brandy.

Onassis and Churchill had known each other for only two years. Sir Winston, who greatly enjoyed luxuries paid for by others, found Onassis to be a generous host as well as an intriguing and intelligent man – one not afraid to voice his opinions loud and strong. With his failing health, the ageing statesman had been spending considerable time in Monte Carlo to escape the damp and cold of the British winter and Onassis had made available to him the magnificent new penthouse of the Hôtel de Paris.

The Churchills had joined Tina and Ari on numerous previous cruises, often including Sir Winston's family members and staff, and *always* Churchill's beloved pet canary, Toby. Churchill had an eye for a pretty woman (although he could do nothing about it, nor, perhaps, would he have done had that been a possibility) and no cruise on the *Christina* was complete without a famous or infamous beauty, who was often Onassis's current amour. 'Ari relished the sexual competitiveness that yachts and beautiful women engendered and life aboard the *Christina* had a constant undercurrent of jealousy and intrigue,' one woman guest was quoted as saying. This never seemed to bother either of the Churchills who found it 'as bracing as the sea air'. But then Sir Winston had been a close witness to the famous affair between Edward VIII and Wallis Simpson, and one of their chief advisers. The old man was wily, worldly and wise, and Clementine Churchill, bright, vocal – certainly her husband's best friend – a handsome woman and a great observer and interpreter of the foibles of people with whom they socialized.

Onassis and Churchill also liked to play word games together.

'If you were an animal, what animal would you be?' Ari was reported as having asked.

'A tiger,' growled Sir Winston. 'And you, Ari, what animal would you choose to be?'

'Your canary, Toby,' Onassis replied.

'Why?' asked the surprised old man.

'I suspect as your constant, silent companion, Toby knows the answers to some of the world's most sought-after secrets.'

Churchill, as always, had brought Toby aboard for the cruise. The golden bird slept in his suite in a cage which was carried up on deck during the afternoon to enjoy the sun under the watchful eye of his owner. 'Every murderer has a canary which he treats kindly,' Sir Winston told Onassis. 'Denmark was Hitler's canary.'

Toby brought back wartime memories to Maria of her own canaries and how much they had meant to her during those desolate days. Sir Winston listened attentively to her stories, especially those about the British soldiers whom the Greeks helped to hide. But generally there was a high level of gaiety aboard and on land.

Churchill loved to talk, 'mostly of the good old days, the Boer War, of course, the First World War … He also talked about the last war, and when the conversation turned on Russia he always had a good word for Stalin. Of all the people he dealt with during the war, he said, Stalin never broke a single promise,' an observer recalled him saying.

On 25 July, just three days out, the *Christina* pulled into the harbour in Capri. Battista, still ailing, tried to persuade Maria to return with him to Milan, but she refused to do so and convinced him to remain, certain that his motion sickness would soon disappear. Then, leaving him on the yacht, she joined the others for a day on the mystical island with its wondrous tints of earth, sky and sea, and the drama of its flaring sunsets and distant, sun-scorched limestone cliffs. The group lunched in a small waterfront restaurant, fishing boats trolling on the horizon. The day sparkled. Everyone was in high spirits, but it was impossible not to notice the special bonding that had occurred between Maria and Onassis, and the cool manner in which Tina accepted it. The great British music hall and film star, Gracie Fields, who had a house on Capri, came on board for dinner and an evening filled with music, during which she sang some of her famous wartime songs and successfully coaxed Maria to join her in several choruses.

Battista remained in their suite the next day when everyone else was on deck to see Stromboli's smoking volcano. He also stayed there when the boat sailed through the Gulf of Corinth on the way to Delphi. By now he did not need to be told that Maria and their host were engaged in a quite public affair, although Tina (who seemed unmindful for the time of the consequences) managed to seek him out and apprise him of the situation. He told her that neither of them had anything to worry about – Maria and Ari were 'just two Greeks enjoying a mild flirtation'. But whenever Maria went back to the suite, voices could be heard in argument, Battista's rising above Maria's, after which she would leave. By the end of the first week she spent little time with Battista and was seen going in and out of Onassis's apartments (which were directly across the hall from her own), often entering late at night and leaving the next morning, freshly dressed.

Maria most enjoyed their days at sea when she soaked up the sun, swam (in the first bikinis she had ever worn), played shuffle board and, when they were anchored, watched Onassis display his expertise on water skis – although she did not take up his challenge to join him. She joked around with him in a coquettish fashion, even when Battista came up on deck for one of his rare 'outings'. Battista had looked shocked the first time Onassis bared his hairy chest. Maria, of course, had already seen him nude and found his hairiness a mark of great virility. Battista called him 'the Gorilla' in private and they had one of their many arguments about this.

The yacht sailed smoothly through the Isthmus of Corinth and on to Epidaurus where even Battista got off to visit the ancient theatre. Maria, thrilled by its history and the fabulous sound of its natural acoustics, stood in the centre and sang a part of 'Col Sorriso' from the final scene of *Il Pirata*, with nearby tourists startled at first, then applauding madly for her to continue. But she merely bowed, waved and turned away.

When they reached the Saronic Gulf, just south of Athens, Greece's

Prime Minister Karamanlis and his wife boarded the *Christina* for dinner. This was the one evening that Maria remained somewhat apart from Onassis and Battista joined the group, looking sullen and seldom speaking. Of course, it was difficult for him, for English was the language most often used, in deference to Churchill and because it was the most common means of communication between the other passengers.

'It was sad to see the marriage [of Ari and Tina] disintegrating, the tenderness fade,' Nonie Montague Browne observed in her diary notes. 'Tina continued to be a sparkling hostess, but one was aware of the well controlled tension – I seemed to be the Pig in the Middle,' she wrote, referring to the fact that both Tina *and* Maria had come to her for advice. 'But I have learned to keep my mouth shut,' she added.

Maria took great pleasure in stretching out seductively on a deck lounger while Onassis smoothed tanning lotion familiarly on her shoulders, back, arms and legs. She quickly turned a beautiful bronze shade, her brief bikini outlined against the milky-white of her protected skin. 'We surely thought either Tina or Meneghini or Meneghini and Callas together would leave the boat when we reached Izmir [the old city of Smyrna and Onassis's childhood traumas] so thick was the tension at this point,' another guest commented. 'It seemed Onassis had made his decision and it was humiliating for both Tina and Meneghini, who looked like he had murder in his eyes – although he would never have been a match for Ari if it ever had come to that...the Churchills seemed to remain above it all, Sir Winston glibly welcoming all the dignitaries who came on board in almost every port to pay him homage.'

On the land tour of Izmir, Onassis took special interest in pointing out the various landmarks and describing the city where he had once so narrowly escaped with his life and where he had left his father to die, feeling he had no alternative but to escort the women in his family to safety. After they had returned to the yacht and dinner had been served, a film was shown in the lounge, but Onassis had decided that he would escort Maria on a personal tour of 'Smyrna'. They were about to go ashore when Battista joined them on deck. In an act totally foreign to his nature, he insisted on accompanying them on to the dock where Onassis's car and driver were waiting. There was nothing to do but for the three of them to take the night tour of 'Smyrna' together. (A number of years later Meneghini claimed that Tina had told him that her husband and his wife were going off the boat alone and that he should do something about it. He said he could not stop Onassis from leaving and that he knew Maria would never have listened to him if he had told her to remain on the yacht, so he decided the best thing to do was to go with them.)

They were an odd trio as Onassis took them through the old, racy ten-derloin district 'telling the stories of his nights in the big brass beds in the cathouses in Demiri Yolu'. They stopped at taverns along the way. 'He [Onassis] got very drunk,' Battista wrote in the tell-all book he would later publish. 'We made merry all night in the company of dealers, prosti-tutes and assorted sinister characters…It was five in the morning before we returned to the *Christina*…He [Onassis] was tighter than a goat. He couldn't stand up, he couldn't talk.' Another member of the party agreed that Onassis reeled in drunk but that Battista was retching so badly that Maria woke up Dr Garofallides (Onassis's brother-in-law) 'to give him some medication and a sleeping potion'. If Battista is to be believed, nothing was said between the two men during the entire bizarre evening about the difficult situation they were caught up in.

The sea was calm, the day golden on the morning of 6 August when the *Christina* anchored in Bosphorus Bay outside the city of Istanbul, the distant mosques shimmering in the bright scene like glittering sand dunes. That afternoon, while at anchor, the *Christina* was visited by Patriarch Athenagoras, the head of the Greek Orthodox Church. On board he bestowed blessings upon Onassis and Maria 'as they knelt side by side on the varnished deck'. He called them 'the world's finest singer and the most famous mariner of the modern world, a modern Ulysses', and gave thanks for the honours they had 'brought to Greece'. The Patriarch seemed oblivious to the fact that the blessings he bestowed were on lovers who were defying the very fibre of the moral code of his religion. When he joined them for lunch afterwards, there was a terrible pall over the table. Onassis's sister, the dark-haired, fiery Artemis, could not contain her fury at 'the sun deck liturgy', which seemed to her too much like a wedding service. She made some strong remarks about the 'hypocrisy of adulterers who pretend to be true to the church'.

Onassis excused himself for a moment. Seconds after he returned to the table, his sister was handed a folded note, which requested she retire to her room. Artemis rose unsteadily, gave her brother a defiant look, Maria a sneering one, apologized to the Patriarch and left the table. Even Sir Winston was becoming uncomfortable at this point. 'That evening…Maria refused to come to bed,' Battista recorded, adding that she had said, 'You can do what you like, I'm staying right here [with Onassis.]'

Then, in the early hours of 12 August, just half a day before the yacht would return to Monte Carlo and all but Onassis and his family happily disembark, Tina, troubled and unable to sleep, went up to the salon and entered to find, on one of the commodious loungers, her husband and

Maria engaged in an act of sex. So involved were they that they neither heard nor saw her.

This was not the first time that Tina had discovered Onassis in the arms of another woman. This time she felt she had had just about enough humiliation and went directly to Battista's suite and pounded on his door. When he finally opened it she burst in to tell him what she had just witnessed. 'I could see by his face that he was beyond doing a thing about it,' she later said. In Battista's recital of the incident he claimed he told her that he was sure it was nothing more than a shipboard romance; Maria would never leave him.

'He has taken her away from you, Battista,' he claimed Tina insisted. 'She'll learn soon enough what kind of man he is – a brutal drunk!' Tina debunked that statement. 'Ari never raised a hand to a woman, I'm sure of that. His brutality was far more violent. He could destroy a woman by his disregard for her. Every woman Ari ever took as a lover was brutalized in this fashion. He showered his women with gifts and disposed of them like the empty boxes in which they had been delivered.'

Battista waited up for Maria to return, which she did not do until morning. He then told her that they had been seen by Tina having sex like 'two animals'. 'How could you have done that, Maria?' he asked.

'I love him,' she replied simply.

'I felt I was going to burst into tears,' Battista wrote later. 'It was as if a fire was devouring them both.' The paparazzi, who had got wind of their affair from people in Izmir, were waiting for them when the *Christina* docked in Monaco. Maria and Battista disembarked together, he tightly holding her hand, unaware that the bracelet she wore on her wrist had been a gift from Onassis – ordered by him in one port and delivered to the *Christina* on their arrival in another. It was a gold circle engraved with the letters TMWL – To Maria With Love. This was the first piece of jewellery she had received from him and she was glad it was not in any way 'flashy' but more like a private token of his love. (He had, in fact, given Tina a similar bracelet engraved TILY – Tina I Love You – shortly before they were married.)

Maria and Battista quickly rode off to Nice airport in a waiting car, the other guests leaving the yacht directly afterwards. Onassis disembarked a short time later; Tina and the children remained on board to continue on to Venice.

The Meneghinis flew from Nice to Milan. Then, at Maria's request (according to Battista), he went to Sirmione while she 'tried to put the happenings on the cruise behind her'. However, the next day Onassis flew in his private Piaggio aircraft to meet her in Milan, out-foxing the paparazzi who thought that would be the last place he would land and were waiting for him in Venice, thus ending Battista's fantasy of a repentant wife.

Two days after the end of the cruise, Maria summoned Battista back from Sirmione. A confrontation between the two men and Maria took place later that same night when Onassis, who had returned to Monaco on business for the day, arrived back in Milan and, taking a circuitous route in an unobtrusive Fiat sedan, drew up in the rear of the Meneghinis' apartment building, entered through a service door and rode the back elevator to their penthouse flat. It was after 10 p.m. For the next five hours they discussed their situation in what Battista later called 'a fairly civilized manner'.

'We are very much in love,' Maria said, as she sat in a chair with Onassis perched on the arm, his hand holding hers. 'We don't want a scandal, but I can't go on living with you as your wife.'

As Battista was the only one who recorded this confrontation and he often coloured the truth with his own preferred interpretation, it is difficult to discern how 'civil' this meeting actually was. But all three certainly knew their best efforts to arrive at an amicable arrangement was to all their advantages. Onassis was a married man and for the moment he did not choose to pursue the idea of divorce. His children were to be considered and he expressed concern on their behalf. Then there was Maria's career; it had to be protected as well as was poss-ible – something with which Battista thoroughly agreed. Money – specifi-cally what Maria earned – was discussed, with Battista insisting that he continue as her manager. He did not, as yet, know that she had been making recent arrangements for her concert fees to be paid into a newly opened Swiss bank account in her name only, arranged for her by Onassis.

Battista seemed quite confident at this time that even if they were to become estranged Maria would remain Signora Meneghini. 'There is no divorce in Italy,' he kept repeating. 'No divorce! Remember that.'

Maria insisted that they could no longer live in the same house and Battista agreed; for *now*, he stressed, he would remain in Sirmione, which was nearer Verona and his mother who was not well. Then Onassis refused to leave the apartment if Battista remained for the night. Finally, the hour now past 2 a.m., both men departed together, Battista to travel to Sirmione by car, Onassis to the private airport where his plane was waiting to return him to Monaco. Maria was left alone with her poodle, Toy, and her very mixed emotions. She did not trust Battista's restraint.

'Money is what matters to him,' she told Bruna. 'He will fight to the death to keep his prize cash cow.'

Onassis flew back the following night, and he and Maria dined alone. The next day the two of them travelled to Sirmione, having obviously decided on a plan of action, and met again with Battista – this time the word 'civility' could not be applied. Onassis had been drinking on the journey up and during dinner, which was a tense, bizarre meal with few words exchanged and, except for Onassis, the participants eating little. Then Battista accused Onassis of 'stinking from alcohol' and repeating the story he said Tina had told him of her husband being 'a brutal drunk'.

'Battista, I beg you to be dignified about this,' Maria intervened. Then she repeated her statement that it was over between them, that she loved Onassis and that there was nothing more to be said – she would never live under the same roof with him again.

'You forget, you belong to me,' he replied.

'I belong to myself!' Maria countered.

Battista became enraged. They were shouting at one another in Italian, he calling her ungrateful, without a conscience. Hadn't he taken her from a dumpy, insecure, obese girl, *yes* with a great voice but little else, and made her into the famous, rich woman she was? Then he called her a whore, at which point Onassis grabbed him by the collar and threw him down in a chair, then, standing over him, dared Battista to do battle. If that had occurred there would have been no real contest, for Onassis was by far the stronger man.

Finally, when Onassis backed away, Battista got to his feet. 'You are beneath contempt,' he claimed he told Onassis. 'You invite me on your yacht and then stab me in the back. When you tire of Maria you'll cast her aside just as you are doing your fine wife.' Then he turned to Maria. 'Can't you see through him? Are you so blinded by your girlish emotions?'

Maria tried to quieten both men to get back to some civility, but it was hopeless. 'Don't you think she deserves a real man?' Onassis later said he asked him, the implication clear.

For a moment it looked as if Battista would pounce on him, but then he drew himself up into a tight bundle of injured dignity. 'You are a whoremonger, a liar and a thief!' he countered.

'Whatever I am, I am not a cocksucker like you!' Onassis replied. 'And I am also a powerful millionaire and the sooner you get it into your head, the better it will be for everybody. I will never give up Maria for anyone or anything... [so] how many millions do you want to let her [go] free? Five? Ten?'

'Out of my house!' Battista claimed he ordered.[1]

Maria said that if Onassis left, she would leave with him, which she finally did, returning to Milan from where she telephoned Battista the next day requesting her passport and her beloved small painting of the Madonna that she always placed in her dressing room before an appearance. He agreed, but then when she told him she did not want him to represent her any more he grew immediately hostile. Maria then said she would have her lawyers handle the matter for her for she now would seek a legal separation.

For the next few days Onassis commuted between Monaco and Milan, dining privately with Maria while they made their plans. Maria was certain she had made the right decision. They were wildly in love – she with him and Onassis, seeming 'freshly minted', looking happier and more relaxed than he had in years. 'It's the real thing this time,' he told Costa Gratsos. Maria had convinced him that they should keep away from any exposure to the press, still afraid of what the scandal might do to her coming engagements, although no longer concerned about Battista and any problems he could make. But on 31 August she finally agreed to accompany Onassis on his private plane back to Monte Carlo, where he arranged for her to have a suite at the Hôtel de Paris. Miraculously, the press were not aware of her presence. Two days later Onassis flew back with her to Milan and then continued on to Venice to meet Tina to discuss his relationship with Maria, warn her that it would soon be common knowledge and assure her that he would protect her and the children as much as he could, and that he did not want a divorce. The following day, after Tina promised to stand by silently, Onassis returned to Turin, where Maria had been driven to avoid the press, Battista having released an angry statement about 'his wife's defection'. Then the couple flew on to Monaco, Tina having left Venice with the children for her parents' luxurious home on the avenue Foch in Paris. 'The plane [Onassis's Piaggio] has never flown so much since Mr Onassis bought it,' its pilot, Angelo Pirotti, confessed.

That same night Maria dined *à deux* with Onassis in his private rooms at the Hôtel de Paris, the press flanked outside the grand façade waiting for a sighting of the now famous adulterous lovers. On 9 September newspapers announced that the Meneghinis were legally separated, the marriage all but over and that Battista would no longer be representing

[1] This confrontation has been recorded by published interviews with Onassis and in Meneghini's memoirs. Callas also gave a version of it to close confidants. What appears here are the quoted words of the parties concerned.

his wife. Battista then made the gratuitous statement that 'she has repaid my love by stabbing me in the back'.

The pressure on Maria was showing. She had a concert engagement in Bilbao on 17 September and a full schedule including London, Berlin, Kansas City and Dallas, before ending her commitments for the year. Onassis decided that what they both needed was a few days of privacy and so he ordered the *Christina* to be prepared for a short, immediate five-day cruise of the Aegean – just he and Maria, and a crew of sixty. Nothing could have intrigued the press more. The *Christina* was called 'the love boat'. From time to time helicopters hovered overhead and Maria and Onassis remained below deck. But then the captain found some sheltered areas along the coast where the yacht could move lazily and its two passengers loll privately on deck and in each other's arms. Maria was the happiest she had ever been, truly in love as she knew she had never been before, certain that everything would now work out as she wished it to.

On their return to Monaco they were greeted by a barrage of reporters and learned that Battista had been making bitter statements, and that Tina had left for New York with Christina and Alexi and would be suing for divorce. Onassis was furious. 'She has kidnapped the children and is demanding $20 million ransom,' he told friends, adding that it was Tina who wanted a divorce, not him.

'He was trying to justify himself,' one close acquaintance reported, 'accusing Tina of carrying on with other men. It was disgusting. I was shocked by the blatancy of his behaviour. I am sorry to say it, but I suspect his real motive was publicity. He had had all the publicity he wanted from Tina who was photographed everywhere she went [because of her beauty and background]. But her usefulness had come to an end ... Onassis never admitted that he craved publicity, but he did.'

Maria closed her eyes to any negative remarks or suggestions. The nay sayers could not, in her opinion, know the truth. Theirs was an historic affair. Never did two people love one another more. Onassis was rightly angered because Tina had gone off with the children, whom he also loved dearly. She told Bruna, 'For the first time I understand what it means to be a woman. My singing, my career – they must come after Ari.'

Not yet, for there were still concerts and an American tour to be dealt with. However, she was seriously considering not renewing any contracts for the coming year, money seeming no longer to be important and time with Onassis the main object in this, her new life.

18

An Historic Affair

'ONASSIS AND I have been caught in this twist of destiny and we cannot fight it. Its force is beyond us,' Maria had told Battista in their final confrontation. But as yet no declaration of the depth of their grand passion had been made public. *Yes*, her marriage had fallen apart. She was legally separated from her husband; Mr Onassis was her 'dearest good friend', who was helping her through these trying days, she insisted to the press. Onassis, also under siege by the paparazzi, finally admitted that he was taking Madame Callas for a short cruise 'because she has had a difficult time and needs a rest'.

'Are you in love?' a reporter shouted at him.

Onassis turned, removed his signature dark glasses momentarily to see the man better, and replied, 'Of course, I would be flattered if a woman with the class of Maria Callas fell in love with someone like me! Who wouldn't?' Then he strode into the building in Monte Carlo where his offices were situated. Only a few hours later Maria, sunglasses in place, hair swept back in a sophisticated coiffure, and holding Toy by a gilded leash, boarded the *Christina* where he was already waiting for her arrival. This time Maria and Onassis occupied his grand suite together.

Battista had returned to Milan where he had methodically packed up all the possessions that he wanted. 'He raped the place of anything of value, even taking several of Maria's fur coats which would end up that winter on the backs of his mother and sisters-in-law,' a former employee of the Meneghinis declared. Bruna, who had remained in Milan, tried to stop him from going through Maria's personal possessions and her jewels, but Meneghini locked her out of the bedroom while he continued his ransacking. 'In Italy, a wife's valuables belong to her husband, and Signora Meneghini is still my wife,' he defended, 'and always will be!'

Unable to reach the lovers for statements, the paparazzi closed in on Battista who dropped all pretences of civility. 'Onassis is a man with an ambition like Hitler!' he declared. 'He wants to own everything with his accursed millions and his accursed cruise and his accursed yacht! He wants to add varnish to his tankers with the name of a great artist!' Then he added,

> We are like three characters in a drama...I cannot forgive Onassis. It was I who made Callas what she is and she showed her gratitude by stabbing me in the back. She was fat and drably dressed, more like a penniless gypsy refugee without career prospects, when she came into my life. Not only did I pay her hotel bill but I also became her guarantor so that she could remain in Italy. This can hardly be described as exploitation of which, apparently, I am now being accused [in the press]. Make no mistake that when it comes to the point of splitting everything down to our poodle, Maria will get the head part and I will end up with the tail!

The press was not sympathetic to Battista's view of the situation. They had never liked the man and however inappropriate his wife's adulterous relationship was with Onassis, they treated her in a more sympathetic light. Few had any doubt but that Battista was bitter, not at the loss of his wife but of her future earnings.

'He told me Onassis had told him to name his figure – $10 million or more – to walk off quietly into the sunset,' one associate said.

> I believe he was sorry he had not accepted that offer when it was made for now, after the statements he had made to the press, Onassis wouldn't give him a dime. The opera world blamed Battista for most of Maria's past difficulties in her business dealings. He was thoroughly disliked by all the managements. And he was a most disagreeable, unattractive man in his late sixties. He could never play Svengali again – if, indeed, that had been his relationship to Maria. He was finished and he knew it. If Maria had gone off with a poor man, his reaction would have been the same, and I am sure he would have held on to all that she had earned during the years of their marriage as well.
>
> But those of us who cared deeply for Maria – and she had many good friends – despite our loathing and disregard for Meneghini did not feel that Onassis would do more than help her make the break, treat her royally for a short time and then move on, driven by his ambition, for someone younger, more famous perhaps, someone who could open doors that were presently closed to him. We weren't prophetic. The man's history pointed to such an eventuality. Onassis was a user of people, who disposed of them when they were no longer useful to him. Love? A grand passion at his age [fifty-nine]? Doubtful. He was a great pretender. He had created his life. But he wanted more fame and more power. Tina could

not bring him the front-page coverage that Maria could. For now Maria was useful. But she could not add to his power. One day he would walk away from her as he had Tina. Her friends saw this. But can anyone discuss such a thing with a woman so besotted, so madly in love as was Maria with Aristotle Onassis? I don't think so.'

The love cruise was interrupted on 16 September, when the *Christina* drew into the bay of Glyfada near Athens where launches brought the directors of Onassis's Olympic Airways back to the yacht for an urgent business meeting. Maria, leaving Toy in the care of the crew, was flown by private jet to Bilbao, Spain, where she was to give a concert the following day, 17 September, at the Coliseo Albia. From the moment she stepped off the plane into the blaring sunlight, she was besieged by reporters and cameramen shouting at her, 'Look this way! Give us a big smile!' They encircled her like a pack of killer dogs. Finally, with two of Onassis's staff buttressing her, they forced their way through the crowd to a limousine. But even as it drew away a man with a camera jumped on the running board and caught a shot of her as she pressed back fearfully against the leather-cushioned rear seat.

Clearly distracted, the first half of the concert was not a prime example of her great talent and her reception by the audience was cool. During intermission she spoke to Onassis from her dressing room, telling him about the poor treatment she had received from the paparazzi upon her arrival. 'I am being looked upon as a scarlet woman,' she cried. Onassis calmed her and she returned for the second half of the concert and sang 'Col Sorisso' from *Il Pirata* magnificently, winning voluminous, enthusiastic applause, and took many curtains. She dined later with Nicola Rescigno, who conducted the concert as he would do for the rest of her 1959 tour commitments. She had great respect for Rescigno, a relatively young man in his forties of Italian origin, who had been her vocal coach after her 1951 tour of South America and, as Laurence Kelly's partner, had been a deciding factor in her appearances with both the Chicago and the Dallas Civic Opera Companies.

Her spirits heightened, she flew back the next morning to the *Christina*. The cruise had been extended for a few more days. They were joined now by Onassis's sister Artemis and his brother-in-law Dr Garofallides, the lovers having been advised it was crucial that they not cruise without 'chaperones', or Battista could bring a charge (valid in Italy) of immorality against them.

Onassis was very much aware that Artemis was on Tina's side in their current struggle and he wanted Maria to be accepted by his family. It is doubtful that Artemis was truly won over, but her brother's happiness and his generous support were of prime concern to her. She was friendly to Maria, the two women spending many hours on this last wing of the cruise talking animatedly. The *Christina* arrived in Monte Carlo on 22 September. On the same day Maria flew alone to London for her concert the following evening at the Royal Festival Hall.

In London, the scandalous paparazzi coverage that was plastered over the front pages of the tabloids seemed only to enervate her audience. They cheered her grandly when she first appeared on stage and remained enthusiastic throughout her entire performance (recorded for the first time from the audience by a hand-held machine operating on battery power). She sang 'Una macchia', Lady Macbeth's sleep-walking scene, and did so to brilliant effect, with vibrant colour and great drama. (John Ardoin was to comment that 'here was a Lady Macbeth bordering on a Medea'.)

A few days later Onassis joined her in Milan. They no longer minded being photographed together, both beaming, Onassis usually with his hand protectively under her arm; or caught by the camera both leaning across a restaurant table seemingly involved in an intimate conversation. She called him Aristo because Tina called him Ari. He often referred to her as his 'beautiful canary', which she thought was affectionate. Even when faced with Battista's ugly, bitter statements and the shock of seeing how he had stripped the Milan apartment of anything of consequential value, Maria could not conceal her obvious happiness. She was a woman in love – and she looked it. She wrote to Battista telling him to keep whatever he had taken, but please to allow her to 'have her life back' and this chance for personal happiness.

Battista's reply was unrelenting. 'For what you have done to me you will pay over and over again for the rest of your days. You will never know happiness; I pity you because you both will pay in hell for this.'

A recent book by Nicholas Gage, the affair of Onassis and Maria as its main theme, drew much sensational publicity with his claim that Maria gave birth to a son by Onassis; the child living only a matter of hours, an allegation suspect at best. Gage gives August 1959 while cruising the *Christina* as the time Maria would have conceived and concludes that the lovers had agreed for Maria to carry full term, keeping her condition and the birth a secret. There is much evidence to contradict this allegation. But taken strictly in the time context that Gage has given, there is great improbability that the lovers would have even considered going through such a duplicitous, complicated and dangerous plan that could have destroyed both their reputations, this being many decades before illegitimacy garnered any social acceptance. They had been lovers for a matter of months. Both were still married to others. Battista would not consent to divorce, which was against his religion. Onassis made it very clear to Maria that he wanted no more children. True, Maria and Onassis were passionate lovers. But Onassis was a cautious man. He had had many lovers. And, as he told Costa Gratsos, 'I shall never be so foolish as to leave myself open to the possibility of a paternity suit. I have two children and that is how it shall remain.' Accidents, of course, do happen. But with Maria's previous health problems, her inability to become pregnant during the good years of her marriage, and the diagnosis of her doctor that due to the position of her womb and related problems, pregnancy would place her and the foetus at risk, it seems illogical that she would continue a pregnancy without being under the care of an obstetrician, which she was not, nor would Onassis with his sexual block toward the mother of his children have wanted her to.

In fact, she returned alone to London on 1 October, to pre-tape a concert to be televised on 7 October, and from that point did a good deal of travelling – appearing in concert in Berlin on 23 October, before flying to the States the very next day for a tour that would take her to Kansas City and Dallas. Onassis remained in Monte Carlo where he had to deal with a difficult confrontation with Prince Rainier who had recently suspended Monaco's Constitution, dissolved its National Council and abrogated the rights of political assembly or demonstration – a veritable *coup d'état* – to remind his subjects that he was an absolute monarch by hereditary divine right. His autocracy assured, Rainier established the Monaco Development Corporation and granted tax-free status to hundreds of foreign companies and investors. This raised the ire of President Charles de Gaulle and the French government who understandably did not want a tax-free state bordering their own, one in which French citizens could fairly easily establish residence to avoid paying French taxes. On 3 October President de Gaulle had given Rainier six months' notice of his intention to abrogate the century-old convention guaranteeing friendly relations between the two countries if he did not retract, or greatly modify, the edict. Onassis's huge financial interest in Monaco was in jeopardy and however much he disliked Rainier, he knew he had to try to help ameliorate the hostile situation between France and Monaco.

This would be the beginning of the end of the shaky partnership of Rainier and Onassis. The Prince greatly resented 'the Greek's' interference and it now became a matter of principle and expediency to get Onassis to sell his shares in the SBM so that all major property in Monaco would be controlled by the Palace. For the next four years it was to be a test of force and not an easy one at that. Maria had a rival for Onassis's attention – Prince Rainier, the husband of Princess Grace, the former American film star Grace Kelly. This promised to be as gritty as any tough Western, but Onassis was a man who loved a battle as much as – or perhaps even more than – he could love a woman.

At the concert on 28 October at Loew's Midland Theatre in Kansas City, Maria was in fine voice, singing 'Regnava nel silenzio' from *Lucia* to a wildly enthusiastic audience. There was a gala reception following the concert at which she wore a red chiffon gown with a wasp waist and looked most glamorous. She was travelling with Nicola Rescigno, her conductor and friend. The two of them flew from Kansas City to Dallas on the 29th for immediate rehearsals for *Lucia de Lammermoor* to be performed on 6 and 8 November with the Dallas Civic Opera at the State Fair Music Hall. 'She was suffering from a sinus infection,' Rescigno noted, 'which she felt had been caused by the air travel, which had created the same problem at other times.' She was given prescribed medication for it. From the moment she stepped out on stage for her first Lucia, Maria was aware that she was in trouble. She had several vocal trips, her voice seeming to fade away. Then, in the mad scene, she missed the crucial high E-flats. She recovered for the second performance but skipped the difficult notes to the disappointment of the knowledgeable opera-goers in the audience.

After the last performance of *Lucia* and before the first rehearsal for *Medea*, her sinus infection still troubling her, she flew to Brescia, Italy for the hearing of her separation suit. On 14 November the court pronounced her separation from Battista legal and devised a financial settlement that was heavily in favour of Meneghini. All Italian real estate – the house in Sirmione and the apartment in Milan, were to be in his name. Artworks and antiques were to be divided (although he had previously taken the lion's share). He was to have no claim on monies she earned from that date. But as Battista had already squirrelled away large sums from her past earnings into his private account, Maria was not in a good financial position. The phone lines rang with calls back and forth to Onassis, who assured her she had no need to worry. He wanted her to spend time with him on the *Christina* (where he lived when in Monaco) and would see about buying a suitable apartment for her in Paris, her residency in Italy no longer necessary.

She returned to Dallas to sing *Medea* on 17 November, the day of the first rehearsal. Her sinus infection seemed to have cleared up and she was in remarkably good voice and form. Her Medea, on 19 November, was

fired with tenderness and fury, her singing impassioned, and both performances were greeted with standing ovations. By the second performance,
on 21 November, her sinus condition flared up again, but she seemed
able to avoid any problems with her voice and in photographs taken at
the opening night reception she looks slim, quite beautiful and is smiling
graciously. The weather in Dallas had been unusually temperate for late
November and Rescigno, feeling she needed a few days' rest before flying
off again to Europe, suggested she remain. But Maria was anxious to
rejoin Onassis in Monaco, having not seen him in over a month.

She arrived in Nice on 25 November and was driven to the yacht
where she planned to stay. No sooner had Onassis greeted her when news
came that Tina had filed suit in the New York State Supreme Court for a
divorce and custody of the children, and had then released a dignified,
civilized, prepared statement, read to him in his office on the *Christina* by
Costa Gratsos.

> It is almost thirteen years since Mr Onassis and I were married in New
> York City. Since then he has become one of the world's richest men, but
> his great wealth has not brought me happiness with him, nor, as the
> world knows, has it brought him happiness with me. After we parted this
> summer in Venice, I had hoped that Mr Onassis loved our children
> enough and respected our privacy sufficiently to meet with me – or,
> through lawyers, with my lawyer – to straighten out our problems. But
> this was not to be.
>
> Mr Onassis knows positively that I want none of his wealth and that I
> am solely concerned with the welfare of our children.[1]
>
> I deeply regret that Mr Onassis leaves me no alternative other than a
> New York suit for divorce. For my part I will always wish Mr Onassis well,
> and I expect that after this action is concluded he will continue to enjoy
> the kind of life which he apparently desires to live, but in which I have
> played no real part.

Tina had filed on the only grounds then acceptable in New York State –
adultery – but she had named a Mrs J.R. – her old friend Jeanne
Rhinelander who had betrayed that friendship several years before in the
South of France – as the other woman. Mrs Rhinelander was appalled and

---

[1] Tina Onassis was a wealthy woman in her own right, her father Stavros Livanos
having established a considerable trust for her in her youth. She also had over $4
million in jewels and the New York Sutton Place apartment and all its contents –
antiques and artworks – were hers. Onassis had set up large trust funds in both
Christina's and Alexander's names, and made them the main beneficiaries in the
advent of his death. He also was responsible for their support until they reached the
age of majority when their trust funds would be payable.

irate, but Maria was immensely relieved. She was also hopeful that both she and Onassis might now be moving closer to a time when they could be married. She expected that he would be pleased that he would soon be free and that they could now concentrate on efforts for her to gain her freedom from Battista, which had to be secured outside Italy.

Instead, Onassis became agitated and short with her. 'I think you should move in [to] the Hôtel Hermitage [in Monte Carlo] right away,' he told her. Maria at first resisted doing so, but finally agreed, departing in a distressed state a short time later. No sooner had she left with her luggage in one of his cars, than he was on the telephone to Tina in New York, tearfully begging her in an hour-long, unsuccessful call, to drop the divorce.

It is impossible to believe that Maria was not aware of his reluctance to make a commitment of marriage to her. And it is equally difficult to accept the notion that Onassis would have tried to dissuade Tina from divorcing him if he knew that Maria was already well into the fourth month of carrying his child. Nor does it seem likely that Maria would have even considered not informing him if she was *enceinte*.

There was no doubt that Onassis – not Maria – was the person who controlled their situation, that he would decide their future. He was no longer 'in love' with Tina – that was evident, Maria believed, because he had told her that they had not gone to bed together in years. Onassis was a man of strong sexual appetites and Maria had fed these with the plenitude of her own long-frustrated passion. But Onassis could also be brutally cold and calculating, a user of people and not one to allow sentiment or the needs of others – wife, lovers, or children – to get in the way of what he wanted.

Maria was living in a state of denial, seeing the man she wanted to see in much the same way as she had done with Battista in the early days of their relationship. Within forty-eight hours of the news of Tina's petition for divorce, Onassis left Monte Carlo on a business trip having to do, he explained, with 'the post-Suez shipping slump'. Maria packed up and returned to Milan and her old apartment, which although she no longer owned it, she still occupied. This gave her a base until Onassis decided what her next move should be. They spoke by telephone daily, but his comings and goings were erratic and there seemed no time for them to be together. Maria was under great stress. Her sinuses continued to give her trouble and she developed painful arthritis in her hands, which she blamed on the dampness of the Milan winter. She also had another pressing problem to settle.

With her break with Battista, she had severed arrangements with the

European managements who had handled her contracts and tours. Her Kansas City and Dallas appearances had ended all the engagements in which Battista might have been involved. Any new contracts she signed placed her solely in control of her own career commitments. Her decisions greatly depended on Onassis. She did not want to sign for another United States or South American tour where he could not be with her. This left only European venues. There had been many offers, all of them a year distant as opera schedules are always set far in advance. Concert offers were forthcoming, but she decided she would wait for a time before signing with a new agency. She wanted to be sure her sinus condition had cleared, but mostly she chose to be available to Onassis.

He agreed to their spending Christmas together in Monte Carlo, but not on the *Christina*, or at the Hôtel de Paris. He arranged for her to have a suite at the nearby luxurious but somewhat more discreet Grand, which was away from the Churchills (who stayed at the Hôtel de Paris) and the other prominent people with whom he had a close personal or business association. This was no doubt bruising to Maria's self-esteem. Why, then, did she accept the situation?

Well, of course, Maria had never been sure of herself off stage with men. Sex, as she had never experienced it before, free, abandoned, bringing her pride in her body and her ability to arouse a man, was perhaps her greatest draw to Onassis. But there was also the excitement of a man whose body never seemed large enough to contain him. Maria could listen for hours to his stories about his life and struggles as a young man. Suddenly he would leap up, unable to talk without striding round the floor, arms flung out to emphasize the drama, the horror, the ecstasy of a particular situation. He would laugh thunderously at himself at times and could see the humour in most things, albeit dry and bitter-sweet.

Onassis was now the same age as Battista had been when she had first met him. There the comparison ended. Onassis was a vigorous man. Age did not seem to touch him. He appeared – much as the partly fictional Zorba the Greek – as though he were immortal and that aura of invincibility was something that Maria wished to share.

She had few friends in Monte Carlo and spent her time in her suite with Bruna and Toy, who had accompanied her to Monaco, while Onassis joined Churchill on visits to friends along the Côte d'Azur, among them the ageing Lord Beaverbrook, the powerful newspaper publisher who had been a member of Churchill's Cabinet during World War Two. But Beaverbrook, with his strong Calvinistic background, had been highly critical of Edward VIII's affair with Wallis Simpson and he was no more approving of Onassis's affair with Maria Callas. To be sure, both men were fascinated by Onassis and thought him 'an invaluable source of financial, political and social gossip'. And Beaverbrook, who cared greatly for Churchill, was 'moved to see Onassis looking so tenderly after Churchill, escorting and supporting him wherever he went, anticipating his every wish and in every way betraying his deep affection'.

Beaverbrook had no love for Prince Rainier, whom he called 'a pompous ass' and 'a despot in fancy clothing', and was most sympathetic to Onassis's side of the Monaco controversy (to persuade Rainier to comply with de Gaulle's demands). Churchill and Onassis often dined with Beaverbrook at his palatial Cap d'Ail villa (a twenty-minute drive from Monaco) and the three men would, as often, spend an afternoon or an evening together on the anchored *Christina* while Maria remained at the hotel.

Relations between Onassis and Rainier were somewhat eased following the Prince's final capitulation to de Gaulle. Rainier now had grand expansion plans for his small principality which, since the country was about the size of London's Hyde Park and had been built 'up' about as far as possible, could only be enlarged by land reclamation from the sea. By the use of landfill, the coastline and inlet directly to the east of the rock upon which the palace stood could be expanded to accommodate a hotel, convention centre and apartment project. For this Rainier needed capital and he was hopeful that Onassis could help him to raise it from some of the tycoons with whom he conducted his business. And so Grace and Rainier, despite their disapproval of Maria's and Onassis's adulterous affair, 'tolerated' Maria. That is, they dined with both Maria and Onassis in restaurants, but did not include Maria in Palace gatherings. The hypocrisy of this was blatant, for Rainier and Grace had had adulterous affairs before they were married – Rainier with the married French actress Gisèle Pascal; Grace with married actors William Holden, Bing Crosby and Ray Milland.

The Rainiers' attitude deeply hurt and disappointed Maria. From the beginning of her affair with Onassis she had been caught up in the glamorous world of which he was a part. 'She had a stupid ambition of becoming a great lady of café society,' Zeffirelli commented. 'You have to go back to the difficult childhood this woman had to understand why she was always dreaming to reach certain positions. First there was that terrible husband of hers; they lived a very suburban, middle-class life. Onassis was a step higher.'

'The world has condemned me for leaving my husband,' Maria told a reporter for *Life* magazine several months later. She then reminded him that it was Meneghini who had sued for a legal separation. 'Battista himself said it was pointless if he had not complete power over me – that's all he wanted, I believe. I didn't want to marry an impresario, and if I had I would have at least married a good one.

'I was kept in a cage so long', she added, 'that when I met Aristo and his friends, so full of life and glamour, I became a different woman. Living with a man so much older than myself, I had become dull.' She did not see the drama her appearance evoked off stage as well as on. There were two Marias – one famous, one just *herself* and that one was riddled with insecurities. Maria was *still* in a cage, another cage – Aristo's golden canary – but she could not see that.

By February 1960 Maria had not sung publicly for two months. She cancelled her last scheduled concert, to have taken place in Belgium in December, so that she could be with Onassis and also because of her sinus problems. Immediately, the press claimed she had lost her voice and would never sing again. This occurred at the same time as her old rival Renata Tebaldi's triumphant return to La Scala in *Tosca*, after which Tebaldi told the press that she had left La Scala four years earlier 'because Callas had monopolized this theatre and, worse still, the attention that was paid to her was too much to take…Afterwards La Scala often asked me to change my mind but I was stubborn and refused to return so long as Maria Callas reigned there.' This was tantamount to saying that Maria was no longer queen, long live the new queen, Renata Tebaldi.

No sooner had Maria dealt with her emotions regarding Tebaldi's comments – which were hurtful – than her mother, in New York and not heard from in the last two years, made a statement to the press regarding her daughter's 'disgraceful deportment with Mr Onassis. Meneghini was a father and mother to Maria,' she declared. 'Now she no longer needs him. Women like Maria can never know real love…I was her first victim. Now it is Meneghini. Maria will marry Onassis to further her boundless ambition; he will be her third victim.'

In epic Judas-like betrayal, it turned out that Litza was about to publish a 'tell-all' book (ghosted by Lawrence Blochman), titled *My Daughter, Maria Callas*. Filled with untruths and inaccuracies, it made Maria out to be a monster who had deserted the one person – her mother – who was responsible for her singing career and was even more venomous in tone and accusation than her past interview with *Time* had been. She portrayed George Callas as 'a feeble layabout' and herself as the main support of herself and her children during their youth. 'To me,' Jackie said, 'the worst part of the book was her suggestion that she had been reduced to penury ['living in a shabby hotel for one dollar a day'] and that her rich and successful daughter refused to help her get out of it. I knew full well that she was leading a reasonably comfortable life and was much fêted in the Greek-American community.'[2]

And what did Litza want of Maria? In one of the many unanswered letters that she wrote to her daughter she cited public recognition by Maria of her part in her success, an apartment befitting the mother of a rich, famous opera diva and a wardrobe suitable to that station. Time and time again she reminded Maria of how she had helped her to fulfil her dream and that now it was Maria's turn to repay this debt. To her Greek-American friends Litza would say that Maria should either go back to her husband or live without a man as she had done. Litza's venom spread to George, who had returned to Athens and finally had married Alexandra, whom Litza referred to in letters to family in Greece as 'the whore'. Maria had never stopped supporting her mother, albeit not as generously as Litza believed was her due and for which she was non-relentingly bitter. The road had ended for Maria and Litza. There would never be a reconciliation. But Maria was not unconscious of her mother's early contribution to her career and could not completely wash her hands of her responsibility. Even with the publication of her mother's vitriolic book, Maria did not stop the delivery of her monthly cheques, meant to supplement Litza's earnings at Jolie Gabor's Madison Avenue shop.

Maria took a suite in the Ritz Hôtel Paris (paid for by Onassis) shortly after the New Year. Onassis had told her he would be in the city (where he owned an apartment) for an extended period of time. But no sooner did she arrive than he flew to Greece on business. Maria was understandably disappointed. She spent time with her good friend Maggie van Zuylen, who was also a friend of Ari's and closer to his age than to Maria's. In early February she had meetings with Michel Glotz, head of Pathé-Marconi, about doing some recordings with the conductor George Prêtre. Glotz, who would soon represent her, also conveyed to her the intense interest the Paris Opéra had in her singing Medea the following season.

Maria went in to the offices of the Opéra to discuss the possibility. She departed leaving the management without an answer. On the way out of the building to her waiting car, she was approached by Marylyse

<hr>

[2] Evangelia Callas was, in fact, at the time living in a rooming house owned by compatriots and friends. She occupied a well-furnished sitting room and bedroom suite, and was treated as a close guest in the home of good friends who refused to take money from her for her accommodation. The 'dollar a day' she claimed she paid out was to the maid who tended to her personal laundry and other chores.

Schaeffer a reporter from *France Soir*, by whom she agreed to be interviewed the next day at her hotel. According to Nicholas Gage's claim, Maria would have been seven months pregnant at this time. Yet Schaeffer refers to her as 'looking so pale in her little black ensemble with her modest make-up, her new short hair', hardly a description that fits a woman seven months along in her pregnancy. Nor does it sound feasible that if that had been her condition, Maria would have gone in for a meeting at the Opéra, and certainly Glotz would have been aware that she was pregnant and would have never sent her in the first place.

Schaeffer came up as planned the next day for the interview, which turned out to be quite lengthy. The only remark she makes about Maria's appearance is that she had some 'arthritic problems evidenced in the joints of her famously beautiful slender hands'. (This was something that had been troubling Maria for some time. She was on medication for it and also had special exercises she did daily.)

After some comments on her relations with the Paris Opéra, when asked about the future Maria replied, 'I want to live and perhaps to have a baby. I'm thirty-six years old, with *no one in my life*, and I do not even know if I am capable of [giving] birth.' She added a bit later, 'Do you understand? What a lovely story to write: La Callas would like a baby.'

Of course, Maria had wanted a baby for many years. This was not news, although *France Soir* gave it the lead in the story. What was news, perhaps, was her statement that there was no one in her life. She was feeling exceptionally bitter as Onassis had spent little time with her since she had come to Paris and she now could see that marriage might not be in their future. Onassis, in fact, had been making endless calls to Tina (to no avail) to work out a possible reconciliation.

Gage offers Maria's statement about wanting a baby as proof that she was announcing to the world her intention of giving up her career 'in order to have a child'. A week after this interview Maria returned to Milan and Gage states that she spoke to her internist, Dr Palmieri (who died in 1992 at the age of ninety and therefore was not interviewed by Gage) and pressured him to deliver the child early by Caesarean section as soon as it was possible to do so and that the doctor had agreed.

Caesarean section is not an optional choice for childbirth unless it is a medical necessity. No responsible doctor would agree to perform the operation, putting at risk the life of a premature seven-month baby at the whim of a mother. It would be unconscionable. Nor would it have been possible in Italy where the father's consent to such an operation would have had to have been given and where a woman could not have a hysterectomy, or any medical treatment that might hinder her chance at childbearing, without her husband's written agreement. Gage states that Maria did not want to be 'swollen and nine months pregnant...' and wanted the operation 'so that she could present her returning lover with a fait accompli'.

Gage asserts that Maria gave birth to a boy on 30 March 1960 late in her seventh month at a Milan clinic and that he died a few hours later. His proof is a picture of a baby bundled up said to be the dead child, although there is no identification on the published picture to establish this, nor can one see in this blurry photograph whether the child is male or female, dead or alive. The papers stated to be certification of a child named Omero Lengrini having died on this date only a few hours after his birth are incomplete and nearly illegible. Nowhere is a parent's name given, or the name of the officiating doctor; all standard information on Italian death certificates. Nor did Gage get anyone actually to say that Maria had given birth to a child. The conclusion is drawn by insinuation and the entirely suspect 'documentation'. He goes to great lengths to establish how familiar he became with Maria's butler, Ferruccio Mezzidri, and includes a photograph of them seated together. But Ferruccio refused to corroborate the story and Bruna, who is claimed to have been a witness to the birth, also refused to do so.

There is a possibility of a secret involved in the short life of the child named Omero Lengrini. He would have been the child of an unmarried mother (social ruin in many circles of Italy at that time), someone in Maria's close employ and Maria might have considered adoption in that case. But it is quite unlikely that it was Maria's child. Doubts exist that such an infant was buried in Milan as claimed. A thorough search of the cemetery records turned up no entry for any infant having been buried there under any name for a period of a month before and after the purported death.

On 8 April Onassis met with Tina in Paris, where they were photographed lunching and dining intimately in public restaurants. Ostensibly, Onassis wanted Tina to drop her suit for divorce. Maria, in Milan, was reduced to a state near nervous collapse. There was press speculation of a reconciliation. Onassis told Costa Gratsos that he was hopeful this would take place. But Tina was determined to end the marriage. She did agree that a messy divorce based on adultery would be harmful to the children and everyone else concerned, and was persuaded, therefore, to abandon the New York action with its obligatory allegation of adultery and to seek a quiet, quickie divorce elsewhere. This took place three weeks later in Alabama on the grounds of mental cruelty. Tina asked for, and was granted, the return of her maiden name – Livanos.

Onassis turned his attention back to Maria. He presented her with a magnificent diamond necklace and matching earrings, then organized another cruise on the *Christina* with his sister and brother-in-law as fellow guests. It was not yet smooth sailing for these star-crossed lovers. Maria had wanted Onassis to include the Churchills on the cruise and he had refused, protesting that her presence 'would embarrass Winston', who was 'genuinely fond of Tina'. She claimed she now understood 'the women she portrayed who died for love'.

In early May the *Christina* sailed through sun-drenched, halcyon days with Maria enjoying ultimate luxury and Onassis's attention, although he kept in constant touch with his business associates on shore and spent several hours a day locked in his study working on papers or talking ship-to-shore. While he was so engaged, Maria read Greek and French gossip magazines, and lolled in an array of bikinis (changing several times a day).[3] When the boat was at anchor they would swim together. In the evening she would dress in flowing silk, fire colours – reds, oranges, deep blues and purple – which Onassis preferred. She was, by her own admission, still 'madly happy' when she was with Onassis and, following the divorce, Onassis began to take on the look of a contented lover.

By mid-summer, her sinus cured, her nerves steadied, she began to long for a return to the stage. Enter her good friend and early mentor, Maestro Tullio Serafin, who had actually always been on hand to talk to her at troubled times in her career and her private life. But despite his sometime position as a surrogate father, it had been seven years since they had worked as a team in the theatre (*Aida* in Verona).

Earlier that year Onassis had promised Maria that he would arrange an engagement at the Opera House in Monte Carlo. But Rainier would agree only on the condition that it would not be under his auspices. In other words, he and Grace would not attend any of the performances. This was totally unacceptable to Maria who could only interpret such an agreement as allowing herself to be the butt of a public insult. More and more, Maria had been thinking about revisiting Greece. She had re-established a correspondence with her father, whom she wanted to see along with Jackie. The previous year she had been approached by the Greek National Opera and the classic Epidaurus Theatre (which she had visited during her first cruise on the *Christina*) to sing *Medea*. Neither the time nor the terms had been right then, but it seemed a perfect choice now. She asked Serafin whether he would conduct if an acceptable offer was made and he

[3] Photographs of Maria sunbathing in a brief bikini were taken by paparazzi using long-range cameras. In them she looks exceptionally slim and trim, and there seem to be no apparent scars from a Caesarean birth or an attempt to hide one if such were the case.

agreed, but suggested she sing *Norma*. Pleased to sign both Maria Callas and Maestro Serafin, the Epidaurus bettered their original terms and two performances, 24 and 28 August 1960, were scheduled.

The ageing Serafin (now eighty-one), who had just coached Joan Sutherland for her successful Covent Garden debut as *Lucia*, had lost none of his energy and went to work rehearsing privately with Maria at the house in Rome where she had first come to him at the beginning of her career. After her problems in Dallas with *Lucia*, and the many months of battling her sinus infection and musical inactivity, Maria was not altogether sure of herself. Serafin did more than help her prepare her role (which, after all, she had sung many times): he helped her to regain her self-confidence.

19

A Family Affair

THE *CHRISTINA*, WITH Maria and Onassis aboard, was anchored at Glyfada, a short distance from both Athens and the vast, ancient, outdoor theatre at Epidaurus where Maria was to sing *Norma*, the first opera to be performed in this great bastion of classic Greek drama. The August sun was bare and relentless. Rehearsals were held after sundown. During the day, Maria remained for the most part on the air-conditioned yacht. The salon had been converted into a temporary music room where she, Serafin, the director Alexis Minotis (who had staged Maria's *Medea* the previous year at the Dallas Civic Opera and was noted for his authentic style of classicism) and the production's three other lead singers – Mirto Picchi, Kiki Morfoniou and Alberta Maziello – worked separately and together. This was a reunion for Maria and Picchi who had sung Pollione opposite Maria's first *Norma* in 1948 at the Comunale in Florence (a production which was also under Serafin's baton), as well as in her 1951 South American tour and at Covent Garden the following year. With Serafin and Picchi, who both admired and worked well with her, Maria's self-confidence was bolstered.

Onassis had not one, but two luxurious homes side by side in Glyfada. Artemis and her husband occupied one and the other he used only occasionally as a pied-à-terre when the weather was too cold or blustery to remain on the *Christina*. (That was also the case in Monte Carlo where he had a grand suite at the Hôtel de Paris.) Artemis managed the household affairs and the staff of four, who acted as extra help for her in her brother's frequent absence. Since Onassis and Maria had been lovers, he used the house even less.

On this trip to Greece business meetings occupied his days, but he seemed to be proud of the musical activity on board and returned to the *Christina*, on the first day he had gone into Athens, to announce to Maria that posters of her as Medea were 'everywhere you looked'.

Her father, now showing his advancing years but still a handsome man, came to visit her on the boat and remained for dinner. Onassis and George Callas got on well and Maria fairly glowed from the renewed warmth she felt for her father. He was happy with Alexandra even though she had not been well. One great advantage of his remarriage, he confessed, was that Litza was no longer in contact with him. He told Maria about the indignities Jackie had had to endure at the hands of Milton's rich, shipbuilding family, the Embiricoses. Despite her many years of sacrifice for him, Jackie had been cut off from any inheritance or support and there was even a good chance that they would succeed in taking from her the small apartment which was her only security. 'You should see your sister and try to patch up your differences,' he prodded her. 'Look how she loved you when you were a little girl.' Maria said she wanted to see Jackie and had written to tell her so. 'Call her,' he insisted. 'She's shy about contacting you first.'

The sisters had not met since twelve years before, when Jackie had visited Maria and Meneghini in Verona. Jackie was hesitant at first, feeling she did not want Maria to offer her pity because of her tragic years with Milton and her current near penurious state. She was able to 'get by' with part-time employment and felt a great independence at achieving this on her own. An appointment was made on the following night for both Jackie and George, and two other old Athenian friends of Maria's, Dr Papatesta and Mrs Xakousti, to be her guests at a waterfront restaurant near the dock where the *Christina* was moored.

One had to take a small launch to get from the yacht to the shore. 'I could see the boat approaching,' Jackie recalled, 'she was there, sitting upright, the image from the [newspaper and magazine] photographs. A sailor helped her ashore and I noticed the assurance with which she moved. Her hands were long and she used them with a sense of drama, her clothes were very stylish and I suddenly realized that I didn't know this woman at all.' Jackie was the last one of her guests whom Maria embraced. At first there was an awkwardness between the sisters, but this soon eased. Sibling closeness was not in evidence, but they were communicating somewhere, in what might be called 'a comfort zone, two old friends grown out of touch but warmed by memory'.

After dinner Maria invited the small group to come back to the *Christina*, its glittering lights now reflected in the calm waters of the Aegean. The launch brought them to the boat. Onassis greeted them as they entered the bar, where he was entertaining some business associates.[1] 'He seemed genuinely interested to meet the sister at last,' Jackie

---

[1] Ironically, one of these men was André Embiricos, an extremely wealthy cousin of Milton's and a long-time friend of Onassis's (he had been best man at the wedding of Onassis and Tina). Jackie and André Embiricos had never met before.

reflected. 'He was short and stocky but clearly tough,' she recalled, 'a man who had fought his way up in a hard world. He made me nervous but I could sense some of the energy Maria evidently found irresistible and for the brief time we were there, he was the life and soul of the party...Once on board father strolled about as if the boat were his and not Onassis's.'

Jackie did not feel that 'at home'. But then, Maria led her to her private suite ('a riot of gold'), which she used as a sitting room, and the years between them faded away. Both had changed considerably. Maria was now a sophisticated woman of the world and looked it; Jackie, although still attractive, appeared dowdy – to the unknowing, a middle-class housewife who might be having hard times. They talked about the family at first, avoiding personal questions. As she looked around at all the splendour and luxury that surrounded them, Jackie asked, 'Are you happy?'

'Oh, I'm happy with Aristo,' Jackie reported her saying, 'but I get tired of this boat. First I'm tired of the sea then I'm tired of being in port with so many people waiting to see me. I'd like to be alone with him more. I'd like to have a baby.[2] And what about you? Are you happy?' Jackie shook her head. Maria placed her arm affectionately round her older sister's shoulders. 'How could you be?' She sighed, recalling from her father's revelations all the sadness in Jackie's life. She insisted that Jackie come to hear her sing, an invitation she had not extended since she was a student performer in Athens. Jackie agreed.

On 23 August, the scheduled day of the first performance, the skies opened. A torrential downpour continued into the night and the opera was cancelled. The following evening was clear, mercifully cool, the great, ruined amphitheatre lit by the stars. Upon her entrance Maria received an ovation and then, with precision timing – before a note was sung – two white doves were released by a member of the audience. The birds, symbolic of hope and love, fluttered to the footlights where they poised briefly, rose and, as though with a graceful bow, disappeared into the night. Maria, obviously moved by what she understood was a gesture of her audience's affection, never lost her composure.

This Norma was a new, more poignant, heroic priestess than Maria had previously portrayed, less shrill, more torn by events rather than enraged by them. She was in exceptional voice, supported magnificently by Serafin and complemented by the others in the cast who gave superb performances. The classic setting, designed by Antonis Fokus to blend

---

[2] This remark about a desire to bear a child was only four months after Nicholas Gage's claim that Callas had and lost a son fathered by Onassis.

naturally with the ancient amphitheatre and so right for a Druid priestess, gave the production a dramatic sense of *théâtre vérité*. This performance was unfortunately not recorded. But ten days later, with Serafin
conducting and a partially fresh (albeit excellent) cast, Maria reproduced
her new version of Norma in a London recording studio with extraordinary success.[3] Serafin was to say that her Epidaurus Norma was Maria's
finest interpretation of the role, her vocal control amazing, her Druid
priestess imbued with increased strength; a powerful, memorable, tragic
figure of gargantuan emotions.

'She acted with her whole being,' Jackie recalled, 'even the sandals on
her feet seemed to project the role.' Later Jackie told Maria, 'Now I understand.' It was clear to her how towering an artist Maria had become, and
that her sister was driven by a different drummer from herself, or most
other people, for that matter. No amount of training, luck, or dedication
ever could have made her 'a second Callas'. Secure in that knowledge,
Jackie could live more harmoniously with herself. But the realization of it
drove a new wedge between the sisters; not bitterness or envy. Jackie was
in awe of Maria, no longer able to associate the artist with her once insecure, pimple-faced, overweight younger sister. Her resentment at being
sacrificed by their mother for Maria and her career now seemed foolish.
Who was she, *what* was she, compared with this woman who was most
probably the greatest singer in the world? The brief intimacy the sisters
had shared aboard the *Christina* could never be recaptured.

'I watched Onassis,' one of his aides recalled of the Epidaurus production of *Norma*. 'He always professed he hated opera. But he sat mesmerized throughout Callas's entire performance. One could see the pride on
his face. And when the opera ended there were tears in his eyes.' The
audience felt the same way. Many were weeping as Maria took her bows,
a laurel wreath placed by one of them at her bare feet. Three days later
she was awarded Greece's Medal of Merit. A new sense of nationalistic
pride was born in her. Previously, she had always considered herself to be
an American of Greek parentage and education. Now, she referred to
herself as 'Greek-American'. She had Onassis look into the possibility of
her becoming a Greek citizen and of obtaining a Greek divorce (which
would not be recognized in Italy). Onassis was also investigating the
possibility of Maria making a film.

Although he was never interested in acting as Maria's manager,
Onassis very much liked the idea that she should become a movie star.

---

[3] This production of *Norma*, with Tullio Serafin conducting, was recorded in a London
studio for EMI 5–12 September (1960), with Franco Corelli (Pollione), Christa Ludwig
(Adalgisa), Nicola Zaccaria (Oroveso), and the orchestra and chorus of Teatro alla Scala.

Films were something he could more easily identify with than opera. He was a movie fan and revelled in the company of Garbo and Dietrich when they cruised with him on the *Christina*. Dietrich would kid him about the way he smoked a cigarette ('So you think you are Jean Gabin, eh? Maybe we should find out'). He was at present toying with the idea of investing in film production. News of this travelled to London where former Hollywood writer-producer Carl Foreman controlled Open Road Films.[4] Foreman held the rights on the Alistair Maclean novel *The Guns of Navarone*, about a group of Allied commandos during World War Two sent to Greece to destroy German fortifications. The film was to have an all-star cast including Gregory Peck, Anthony Quinn and David Niven (representing American, Greek and British forces), but the two major female roles had not yet been set and one – a Greek woman who helps the commandos – seemed to be the kind of dramatic role tailor-made for Maria. 'You couldn't *buy* that kind of publicity!' Foreman told his associate, Leon Becker.

The two men went down to Monte Carlo on their way to Greece to scout locations. They first met Onassis who, to Foreman's surprise, tried to convince him to cast Maria when he was already wildly enthusiastic. Onassis offered to cover all expenses if after ten days they found out that she was wrong for the role. 'That would be a great deal of money,' Foreman was reported as replying. 'I'm a very rich man,' Onassis assured him. Actually, it was Maria who needed to be won over. Foreman offered to do a private film test so that she could see for herself what he believed to be the case – the camera would love her.

Maria, to Aristo's anger, still remained negative. She simply was not keen on the idea of performing before a camera, particularly in a non-singing role. Onassis insisted she at least read the script. 'I have sympathy for the woman,' she told Foreman and Becker later, 'but this is not a star role. The men and the guns are the centre of the story.' Foreman tried to convince her that he could rewrite the part with stronger scenes for the character and assured her it would be of Academy Award calibre. Maria still said, 'No, thank you,' much to Onassis's disappointment.[5]

Suddenly Visconti re-entered Maria's life. For her, it was to be a

---

[4] Carl Foreman moved from Hollywood to England in 1951 at the time of the House UnAmerican Activities Committee hearings.

[5] The fine Greek actress Irene Papas was cast in the role originally offered to Maria Callas. *The Guns of Navarone* (1961) was nominated for Academy Awards in seven categories (Best Picture, Best Director, Screenplay Adaptation, Music, Film Editing, Special Effects and Sound) and lost in all of them. Although the movie was hugely successful, no member of the cast was nominated.

defining moment, but only that – for almost as soon as he appeared on the scene he would withdraw and disappear once again. Visconti had for some time been intrigued with the idea of reviving Donizetti's *Poliuto*, which had not been performed in a major opera house for over a century. His revisionist take on the libretto was to centre the story of early Christianity not on Poliuto, but on his wife Paolina, a Christian convert whose intense love for her husband is instrumental in her finding her faith and who eventually makes the sublime sacrifice of following him to her death. Two of Donizetti's most lasting tragedies – *Lucrezia Borgia* and *Lucia di Lammermoor* – were composed just preceding *Poliuto* which, due to its fatalistic view of the faith, was banned in 1839 by the Naples censor. The opera had a chequered performance record after that, being produced in Paris the following year as *Les Martyrs*, then in New Orleans in 1846 (in an Italian translation) as *I Martiri*, with only rare, sporadic productions since that time.

Visconti believed from the start that Maria was the ideal Paolina and that by casting her in the role the opera would transmogrify almost naturally into his conception. He approached Ghiringhelli and La Scala, following Maria's triumphant *Norma* at Epidaurus. Ghiringhelli, reassured by that performance that Maria was as great as ever, was less confident that she would choose to return to his opera house 'what with Tebaldi's current popularity'.

Visconti sent Maria the libretto and score. Paolina captured her imagination. There was also the intrigue and challenge of working again with Visconti, who travelled to Monaco to see her and, as it turned out, Onassis as well. The two men disliked each other almost upon first handshake. 'Your taste in men baffles me,' Visconti told a bristling Maria. 'You are throwing yourself away.'

Despite the brutality of his comments and her renewed dislike of his arrogance, Maria decided she would do the opera under Visconti's direction, fully believing in his ability to make a grand success of it. The terms offered by La Scala were excellent. Corelli was to appear in the title role and Nicola Zaccaria as Callistene. They were two singers with whom she had sung many times and with whom she had an outstanding musical rapport. This would also be a new production, designed especially for her and masterminded by Visconti. It would, she decided, be an excellent vehicle to whisk her back, centre stage, at La Scala. In truth, Maria had felt the pressure of losing her place in two of the greatest opera houses in the world – the Metropolitan and La Scala. So she signed, rehearsals to begin almost immediately as the opera was scheduled for 7–12 December 1960, filling the spot of a cancelled production.

The next three months were an emotional see-saw for her. She confided to Stelios Galatopoulos, 'Spiritually, I never left La Scala but physically, I was returning there as an estranged artist. Would the public
accept me on these terms? I was very nervous about this as it had nothing
to do with my artistic capabilities.'

There was also the almost palpable shadow of Tebaldi haunting her.
With both divas singing in the same opera house, would the media turn
this into a contest? That was something Maria did not wish to happen.
She would also be separated from Onassis for an extended period and
would be in Italy where Battista, whose rancour knew no bounds, might
decide to file a charge of immorality against her. Nonetheless, her desire
to regain her stature at La Scala overcame all these objections and she
dedicated herself to the success of her performance and of the opera.
What Maria had not anticipated were problems with Visconti's absen-
teeism. No sooner had rehearsals begun than he was drawn into government censorship complications regarding his two most recent projects –
the film *Rocco and His Brothers* and the play *L'Arialda*, which had been
banned in Italy on grounds of obscenity.

Instead of being in Milan overseeing the production, he was in Rome
and almost impossible even to reach on the telephone. Without his
strong hand and artistic vision, Maria felt unprotected. On 15 November,
just three weeks before the première, he sent two telegrams – one to
Ghiringhelli withdrawing from the production and one to Maria, apolo-
gizing profusely for what looked like his desertion but, he assured her,
was not. He simply had to make a political stand about government
intervention in the arts and so would publicly declare that he could not
in good conscience work for a state-subsidized theatre (which would
include La Scala). 'I am sure you will understand my predicament and
approve of my decision.' She replied that she did, but it was a great
disappointment. A crutch had been removed.

Herbert Graf, the Austrian-American son of the famous Viennese critic
Max Graf, stepped in. Graf had staged many operas at the Met, produced
regularly at La Scala and had just been named Director of the Zurich
Opera. He did an excellent job of taking over from Visconti and Maria got
on well with him. Her personal reviews were excellent. She was in good
voice and endowed Paolina with extraordinary grace and pathos. But
Poliuto did not loom as one of her great theatrical triumphs and it seemed
unlikely that it would be retained in La Scala's regular repertoire. Onassis,
this time visibly restless, his dark glasses in place and possibly concealing
his lowered lids, sat in the front row on opening night surrounded by a
host of important and socially prominent friends who all attended the

grand party he gave in Maria's honour directly following the performance. (Later, he was to say scoffingly to Artemis, 'They should have reviewed the party, not the opera.')

Ghiringhelli was not displeased. If Callas could sell out the house with *Poliuto*, he was confident that she could still receive much acclaim and be as great an asset to La Scala as she once had been. He discussed the possibility of several operas for the 1961 season. Sander Gorlinsky, who had handled Maria's British appearances for years, was now (since her severed relations with Battista) her exclusive agent. He tried to convince her seriously to consider La Scala's offer but to no avail. Maria was not yet ready to make a commitment that would mean a long separation from Onassis and, on his part, he showed no enthusiasm for her to sign with La Scala. He liked her being famous. Opera simply did not interest him.

Following *Poliuto,* Sander Gorlinsky received offers from all over the world for Maria. 'The canary chooses only to sing for her master,' a frequent guest on the *Christina* commented. This was the time of Maria's most romantic feelings towards Onassis and his for her.

> There was no doubt that they enjoyed sex together. They often disappeared, sometimes twice in one afternoon, behind the locked doors of 'Chios', not to be seen on deck again for an hour or two, seldom in the same clothes they had been wearing, Maria's hairdo rearranged. Within the comparative privacy of the *Christina*, they felt able to express their feelings tangibly. There was a lot of body touching – his hand on her bare upper thigh, hers stroking his arm or resting suggestively close to his 'manhood'. No one minded. It somehow did not seem vulgar. They were so obviously in love. They were, of course, much more circumspect in public. Although Onassis had a possessive way of holding her, his hand slipping down her back when they went dancing.

Once they were caught by a paparazzo kissing lightly, lips brushing, and the photograph appeared on the front page of several tabloids.

Only a few days later Battista filed a new order with the Civic Tribunal in Milan to annul the original separation by mutual consent and replace it with one that named Maria as the guilty party in the break-up of their marriage. 'I want to whiten my name,' Meneghini told the press, 'and I want to proclaim that it was because of her that our marriage was destroyed…She's not behaving like a women of her position [and] has made nonsense of the court order that we should remain faithful to one another.' Battista did not name Onassis as his wife's lover, perhaps because he still had expectations that 'the snake', as he privately referred to him, would uncoil long enough to reconsider his offer of a pay-off, this time to refrain from further legal action, for surely Battista was aware Maria would never return to him. Onassis convinced Maria that silence in the matter was her best weapon of retaliation. She was, however, so happy in her new life that even Battista's public vitriol could not ruffle it.

Ostensibly she was living in Monte Carlo where the *Christina* occupied the prime berth in the harbour. The sixty-member crew referred to her privately as *la patronne*. She conferred on the daily menus with the head chef, was hostess at their small, on-board dinner parties and occupied Onassis's bed in 'Chios'. A second suite (redecorated in the gilded opulence that had so impressed Jackie) had been converted for her use as a private sitting and dressing room. Bruna was on hand, as was Toy wearing a jaunty 'sailor's' jacket for his night-time walks along the harbour (Maria had, indeed, taken 'the head and the tail' of their pet as Battista had predicted). She and Onassis dined often at the Maona, a new nightclub in the heart of Monte Carlo where they danced in a tight embrace ('It is impossible for them to dance cheek to cheek,' London *Daily Express* columnist William Hickey reported, 'as Miss Callas is slightly taller than Mr Onassis').[6]

There was no need for them now to speak secretly to each other in Greek as their relationship was no longer conspiratorial. Each had had a profound impact on the other's habits and dress. Maria had cut her hair in a chic younger style, to please Onassis and, although attractive, it deprived her unique face of some of its great drama. But she expressed her true self in her clothes. She had created a style that was inimitably her own. Evening gowns in flowing chiffon with bat sleeves that created a marvellous wing of colour whenever she raised her arms; stiletto knee-high boots for daytime to hide her legs, which she always felt were not shapely enough. She perfectly portrayed a woman of class, poise, elegance and passion. Much of her style had been inspired by Visconti. But she now moulded it to Onassis's need to be surrounded by glamour.

He, too, dressed more conservatively. 'There had been a touch of mafioso tailoring about his suits and ties before Maria,' one friend noted. He was a heavy smoker, three packs a day, his faintly rasping, carefully modulated voice reflecting its effects. Maria was a non-smoker and cigarette fumes irritated her throat. Onassis did not stop smoking, but when they were together he smoked less.

When they weren't exchanging gossip (something Onassis dearly

---

[6] Onassis had an interest in the Maona, which was named, it was largely supposed, by combining the first two letters of Maria with the first three of Onassis.

loved), conversations centred not on music and the world of opera but on politics, big business and his problems with Prince Rainier. Onassis became her college of one – but the subjects he taught had only to do with himself.

Although Tina had custody of the children, she never stood in the way of Onassis having them whenever he chose. In the winters Christina and Alexander attended school in Paris near Onassis's apartment at 84 avenue Foch, and for now this regime was maintained. When he was in France it was understood that they would spend the weekends with him; during the week they were at the grand Paris apartment of their maternal grand-parents, while Tina was either skiing in Switzerland or visiting in New York with her sister Eugenie and her husband, Onassis's hated rival, Stavros Niarchos. Onassis never trusted his brother-in-law who displayed a lecherous eye for Tina, and who he always suspected had attempted to seduce her as revenge on Onassis who had won over him in many a busi-ness deal. Therefore Onassis was never happy when Tina planned to take the children on a visit to Eugenie, even now that they were divorced.

For Christmas 1960 the youngsters joined Onassis and Maria in Monte Carlo, where they occupied the newly decorated and renamed children's room (as they had outgrown a nursery). At twelve, Alexander openly dis-played the signs of the hostile, rebellious teenager he would soon become. Christina, three years his junior, remained a sullen, withdrawn girl already on the road to serious eating disorders and manic depression. Maria had never been able to bond with young children despite her con-stant cries that she desperately wanted a baby. Alexander and Christina presented a challenge that, try as she might, she could not overcome.

Her first attempt to win them over had not been successful. She went on an extensive shopping spree before they were to arrive and left all the gaily wrapped packages in the main lounge of the *Christina* where she had planned a special afternoon tea, requesting the pastry chef to make all their favourite sweets. That occasion turned out be one of the worst hours Maria was to spend. Christina fell back into a kind of mutism she had suffered as a small child – saying nothing, not answering when anyone spoke to her, father, brother or Maria. Her expression taut, she refused the specially made tea cakes by simply pushing the plate away without even glancing down at it. Neither child ever acknowledged her presence and when the ghastly hour was over they left the lounge – the gift packages unopened and deserted despite Maria's prodding that they 'please open them, there will be more for Christmas'.

Both children blamed Maria for their parents' divorce and the loss of the small bit of security they had known. They had experienced the bitter

disappointment of a form of parental abuse only exercised by the very
rich: money, gifts and an array of caretakers substituting for a parent's
attention. Christina's school friends say that she cried herself to sleep
every night before and after her parents' divorce. Neither of Onassis's offspring could be bought with an expensive present. Scattered among their
many homes were enough toys and clothes to fill a department store.
Presents were given by both Tina and Onassis to compensate for long
stretches of neglect – the longer the stretch, the more lavish the gift.

Alexander pointedly referred to Maria as 'the singer', refusing to call
her by name. When Onassis castigated him for this the boy got up and
strode out of the room, slamming the door as he went. Christina raised
her soulful eyes to her father, who was furious with his son, but did
nothing to follow. 'Can I leave, too?' she asked.

'You are both to remain in your cabins for dinner,' he said harshly to
her. Christina said nothing as she turned and left the room.

'They hate me.' Maria sighed, her voice near breaking.

'They'll come round,' Onassis replied.

They never did, no matter how hard Maria tried, the insults she overlooked, the number of presents she continued to buy for them, which
they ignored and never thanked her for. His children had deep-seated
problems and Maria attempted to discuss this with Onassis, but he
became gruffly dismissive, his copper-coloured eyes hardening to cold
metal. This unnerved her, and she would immediately change the subject
to something light and frothy so she could see the light come back into
his eyes and hear the sound of loving familiarity in his voice. She wanted
to talk to him about marriage, about having a child together, to remind
him that her biological clock was ticking fast. The time seemed wrong. It
would perhaps never be right, but she had *now* and that was better than
anything she had ever experienced before – except when she was on stage
and the shouts and cheers of an audience enveloped her with acceptance.
That was not real love, however, and Maria, more like Christina than
either of them perceived, desperately needed the love that signified her as
a special person in Onassis's life.

Onassis was a willing giver, an eager partner. He felt comfortable with
Maria, sure of her loyalty to him. There was a sense of belonging that he
had never before experienced in the women he had known. Despite his
friendships with Winston Churchill and the many famous people he
courted, there were only two persons in his life he was actually close to –
his sister Artemis and his oldest friend Costa Gratsos. Artemis was
'blood', a tight bond with Greek men. Gratsos had been his confidant
since the 1920s. 'Costa knows every crime I've ever committed,' he told

Maria. Gratsos was born in Ithaca of a shipbuilding family and had attended the London School of Economics before he decided to become a sailor and see something of life. Burly, tough, yet intelligent, he could fight with his fists as well as he could outwit with his mind. Maria tried to win over both Artemis and Gratsos. Artemis would always remain somewhat indifferent to her approaches. Gratsos was another matter. He liked Maria, perhaps because she was Greek, more likely as he could see how content Onassis was in her company. He even posed the idea that Onassis should marry her.

'Marriage to Maria would be a commitment to the gods that I could never break,' Onassis told his friend. Tina was a possession and he hated to lose what he owned. But he could not belong to anyone. That was the keystone of his personal creed. He had to be the person in control. 'It's not just lust,' he went on. 'I love Maria and that places me in grave danger.' The danger was evident for Maria as well.

20

A Loss of Innocence

ON THE MORNING of 27 April 1962 Maria awoke in the suite Onassis kept at the Dorchester Hotel in London to learn that a cadre of newspaper reporters were waiting in reception to speak with her about her mother's failed suicide attempt the previous day. It was the first she had heard of the incident. Moments later, Jackie called from Athens. Litza had consumed a potentially lethal number of sleeping pills. When she had not showed up for a luncheon date with a friend and the woman was unable to reach her by telephone, she came running over to the new studio apartment in mid-Manhattan where Litza now lived and got the management to open the door. Litza, fully dressed, make-up neatly applied, was unconscious on the bed. On the table beside her were some token gifts to her friends (bits of her jewellery) and an envelope addressed to 'My Daughter Maria Callas'. Rushed to nearby Roosevelt Hospital, her stomach was pumped and she was placed under twenty-four-hour surveillance and the care of a psychiatrist.

Dr Lantzounis had gone over to the hospital immediately to see her and then called Maria who, having been told her mother would survive, asked him to read the contents of the envelope. 'I am sure you will shed no tears for the woman who gave you life and sacrificed her own so that you might one day be famous,' it began. Dr Lantzounis assured Maria that her mother would fully recover from the effects of the overdose. She would, however, need extended psychiatric care.

'In a hospital?' Maria asked.

'No, not at this time. But she should not be living on her own.'

Arrangements were made for Litza to move in, once again, with her Greek-American friends. Maria agreed to pay for her upkeep and for the psychiatric care that was required. Litza had asked Dr Lantzounis to tell Maria she 'would forgive her if she only would come to see her dying mother'.

Maria refused to be snared in Litza's trap, carefully woven of guilt and pity. 'It is over,' Maria told her old friend and godfather Dr Lantzounis. 'I cannot totally desert her, but I never want to see her again. Being my mother does not exempt her from the many times she has betrayed me.' Perhaps Litza's most perverse action was an added line in her 'suicide note' bequeathing to Maria the royalties from her book, *My Daughter, Maria Callas* (which had not been a best-seller, but had appeared in excerpt form, been a featured selection of a bookclub and earned a respectable advance).

Maria and Onassis had now been together for three years. Her passion for him had not waned and he seemed just as smitten by her. Still, their relationship had not moved forward. After looking at villas outside Paris for several months, Onassis had finally bought for her a beautiful flat at 36 avenue Georges Mandel. To Maria's disappointment, it was to be her own apartment; Onassis was retaining his on avenue Foch. Aware that the world thought of her as Onassis's mistress, she nonetheless sustained the hope that she would one day be his wife.

Tina had married 'Sunny', Marquess of Blandford, the Duke of Marlborough's thirty-five-year-old heir, on 23 October 1961, sixteen months after her divorce from Onassis, and was now a marchioness, the chatelaine of a great house – Lee Place – and, when her new husband succeeded his father, would be a duchess, with one of the grandest and most famous homes in all of Great Britain, Blenheim Palace. Sunny Blandford, who was divorced and the father of two children, was a mild-mannered man, aristocratic, kin of the Churchills and the Spencers, and well accepted in royal circles (he had, in fact, once been considered a possible suitor for Princess Margaret's hand). Onassis had never met Blandford, but he had spoken to numerous people about him. 'She doesn't love him,' he told Gratsos. 'Too quiet, too refined.'

'You know what they say about still water?'

'She won't stay with him long enough to find out,' Onassis predicted, intimating that he knew Tina better than she knew herself. The idea that his children now had a stepfather – albeit a man with royal connections – did not go down well with him although he retained a possessive attitude towards Tina. 'She is, after all, the mother of my children. We will always be bound by that,' he told Maria. 'I will always be there if she needs me.'

Maria had greatly curtailed her singing engagements, but she had made some important recent appearances following the concert on 30 May 1961 at St James's Palace. On 6 and 13 August that same year, she returned to the Epidaurus to sing Medea: a Greek woman singing the quintessential opera dealing with Greek legend in the hallowed, ancient remains of a Greek theatre. Her preparation for *Medea* was so intense that Onassis found the excuse of some business dealings in Alexandria to leave her to it on her own. Of course, she was not really on her own, for she had great faith in Alexis Minotis, who had also directed her successful *Medea* in Dallas, and in the exceptional Jon Vickers who sang Jason then and would now do so again.

Maria insisted upon numerous extra rehearsals. She appeared tireless, working well into the night, while everyone else was exhausted. This *had* to be her ultimate performance of Medea and there were many difficulties to overcome, not least the open-air arena itself, which despite its remarkable acoustics could not shelter her from small flying bugs, the heat, the humidity, or the personal agenda that her audience would bring to this famous Greek legend.[1] There was not one step or hand movement that she did not rehearse several times. Every recitative and aria was repeated and repeated again and again as she discovered new layers of meaning. The cast grumbled but her old friend, and her conductor, Nicola Rescigno managed to keep the peace.

Maria's dedication became so extreme that the night before the first performance she had a bed brought to the museum enclosure near the theatre and slept there for a few hours, waking at dawn and going out on the stage alone, walking through the scenes which presented the greatest technical problems. It was there, by herself, on the stage of that ancient theatre that she felt her Greek roots the strongest, she later told Rescigno.

There had been rain in the days before, but the night of 9 August was clear, the stars high and brilliant, and the air tinged with only a gentle, cooling breeze. The expectation of the audience, who had driven from all over Greece for this special occasion, was almost tangible. There was not a spare seat in the amphitheatre, which held over 20,000. Several thousands more, unable to buy a ticket, stood outside the seating area, pleased just to be able to be a part of such an historic occasion. Onassis had not returned from Alexandria for the performance, but Maria did not seem to be greatly disturbed by this. 'He has his business and I have mine,' she told Minotis, 'and sometimes the timing isn't perfect.'

Maria was at the top of her form both vocally and dramatically. She not only gave a stunning performance, she infused Medea with a fresh interpretation. She took seventeen curtains and could not make her way

---

[1] In Greek legend, Medea was a sorceress who helped Jason to win the Golden Fleece. She escapes with him, avoiding pursuit by casting the legs of her brother behind her to delay the king their father, Aeëtes, the keeper of the Golden Fleece. When Jason later deserts her, she kills his two children and poisons his new wife, Creusa; then flees to Athens, where she marries King Aegeus (for whom the Aegean Sea was named).

through the crowds of fans who were waiting for her to emerge from backstage until a man stood up on another man's shoulders and shouted (in Greek), 'Make way! Make way for Greece's Queen of Opera!' Suddenly a path was cleared for her to pass. Cries of 'Maria! Maria! Queen Maria!' rose on both sides as she walked to a waiting car, Minotis on one side of her, his wife Katrina Paxinou, on the other. Behind them was Ghiringhelli who had come from Milan to see for himself if Maria could carry a strenuous opera like *Medea*, for he had engaged her to sing the role at La Scala in December, just four months later.

She was nervous about her return to La Scala after what she considered the lukewarm reception of *Poliuto*. Milan, with the possibility of more legal problems arising by way of Battista, was no longer a safe haven or a home, because she and Onassis could not stay together there. She had thought that the same team who had been with her at Epidaurus would be with her at the La Scala production. However, Rescigno had to back out due to a conflicting schedule. Ghiringhelli signed Thomas Schippers, a young American (thirty-one), who was closely associated with Gian Carlo Menotti (they were, in fact, lovers), for whom he had conducted the première performance of *The Consul* (1950) as well as *Amahl and the Night Visitors* (1951) and *The Saint of Bleecker Street* (1954), before helping Menotti found the Festival of Two Worlds in Spoleto in 1958. Schippers had never before conducted Cherubini's music, which was somewhat severe but with a distinct purity and originality, and it was immediately obvious that he and Maria did not see things alike. Tempers often flared and it took all of Alexis Minotis's skill as a mediator to quieten them. But Maria did not have confidence in Schippers's baton and because of it her own self-confidence began to erode.

Onassis, claiming previous business meetings that could not be broken, did not attend the first performance on 11 December. Maria was disappointed, but she put on a brave front and, before the performance, seemed in excellent spirits, if a bit nervous. Even through the last re-hearsal she had been concerned about the way Schippers 'set pieces by tempi which divided instead of joined'. Minotis had assured her that it would be all right, but she had noted that he had not looked too pleased himself and that he had huddled privately for a long while with Schippers right after he spoke with her.

The usual red roses arrived from Onassis on opening night and he called to wish her well and send her his love. Ghiringhelli stopped by her dressing room, as did Minotis. Bruna was there to assist the dresser and to walk with Maria backstage to the wings as she prepared for her entering recitative. All seemed well and she began her first aria 'Dei tuoi figli' with her usual dramatic intensity. Then, suddenly, 'from the top of the gallery', Schippers recalled, 'came an awful hissing sound'. Maria was taken aback. Her first thought was that a Tebaldi claque had decided there could be only one queen at La Scala and it would not be Maria.[2] She continued and so did the hissing. 'When she came to the words "Ho dato tutto a te" ("I have given all for you"), she shook her fist at the gallery instead of at Jason [Vickers],' Schippers continued. 'She sang the word "Crudel" ("Cruel man") and then stopped completely, creating a suspense-filled pause.' The hissing grew louder. 'She glared up at the gallery and then sang the second "Crudel" directly at the public, forcing it into a deadly silence. There was no more hissing nor was there any vocal insecurity in Maria's singing. She was very successful and the audience responded favourably, appreciating all the new refinements which she brought to this great role.'

The recording made of the performance that evening has expunged the hissing. What could not be excised is the weak support and flabby tempi under Schippers's baton. Maria does not take command until Act Two ('though Schippers draws out "Ebben! tutto mi manca" to interminable lengths'), and Vickers appears to be having some of the same problems as Maria in his arias. It seems obvious that some conversations passed from backstage to the podium between Act Two and Act Three, because the tempo suddenly picks up and Maria is once again in excellent form, vocally secure and, if anything, singing more strongly and even better than she had at Epidaurus. There was no hissing, only bravas as the curtain fell on the last scene and Maria came out for her solo bow to be called back for seven more.

She spent Christmas in Paris with Onassis, Alexander and Christina (Tina was in St Moritz with her new husband). With their mother's remarriage and being whisked off to the rather more disciplined routine of English schools, the children's hostility towards Maria had not eased. She understood their unhappiness, a need to thrash out, to blame someone. It was unfortunate that she was the target of their abuse. Her only hope was that once they had settled into their new life they would come to terms with their father's current life as well.

This was a reflective time for Maria. She was approaching forty. Her youth was gone, her innocence lost (years before). There was every sign that despite his obvious affection for her, Aristo might never marry her. The chances of her having a child of her own looked bleak. And she had come to accept the cruel truth about fame. The same people who loved you one day, could turn on you the next if you somehow missed a step

---

[2] This was never proven to be the case.

and did not keep up with their vision of what they wanted you to be. While the Epidaurus *Medea* had been one of the greatest triumphs of her career, her lukewarm return to La Scala had filled her with apprehension.

She believed that if she cared for it well, her voice would not desert her – not for a number of years, at least. Many famous singers had remained at their peak into their fifties. At forty-four Birgit Nilsson had just made her debut at the Met, which had warranted a sizeable front-page story and a picture in the *New York Times*.[3] No, despite the critics of her vocal technique, those who found her tone sometimes unpleasant and those who kept prophesying the imminent decline of her voice, Maria had confidence that it would not betray her if she did not betray it. Nor was she intimidated by the fine younger singers coming up – Anna Moffo, Leontyne Price – or Joan Sutherland, who by now had established herself as a dramatic coloratura soprano with her hugely successful 1959 *Lucia* (conducted by Serafin). Maria realized that her quarrel with Tebaldi was more a personal than a professional matter. She respected the talents of her peers and that included Renata Tebaldi. That she considered her long-time rival greedy, false-faced and mean-spirited was something else.

It was her heart, not her voice, that was the cause for her confusion and any self-doubts she had. Onassis was the father she had lost as a child, the lover she had sought her entire life. What she yearned for far more than the public's approval was his pride in what she could accomplish. He gave this to her, but for reasons that had nothing to do with her singing talent (except that it had brought her fame). Onassis believed she was tough, as he was, a Greek who had survived war and poverty to become one of the most successful, well-known women in the world, as he had fought war and poverty to become one of the most successful, well-known men in the world. 'We are some pair!' he would say to her proudly. Yet, he avoided any discussion of marriage. Nor did he press for her to get a divorce. 'I'm not sure you should renounce your American citizenship,' he hedged, knowing full well that to do so would enable her to get a divorce in Greece. 'The American government can be difficult in such a situation. It might make it hard for you to get a visa to either sing or live there.'

What she wanted was to have a true home with him. She was aware now that his rootlessness had also been his problem with Tina. Onassis could never settle into one place. The reason he loved the *Christina* so was that it was a *moving* home, one he could unmoor at any time he chose and go elsewhere. Still, she did not stop hoping he would wake up

[3] The *New York Times* reported that 'Miss Nilsson proved herself to be the greatest of rarities, a performer – like Flagstad before her and Caruso before *her* – to whom the size of the Metropolitan was not a hazard, but an advantage.'

one morning with a new attitude and a desire to marry her and 'settle down'. It was her dream and that dream had become her entire purpose in life, an obsession, just as maintaining her position as one of the greatest opera stars of her time had been until she fell in love with him.

Apart from her contract to sing *Medea* at La Scala again in the early summer, she confined herself to the concert form, the Royal Festival Hall on 27 February 1962 and four concerts in Germany (Munich, Hamburg, Essen and Bonn) in March. She started the year off in Monte Carlo where she and Aristo had some private time together on the *Christina*. She was not intending to take on any additional engagements in order to return to Paris with him and initiate work on her apartment. Then she received an invitation to sing at Madison Square Garden, New York, for President John F. Kennedy's forty-fifth birthday celebration on 17 May. As this would have to be sandwiched between the German tour and the La Scala *Medea*, thus lengthening her separation from Onassis, her original instinct was to say no.

Maria had never met President Kennedy, but in the summer of 1958 when he was a senator from Massachusetts, Onassis had entertained Kennedy and his wife, Jacqueline, for cocktails aboard the *Christina*, when Winston Churchill had also been his guest. The yacht had docked for the night in the Bahamas where Senator and Mrs Kennedy were on holiday. Churchill had known Kennedy's father Joe, when he was United States ambassador to Great Britain in 1940 and had regarded the millionaire entrepreneur and sometime diplomat with 'a certain fondness'. Recently, there had been stories that old Joe was setting in motion plans for his son 'Jack' to make a bid for the presidency. 'They tell me he is presidential timber,' Churchill told Onassis. 'I'd like to meet this presidential timber.'

His host immediately obliged and an appointment for cocktails aboard the *Christina* was arranged, Kennedy perhaps more thrilled to be meeting Churchill than the other way round. Onassis was not as impressed with the husband as he was by the wife, whom he considered a real charmer. The youthful Jackie (then twenty-nine) came aboard stunningly dressed in a white trapeze-style, St Laurent dress, the hem just above her shapely knees. An aura of elegance clung to her as the soft evening breeze caught her short dark hair. Onassis liked her lilting voice, the way she so easily switched from English to French and back again when introduced to some of his French-speaking guests. Jackie had that 'royal way' of looking at a person when she was in conversation with them – eyes intent, full concentration, small, natural approving smile when required. Yet he sensed something else about her – 'something damned *wilful*... something provocative... She's got a carnal soul,' he told Gratsos.

Now that Kennedy was president of the most powerful country in the world, Onassis was sorry that he had not been more gracious to him that evening on the *Christina* and invited him to remain for dinner. He did not plan to accompany Maria to New York, but he encouraged her to accept the invitation to sing at the President's birthday celebration. Costa Gratsos headed the Manhattan office and would look after her while she was in the city alone. Maria wrote to Dr Lantzounis about her intended visit and asked him to inform her mother that she would neither call nor see her while she was there.

Madison Square Garden was, and is, like no other arena in the world. This has more to do with its audience than its size, although it is massive and can hold over 20,000 people. The New Yorker is conditioned to crowds. He feels at home and his guard is down. He can let out all his suppressed emotions – excitement, anger, happiness. What is one shout among 20,000? Pejoratives fly through the place like baseballs at batting practice and so are not noticed much. The Garden gathers to it obsessive crowds of eclectic tastes. It is the ultimate battlefield for championship boxers, wrestlers, baseball, basketball and hockey teams. Political rallies, dog shows and circuses are held there. Pop singers and evangelists hold sway over their fervent followers. There is none of the hush of theatres, concert halls and opera houses before a performance. The ticketed crowd are almost always noisy and irreverent until they are called to order over a loudspeaker system that blasts out over all the din.

As she looked out from backstage, Maria wondered how she would be able to hold the attention of such a high-spirited crowd with an operatic aria. Cigar and cigarette smoke wafted unpleasantly through the Garden as the 15,000 Democrats, who had paid a record price to attend and donate to the Party, waited impatiently for the music of 'Hail to the Chief' that would indicate the President's arrival. Kennedy's brother-in-law, the actor Peter Lawford, was the Master of Ceremonies and, in addition to Maria, the other celebrity performers were Ella Fitzgerald, Peggy Lee, Jimmy Durante, Jack Benny and Marilyn Monroe.[4] The platinum-haired star was nowhere to be seen even as Kennedy was being ushered to

---

[4] Frank Sinatra, previously an ardent Kennedy supporter, was originally to sing. But he and the President had a falling out not long before the event. Kennedy had made plans to spend time in Palm Springs with Sinatra, who redid a wing of his home there to accommodate the President and his security needs. A few days before Kennedy was due to arrive, Robert Kennedy called Sinatra to tell him that the President would be staying with Bing Crosby (who also had a home in Palm Springs) as they were worried there might be talk about Sinatra's 'mob connections'. Sinatra was furious. 'Crosby's a Republican, for chrissakes!' he boomed over the telephone and hung up.

his seat of honour, surrounded by members of his family – his brothers Robert and Ted, his mother Rose, sisters Pat (Lawford's wife), Eunice (married to Sargent Shriver) and Robert's wife Ethel, as well as Vice-President Lyndon Johnson. The First Lady was glaringly absent. She had claimed a previous commitment to compete in the Loudoun Hunt horse show (where she was to take third place). The cognoscenti knew better.

Jack Kennedy was a serial womanizer. Jackie retained a dignified front, although she was well aware of the other women who shared his bed. Recently, Marilyn Monroe had been 'in the girlfriend category. Jack never considered her on a par with Jackie,' a Kennedy associate asserted. Nonetheless, Marilyn had flown on Air Force One with the President and made some private visits to the White House when Jackie was elsewhere. The First Lady did not want to be in the position of sitting next to her husband while one of his lady friends sang to him in front of 15,000 people. 'It's either me or her,' she said in effect to Lawford, who was organizing the performers. He replied that it would be handing a damaging news story to the media if he cancelled Marilyn's participation, which was expected by the tickets holders and had already been announced in the press. So Jackie found a convenient previous engagement, but there was a disconcerting buzz in the audience as her absence was realized.

Lawford, knowing that Marilyn had not yet arrived (she was famous for being hours late for every appearance), decided to make a joke of it. 'Mr President, on this occasion of your birthday, this lovely lady is not only pulchritudinous but punctual. Mr President – Marilyn Monroe!' There was thunderous applause, then whistles and catcalls, but no Marilyn. Lawford held out his arms and grimaced. 'Mr President,' he then announced, 'Miss Ella Fitzgerald' (who was not amused).

Lawford repeated this 'gag' before the introduction of each guest performer. Maria was the last on the programme and by now she was deeply sorry she had come. She received a good hand of applause, but it was obvious that the audience had grown impatient that Monroe remained among the missing.

Maria looked elegantly glamorous in her preferred red chiffon, her hair coiffed in a bouffant style, her diamond necklace a dazzling circle round her long, sculptured neck. She sang, in extremely good French, the Habanera and Seguidilla from *Carmen*. Visconti had, of course, always wanted her to sing Carmen and she had resolutely refused to do so. Lately, she had warmed to the idea and had decided to experiment with these two arias. Her voice was light and quick in the Habanera, confidant and sensual in the Seguidilla, her 'come on' to Don José near the end of the first act of *Carmen*. She received an enthusiastic ovation. But before she finished her bows, Lawford strode out, took the microphone in his hand and, with a flourish, announced: 'Because, Mr President, in the history of show business, perhaps there has been no one female who has meant so much...who has done more...Mr President, the late – *the very late* – Marilyn Monroe!'

Maria had just walked off stage when Marilyn slithered seductively on stage wearing what Adlai Stevenson (the one-time Democratic presidential nominee) called 'skin and beads'. Actually, it was a gown designed by Jean Louis, made of fine, nude netting moulded to her body and covered in thousands of glittering, hand-stitched beads, the final seams sewn on her just before she stepped out on stage 'for a perfect fit'. In a throaty voice she sang 'Thanks for the Memory', then followed it with the most famous rendition of 'Happy Birthday [Mr Pres-i-dent]' ever heard in a public venue. It was obvious by now that Marilyn was either on drugs or had had too much to drink. The words came out slow, seductive, slurred as she stared at Kennedy and at the end she pursed her voluptuous lips in a way that sent a kiss floating through the haze of smoke towards Kennedy.

Moments later 'Mr Pres-i-dent' was standing next to Hollywood's most famous sex symbol as a huge birthday cake was wheeled out on stage. 'I can now retire from politics,' he said, 'after having had "Happy Birthday" sung to me in such a sweet, wholesome way.' The audience went wild with laughter and applause.

Maria, against her first instincts, with Costa Gratsos at her side, attended the gala party after the Madison Square Garden celebration, given by Arthur Krim, the head of United Artists (and a dedicated Democrat) at his magnificent mid-Manhattan town house. She had been there, obviously uncomfortable, for about half an hour when, at her request, Gratsos went to organize their departure. Kennedy caught sight of her standing alone and told *Time* correspondent William Walton, 'Go talk to Callas. No one's talking to her. She's pouting.'[5]

Maria returned to Milan for rehearsals and the two performances of *Medea* (29 May, 3 June) at La Scala. The weather was unseasonably damp, the days grey and although she had Toy and Bruna, Onassis was in

[5] After the Krim party, Kennedy and Monroe were known to have gone to his penthouse suite at the Carlyle Hotel where they spent several hours alone. The President's men had learned that Peter Lawford's beach house in California, where they had met several times in the course of their affair, had been taped by the Mafia. That night Kennedy ended the affair. They were never to see each other again (although Monroe then became involved with Robert Kennedy). On 5 August 1962 Monroe died of an apparent drug overdose (whether this was suicide or murder remains a mystery). Fifteen months later, on 22 November 1963, President Kennedy was assassinated.

Greece, involved in a new enterprise with fierce dedication. He had bought a formerly uninhabited island in the Ionian Sea about seven miles off the coast of Ithaca (where so many of his friends and staff, including Costa Gratsos, were from), which he called Skorpios because 'it is shaped like a scorpion'.

After only a few days in Milan, Maria's previous sinus problems returned with a vengeance. Rehearsals went badly. Once again Schippers was conducting and it was clear that the two of them did not share the same musical instincts. Maria met privately with Ghiringhelli to see if someone else, perhaps Rescigno, could take over the baton. It was not possible, Ghiringhelli told her. It would be too costly at this late date and Schippers had a contract that would be too expensive to break. Somehow, news of this 'secret' meeting got back to the conductor, putting a definite edge on his relationship with Maria.

The production seemed as doomed as the eponymous Medea. The late spring cold spell had driven many of Milan's opera lovers to leave earlier than usual for their summer homes. Ticket sales were off. Maria's sinus condition worsened and she had to undergo painful treatment. Onassis was often difficult to reach by telephone, spinning her into spells of depression. Minotis and Vickers (singing Jason) did all they could to buoy her spirits, but her heart was elsewhere and that was where she wanted to be. It was time, she confessed to Bruna, that she concentrated more on Maria the woman and not on Maria the performer.

There was no hissing in the audience this time, but her voice was not in top form in the first performance and broke during a crucial aria in the second. The critics were less kind. There were blatant insinuations that, although her acting remained extraordinary, her vocal powers were possibly diminishing. Maria herself feared the same thing and was in a terrible state as Bruna helped her to pack so that she could rejoin Onassis on the *Christina* for the usual round of summer cruising. Then her beloved Toy, who for several days seemed to have suffered *le cafard* along with Maria, died suddenly of a heart attack.

When Maria left Milan this time she had Bruna pack the few personal possessions that she wanted to keep. Milan and La Scala were the past. It was time to move on.

21
〜

Enter: the Temptress
and the President's Lady

PARIS WAS MARIA'S new home. She loved the tempo of the city, the language, the style. Onassis remained a man on the move, business occupying a large slice of his life. However, they were together for sizeable lengths of time in Monte Carlo and on the various cruises they took on the *Christina*. She also joined him in London and they were together in Paris, although in the latter he lodged in his apartment on the avenue Foch. Her passion for him was undiminished. He remained the centre, the mainstay of her life. He appeared to be devoted to her. His gifts were lavish (a set of emeralds for her last birthday). The rising bills for the antiques and decoration she chose for her apartment were never questioned. ('Just pay them,' Onassis ordered his complaining accountant.) He listened sensitively to Maria's problems – career, family, household – and dispensed caring advice.

Still, he had somehow distanced himself. One could not identify or isolate the examples. Their relationship was simply not the same as it had been in the previous four years. He avoided any discussion of marriage or their future together and she no longer pressed, fearing she might stand to lose what she did have. 'Maybe our lives have not turned out so different after all,' she confessed to her sister, a reference to Jackie's long-time affair with Milton Embiricos. It was ironic that both their lovers were shipbuilders and tragic that Embiricos, unlike Onassis, had never given Jackie any monetary recognition of her status in his life. Maria's high income from records and appearances gave her a sense of independence and enabled her to look upon Onassis's lavish outlays on her behalf as gifts which a man of his great wealth could easily afford. She did not feel compromised. If anything his largesse simply illustrated how deep his caring went.

She scheduled only concerts for 1963, all of them in the spring and early summer. Onassis joined her for the ones in Paris and

London,[1] leaving her free for almost the entire second half of the year to be with him whenever possible. When they were not together she occupied herself with the business of decorating her apartment, or she worked with an accompanist to keep her voice in shape. She did not have many women friends. There were Maggie van Zuylen and a few others, but she had not been accepted in Paris society as she had hoped would happen. Bruna was nurse, mother, sister and friend to her, but there was still a class code that divided them. 'The day is easy to live through,' she said of her Paris life when Onassis was unavailable. 'What about the evening? What about when you shut your door to your bedroom and you are all alone?' She slept poorly when he was not with her. 'I'm used to working at night,' she explained, 'used to thinking then. It's my job, my chemistry. But at night you get lots of funny ideas, pessimistic ideas, and I'd like to shake them. But [in Paris, late at night] can you go for a walk, really walk your feet off, get tired, do something? A woman can't do that. Take a train? Go some place when you get desperate? What does a woman do?'

She desperately wanted Onassis to marry her, although that would not have guaranteed his nightly presence. She still wanted a baby, or so she thought. 'Maybe I would make a terrible mother,' she confessed, 'but at least I would never have to be alone.' In the hopes that this miracle might occur, she left one small room empty, using it for the present as a box room, ready for occupancy should a miracle take place.

The avenue Georges Mandel had only recently been named for Louis-Georges Rothschild Mandel, a Cabinet minister before World War Two, staunchly opposed to Nazi Germany, who was executed by the collaborationist French Vichy government in 1944. As befitted a Rothschild, it was a wide avenue, bordered by flowering chestnut trees, in an elegant section of the city (the 16th arrondissement). With the help of designer Georges Grandpierre (who also worked for the Paris Opéra), Maria furnished and decorated the luxurious second-floor flat in Louis Quinze style, each high-ceilinged room resembling a possible set for Mozart's eighteenth-century opera Le Nozze di Figaro.

The living room, truly a grand salon, was used as a music room. Floor-to-ceiling windows, draped in 'a vibrant burgundy-red velvet the pelmet stretched across most of the wall, golden cords holding back the heavy material to disclose an inner pair of oyster-coloured raw silk'. Under this was white voile netting 'suggesting the proscenium curtains of a grand

---

[1] Her concerts in 1963 were: Deutsche Oper, Berlin, 17 May, Rheinhalle, Düsseldorf, 20 May, Liederhalle, Stuttgart, 23 May, Royal Festival Hall, London, 31 May, Théâtre des Champs-Elysées, Paris, 5 June and Falkoner Centret, Copenhagen, 9 July.

opera house'. A Steinway concert grand battled with the draperies to dominate the room, the windows of which opened on to a wrought-iron, trellised balcony overlooking the tree-lined avenue. There was one fine painting by the eighteenth-century artist Jean Baptiste Greuze and several allegorical scenes of an earlier period and of uncertain attribution. Over the elaborately carved Louis Quinze marble fireplace was a fitted mirror outlined in gilt to match the decoration on the cream-coloured wood panelling. A magnificent patterned Aubusson carpet in the Empire style covered the floor. Chairs were upholstered in golden silk-velvet. Tables, fine woods beneath, were mainly covered in glass for protection, the tops holding numerous silver Ronson lighters and antique Chinese plates to be used as ashtrays – Maria's bow to Onassis's compulsive chain-smoking habit. There was always a large bouquet of long-stemmed red roses, replaced the moment a single blossom drooped.

Grandpierre, a meticulous man of autocratic bearing, had cleverly hidden stereo loudspeakers behind the curtains (to be drawn back when in use) on each side of the large windows, and a yellow-lacquered rococo commode housed 'a barrage of hi-fi equipment... [so that] when necessary, the whole room could be converted in a few moments into a musician's studio'. But, said her future accompanist Robert Sutherland, 'It was a comfortable, enhancing environment, with no hint of the aloof inhospitable chill of many formal rooms. There was an extraordinary air of ease, everything radiating an atmosphere of warm opulence.'

Doors, painted in the Venetian style of the eighteenth century, separated the grand salon from a smaller room, the salon rouge: its petit point flowered rug of fine woven silk, the red walls hung with several early Fragonards in elaborate gold frames. Tables and niches displayed Maria's growing collection of antique Chinese cloisonné and bronze – elephants, dogs, pagodas. Grandpierre had moved to Louis Seize in the dining room where a large display cabinet[2] held Maria's prize set of Sèvres dinnerware. One of the few pieces of furniture Maria had taken from Milan had been the eighteenth-century Italian double bed (a painted scene of Venice inset into its petit point, five-foot-high headboard with its rococo, gold-scrolled frame) that Battista had bought for their first apartment in Verona. On the wall facing the bed was a large, gracefully rendered oil portrait of Toy, painted after the animal's death.

The bathroom (mostly of Maria's design) was the pièce de résistance, all mirrors and pink and white marble, and fitted out with a deep, rose-coloured velvet settee and armchair, a glass-topped table holding a record

---

[2] Referred to as a 'breakfront' in the United States.

player and telephone, the cord of which reached conveniently to the bath where Maria could luxuriate until the water turned tepid.

Bruna had her own small suite on the opposite side of the apartment, behind the kitchen. The staff also consisted of Consuelo, the cook, and Ferruccio, the butler ('a handsome, gentle Italian') who drove the Mercedes that Onassis supplied. The main additions to the household were two female miniature poodles –white Pixie and brown Djedda – that Onassis had bought Maria soon after Toy's death. Maria loved them both. They jumped wildly, trying to lick her face when she returned home from even a short shopping excursion; followed her wherever she went in the apartment and, placed at the foot of Maria's bed at night, often ended up in the morning on the pillow beside her own. Pixie was well named and perhaps her favourite. Whenever Maria would practise in the middle range, Pixie would sing along 'in a sustained wail'. This amused Maria, who swore that Pixie must have been a failed singer in an earlier life. She would encourage the small dog to perform whenever there was a guest who she thought might be entertained. But then, when serious practising was required, Pixie would have to be closed into the bathroom so that her whines could not be heard.

Onassis was obsessed with his own new home – the four-hundred-and-some-acre island Skorpios (about the same size as Prince Rainier's minuscule principality of Monaco) – which he was converting into an example of 'feudal opulence'. At this early time the island – the buildings consisting only of a small, crude chapel and some fishermen's cottages – was not yet ready to bring guests to and even Maria seldom journeyed there with him. 'In the beginning,' he later recalled, 'the island was covered in olive trees.' Within a short time he added 'all the trees of the Bible... almonds, bramble, pine, oleander, figs'. The first time Maria saw him 'stripped down to his shorts... planting trees himself, sweating in the sun, digging with his workers, telling them about the flowers, the fruits and the trees they were planting', she felt she had witnessed the unveiling of the *true* man she loved.

He would repeat the stories his grandmother had told him when he was a child. 'To sit beneath one's own fig tree is the Jewish ideal of peace and prosperity... when the cone of the pine is cut lengthwise, the mark on its surface resembles the hand of Christ, a sign of His blessing on the tree that sheltered the Virgin Mary when she was in flight with her family from Herod's troops.'

While Maria was buying Louis Quinze antiques, Onassis was supervising the construction of many miles of roads curving around, and carved into, the white rock hillsides, and the building of a main house, six guest cottages and servants' accommodation (mostly the converted former fishermen's homes). He had one side of the sea coast of the island dredged and two harbours built, one for the *Christina*, the other for those guests who might arrive in their own yachts. He slept on the *Christina*, as he would always do – the other buildings were for his guests. But his pride in the island, his entire and sole domain, was great.

Maria was pleased when Onassis, whom she felt she had not seen enough of that spring (1963) due to three concerts in Berlin and one at Covent Garden and his many business meetings, suggested they take a cruise in between her upcoming concerts in Paris (5 June) and Copenhagen (9 July), which would allow them four weeks together. To her added delight, this time Sir Winston and Lady Churchill, as well as the great ballerina Margot Fonteyn, would be cruising with them along the Italian coast. Also in the yachting party would be Prince Stanislas Radziwill ('Stas', pronounced 'Stash') and his wife Lee, née Bouvier, younger sister of Jacqueline Kennedy. The Radziwills had entertained Maria and Onassis several times at their London home in Buckingham Place, an unpretentious side street near Victoria Station, and Maria had been impressed by how Lee had turned a modest house into one with touches of great elegance. Even more daunting was the opulent table the hostess set for an interesting, eclectic group of people including Cecil Beaton (who then asked if he could photograph Maria), other members of displaced royalty, literary glitterati and society figures.

Maria found the ebullient Lee, who always travelled with a fresh supply of current gossip, bright and entertaining; her husband, a charming 'pretender'. Actually, Stas was the fourth son of a Polish aristocrat, whose fabulously rich and powerful ancestors reigned over Poland between the fourteenth and sixteenth centuries. Their fortunes waned through the years; their power disappeared. Stas had a privileged childhood until the Soviets confiscated all his family's property. Forced to flee the oncoming German Army during World War Two, Stas arrived penniless in Great Britain in 1946, settling in London, and became a British citizen a few years later, which in effect meant he had forfeited his foreign title as a form of address. Nonetheless, he did use it (as did many of Europe's other displaced aristocrats), because it was of great value to him in his real estate business and social ambitions. Lee was smitten with the idea of being a princess, especially after Jackie (with whom she shared a biting sibling rivalry) became First Lady, but she hated not being rich.

Maria cared little about Lee's adopted title, but she was impressed to be friends with President Kennedy's sister-in-law. What she did not know was that Princess Lee Radziwill and Onassis were secret lovers at this time, although it was quite obvious that the Radziwills' marriage was presently rocky.

Lee had been in search of who she wanted to be since youth. She dumped her first husband, Michael Canfield, when she met Stas, married then to the rich Grace Kolin. Backs had been turned on her when she entered into an affair with the 'Pauper Prince' who left Grace when Lee became pregnant. The social world Lee so desperately wanted to enter would not let her forget this ignominious act and closed ranks. Lee was smart, but not as clever as Jackie, and although prettier than her older sister, her reputation was as a seductress, social climber and clothes horse. Designer Oleg Cassini (who also dressed and nearly married Grace Kelly before she became a princess) called Lee '*Dégagée*…a very chic woman. She wore an elegant mask. I could imagine both her and her sister at the court of Louis XV. Destiny had separated them. It was Jackie who became the historic figure and Lee the society woman.'

It was also her brother-in-law's rise to the American presidency that finally helped Lee break back into a few formerly closed social conclaves. 'Had lunch with your new friend, Princess Lee,' Truman Capote wrote to Cecil Beaton in the spring of 1963. 'My God, how jealous she is of Jackie. I never knew. Understand her marriage is all but finito.' She told Capote that she felt very much eclipsed by Jackie and that Stas did not understand her. He was also dependent upon his (or her) social connections to find 'suitable' employment and to underwrite the luxuries they both so enjoyed. It did not help that Stas suffered 'deep, black spells' and was taking a frightening number of Valium and submitting to injections laced with amphetamines.

Lee wanted a divorce – but not without a man to go to who could give her the lifestyle to which she was most anxious to become accustomed. She made a deliberate play for Onassis, who had a difficult enough time ignoring a beautiful woman's overtures and Lee had more to offer than just sex and games. She was the sister-in-law of the American President (who seemed to like her too much to please Jackie) and Onassis was having a long-standing problem with his shipping interests in the States and wanted very much to get on more personal terms with Kennedy. His affair with Lee had been going on for several months and, as he feared the media might get hold of the story, he decided to counteract it before that could happen. Therefore the cruise with Lee and her husband, Maria and the Churchills aboard, making any gossip that he and Lee were lovers seem highly illogical – or so he thought. However, in the early days of his pursuit of Maria he had done exactly that (except that Tina was his wife, not his mistress) and should have known how difficult it would be to keep a good story from the paparazzi.

Lee did not remain on board long enough for Maria, or the press, to guess the truth. On the third day at sea, after receiving a radiogram from President Kennedy's secretary Evelyn Lincoln, she disembarked at the small port of Fiumicino on the Italian coast, to fly to Bonn, Germany where she had been asked to stand in for a pregnant Jackie at a hastily arranged dinner Kennedy was hosting for the German president. Unbeknown to Maria, Onassis and Lee had liaisons during the following eight weeks in London, Paris and Athens. In this time Onassis had made Stas a director of Olympic Airways with a comfortable stipend. ('Now I can live on an airplane with my secretary and keep going around the world, and I won't have to pay any tax!' Radziwill declared.)

By now, rumours had reached Maria, but she refused to credit them. She was much looking forward to an early August cruise on the *Christina*, which she regarded as a romantic voyage, a celebration of the four years she and Aristo had been together. To her surprise, Lee joined them in Glyfada on the day of their departure. On the first afternoon, as the *Christina* cut through the smooth summer water of the Aegean, Maria observed that Lee and Onassis were on very familiar terms, his arm too easily about her waist, his glance following her shapely, bare, bronzed legs as she walked on deck. Unsure of what she should do, through the next few days Maria kept her troubled thoughts to herself and tried to act as if everything were 'as usual'. This time, on the fourth day of the cruise, Lee received another radiogram notifying her of the death of Jackie's newborn son, Patrick. She immediately went ashore and flew in Onassis's private jet to Otis Air Force Base, where her sister was convalescing. Maria felt relieved. Onassis's close attention to her from the time of Lee's departure made her doubt her suspicions and she was happy that she had not given in to her jealous emotions.

When the cruise ended on 15 August Onassis, playing a game of sexual musical chairs, escorted Maria, the Churchills and Margot Fonteyn to London on his jet. Lee arrived back in Athens on 16 August, where Artemis had readied the Glyfada house for her use and where Onassis had arranged to meet her six days later, Maria having returned to Paris. Bored with sitting it out in Glyfada despite Artemis's attention, Lee called Taki Theodoracopulos (later a London newspaper and magazine columnist, but then a self-described 'young good-for-nothing playboy, scion of a Greek shipping fortune and professional athlete') who was playing in the final rounds of the Greek tennis championships in Athens. 'I'm going crazy!' she told him. 'Please, let's have dinner.'

'So we had dinner by the sea right next to my house,' he recalled. 'Lee was going nuts. She was very lonely and wanted company. "Where's your boyfriend?" I asked. She got very angry.'

Onassis returned to Glyfada, where the *Christina* was docked, the following day. That night he attended the opening of the new Athens Hilton with Lee and then dined alone with her at one of Athens's most exclusive restaurants. Two days later an item appeared in Drew Pearson's column in the *Washington Post* that they had been seen tête-à-tête. 'Does the ambitious Greek tycoon hope to become the brother-in-law of the American President?' he posed. Lee was shocked at the 'leak', which seemed to have come from Onassis's own publicity agent.

'Lee had quite a lot of affairs,' a friend of hers commented. 'It was all very discreet. But Ari was very much out in the open because he revelled in publicity. One couldn't be discreet with Onassis.'

When a friend brought Pearson's column to Maria's attention, she immediately called Onassis who explained that Lee was alone in Athens and he had thought the least he could do was to take her to dinner. There was nothing more to it. Maria accepted the explanation because she did not want to believe the alternative.

Whatever fantasy Lee might have had about Onassis, it seems fairly clear that he never had marriage to Lee on his mind. But without question, her relationship to Kennedy was a major force in the affair. Onassis wanted to make 'the Kennedy connection' and what better way could that be accomplished than through the First Lady's sister – especially if all he had to do was entertain Lee and, as one close associate crudely put it, 'fuck her a few times'. He wasted no time, either. For during their stay together in Glyfada, Lee confided to Onassis how depressed Jackie had been after little Patrick's death. This was Onassis's grand opening. She must tell her sister that the *Christina* was hers to use for a cruise (without his presence) which would hopefully help her to recuperate more fully from her recent tragedy. He suggested early October in the warm Aegean waters. Lee relayed this invitation to Jackie and Onassis followed up with a gracious note to the First Lady, saying how happy he would be if such a cruise would be acceptable to her – and it was.

'Lee had a sort of a romance going with Onassis,' Evelyn Lincoln, Kennedy's personal secretary, said. 'At first Jack didn't like the idea [of Jackie going on the *Christina*] but then he thought maybe it would do her some good.'

At this point Onassis told Maria what had transpired and that he would not be hosting the First Lady and her party (which would include the Radziwills, Under Secretary of Commerce Franklin D. Roosevelt, Jr and his wife, Suzanne) aboard the *Christina*. He suggested to Maria that they might go to London to see Fonteyn and Nureyev dance at Covent Garden during the time that Mrs Kennedy had the use of the yacht.

Maria was appeased. She well understood Onassis's deep-seated wish to become friendly with President Kennedy. Lending his wife a luxurious, all expenses paid cruise at an emotional time in her life would place him in a good position for a payback if he wanted it – and obviously he did.[3] Jackie wrote to Onassis that it seemed wrong and far too generous of him not to accompany her and her friends, and begged him to reconsider. Two weeks before the cruise was due to depart from Glyfada, sail to the Greek Islands of Lesbos, Crete and Ithaca and then on to Istanbul, Onassis decided to join his guests.

There followed a difficult scene in Paris with Maria when Onassis told her that she could not be with him on the cruise as 'it was unseemly for him to have his married mistress on board with the First Lady of the United States'. Tears followed. Maria was humiliated. She had not forgotten that once he had not wanted her on board with Sir Winston. That had cut her deeply. This was even more painful. She very much wanted to meet Jackie Kennedy and she was not happy that Lee would be on the cruise. Her jealousy was somewhat assuaged with the knowledge that Stas Radziwill would also be on board. Nonetheless, there were lurking doubts as she remembered the fatal cruise on the *Christina* when Battista *and* Tina had been present, and that it had not stopped Onassis from pursuing her, nor her from allowing him to make love to her.

Had Maria gone on the cruise she might have been more troubled by Aristo's attention to the First Lady. Always something of a flirt, Jackie was openly receptive to his company. They took evening walks alone along the shore when they were in dock, and when they moored at Skorpios (not yet ready to receive sleep-over guests) he took her on a personal tour of 'his' island and listened to her suggestions. In Istanbul, he gave her a diamond and ruby necklace that came apart to become two bracelets (worth, it was estimated, over $50,000).

'I can't stand it,' Lee wrote to her brother-in-law the President. 'He gave me three dinky little bracelets that Caroline [aged five] wouldn't even wear to her own birthday party.'

Kennedy radiogrammed his wife to leave the cruise in Istanbul. Strong-

[3] There is an eerie resemblance between Onassis's offer of a cruise to Jacqueline Kennedy and Mohammed Al Fayed's similar invitation to Princess Diana in the summer of 1997. Both men were genuinely concerned for the health of these two women, but they were also using the gift of a luxury cruise to gain special favours from their guests.

minded as she was, she refused to do so. 'How would it look?' she told
Lee. 'The man has been so kind.'

'If there was anything going on [aboard the *Christina*] it was between
Ari and Lee,' fellow passenger Franklin D. Roosevelt Jr later reported.
'Maria Callas wasn't there for the first time in four years…Stas left during
the trip [in Ithaca, to return to Athens for a suddenly called Olympic
Airline meeting]…there was definitely a relationship between Lee and
Ari. But while that was going on, Jackie was there simply for the rest.'

A photograph, taken by paparazzi with a zoom lens, shows Jackie on
deck, sunbathing in a bikini. Another paparazzo, travelling close to the
Christina in a motor boat, reported that loud music blared from the yacht
every evening, where the pool cover served as a dance floor, and that
Jackie was dancing until the early hours of the morning with Onassis.
'Does this sort of behavior seem fitting for a woman in mourning [for her
infant son]?' an editorial in the *Boston Globe* asked.

The reports of Onassis's attentions to Jackie were actually a relief to
Maria, who knew that he would never have an affair with the President's
wife; Kennedy's possible friendship meant too much to him to jeopar-
dize. No, Aristo's overtures to Jackie suggested two things to Maria. He
wanted Jackie to go back to Kennedy and sing his praises *and* he was not
having an affair with Lee. She was right about Jackie, but not about Lee.

Life changed for every one of the members of that October 1963 cruise
on the *Christina*, and for Maria as well, a month later when, on Friday, 22
November, President John F. Kennedy, riding through the streets of
Dallas in the back of an open car, Jackie beside him and cheering crowds
on each side, gunshots rang out and the President was assassinated. The
world was in shock. Many watched the murder replay over and over on
their television screens, Maria among them. Lee immediately flew to
Washington (Stas followed the next day) to be with Jackie upon her
return on Air Force One, her days of being First Lady tragically ended.
Onassis joined Maria in Paris and spent the evening with her at her apartment where he sat for several hours in the salon rouge watching television intently and offering his theories. When images of Jackie were
shown – cradling her dead husband's bloodied head in her lap in the
back seat of the topless limousine, blood streaked on her clothes, and
later as she stood next to Vice-President Lyndon Baines Johnson in Air
Force One as he was sworn in as the new President of the United States,
he kept repeating, 'She is so brave, so courageous.' He was also with Maria
on 25 November, the day of the President's funeral, and watched as the
camera focused on Jackie, standing erect in front of the steps of the

White House, veiled in black, three-year-old John-John and five-year-old Caroline on either side of her as the riderless horse and the coffin of her husband passed before her and her small son, whose birthday it was that day, saluted at his mother's request.

The former First Lady had poignant grace. She was a symbol of strength. 'There's something Greek about Jackie,' Onassis noted. Maria did not place any importance on those words until several years later.

During the month of December Maria was busy recording for EMI in Paris with Nicola Rescigno conducting. She had been working diligently for several months on her middle voice, which she felt had slipped at the time of the spring concerts, and these recordings[4] show how masterfully she had overcome most of her major problems. 'Only Elisabeth Schwarzkopf comes close to matching the fire and recrimination that lights up Callas's voice, or her scalpel-sharp attacks,' John Ardoin commented on the Beethoven concert aria that she sang.

Maria found recording in a studio satisfying. She had long ago mastered the art of the microphone and singing in a restricted space without an audience. She quite liked it, in fact. The demands were no less than singing on a stage either in concert or in a theatre. However, she had a chance in this medium to correct errors she might make. There was no fear that her voice might break or be lost completely. If it happened, she could repeat the aria until she was fairly confident it was the best she could do at the time. Recordings were also beginning to bring in high revenues. But she was nervous about the upcoming new Zeffirelli production of *Tosca*, which she was scheduled to sing at Covent Garden on 21, 24, 27 and 30 January, and 1 and 5 February (1964) under the baton of Carlo Felice Cillario, with Tito Gobbi as Scarpia and Renato Cioni as Cavaradossi. Although Tosca had never been one of Maria's favourite roles, she had a strong affinity for this very theatrical woman who would commit murder in the belief that she was saving the life of the man she loved. Tosca's range did not present too great a risk for a singer trained, as Maria had been, in bel canto music and she liked Zeffirelli's concept of a warmer, more humanized, yet grander Tosca than had previously been portrayed.

She was therefore hard at work over the holidays and saw very little of Onassis. They spent a few days at Christmas in Monte Carlo and stood, hand in hand, on the deck of the *Christina* at midnight on 31 December,

---

[4] There were two albums recorded in Paris over 6 December 1963–21 February 1964. They included Beethoven's 'Ah! perfido!', excerpts from Mozart's *Don Giovanni* and *Le Nozze di Figaro*, Weber's *Oberon* and arias from Verdi's *Otello*, *Aroldo* and *Don Carlos*.

to toast the New Year in and watch the magnificent, extravagant display of fireworks that Prince Rainier had ordered. To add to her excitement she told Onassis that she believed she was pregnant.

He was dumbfounded. 'But, Maria, you are forty-one and we are not married,' Maria reported that Onassis told her.

'The first I can do nothing about. The second, we can, Aristo,' she answered.

He made no reply, but he held her close to him and she thought he was just too surprised to express his happiness.

22

The Turning Point

SEVEN DAYS AFTER Maria had announced to Onassis that she was pregnant with his child, she entered a Paris hospital, ostensibly for a hernia operation, but in fact to submit to an abortion. To abort a child she so desperately wanted was one of the most difficult decisions of her life. She had believed her late conception was a miracle and by bearing his child she would be giving Onassis the greatest gift in a woman's power. Onassis said little about his views until the following day, when he quietly and persuasively explained to her how impossible it would be for her to carry the pregnancy to full term. It would be months, perhaps years, before she could become a Greek citizen and obtain a divorce from Battista. There were other alternatives. She could retain her American citizenship and go to Reno, or Mexico. But she was one of the most famous women in the world. Their offspring would be a known bastard. How would that be for the child?

As they sat in the grand salon of the *Christina* where only five years earlier they had consummated their love, Maria wept as Onassis cajoled. She was all he wanted, he told her. A baby, a child, could well come between them. He reminded her of his sexual problems with Tina after the birth of their children. 'We are happy as we are,' he insisted, as Maria later recalled. 'Do we want to get married under such unexpected and difficult conditions?' He went on to tell her he, at least, was too old, sixty-four, to become a father. Christina and Alexander were to be considered. And, not least, a child would keep her inactive for a year and endanger her career and her health.[1]

---

[1] In 1965, Maria told Panaghis Vergottis (a Greek shipowner and Onassis's friend of thirty years) that she was pregnant with Onassis's child. Bruna later confirmed this, as did Onassis's sister, Artemis Garofallides, and Maggie van Zuylen, whom Maria did indeed confide in and considered to be her most intimate and trusted friend. It is this

Maria finally agreed and Onassis told her not to worry, he would take care of everything. She returned immediately to Paris where, within twenty-four hours, she entered a private clinic, a grand suite filled with bouquets of red roses awaiting her arrival. Bruna accompanied her and remained on 'twenty-four-hour duty'. The abortion did not go as smoothly as promised. Maria bled profusely and suffered post-operative depression. Bruna never left her bedside. 'She didn't even want the nurse to touch me,' Maria later said. 'Imagine that creatures like that should still exist!...Ashamed to humiliate me to a nurse, cleaning me in private instead.'

A pearl and diamond necklace was delivered to avenue Georges Mandel upon her return. Onassis had not come to see her in hospital. He had remained in Monaco where he was in the final throes of a battle to retain his control over the SBM. Until New Year's day 1964, Rainier had been hopeful that Onassis would support his plan for land reclamation, the only scheme he could envision to increase the size and the potential development of his principality. Onassis, sincere in his belief that such a plan would devalue his holdings, gave the Prince his negative response shortly after Christmas. On New Year's Day Rainier, in his annual address to his subjects, made a slurring remark about Onassis being responsible for the falling assets of the SBM (which controlled most of the hotels, clubs and tourist attractions in the small country). It was a clear signal.

While Maria was going through her ordeal in a Paris clinic, Onassis and Rainier reached the end of their long association. Rainier, in a scheme that Onassis's Monégasque office referred to as *loi gangster*, created 600,000 shares of SBM controlled by the state, thereby becoming its major stockholder. As Rainier had total power over his courts, Onassis was helpless to do anything. He had lost his edge and his right as the major shareholder to veto. To add to his fury and humiliation, Rainier sent a representative to his office to tell him that the Prince was buying out all his shares. A cheque in French francs equal to $10 million (about

pregnancy which seems to have inspired the story of 'a secret son' at an earlier date.

After Maria's death, Meneghini would claim that it was only rumour that she had become pregnant with Onassis's child because, without an operation to correct a malformation of the womb, Callas was incapable of becoming pregnant. He produced a document to one biographer, signed by Dr Carlo Palmieri, that substantiated the fact that in 1957, *when he last examined her*, Maria had a *malformazione dell'utero*. This, in fact, does not mean that a woman with this condition cannot become pregnant. It does indicate that the pregnancy would be painful and difficult, and that it posed possible danger to the life of the mother and the child. Maria was given hormone shots to regulate her periods but no corrective surgery was prescribed.

Dr Palmieri is thus stating that he had not examined Maria after 1957, that is two years before Nicholas Gage claims he performed a Caesarean section on her.

one-third their worth) was then presented to him with a notice that the rights to his private berth for the *Christina* had been rescinded, an order that would take effect within ten days. A week later the *Christina* lifted anchor and sailed out of Monaco. Onassis went below deck so that he did not have to see the town where he had held so much power and that had been his primary home for over a decade slip into the distance and fade from view.

Knowing the pain that Onassis was suffering in this face-off with Prince Rainier, Maria could not find it in her heart to burden him with her own grief. She turned for solace to her work, throwing herself with surprising energy into the final rehearsals of *Tosca*, which began in London only ten days after she was released from hospital. Preliminary rehearsals had been conducted in Paris and London in December.

This would be the first time Maria and Tito Gobbi were to sing the complete opera together, having previously sung only excerpts in concerts. The production, a new one, was directed by her good friend Franco Zeffirelli and there is no doubt that he and Gobbi had a salubrious effect on Maria. No one in the company knew what she had just been through. Bruna was with her, making sure that she was well cared for, but Maria asked for no special attention (other than what she was always given in rehearsal). She arrived in London where she was staying at Claridge's, suffering from depression. This, however, was Maria the woman. Callas the great opera diva, on the other hand, had come out of a two-year period of near inactivity, her voice back in top form, her courage bolstered that it would not fail her. 'I got so many complexes from the continual negative criticism which contributed to what I admit was a vocal crisis,' she said of the time directly leading up to her two-year hiatus. 'I had a big wobble in my voice.... And I pushed and opened my mouth too much. The sound just poured out without control.'

The person most responsible for her regained confidence in her voice was Michel Glotz, the artistic director of EMI, Paris, who also represented some of opera's star directors, conductors and singers. It was Glotz who was responsible for Maria's recordings during this period and for her agreeing to sing *Tosca* at Covent Garden. Throughout 1963 and during the year that would follow, Glotz was her main support, comforter and inspiration. She would later say that she could never have made it through this troubled period of her life without Glotz's backing and encouragement and, although it cost him precious time away from his Paris office, he was with her in London during the greater part of Zeffirelli's production of *Tosca*. Lord Harewood was also nearby whenever she needed a knowledgeable ear and a comforting friend.

It had taken several years for Zeffirelli to be convinced to mount a new *Tosca* for Covent Garden. 'That is because I needed in the soprano a personality who could comprehend my approach,' he has said. 'My conception of Tosca was that of an exuberant, warm-hearted, casual woman and not the grand diva who arrives at the church with four dozen roses, a walking stick, wearing a large hat with feathers, et cetera. Tosca was never like this. It was amazing how fast Maria brought her to life in the way only she could.'

Maria responded to Zeffirelli and his artistic vision. He was a totally outgoing personality, egocentric, but in no way stuffy or dictatorial. Instead of roses, Zeffirelli had Tosca, in her first scene, buy 'a colourful, confused bouquet of flowers that she carries lightly, with no formality, in her hand. She arrives [at the church to see her lover, the artist Mario Cavaradossi] and is like a ray of sunlight in the dark church, very feminine in a lace veil and yards of pink chiffon. She was free – no corset or brassiere, for in that period dresses were cut to give women support.'

Zeffirelli was the kind of man who invited so many guests to his summer cottage in Italy that three people (once including Joan Sutherland) would have to share a double bed and yet no one complained or left abruptly. He was known for forgetting to pay his utility and telephone bills, and having them disconnected so that he had to make calls at a nearby telephone box and dress in the evening by candlelight until his cheques for payment were received. Friends were especially attracted to his Bohemianism and vigour, and his common-sense approach to both his life and his art. 'I adored Maria,' he confessed.

> I wanted her to be at her best. So everything I did was to emphasize her qualities. I never dreamt of showing her a gesture or anything like that. I always fed her imagination with visual images. You know, the less you speak to artists, actors or actresses, the less you fill their minds with 'concepts', the less you look for trouble. You must give them very precise and very clear, simple essential indications – love, hate, happiness, resentment – whatever you like, but it must be as for children. Beyond that they are their own personalities. How much can you change a Callas in a production? Ninety per cent of what goes on stage is what she has accumulated through the years. It's what has been given by God. A director can build something around her, make her go in one direction or another, but she will remain herself.

Maria relaxed with Zeffirelli at the helm and followed her best instincts, which in this production seemed exactly right. 'With Maria,' Tito Gobbi recalled, 'I discovered an artist who also asked why and who understood what it means to be an actor. We reached a hundred per cent together…She was Tosca and I was Scarpia. Not Maria and Tito.…Everything came spontaneously.' This was exactly what Zeffirelli wanted. 'And for once,' Gobbi added, 'there was the right distance maintained between Tosca and Scarpia – not too close, not too far.…Maria was Tosca every second of the performance. The way she moved and sang, the way she listened to colleagues when *they* sang. She filled dramatic pauses with her presence, her ability to sustain tension. She was genuine, authentic, without the old clichés. [A Tosca] better than Callas we will never see.'

Her concentration on the role was monumental and, through it, each day her depression waned. At the dress rehearsal she was so deeply immersed in her portrayal of Tosca that in the scene in Scarpia's office she leaned across his desk as she sang 'Vissi d'arte' and did not realize that her long, black fall had caught fire from the candles burning to one side. 'People ran on stage [and put the fire out with hastily dampened cloths],' Zeffirelli remembered. 'But she went on singing. Never stopped.'

Opening night, 21 January, was a triumph. 'How superb the whole delivery in the first act,' the *Guardian* critic wrote. 'What detail, what caressing and isolating of key words. All the detail was lovely; some of it unforgettably striking. I have not known Callas so magnificently in control of the situation (if not at the top of her voice) for a long time.'

There were times during the performance when some wobbling in her voice occurred but, as another critic put it, 'Callas's voice is so much part of the whole of a Callas performance that one cannot really separate it from the acting. She colours her voice such as a painter does his canvas, and if it is not as large and sumptuous as it once was, it still is an amazing instrument, and its timbre highly individual.'

Gobbi came in for high praise, which he attributed in large measure to the rapport he had with Maria.

> I shall never forget the moment [when] Scarpia agrees to write a safe-conduct for Cavaradossi as payment for Tosca [giving herself to him]. At that moment I tried to caress Maria, but she grew rigid, like stone, refusing any concession until she got the permit. I went to write out the document and when I asked by what port she wanted to depart, she replied 'Civitavecchia' coming close to watch me, her hand touching the desk. I looked at her with lust, running my feather quill all the way up and down her beautiful long white arm. Maria froze, petrified. Stupendous. Now everyone asks me to retain this bit of action, but it can never be the same without Maria to respond.

With each performance, Maria grew ever more confident, her voice responding, her acting not seeming to be acting at all. Commenting on the second, 24 January, performance, Ardoin wrote of the moment in Act Three when Tosca discovers she has been betrayed and Cavaradossi is dead: 'Callas' suddenly wrenching screams followed by sobbing cries of Mario's name take one beyond the theatre into reality. You have to pause and remember this is only pretence.'

Michel Glotz had arranged a series of studio recordings, which began almost immediately upon Maria's February return to Paris. She looked and sounded better than she had in many months, but being alone in Paris while Onassis was conducting business elsewhere brought back some of her earlier depression.

After President Kennedy's assassination and his departure from Monte Carlo, Onassis abruptly stopped seeing Lee, who was puzzled but seemingly unable to rekindle their past passion. There was no woman except Maria in Onassis's life. However, he had lost prestige and a large amount of money in the Rainier/Monaco break-up and was wandering around the world on the *Christina*, a bit like the man without a country. Maria could feel his sense of loss, but was unable to ease it for him. 'He lost Monaco and I lost my one chance for motherhood. Perhaps that was God's justice,' she would say uncharitably at a later time. But in 1964 she felt she had failed him and not the other way round.

She had signed to sing eight performances of *Norma* in May and June at the Paris Opéra, all to be directed by Zeffirelli and with Corelli to reprise the role of Pollione, which he had sung opposite her previously. Maria seemed never to tire of Norma, a role she had sung nearly eighty times and still found challenging. Norma was a woman of warring feelings, a Jekyll and Hyde, daring for her time and relevant to the present; a woman in an exalted position whose private life is scandalous. In the end, she has the courage to confess her sins and to sacrifice her life. There is a moving scene when, on her knees, she begs her father's forgiveness and his promise that he will take care of her two children after she kills herself. Knowing he will, she walks to her immolation into the flames of her funeral pyre. Pollione, the father of her children, is so overcome with remorse that he follows her into death.

'Maria was at her greatest in these final moments,' Zeffirelli said later. 'So intensely moving. I think she identified with Norma greatly. In a way it was her own story. Maria, after all, is…the high priestess of her art. Yet, at the same time, she is the most fallible of women. Very human. As Norma, Maria created the maximum of what opera can be. In a lifetime, one can see many great things in the theatre. But to see Maria Callas in *Norma*, what is there to compare to it?'

Maria's scenes with Norma's two illegitimate sons were more powerful-
ly moving than in her previous productions. Silhouetted by the moon,
dressed in a deep purple gown of Egyptian silk, a flowing cloak about her
shoulders, this Norma draws the dagger with which she plans to murder
her two sleeping children, but is overcome by maternal love. There was
an elongated moment of agony, almost unbearably moving. Slowly she
pulls back the weapon, drops it as she kneels beside her sons, awakens
them and emotionally gathers them to her, unable to take their young
lives in revenge for their father's betrayal of her.

During rehearsals Maria told Zeffirelli that she did not want to get 'too
familiar' with the children playing the roles. Stage children could be too
easily conditioned and their reactions become 'stagy'. What she wanted
with the two child actors was a good relationship, to avoid any
strangeness, but to let her final emotion and tenderness with them reveal
itself in actual performance, so that they would react with greater
naturalness.

The night of the première the scene was exquisite. The youngsters
were immensely moved by the unexpectedness of Maria's affection and
the scene took on a stunning reality. 'My God, what a pity this woman
never had a child,' Zeffirelli exclaimed, unaware of her recent loss.
'Really, she would have been...well, perhaps her child is her work. After
all, artists of her stature cannot have complete fulfilment in their private
lives. Otherwise they would never attain the kind of desperate extra
dimension that sets them apart.'

Onassis missed the opening night, attending instead the fourth performance on Saturday, 6 June, the twentieth anniversary of the Allied invasion of Normandy and a special gala performance with an array of
celebrities in the audience, Charles and Oona Chaplin, Jean Seberg,
David Niven, Begum Aga Khan, Jean-Paul Belmondo, Jeanne Moreau,
and Catherine Deneuve among them. Also attending was Rudolf Bing,
there at the invitation of Michel Glotz who was attempting to ameliorate
the past ill feelings between Bing and Callas in the hopes that Maria
could once again sing at the Metropolitan.

Maria had been at her best at the première, but this night her phrasing
and timing were off and in the last act she broke on a high C. 'It was the
signal the anti-Callas claque had been waiting for. Amid the catcalls, she
stopped the orchestra and told the conductor to begin again. It was the
kind of risk that Callas at her peak would have taken with contempt.
Now it was akin to madness. The sudden silence – the sort of quiet the
mob probably made as the guillotine shivered before its descent,' Rudolf
Bing recalled, 'was awesome.' Maria hit the note and held it with perfect

control. Suddenly, a fight broke out in the balcony between two groups of men – 'those who applauded her courage and those who resented it'.[2]

Onassis rose to his feet and cheered her, never prouder of Maria than he was at that moment. 'You showed a lot of courage out there tonight,' he told her later.

'It was mostly impudence,' she replied.

'I think we need to build some time together,' he admitted. To her great joy, he suggested that as she would be free for the entire summer, they spend it together in Skorpios on the *Christina*. Major construction on the island had just been completed and it was to be the most intimate time they were to share since the early days of their relationship.

Maria bought an entirely new summer wardrobe, lighter and freer than in the past. They carefully put together the list of the few people they would invite for short stays on the Island – Zeffirelli, Maggie van Zuylen, Panaghis Vergottis, Costa Gratsos, Michel Glotz, Alexander and Christina (during their August school holidays), the ageing Serafin, his wife and Elvira de Hidalgo. They chose not to invite the high-profile celebrities who so often were passengers on the *Christina*. For one thing, Skorpios was not yet ready for entertaining on a grand scale. More important, Maria and Onassis wanted more time to themselves than playing host to such famous guests would permit. There were dinners on the *Christina*, open-pit barbecues on the beach (which was now covered in beautiful white sand imported by Onassis) and cocktails on the terrace of the main house on the island.

Often Maria and Onassis would wander off alone and be seen walking along the ocean front hand in hand in the moonlight. They were like honeymooners and their loving mood was felt and reflected by both staff and guests, and Bruna was present to see personally to Maria. The two poodles were kept on board and carefully tended when they were ashore for fear that they might be attacked by one of the small wild animals who still inhabited the island. Maria was surrounded by people who cared about *her*, not her fame, and it did wonders in making her feel at ease, perhaps for one of the few times in her life. There seemed also always to be present an elderly surrogate father figure, like Serafin and Vergottis, with whom she could discuss her most private concerns: with Serafin her voice, with Vergottis her relationship – now more passionate than ever – with Aristo.

[2] In his book, *5,000 Nights at the Opera*, Bing was to recall of that incident: 'I went backstage to [Maria's] dressing room afterward, and I didn't know whether to refer to this episode or not – it's like a woman wearing a very low-cut dress, you're not sure whether it's more rude to look or not to look. I decided not to mention it, and she never mentioned it either.'

Panaghis Vergottis was a decade older than Onassis. A tall, lean, elegant man, born into a wealthy shipowning Greek family, he had never married, rumours of a homosexual nature abounded (although he had had a string of beautiful mistresses), one that involved him and Onassis during their younger days, which were never proven. Vergottis kept a suite of rooms at the Ritz Hotels in London and Paris, was often a guest on the *Christina* and had been in on several business deals with Onassis. He was genuinely concerned about Maria's future. He knew Onassis well and feared Maria's strong belief that they would eventually marry was not likely to happen. He never doubted his old friend's love for Maria, which was – as he told other intimates – '*historic* or *histrionic*, I'm not sure which. Ari has never loved any woman as deeply. He doesn't realize now how much he needs her. She is as though of his flesh. But he is always in battle with who he really is and who he wants to be. Sadly, the lure of the fiction invariably wins over the reality. Right now, Maria only has love to give him and that is not enough for Ari.'

Maria's financial situation at this time was such that she could not have supported her luxurious lifestyle *without* Onassis's generous help. Vergottis advised her to become more independent, financially secure. His idea was for her to become a shipowner in her own right. This was agreed to by Onassis after some private discussions between the two men. Vergottis promised to scout out a purchase for a vessel that looked good. In early September he heard of a carrier nearing completion at a shipyard in Spain, which had been abandoned when the builder defaulted on his loans. It could be bought for far less than what it was worth and, when work was finished on it, would be able to bring in a considerable, hefty annual profit.

Onassis agreed to put up, in Maria's name, twenty-five per cent of the vessel's $3.4 million price tag (the cash that was required to close the deal). The two men would then take over the mortgage for the remaining money, for which Vergottis would have a twenty-five per cent interest and Onassis fifty per cent. A guarantee was then drawn up that Maria would receive an additional twenty-six per cent of Onassis's share upon his death, which would then give her the controlling interest and protect her against any interference from his other heirs.

To Maria's enormous delight, the contracts were signed on 27 October. She was now part-owner of a 28,000-ton bulk carrier named *Artimission*, which was held in a Liberian corporation. The three partners held a cele-bratory dinner at Maxims in Paris. No sooner was the ship launched, than it developed complicated engine trouble on its maiden voyage to Japan. On 8 January 1965, while Onassis was in Glyfada, Vergottis took

Maria back to Maxims where they discussed 'some serious matters' over dinner. The future earnings of the *Artimission* looked less profitable than first thought. It would be in her best interest, he advised, if her original investment ($168,000) be converted to a loan, which would pay her a guaranteed 6.5 per cent interest.

'As I love you very much,' she reported him having said, 'I think this is a better way...if the ship does not do well, you can always pull out and you will have had the interest on your money. And, of course, you would still be able to exercise the option on your share in the company.' Maria, not knowledgeable about such matters but trusting Vergottis implicitly, replied, 'Thank you, Panaghis. That is very nice of you' and signed the paper he handed her.

Onassis had already transferred the promised additional twenty-six per cent to her, the remaining twenty-four per cent to be equally divided among his sister's four sons. When advised the next morning by Maria of what she had just done, he became outraged. Maria thought it unlikely that such a good friend, who was also a very rich man, obviously terribly fond of both, would ever treat them dishonestly. Onassis was much wiser and wilier and, to her humiliation, he thought her naive and stupidly malleable for signing the paper before consulting him.

The disturbing episode over Vergottis (who had also promised financing for a film version of Zeffirelli's *Tosca* to star Maria) was soon pushed aside as Maria found herself once again with an active performance schedule. She repeated the Covent Garden *Tosca* production at the Paris Opéra for nine performances from 19 February through 13 March 1965, and then – with private fears and great joy – flew directly to New York where, on 19 March, she would be returning to the Metropolitan for the first time in six years, a rapprochement made possible by Michel Glotz. She would again be singing Tosca with Gobbi as Scarpia. Corelli would sing Cavaradossi on the opening night, Richard Tucker on 25 March, the second and last performance. Upon her return to Paris, there would be five performances of Zeffirelli's production of *Norma* at the Opéra, the season ending on 5 July with *Tosca* at Covent Garden.

Maria's performance of *Tosca* would be one of the last operas to be sung at the old Metropolitan on 39th Street, for the new opera house further uptown in Lincoln Center would open for the following season. There had been an active campaign to save the old Met, which had failed, despite the success of its final season which featured the return of some of the veteran building's greatest singers, Maria included, of course, and introduced an unprecedented and impressive list of brilliant debuts – Elisabeth Schwarzkopf as the Marschallin in *Der Rosenkavalier*, Mirella

Freni and Gianni Raimondi as the lovers in *La Bohème*, Montserrat Caballé, Sherrill Milnes and Nicolai Ghiaurov in *Faust*. Bing had also signed the tempestuous Grace Bumbry who would become a legendary Aida, and the brilliant young conductor Zubin Mehta.

Being separated from Onassis while she was in New York had a discomforting effect on Maria. The tangible intimacy they had known the previous summer had dissipated. Maria sensed his anger at her for her private dealings with Vergottis. But she also knew he was disturbed by his sudden, humiliating departure from Monaco. He had not won that battle and for Onassis, winning was everything. 'I should be with him now,' she told Bruna. Much to Michel Glotz's disappointment, she refused to sign for anything other than recordings to be made in Paris, in the year to come. Nothing, not her career, nor her voice, meant as much to her as did Aristo and her need to be with him.

Banners reading 'Welcome home, Maria' greeted her upon her first rehearsal of *Tosca* at the Metropolitan. Her immediate reaction as work began was the seediness of the production and the sad decline of the opera house since her last appearance there seven years earlier. Rehearsals were slipshod; only one piano rehearsal and no dress on stage. Sets were shabby, costumes lacklustre, a startling opposite from the brilliance and freshness Zeffirelli had brought to his production. Bing's attention was on the new, not on the old, opera house; his young, promising singers, not the artists who had given the Metropolitan its worldwide reputation. As General Manager the fault had to stop at his door.

Maria and the rest of the cast soldiered on, but she was extraordinarily nervous on opening night and disappointed that for the first time in memory there were no red roses from Aristo. She need not have worried about her reception. Upon her entrance there was wild applause. For six full minutes she stood frozen on stage waiting for the cheers and the rhythmic clapping to stop so that the performance could continue.

'She did not sing well,' Bing later wrote, 'but it made no difference whatever – never had there been such a *Tosca*. I never fully enjoyed any other artist in one of her roles after she did it…She and Herbert von Karajan were the complete artists of my time at the Metropolitan, and I can criticize myself most effectively by complaining how few performances we had from either – from Callas, only twenty-one altogether, seven of Lucia, six each of Norma and Tosca, two of Violetta.'

Alan Rich's *Herald Tribune* review of Maria's opening night of *Tosca* did not demean her voice. It was, instead, filled with laudatory reverence. 'The voice I heard last night had a creamy lightness to it which summoned up memories of her earliest recordings. She has somehow achieved this without losing her astounding ability to make the voice the servant of the drama. It was – simply as singing – one of the most remarkable vocal achievements in my memory.'

The same morning the front page of the *New York Times* carried a review (a rare occurrence) by Harold Schonberg that proclaimed: 'Her conception of the role was electrical. Everything at her command was put into striking use. She was a woman in love, a tiger cat, a woman possessed by jealousy...this was supreme acting, unforgettable action.'

After the opening night performance, Bing hosted a reception for all the stellar artists in the cast, but it was obvious that Maria was the unproclaimed guest of honour. Jackie Kennedy had been in the audience and had cheered along with everyone else. Her dark hair carefully coiffed and wearing a stunning white satin Dior gown, Jackie was ushered by Bing to where Maria stood greeting well-wishers. 'Madame Callas, this was one of the most thrilling nights I have ever had at the opera,' Jackie said, eyes glittering with unfeigned enthusiasm.

Maria took her hand and shook it lightly. It would be the first and only time the two women would meet.

23

An Historic Hiatus

ARIA ARRIVED BACK in Paris in frail health, her energy minimal, her weight having dipped to a new low. It was not something she cared to discuss at this moment with her private physician who, as yet, did not know that she had undergone a recent abortion. She took an alphabet list of vitamins, self-prescribed, and threw herself into rehearsals at the Opéra for *Norma*, which began almost immediately upon her return. Gianfranco Cecchele replaced Franco Corelli as Pollione, but otherwise the production was the same as it had been the previous year.

The first-night audience, though perhaps not as glittering, was awaiting her entrance excitedly. There was speculation that she might never sing in Paris again. Rumours circulated that she was retiring finally to marry Onassis. Most outsiders assumed that it was her career that had kept this from already happening. The audience glanced about for a glimpse of 'the Greek', but he was missing. Perhaps he was backstage, some speculated. He was actually in New York, having flown there shortly after Maria's return to Paris. There was, however, a huge basket of red roses and Zeffirelli had been a magnificent support, both personally and professionally, throughout the rehearsal process.

An hour before curtain up Maria felt suddenly faint. There was much excitement and confusion backstage as to whether she could sing. 'No, no. I won't disappoint,' she insisted as she prepared to make her entrance. Before the curtain was raised, the house manager appeared at the corner of the stage. Silence fell on the opera house, the audience fearing a cancelled performance. Instead, he informed them that though she was feeling somewhat unwell, Madame Callas would sing but begged their indulgence and awareness of her condition.

In fact, she gave a more than creditable performance and there were some extraordinary moments – the scene with the children, of course, the ennobling ending, the poignancy of her middle-voice passages. She exchanged some of the many high Cs in her role with B-flats (and in one case with an A), but her voice was stable and if this was not the most powerful Norma she had ever sung, it was an electrifying experience for the audience who gave her a long standing ovation through a dozen curtains.

As she approached the fifth and last performance on 29 May, she appeared to have overcome most of her vocal problems. Privately, her strength was ebbing, her haemorrhaging remaining a serious problem. Just before the curtain was to rise on Act Three, she stumbled as she made her way to the wings and was caught and supported by those closest to her. 'Are you sure you are all right?' the stage manager asked.

She simply nodded her head in assent and brushed by him. About ten minutes into the act, a small gasp could be heard as her long, expressive hand rose to her throat. In that moment it seemed the gesture and the sound had been part of her performance. But then, to the horror of everyone, she collapsed into a heap on to the floor. 'Lower the curtain!' the stage manager ordered and, as cast and crew hovered around her momentarily unconscious form, the performance of *Norma* ended, the audience not knowing if Callas had been mortally struck or simply had fainted (the latter having been closer to the truth). She was carried back to her dressing room in a semi-conscious state and the physician she had been loath to see was called.

The doctor arrived within half an hour and ordered her transferred to hospital. 'Not in an ambulance,' Maria insisted. An hour later, still weak and woozy, she was helped out of the theatre where a large crowd greeted her as she came through the stage door. 'I know I've let you down,' she managed to say, her hand tightly gripping Michel Glotz's arm. 'I'm so sorry. I promise you that one day I shall return to win your forgiveness and satisfy your love.' There were tears in the eyes of many of her fans as she made her way, in a kind of stupor, to her waiting car.

The press were told that she had suffered from low blood pressure, a partial truth. Her haemoglobin count had dropped dangerously low from her loss of blood. A cauterization was performed and she received a blood transfusion. Onassis rushed back to Paris to her side. For two weeks she had total rest at home, few visitors and no practice sessions. There were discussions about possibly cancelling the 5 July performance of *Tosca* at Covent Garden, but she insisted she would be able to appear. Onassis promised that after this performance they would go to Skorpios for the remainder of the summer where she could do nothing more than lie in the sun if she so wished.

There is every chance that he was feeling some guilt for her condition. Whatever the cause, Maria was delighted with the effect. She and Onassis would have time together. 'This will be the time for both a proposal and a quiet wedding,' she assured Maggie van Zuylen. Onassis went with her to London for the Covent Garden *Tosca*, which was to be sung in the presence of the Queen, the Queen Mother and Prince Philip. Perhaps this was not the most fiery of her *Tosca* performances, but 'Vissi d'arte' was sung exquisitely, her Tosca came vividly to life and her voice, although not as full as it might have been if she had been in better health, never failed her. She had no idea that this would be the last *Tosca*, or any operatic role, she would sing. Michel Glotz was negotiating terms for a return to Paris with *Norma* and other productions. *Traviata* and *Medea* had been offered, and Zeffirelli was keen on a plan to film *Tosca* – a project that Vergottis (in an effort to show his good faith) had already agreed to help finance.

Maria had looked forward to her stay with Onassis on Skorpios as a 'second honeymoon', a chance for the two of them to relive the happiness of the previous summer. The guest list was even more select than it had been then. There would be less entertaining, more privacy for them. Onassis also needed time to heal. Sir Winston Churchill had recently died and Onassis was still mourning his loss. At the funeral service at St Paul's he had sobbed so uncontrollably that Nonie Montague Browne tried to calm him with a tranquillizer, which he was unable to swallow. On the way back from the cathedral in his limousine with several other mourners, he insisted his chauffeur stop at a pub in the Strand where he held his own private memorial tribute. Everyone was served the great man's favourite brandy as they contributed fond and colourful memories of him. Onassis continued to mourn. For many months afterwards, Maria would find him sitting alone at his desk in his office on the *Christina* rereading Churchill's letters to him, his eyes brimming.

'Churchill was the father he had lost so early in his life and under such tragic circumstances,' one intimate noted.

'Ari's mood that summer was very dark, very Greek,' another friend added. 'Most of the time he ignored [Maria] utterly, as if she simply wasn't there. Then he would explode in a terrible rage against her for no reason at all that anyone could fathom.'

Maria was puzzled and at times desperate. This was a period in both their lives when their response to each other should have been the greatest. Each was mourning a loss and each feared what they might have to face in the near future – Onassis a declining grasp on power (having lost control of Monaco) and Maria the instability of her voice. Instead, they were constantly 'at each other' and Maria would end up retreating to a private corner of the *Christina* while Onassis wandered aimlessly over his new domain – the island of Skorpios.

'Once you knew that they always had a good time in bed, even when they fought. Just to look at them you knew the sex was fine,' a close observer said. 'But now he acted as if he couldn't stand to be near her.' Zeffirelli came for a week's stay on Skorpios and left after a few days, unable to see Onassis treat Maria in such a cruel manner and feeling helpless to do anything to ease her obvious pain.

Onassis put up little resistance when in mid-August Maria told him she had decided to go to London to attend the funeral of Vergottis's brother, of whom she had been especially fond, and to meet with Zeffirelli about his proposed film of *Tosca*. She flew out of Skorpios on Onassis's private jet.

'Her departure only deepened Ari's depression,' a remaining guest remarked. 'We [his close friends] all agreed that Maria was the real love of his life, but for reasons that no one could fathom at the time, he had decided to end the relationship but did not know how to do so and, deep down, really did not want to let go.'

While Maria was in London, the *Tosca* film deal shaped up into a property set to go. Zeffirelli, of course, would direct, Tito Gobbi had agreed to sing Scarpia and space at Shepperton Studios had been booked. In an arrangement made by Vergottis, the German company, Beta Films, would produce. Sander Gorlinsky was representing Maria's interests, which at this time would have given her a fee of $100,000 plus expenses and ten per cent of the gross (not a usual arrangement then, when major film actors received percentages of the *net*, seldom on the gross).

Maria had been in daily contact with Onassis, who seemed to enjoy being able this once to pull the strings, for he had never before involved himself with Maria's contractual negotiations. She rejoined him on Skorpios two weeks later, from which point he took over the calling of the terms. Maria was to receive $250,000 plus expenses and twenty-five per cent of the gross. Zeffirelli and Gorlinsky flew down to Skorpios to see if they could talk some sense into Maria – for with the figures she now placed in negotiation the film could not be made.

Onassis took over the meeting, which turned into a shouting match with him yelling at Maria to 'Shut up! Be quiet! You are nothing but a nightclub singer!'

'I was hoping she would pick up the nearest bottle [in the bar of the *Christina* where they were gathered] and throw it at him, but no, she just got up and walked out. She was totally under his thumb,' Gorlinsky said.

Later Maria refuted this. 'Yes, of course, Ari wanted to deal with the film contract himself and with his tongue in cheek made that grossly exaggerated remark in order to give me the excuse of walking out and leaving him to handle the situation. We did rehearse it but he surprised me when he mentioned nightclubs. We both laughed about it later … Let's face it, in business matters he was second to none.'

He had convinced Maria that it would be a better business investment if they produced the film themselves – with Zeffirelli directing, but not tied to Beta Films or Vergottis, with whom he now had something of a vendetta going. Gorlinsky dutifully (but not happily) went back to the producers and asked how much they would want to sell all their rights in the property. Beta refused to sell and for several weeks hostilities, rather than negotiations, were the norm. On 4 October, Maria released a statement to the press that she was withdrawing from the project. Vergottis instantly rang her to tell her that Onassis had ruined what would have been her golden opportunity to put one of her finest roles on film for future generations to see how truly great she was. At the same time she would have opened new doors for herself to far greater revenues, and less stress, than singing in an opera house produced.

'It was I who withdrew,' Maria said. She claimed that Onassis never interfered with her art, 'except to tell me that I should not feel any obligation to continue my singing career'. Onassis recognized, perhaps as few others did at the time, how stressed Maria was about her voice, and how frail she was physically. Both these impediments to her health and wellbeing were of concern to him, even though he seemed to be attempting to manipulate her – which he most certainly was doing, knowing that no one would have as much power over her decisions as he had. His true reasons are murky. Not so Maria's response in backing out of a project that she had greeted enthusiastically and honestly wanted to do.

It seemed to her that Onassis chose to have her *not* sing so that she could be with him and that if she did elect to appear – either in opera or on film – she should be compensated as the star she was. 'Think, Maria, think!' he told her. 'Without you there is no film of *Tosca*. They will all be making money on you, because of you. Why shouldn't you get the largest cut of the pie?'

Maria continued to insist that 'neither Ari nor anybody else could have influenced me during that stage of my career… As far as my artistic career is concerned I always took the decisions.' This seems naive in face of all the evidence to the contrary. Maria was desperately seeking Onassis's approval, a way to win her way back fully to his heart. Placing herself in his control seemed a wise choice. He liked playing the protector, winning the battle for his lady. He had resented her continuing friendship with Vergottis, considering it a betrayal of sorts – since he had fallen out with him.

So what does Maria do, just a few weeks after withdrawing from the Zeffirelli film? She contacts Vergottis and notifies him that she wants her loan on the *Artimission* to be converted back to shares. Not a request she would have been likely to have made without coaching from Onassis. Vergottis refused. A few days later the two men met by accident in London in the restaurant of Claridge's Hotel at lunch one day and nearly came to blows. Onassis called Vergottis a blackmailer and a swindler, and threatened a criminal lawsuit. They had to be separated by appalled restaurant staff as Vergottis, poised to throw a bottle of wine wrested from a nearby waiter's hand, promised a scandal in court if Onassis dared such a thing. 'You will be the cause of Maria's humiliation as you are of her unhappiness!' Vergottis vowed as Onassis straightened, put on his sunglasses (although it was a typically grey English November afternoon), spat on the floor (to the dismay of staff and diners) and strode out of the hotel.

He cooled down later and even met Vergottis to pressure him to take the matter (of Maria's right to have the shares returned to her) to arbitration before an independent panel of lawyers. 'I think we should avoid the publicity of a public trial, don't you?' he told Vergottis. Vergottis thought otherwise. Legal work went forward, but it would be a year before the two men would have a final face-off.

In the early days of April 1966 Maria released a statement that she was renouncing her American citizenship. 'After seven years of struggling with divorce proceedings,' she said, 'my lawyers discovered that by taking Greek nationality my marriage becomes simply non-existent throughout the world – except in Italy.' This was not exactly true. Her legal representatives were not ignorant of the Greek law that had been passed in 1946, three years before her marriage to Meneghini, which stated that no marriage of a Greek citizen was valid unless it was performed in a Greek Orthodox Church. What they had to prove was that her Greek citizenship could be established at the time of her marriage. True, her parents were Greek. However, her father had renounced his citizenship to become an American citizen when she was a small child. Somehow, the lawyers overcame that obstacle, although it had taken a good deal of time and expense. The end result was that Maria was free (Meneghini refused to accept the judge's decision in the matter) and could, if she so wished, marry again.

The way was open for them finally to seal their troth. Friends waited expectantly (as did Maria's sister Jackie and their father) for an announcement to be made. None was forthcoming, which was troubling to those closest to Maria, who knew how much she wanted to become Mrs Onassis. Maria later told Stelios Galatopoulos that her love for Onassis was very strong, 'but my intuition, or whatever you call it, told me that I would have lost him the moment I married him – he would have turned his interest to some other younger woman'. This is a curious rationalization, if Maria was speaking truthfully. She was well aware that Onassis had only been faithful to her during the earliest stages of their affair. She had spoken frankly to Maggie van Zuylen about his womanizing and been advised by her friend, in effect, to overlook it and never bring it up with him but to make him grateful to return to her loyal friendship, her comforting arms and her sexual companionship (Maggie often gave her advice on how to hold her man, which she respected).

Onassis was by nature a serial womanizer. When a young man, he had spent a good deal of time in whorehouses. As one of the richest unmarried men in the world, women were constantly throwing themselves at him and he was not one to resist the charms of a beautiful female when they were offered to him. Maria nurtured contradictory, and highly hypocritical, views on her lover's 'addiction'. Despite her history of adultery with Onassis, and their long, illicit affair, she claimed that, because of her religion and her moral background, she could not enter into a marriage and covenant with a husband who was having affairs. 'Our marriage probably would have become, before long, a squalid argument,' she later said. 'How can a man who really loves you have affairs with other women?' she mused, when talking to Stelios Galatopoulos. 'He couldn't possibly love them all.' She always tried to dismiss her suspicions. 'Evidently I could not and it was out of the question to accept it into my moral code.' Maggie, she claimed, 'was like a mother, sister, friend', explaining to her that a man like that genuinely loved his wife 'or the woman in his life. To his way of thinking these extramarital affairs are no more than biological infidelities.' What Maria appears to be saying is that she could cope with an unfaithful lover but not a straying husband. 'The role of the betrayed wife was not in my repertoire,' she would say later. 'Ari...knew that sooner or later we would have been at daggers drawn had we married (that may sound rather eccentric but I have to accept that it was his way of thinking and therefore not necessarily wrong).'

The truth was that any mention of marriage to Onassis brought on one of his cold, detached moods and Maria knew she dared not press it further without endangering what they had. Theirs, she firmly believed, was a special love, an *historic* love. She convinced herself that Onassis did

not love these other women. Those relationships had only to do with sex
or, if she was not with him, simple boredom. On the one hand she
claimed he gave her freedom, independence, the ability to be her own
woman; on the other she appeared to be blind to what was a blatant loss
of freedom and independence. And now that there was an hiatus in her
career, she was wholly dependent upon Onassis for whatever happiness
she enjoyed. She did have substantial holdings: the apartment on avenue
Georges Mandel, jewellery, antiques, enough royalties from her recordings to live on comfortably – if not luxuriously – and stocks and cash that
ensured she could maintain her current status quo. But without Onassis
that would mean very little.

When Serafin once asked why she didn't leave Onassis, she replied,
'Will you be there at three o'clock in the morning when I am all alone?'

'But you are a beautiful, talented woman. What makes you think you
would be alone?' he queried.

'Without Onassis I am nothing. It is only in his eyes that I become a
woman. So why would I interest another man?' she answered.

On 17 April 1967 the case of Vergottis versus Onassis (which the judge
later claimed had 'many of the elements of a Sophoclean tragedy about it')
came before Mr Justice Roskill in the Queen's Bench division in London.
Maria entered the courtroom on Onassis's arm, dressed as though she
were about to appear in a theatrical production, a dramatic scarf flung
over the shoulder of her scarlet dress, her hair hidden inside an exotic
white turban, her skin chalky, her large, expressive eyes lined with kohl.

'I am sorry to say that Mr Vergottis said that if either Mr Onassis or
Mme Callas dared to appear in the witness box they would be faced with
a great deal of scandal, both in court and in the press,' began their representative, Sir Milner Holland, in his opening statement. 'It is perhaps
natural that Mr Onassis stigmatized that as blackmail and that Mr
Vergottis laughed. The breach between the two gentlemen has not been
healed from that day.'

Vergottis would have his revenge. As soon as Onassis was in the
witness box, his counsel, Mr Peter Bristow, asked him: 'After you got to
know Madame Callas did you part from your wife and did Madame
Callas part from her husband?'

'Yes, sir. Nothing to do with our meeting. Just coincidence,' Onassis
replied.

'Do you regard her as being in a position equivalent to being your
wife, if she was free?'

'No. If that were the case I have no problem marrying her, neither has
she any problem marrying me.'

'Do you feel any obligations towards her other than those of mere friendship?'

Without hesitation, and to the entire shock of almost everyone in the courtroom, Onassis answered, 'None whatsoever.'

Again to Galatopoulos, in a long interview late in her life, Maria fell back to rationalization. 'What Ari said in court was absolutely correct. He was referring to the case and as far as that was concerned he had no other obligations... Ari was a far too shrewd man to let Vergottis's lawyer get the better of him. It was quite clear that Vergottis thought that he would win his case by exposing my relationship with Ari and creating a scandal.'[1]

The case, which received worldwide coverage and front-page tabloid photographs of the players, marked the end of Maria's friendship with Vergottis, whom she would never speak to again. It also signalled the start of what Maria called 'Aristo's restless wanderings'. During the winter of 1967–8 he was almost constantly on the go and always without Maria, who returned to Paris and the cloistered comfort of her grand apartment, seeing friends like Maggie van Zuylen and Zeffirelli but seldom venturing far from the avenue Georges Mandel.

Maria and Onassis had been drawn closer by the Vergottis ordeal, but the evening before she returned to Paris she was conscious of a change in Onassis's attitude towards her. At dinner with Lord Harewood and other friends, Onassis made the statement, 'The only free people are those who love nobody.'

'That's too high a price to pay,' she replied.

He then asked her what she wanted most for herself.

'I just want to be on good terms with myself,' was her answer.

Their guests noted a change in their body language. There was no hand-holding as was often the case. His arm did not slip casually round her waist or shoulder. She seemed distracted and he seemed not to notice.

With the utmost secrecy, Maria not even suspecting, Onassis had been seeing the widowed Jackie Kennedy on sudden and unannounced trips to New York throughout 1966 and 1967, where she privately entertained him at her Fifth Avenue duplex apartment. There were constant rumours flying around Jackie. The American public, who had already turned her into an icon, did not want her to become a professional widow. At the

[1] It would take another year for the case to be settled eventually in favour of Maria and Onassis, who gained little financially from the outcome but, at least in Onassis's case, enjoyed the victory.

same time they felt proprietary about her, obsessed with the eligibility or non-eligibility of the men with whom she was seen and photographed by the squads of paparazzi who hunted her as they would, twenty-some years hence, hunt Princess Diana.

The widowed David Ormsby-Gore (Lord Harlech), former British ambassador to the United States and a good friend of the Kennedy family, was one of her suitors who seemed acceptable by public standards, despite the fact that he was a 'foreigner', for the majority wanted Jackie to remarry, if she must, but to an American. She was photographed dining with Roswell Gilpatric, former Under-Secretary of Defense in her husband's administration, Mike Nichols, the financier André Meyer and Arthur Schlesinger Jr. She also had a circle of gay friends like Truman Capote and Rudolf Nureyev. Speculation about Jackie's personal life filled gossip columns and was discussed at luncheon and dinner tables almost every time interested parties gathered – and that seemed to include many thousands of people.

As late as January 1968 the relationship between Jackie and Onassis was guarded with such secrecy and care that neither the members of the Kennedy family nor Maria was aware of the serious stage that it had reached. Until then they met in private – Onassis would fly in to New York on a supposedly strictly business trip and would see Jackie at her home, entering the building through the service door and taking the back elevator to her apartment. Jackie had managed to spend time with Onassis on Skorpios without detection and come to Paris, where they rendezvoused at his apartment on the avenue Foch without Maria's knowledge.

Privacy was a must for Jackie, who remained at this time greatly under the influence of the Kennedy family and most especially Robert 'Bobby' Kennedy, who was planning to declare himself a candidate for the presidency in the summer of the 1968 Democratic convention. The image of his martyred brother's widow by his side was a potent vote getter and Bobby had warned Jackie of the danger to his campaign and to the Kennedy name, if she had indiscreet and 'unacceptable' liaisons. But the very incongruity of an affair between Jackie and Onassis appeared to keep Bobby from guessing the true mystery man in her life (for he did suspect there was someone).

Then, suddenly, they seemed to be seen everywhere – dining at El Morocco and '21', at Dionysus and Mykonos, two well-known Greek restaurants in New York, and at Maxims in Paris, which had always been where he and Maria had gone on special occasions.

It was in March 1968, while Bobby Kennedy was immersed in the hard push of the primaries that, at a cocktail party at the George V Hôtel in Paris, a woman, known to feed items to gossip columnists, asked Onassis who he thought was the consummate woman – 'Garbo? Eva Perón? Maria Callas?'

He did not hesitate: 'Jacqueline Kennedy. She is a totally misunderstood woman. Perhaps she even misunderstands herself. She's being held up as a model of propriety, constancy and so many of those boring American female virtues. She's now utterly devoid of mystery. She needs a small scandal to bring her alive. A peccadillo, an indiscretion. Something should happen to her to win [the world's] fresh compassion. The world loves to pity fallen grandeur.'

The press picked up the implication. Onassis and Jackie were an item.

'I guess it's a family weakness,' Bobby quipped when informed of Onassis's remark, making reference to Lee's former liaison with Onassis. 'I guess you know this could cost me five states,' he added.

Maria was stunned. Onassis told her frankly that he had proposed to Jackie and hoped she would marry him. 'It is not love,' he insisted. 'I love you, I need Jackie.' And he went on to explain that the American market had been denied him for twenty years when, in 1946, the Federal Government accused him of not paying income tax on his oil tankers that had used US docks. Marriage to Jackie would eventually bring him into the Kennedy fold and with Bobby seeming a certainty to be the next Kennedy in the White House, the obstacle for access to the American market would be removed. *And if Robert Kennedy did not win the election*? He would finance a campaign for the younger brother, Teddy, which should do it.

Jackie did not love him either, he claimed. She wanted to leave the United States where she had no privacy any more. 'She had dreams of being murdered and worried constantly that her children would be kidnapped or harmed. Assassination was her shaping experience.' He promised her homes abroad, bodyguards night and day more vigilant than the few FBI men who guarded her now (and whom she had been clever enough to elude for her private meetings with Onassis). In America she remained Kennedy's widow, her life enveloped in an aura of sadness. In Europe, and with him, she was the light-hearted Jackie of earlier days. She had become aware of herself as a woman, you could see it in her step, in the mischievous smile, in the return of the sexy voice that Maria had called 'Marilyn Monroe playing Ophelia'.

Maria was anything but appeased. The hurt was deep and the pain increased when she realized that Onassis had come to tell her that they could not meet in public or be with each other again in the biblical sense – at least for the present time – but that he would always love her and care for her, and be there for her if she should need his help or counsel. Maria felt betrayed, more puzzled than bitter. After so many years together and the depth of their mutual passion, it was difficult for her to understand why he would want to marry a woman whom he did not love – even given the special circumstances of what his alliance with Jackie would engender.

In May Onassis took several close friends, associates and the now teenage Christina on a cruise to the Virgin Islands. The majority of the guests appeared to be a cover, for they disembarked from the *Christina* in St John the day 'before the mysterious new arrival was due'. The mystery guest was Jackie, to be greeted by a staff who had been warned that whoever was coming 'had the clout to dismiss anyone deemed unsuitable'. Portraits of Jack and Jackie in their Camelot days were hung in the grand salon and the smoking room. Onassis vacated his suite and in one day managed to have the decoration redone in a more feminine fashion. Large bottles of Jackie's favourite perfumes were placed in the dressing room. Massive pink and scarlet peonies (which she adored) replaced the usual red roses that had been Maria's flower of choice.

Along with Christina, Joan Thring, Nureyev's personal assistant and a good friend of Jackie's and of Onassis, was one of the few guests remaining on board. 'For Christ's sake', Onassis warned her, 'stick close. Don't leave her side. I don't want any sons of bitches getting any of those Peeping Tom pictures of just the two of us, making it look like we're horsing around alone out here.'

Thring recalled that the two of them secreted themselves every afternoon at teatime in a private corner of the yacht to discuss their marriage plans, yet they did not seem like lovers in the same way that Maria and Onassis had appeared to be. Jackie and Onassis were in constant touch with Bobby who was acting as Jackie's marriage broker as he moved energetically along the campaign trail. Halfway through the negotiations (for they were exactly that), Onassis declared that Bobby was 'making it too fucking easy' and he suspected trouble ahead.

Although it seemed as though Jackie and Onassis had a deal, she had promised Bobby that she would not make any announcement until after the election. This meant seven months of waiting and, from Onassis's point of view, no deal was sure with such a wide time frame. 'As long as Bobby has a political bone in his body,' Onassis grumped, 'Jackie will be under his influence.'

Only three weeks later, on 5 June, Robert F. Kennedy was assassinated at the Ambassador Hotel in Los Angeles at a fund-raising affair. A London associate of Onassis's is claimed to have been told by him: 'She's free of the Kennedys, the last link is broken.' He seemed genuinely moved by the ghastly tragedy, yet relieved that 'his biggest headache had been eliminated'. Onassis was now Jackie's only hope to escape from what she called 'the vendetta against the Kennedys...If they're killing Kennedys, my kids are number one targets. I want to get out of the country.'

Jackie accepted his proposal, although the financial arrangements were not yet concluded (Teddy Kennedy took these over from Bobby). A tentative date in October was chosen for a marriage to take place on Skorpios. When Lee Radziwill was told, she was so frenzied she rang Truman Capote in the United States, 'screaming and crying and carrying on. "How could she do this to me! How could she! How could this happen!"' Capote tried to calm her down, but she was sobbing hysterically. He waited until she 'came up for air' and then told her he would call her back – which he did, when she was reasonably in control, but no less bitter. 'Lee really thought she had Onassis nailed down,' Capote later said. 'She wasn't in love with him but she liked all those tankers.'

Not until three days prior to the wedding was a public announcement made that Jacqueline Bouvier Kennedy would marry Aristotle Onassis on 20 October 1968 in a ceremony to be held in the chapel on the island of Skorpios.

Maria immediately went into isolation, refusing to answer the telephone or see anyone except Maggie. The curtains in her apartment were drawn night and day because paparazzi had managed to climb one of the tall chestnut trees outside the building and was caught perched on a limb with a long-range camera aimed at the windows of her grand salon. She bolted the french doors, fearing that with one Tarzan-like swing another photographer could make it on to her balcony and enter the apartment.

She was beyond distraught. 'After nine years, not a child, not a family, not a friend,' she sobbed many years later to John Ardoin, whom she much respected. 'That's very little, you know. And you say, "God, why? Why should these things happen...How could anyone be so cruel?... How can a man be so dishonest? So, I don't know, so crazy? Poor man..."'

'He doesn't love her,' she kept protesting. 'It's a business arrangement.' In her heart she did not fully believe this, for on the day of the wedding she gave orders that neither the radio nor the television should be turned on. She did not want to see the daily papers or speak to anyone on the telephone. She closed herself in her bedroom with the two poodles, locked the door and could be heard sobbing by the staff (who kept coming close to the door to make sure she was not going to do herself harm). 'Her mood was dark, *very dark*,' one of them said. 'No one wanted to say it, but we did worry that she might do something foolish.'

Maria was, however, a survivor. She had come through a lot in her life: the war, near starvation, her mother's and Battista's betrayals. By the next morning she was talking to Michel Glotz and Sander Gorlinsky about getting her career back on track, which did not mean that she had survived intact. A part of her had died when Onassis married Jackie Kennedy and what remained would be tinged for ever with sadness.

24

By Herself

SHE MIGHT HAVE wallowed in self-pity. She would always love Aristo. No man would ever mean to her what he did. His photographs were displayed in every room of the apartment. Her favourite was one which she kept on her night table – the two of them holding hands and smiling on the deck of the *Christina*. She avoided reading any of the current magazines and tabloids that covered the wedding, the post-wedding and then just the everyday social life of Jackie and Onassis, which was monitored assiduously by the paparazzi.

Her heart grew heavier with news of Tullio Serafin's death. He had been her greatest teacher, perhaps her best friend. 'It was Serafin who taught me the meaning of art,' she confessed, 'and who guided me to discover it for myself…He opened my eyes, showing me that there was a reason for everything in music. Nothing escaped his attention. He was just like a sly fox – every movement, every word, every breath, every little detail was important.' It was from Serafin that she learned the proportions of recitative, the basic principle of bel canto (to prepare 'a phrase in your soul before you sing it'); he taught her gestures, to listen to the music, to act accordingly to a pause, a chord, a crescendo. 'And so I learned exactly the depth and justification of music. That is why I tried to absorb, like a sponge, all I could from this great man. [When he conducted] he was breathing with you, living the music with you, loving it with you.'

Serafin gave just as deeply and sensitively to their friendship. She picked up the telephone often, forgetting for a brief moment that he was gone. 'He was the wisest man I ever knew and he was always there when I needed him,' she said. 'I cannot think of another person whom I can say that about. To have had such a man as a friend and mentor may have been my greatest blessing. I shall never stop missing him.' Nonetheless, by Christmas 1968, whatever ghosts of times past haunted her privately,

Maria made a tremendous effort to show a different face to the friends who rallied around her. On 2 December, her forty-fifth birthday, she had received a package from Onassis containing a beautiful, small, jewelled and enamelled Cartier clock, which had been in her dressing room on the *Christina*. She returned it without a note.

There seemed little left for her except to hold on to her dignity. The past had slipped darkly round an unknown corner and was lost. What she feared most was inactivity, which she knew would be devastating to her. A likely project would reach the discussion stage and then dissolve into nothingness. She was humble, grateful, responsive to the smallest kindness shown to her. Bruna and Ferruccio, her butler, were her guardians, her protectors. The paparazzi gave her little peace. They appeared from behind trees and cars. Stolen pictures of her walking the dogs, entering a limousine, or leaving her hairdresser's appeared in tabloids with captions referring to her not as Maria Callas, the opera diva, but as the woman Onassis had jilted for Jackie. She received hundreds of letters of 'condolence'.

'If they think I am going to curl up and die', she told her good friend Hélène Rochas, the perfume mogul, 'they will be greatly disappointed.'

After only five months of his marriage to Jackie, Onassis turned back to Maria, trying to woo her once again into his life and his bed. The marriage he had thought would bring him the prestige and connections that would exalt his position was a disaster. The passion Jackie had shown for him in the early days, when he was presenting her with expensive jewels almost daily, had disappeared. She was always going somewhere where he was not. When they were together she belittled him in public. Her spending was outrageous – within five months, $7 million to redecorate the *Christina*, the new house on Skorpios, the Paris apartment and the house in Glyfada [this would escalate to nearly $20 million within a year]. Her monthly allowance of $30,000 was usually spent by the end of the third week and where it went he could not understand as she ran up astronomical charge accounts, bills for her decorator and personal staff, and her travel arrangements, which were paid for by his office.[1]

Onassis might not have minded the staggering expenses he was now incurring if it had been an investment that would pay off. But he complained that the Kennedys treated him like some dance-hall gigolo. He was an outsider, a foreigner, and he was quickly attuned to the fact that

---

[1] Aristotle Onassis's official worth at this time was listed by Forbes as $500 million. That amount did not take into account the actual real estate value, now that it was developed, of Skorpios, nor were there any appraisals available of the antiques, paintings and jewels in his possession.

he would remain exactly that. With Bobby dead there was no powerful insider to help him re-establish his shipping business in the United States. Richard Nixon was in the White House, and Nixon made his dislike and distrust of Onassis clearly known. Onassis had made a bad calculation and he hated to be a loser.

'A short time after his marriage to Jackie, he began to see Maria again,' Baroness Marie-Hélène de Rothschild, Maggie van Zuylen's daughter, recalled. 'My mother acted as intermediary. We told Maria that if she wanted to conquer Ari she had to be more elusive. She was always there for him, always at his disposal. I once made her hide out at my country house so he wouldn't find her. This agitated him, made him edgy. But the effect quickly wore off because within a week she was again grovelling at his feet.'

Maria did not quite see it that way.

> At first I would not let him into the house but, would you believe it, one day he persistently kept on whistling outside my apartment, as young men used to do in Greece fifty years ago [this was said in the mid-1970s] – they wooed their sweethearts with song. So I had to let him in before the press realized what was going on in avenue Georges Mandel.
>
> With his return, so soon after his marriage, my confusion changed into a mixture of elation and frustration. Although I never admitted to him that I believed he was going to divorce his wife, I felt that as our friendship at least had survived his marriage, however weak its foundations, his principles regarding human relationships were changing.

Their meetings were sporadic and there was always the secrecy that had to surround them. For now, Onassis gave no indication that he would leave Jackie. He was volatile in his insistence that they no longer had any sexual contact. (Only a short time before, he had boasted to Pierre Salinger, John F. Kennedy's former press secretary who was then working for ABC-TV in Paris, that he had sex with Jackie five times a night. 'He could get very vivid in his descriptions of his physical relationship with her,' Salinger recalled.) Christina and Alexander loathed Jackie ('the widow' they called her), Onassis told Maria, and this was making life difficult for him. They were both adults now and he was unhappy with the way they were living their lives and could not look to their father as an example. Nor could they look to their mother.

Maria listened to his woes and sympathized. They became lovers again. But she was, once more (as she had been in the beginning), 'the other woman', their meetings mostly clandestine, an incredibly difficult situation for Maria to accept after the many years when she had been treated as if she were his wife. Maggie van Zuylen hosted intimate dinner parties with Maria and Onassis, and close personal friends, as did her daughter and Hélène Rochas, at which they were able to relax and be themselves. Onassis was now a man in his sixties, his black shiny hair almost all grey and beginning to thin. His eyes had not lost their sharp look of perennial speculation, his whisky voice had thickened some. There was about him now, more than ever, the look of a Mafia don. He had not lost his charismatic sexual appeal, nor his hold on Maria.

'Maria was [still] madly in love with Ari, sincerely in love with him,' Baroness Hélène-Marie de Rothschild recalled. 'She had a mad passion for him. They were like two wild beasts together,' unable to be together without some body contact. Although Maggie and her daughter had helped reunite them, both now questioned whether this had been a good thing for Maria who, unlike Onassis, was not able easily to accept their relationship on a 'we'll-see-each-other-when-it's-convenient' basis.

On the morning of 26 May 1969, Bruna found Maria unconscious in bed. She had taken an overdose of sleeping tablets and was rushed to the American Hospital. She swore it was an accident, that she had not been able to sleep, taken her usual dosage and an hour later took more, as she still was awake. Bruna, out of concern for her, had overreacted. Whatever the truth, the damage had been done. CALLAS ATTEMPTED SUICIDE OVER ONASSIS read the tabloid headlines. Maria was horrified, but Onassis was supportive, if not publicly so. His position was that they should not be seen together for a short time. She thought she might have lost him again, as pictures of Jackie and Onassis at various social affairs began to appear.

Salvation came to her in a production of *Medea* (based on the legend and not on the various operas that had been written throughout the past two centuries) that Pier Paolo Pasolini was developing for the screen. A brilliant, hollow-cheeked, intense homosexual, Pasolini had made a name for himself with films like *The Gospel According to St Matthew* (1964), an unconventional, austere movie which had been made with an amateur cast, including his mother, and was hailed almost immediately as a masterpiece. *Gospel* had displayed a strong directorial presence; an austere, haunting dignity, the camera using shadow and light to great effect. His film *Oedipus Rex* (1967) in which he played the High Priest and Sylvana Magnano, Franco Citto and Alida Valli were co-starred, had more than confirmed his distinctive talent and the classic way in which he / dealt with passion and violence. Maria had met Pasolini at one of Maggie's dinner parties. Surprisingly (noting the subjects of his films), he was a dedicated Marxist and although his work had a sombre quality to it, personally he could be a man of extravagant moods.

Maria was quite taken with Pasolini and when he sent her the script of *Medea* – which had almost no dialogue, the story being told mostly in the camera direction – she was intrigued. This was *Medea* told as a pure Greek legend, a tragedy of enormous pathos. She was much aware that if she did play the role, there would be comparisons between her affair with Onassis and the passionate, violent love Medea had felt for Jason. Except for a lullaby sung to the children she would not have to sing. This removed the pressure such a project might have had if filmed as an opera.

Pasolini asked if she would agree to a film test. Maria invited him to dine with her at home so that they could talk privately about it. She agreed to the test with the condition that it would not be shown *ever* in a public venue. Pasolini promised that would be the case and from that point the evening was a resounding success, filled with much laughter. According to members of the camera crew, Maria gave an amazing performance before the camera the very next day, with Pasolini directing the test. He saw in her, in one sense, 'the most modern of women, but there lives in her an ancient woman – mysterious, magical – whose sensibilities create a tremendous conflict for her', he told a reporter for *Opera News*.

She was to star in a movie. The idea thrilled her and it pleased Onassis who had always believed this was a good venue for her. He did not, however, as he had done in times past, become involved in any of the negotiations, which were handled by Michel Glotz, her lawyers and herself. According to film standards, her requests were simple enough and straightforward. Pasolini did not work on the kind of budgets that financed commercial films. *Medea*, he hoped, would gain a popular showing, but it was essentially an art film. Maria had a participation deal with the modest performance salary (for a star of her calibre) of $65,000. Her expenses would be generous, and would include the services to her of Bruna and Ferruccio during the making of the movie, and the company would engage and pay for a secretary. She would also have approval of all stills released to the press.

The 'secretary' turned out to be Nadia Stancioff, a tall, striking, intelligent blonde woman, who had been the past public relations director for the Spoleto and Venice festivals, and was not a secretary at all. 'I don't need a public relations person,' Maria complained to Pasolini. 'I need someone to write letters and take care of small personal tasks for me.' Pasolini believed otherwise, and Nadia remained to do duty as both secretary and press representative. The relationship turned out to be serendipitous for both women, who seemed such opposites and yet were very soon in close accord.

Costume fittings began in Rome in May where some of the interiors would be shot at Cinecittà's studios. The designs were by Piero Tosi, who had created Maria's costumes for her La Scala 1955 production of *La Sonnambula*. In early June Maria and the company were transported to Goremme, a remote corner of Turkey which had as a backdrop 'monolithic hills of rock and clay, dazzling blanched dunes and deserts resembling moonscapes, infinite mudflats baked by the sun'. Pasolini wanted to create 'a lost, unknown, mystical world' and in Goremme he did so, with astonishing effect.

The heat was often unbearable and Maria's costumes, heavy fabrics encrusted with huge ropes of pagan jewels, weighed over fifteen pounds. Her hair was worn loose with added crimped pieces that gave her a wild, primitive look. Pasolini worked with very little dialogue. He encouraged improvisation, hoping for a rare interpretation that Maria and the other cast members would bring to a scene. Rehearsals were few and often the first take was the final one. During the shooting of one scene the temperature had soared to over 100 degrees and Maria had to run frantically – as if driven by some mad demon – back and forth through a mudflat, the bottom of her massive skirt caking with mud and weighing her down so that she had to use enormous strength to keep moving. Finally the effort was too much. She collapsed and was carried by two of the crew to the protection of a tent. When she regained consciousness, she cried, 'Please forgive me! I'm so stupid. I shouldn't have done that. It's cost everyone so much time and money.'

She was intent on making a success of this endeavour. She trusted Pasolini, yet at the same time she was unhappy when she saw the rushes, feeling he had shot too many close-ups of her, which would slow down the film. 'Shoot from far away, for me!' she begged him. They argued about this. Maria felt he was concentrating on her face 'so like a Greek mask' when movement and action shots would often be more telling. She did not win these arguments, which was unfortunate, because the film grew very static, often deadly so.

'Pasolini destroyed Maria,' Zeffirelli said later, 'tried to make her look different from what she is…you could spend years looking at her. It was tremendous that half-smile of hers, the mouth, the eyes. She was enchanting, living music, the perfect illumination of the music. No director taught her this, she was born with it, she found this way of trusting herself, the right gesture, the right moment, not one motion more or less than was necessary. A director had to trust her instincts. Pasolini did not.'

'[Medea] was a semi-goddess who put all her beliefs in a man. At the same time she is a woman with all the experiences of a woman, only bigger – bigger sacrifices, bigger hurts,' Maria told an interviewer during time out from shooting. 'She went through all these trying to survive. You can't put these things into words... I began to look into the depths of the soul of Medea.'

Towards the last weeks of shooting, which were on location in Pisa, the islands of Grado and Tor Caldara, Tor Calbona (near Rome) and Aleppo in Syria, she began to lose confidence in herself. 'Tell me,' she would plead with Pasolini. 'Is this gesture too grand? Too operatic?' She was unsure of how the camera was reacting to her.

Whenever she could pull away for a weekend from the killing shooting schedule she returned to Paris. She spent time with Elizabeth Taylor, on location there for *The Only Game in Town*, and her husband, Richard Burton, who gave Maria advice on camera angles and the film technique of acting.

Shooting was completed by the first week in August. She wanted Nadia, whom she had bonded with by the end of the filming, to remain with her in Paris, but Nadia did not envision herself in what would be a purely secretarial post and she knew that without the demands of work, Maria would not be easy to deal with. They remained friends, but she went her own way.

In December Maria went to Rome to view the first cut of the movie. She recognized the artistry of Pasolini's film, but she was not really sure what to make of it. There were all those interminable close-ups of her, an emphasis on all the violence, the blood and gore. She was moved by the scene of the murder of her sons, the lullaby she sings as she puts one to sleep and then holds him in her arms and stabs him swiftly in the back so that his limp head falls against her shoulder, as though sheltered there like a sleeping child, not a dead one.

As 1969 drew to a close, Onassis's relationship with Jackie worsened. He told Maria that Jackie had only wanted his money and she had got her hands on a good chunk of it. She was 'cold-hearted and shallow'. Onassis and Maria were now seen together publicly. One evening they were photographed dining tête-á-tête at their old haunt, Maxims. When the photograph appeared in newspapers around the world the following day, Jackie flew from London (where she had been shopping with Lee) to Paris and insisted that Onassis take her to dinner at Maxims to counter the gossip. He did so reluctantly, he told Maria, adding that she more or less threatened to name Maria in a divorce suit if he refused.

Onassis was privately besieged on all sides – the situation with Jackie, and Christina, twenty-one, frightened, rebellious and desperately needing love, wanted to marry a man, Joseph Bolker, forty-eight and recently divorced, who Onassis felt was only after his daughter's money. Christina, unable to communicate with her mother who seemed too frequently under the influence of drugs, distanced herself against her father's interference in her life, spending much of her time in Monte Carlo where she knew he would not follow her. His son Alexander – handsome, adventurous, intelligent – was uninterested in learning his father's business and was deeply involved with Baroness Fiona Thyssen-Bornemisza, a woman fifteen years his senior. Added to all this, Onassis was trying to balance several high-rolling, floundering business deals.

Maria was only too happy, as an escape shortly after the New Year, to accompany Pasolini to Argentina to present *Medea* at the Festival of Mar del Plata, where it had a disappointing reception but she was treated royally. She returned to Paris and Pasolini to Rome for further cutting on the film to prepare it for a gala première at L'Opéra on 28 January. Maria was thrilled and anxious. Onassis had reserved a box – Maggie van Zuylen and other mutual guests were to join them for the grand occasion. At the last moment Onassis had to fly to New York.

Much of Paris society turned out for the occasion. Maria received a standing ovation when she entered, dressed regally and wearing many of the magnificent jewels that Onassis had given her through the years. She was extremely nervous during the screening of the film. From the box where she sat, she looked down on a restless, bored audience, or at the huge screen, the things that had previously appeared wrong to her grotesquely magnified. She kept up a spirited front during the supper that followed, but she knew that her initial appearance in a film would be her last. *Medea* was, perhaps, a *succès d'estime*, but it would never gain a general release and so would be seen by only a limited audience.

In the summer of 1971 Maria accepted an invitation from Peter Mennin, president of the famed Juilliard School of Music in New York City, to conduct a series of master classes with a select group of talented young performers. The classes were to be held over a twelve-week period between October 1971 and March 1972. There would be two sessions a week with twenty-five singers who had been chosen by audition from three hundred hopeful applicants. She was tremendously enthusiastic about the opportunity to pass on her knowledge to a new generation of singers.

Life had not been easy for her in Paris. Onassis was preoccupied and his visits infrequent. She was lonely and somewhat frightened. Her eyesight was weakening and glaucoma was diagnosed. She wore a watch that had an alarm set so that she would not miss taking the essential eye drops every two hours. Most terrifying was the decline she heard in her Voice, the companion she had always trusted to be there; 'God's gift, my responsibility,' she often said. She needed to regain her self-confidence and the master classes at the Juilliard seemed a good place to begin. In the weeks before she departed for New York she worked hard on what she would teach, consulting her old teacher, Elvira de Hidalgo. She arrived in New York a week before the start of her classes, excited as she had not been since *Medea* about a coming project.[2]

'A singer's career is essentially built on youth,' she once wrote. 'Wisdom comes later. Unfortunately we cannot go on as long as conductors, for example … A beautiful sound is not enough … You must take that voice and break it up into a thousand pieces so that it can be made to serve the needs of music, of expression.'

John Ardoin, who was present at the classes, wrote, 'She approached her role as a teacher more as a friend or colleague who was anxious to help her students over the pitfalls they were certain to encounter' and adds that she was 'soft-spoken, frank, and chary with praise'.

The experience of teaching was extremely moving for her. The master classes had enabled her to rarify and recount all that she had learned through her years as a singer. ('When it comes to music,' she told Ardoin, 'we are students throughout our lives.') They also helped Maria to gain her confidence before an audience, rather large ones with some of the music world's greatest singers and musicians in attendance to hear what she had to impart. Placido Domingo and Luciano Pavarotti were there, as well as Grace Bumbry and many others.

Giuseppe di Stefano, now fifty, a bit paunchy but ever the Lothario, happened to be in New York at this time. Their relationship had not always been smooth. Di Stefano was an arrogant man, a lazy musician, filled with his own importance as a leading, gifted lyric tenor. But things had not been going too well for him of late. There had been troubles with

---

[2] *Callas at Juilliard: The Master Classes* by John Ardoin is a masterwork in itself and gives a full and fascinating coverage of the classes, and of Callas's programme, her work with the young professionals under her tutelage, and her words 'on music and on creating drama out of music'. It is a true and faithful homage to Callas's important, serious and conscientious master classes.

The play *Master Class* by Terrence McNalley, which presents 'Maria Callas' as the main character, on the other hand, is pure fiction, as it was obviously meant to be. It is a dramatic work and good theatre. But Callas never belittled or berated her students in the way portrayed (quite the opposite, in fact), nor was she in an hysterical state during any part of the classes. Her students say she was always controlled, always patient and that the classes were instrumental in their gaining a greater knowledge of their voice, the use of it and the music they hoped to sing professionally.

his voice and difficulties in his personal life. His long-suffering wife, Maria, was no longer as complacent as she once had been and his young daughter, Luisa, was struggling with pervasive cancer. His career was in a financial slump, just at a time when he desperately needed money to pay for Luisa's expensive and ongoing medical care.

Di Stefano was on his way to his home in Milan after a disappointing concert tour that had taken him to Japan. While there, an agent had suggested to him that he would be better able to fill a concert hall if he appeared with a famous soprano. The agent offered him another tour and a bonus (a finder's fee, so to speak): $5000 for Anna Moffo, $10,000 for Renata Tebaldi, but $15,000 for Maria Callas. It was, therefore, not by accident that he stopped off in New York where Maria was giving her much-publicized master classes, nor was it pure fondness that incited him to send her a large bouquet of red roses with a card signed 'Felicità, Pippo', which was what she always had called him.

Maria was pleased to have an old friend with whom to talk and share some gossip. Di Stefano made his way carefully to the subject of a dual concert tour. 'No! No!' she countered. 'It's impossible!' He said she was wrong. It would be the best thing she could do to get back on stage and to retrain her voice. He (who often coached singers) would help her. They would sing duets and each sing only two, or three at the most, solo arias – certainly not a strain. He was most persuasive and Maria agreed that she *might* do it. They would talk when she got home to Paris. But it would have to be handled by Sander Gorlinsky, who would set her terms.

Maria returned to Paris in the spring of 1972, feeling greatly revitalized. The idea of the tour had given her something to which to look forward. Also, she had found di Stefano far more appealing than she ever had before. She had never felt free about casual sex once she had married Meneghini, and had been assiduously true to Onassis, but with his marriage and his current preoccupation that seemed foolish of her. Di Stefano sensed her loneliness and her hunger. It was not difficult to take advantage of the situation. Anyway, di Stefano was not a man to pass up a chance to confirm his opinion of himself as a great lover.

The master classes had helped Maria in her ability to communicate with young people. Obviously some of them felt that way as well, for both Alexander and Christina (who had in this brief time married and divorced Bolker) made an effort to establish a connection with her. She met Alexander several times, having him for tea at her apartment where their conversations would last well into the evening. Alexander now had a growing regard for Maria. Originally he had felt that she was the cause of his parents' divorce. He knew differently now, saw his mother's and his father's part in it with clearer, more mature eyes and recognized Maria 'as a worthy companion and adversary' for his father.

Maria encouraged these meetings. Alexander was the most important person in Onassis's world at this time. He was his only son, his guarantee of immortality, the heir to his vast fortune. But the significance of their relationship did not fully strike him until the boy had grown into manhood and they had become, if not estranged then *distanced*, and this was a source of great pain to Onassis. Alexander bore some resemblance in appearance to his father, although he was taller, slimmer and somewhat more boyish in his looks than Onassis had been as a young man. Like Maria, he was seriously near-sighted and wore heavy horn-rimmed glasses. 'You and I see the world blurred, often distorted,' she once told him. 'I understand how that can affect your life.'

He was withdrawn and found it difficult to talk to his bombastic father. He was interested in planes, in flying, in boats and machinery. He knew Onassis planned to leave him the management of his empire and the idea terrified him. He felt trapped. His father still kept him on an allowance – an extremely generous one at that – and he resented it, for he was at present in an executive position at Olympic Airways and felt he should, instead, receive a decent salary. With his lover Fiona's prodding and Maria's encouragement, he decided he would privately (without his father's knowledge) pursue his studies (which he had deserted) at university level eventually to gain a degree in aeronautical engineering. His greatest disappointment in life was that due to his poor vision, he would never be able to qualify as a commercial pilot. He was a trained pilot, however, and often flew his father's private planes illegally.

At 3.30 p.m. on Monday, 22 January 1973, Alexander, with co-pilots Donald McCusker and Donald McGregor, took off on a round-trip flight from Athens to several of the Greek islands. A few seconds later, having only attained an altitude of 100 feet, the plane veered to the right and slammed into the ground, cartwheeling for another 400 feet. When the emergency crew reached the crash sight, Alexander's head injuries were so severe that he could only be identified by the monogram on the bloodstained handkerchief in his pocket. The two other men were seriously injured but stood a better chance of recovery. After desperate surgery (ordered by Onassis and performed by a Boston neurosurgeon flown to Athens) was performed, it was clear that Alexander would not survive. He died at 6.55 p.m. on 23 January with his father, Jackie, Christina and Fiona by his side.

Onassis was inconsolable, certain that his son's death had not been an accident but the vicious work of one of his enemies – which one, he could not name, for there had been many through the years. More than anything, Maria wanted to be there to share his sorrow. She had been told she could not come to the funeral, which was held on Skorpios where Alexander was buried beside the chapel (Greek Orthodox law forbade anyone but a saint to be buried inside a chapel). Maria did not see Onassis for several months as he sailed the *Christina* from port to port, walking its decks alone like the Flying Dutchman of Wagner's opera.

To Maria's distress, Alexander's death had brought a brief renewal of tenderness between Onassis and Jackie, who knew the grief of a dear one's sudden death well. But before long Jackie bolted, returning to New York, where her own children attended school, and Onassis was once again back in Maria's arms. She comforted him as best she could, but she had her own family grief with which to cope.

In November 1972 Maria had received a call from her sister Jackie, informing her that their eighty-six-year-old father was dying.

'Have you had any reporters around?' Jackie reported Maria as asking.

'I told her that no one knew so far and she seemed relieved.'

'I can't come just now, I'm working again – recordings, can't interrupt them. You understand.' She enquired whether their father was conscious. Jackie reported that he was – and, sick as he was, insisted on shaving every morning and keeping his moustache trimmed.

Maria was quiet for a time. 'I just can't come, Jackie,' she finally said. 'Can you explain for me?'

Jackie, who now had Litza back in Athens to care for as well as Alexandra and their father, said she would try. When George Kalogeropoulos died the following month from complications of pneumonia, Jackie called Maria to give her details of the funeral.

'I had expected that she would at least come back for that,' Jackie wrote at a later time, 'but no. Once again she was worried that the press would get hold of the story that she had ignored her dying father and was not coming to his funeral.

'"You know that's not true," she denied. "It's just these recordings. What can I do?"'

Paparazzi did show up in force at the small, humble funeral, with only a handful of mourners present. Jackie told them that Maria was desolate but that she had recording engagements that could not be broken. The truth was more brutal. Onassis and Jackie were also in Athens, on their way to Skorpios for the holidays. Yes, there were recordings, but Maria could certainly have interrupted them for the death of her father. What she could not bear to do was to be in Athens at the same time as Onassis and Jackie, a situation that she knew the press would play up. It was a decision that would haunt her for years. Bruna once found her sitting in her bedroom with a picture of George in her lap and crying bitterly, 'I've been such a bad daughter. I never even went to see him when he was dying.' Then she looked up. 'He would forgive me, you know. But I don't think God will.'

25

⤷

Touring Days

T HE RECORDING SESSIONS that were Maria's explanation for not
seeing her dying father were made for Philips in London from 30
November to 20 December 1972, with Giuseppe di Stefano and
the London Symphony Orchestra, and were the precursor to the tour that
the two of them would embark upon in the autumn of 1973. The two
singers recorded five sessions of Verdi operas when Maria, alarmed by
what she heard in playback even after editing, insisted they be shelved.
Her voice was hollow, her breathing erratic and she was frequently off
pitch. Di Stefano had tremendous problems, his voice scooping and
sliding in a careless way. A tape does exist, and on it is Maria's sole performance of 'Io vengo a domandar', the powerful love duet from Act One
of *Don Carlos*. But even this is sadly ineffectual, missing her former ability
to bring lightness and meaningful exuberance to such an aria. One thing
was clear, she must get her voice in shape within the next six months, or
the tour would have to be cancelled. No one would expect it to be of the
same calibre as it had been seven years before during her Paris and
London *Toscas*. They would come to see Callas once again, fearing this
might be their last opportunity to do so. But she had to give them the
very best she had.

After his son's sudden tragic death, Onassis seldom called. He was in a
deep state of grief and remained so for many months. Maria felt isolated,
deserted, so it was easy to turn to di Stefano for comfort and reassurance.
The tour, under Gorlinsky's entrepreneurial guidance, had been sched-
uled, with Ivor Newton as accompanist, to kick off in September at the
Royal Festival Hall. From there they would go to Hamburg, Berlin,
Düsseldorf, Munich, Frankfurt and Mannheim, Germany, then to
Madrid, Paris and Amsterdam. The year-end holidays would give her an
opportunity to relax before departing on a twenty-city tour of the United
States and Canada, ending in the autumn of 1974 in the Far East: Seoul,

Korea, Tokyo, Osaka, Hiroshima and finally, on 11 November, Sapporo, Japan.[1]

The sheer extent of the tour would have taxed the energy of a much younger performer: so many flights, time and climate changes, thirty-six cities and three continents, receptions and press interviews, the acoustical differences of the theatres, hotel living and restaurant food, often eaten at off-hours, and always the pressure each time – *will my voice be there for me*? Maria would celebrate her fiftieth birthday before leaving on the arduous American wing of the tour and she was plagued with low blood pressure and a recently ruptured hernia, which could cause internal bleeding. In most ways it seemed foolish of her to agree to such a brutal schedule. But since the Juilliard master classes her world had narrowed. Without Onassis, her audiences and her *Voice* (which she spoke about often as if it were her child – and perhaps it was), Paris had become airless and her apartment a cage.

Sander Gorlinsky, who was arranging the tour, had first represented her in England twenty years earlier. He was now as powerful in Europe as Sol Hurok was in America. Maria had a love–hate relationship with Gorlinsky: Russian-born, bespectacled, a cigar seemingly permanently planted between his lips, a somewhat vulgar man, kin to the Hollywood moguls who ran the studios in tyrannical fashion. However, Gorlinsky was able to command high figures for his artists – who included Tebaldi, Gobbi, Nureyev and Callas. For this tour he had negotiated a fee for Maria of $15,000 a concert, all expenses paid, hotel suites wherever possible, and the salary and expenses (first class on all flights) of the young Italian maid, Elena, who would accompany her (Bruna and Ferruccio remaining in Paris). She was even assured she could travel with the poodles – at least in Europe. Di Stefano would be receiving $5000 per performance, a discrepancy that caused him no end of irritation.

Did Maria need the money? Not really, but she was dying inside for the lack of an audience. Then there was the promise of di Stefano's company. Their past relationship had been strained. Yet there had always been a sexual attraction that neither of them had pursued until di Stefano had come to see her in Paris (from Milan where he lived with his wife and his three children) to try to persuade her to do the tour with him. He flattered her madly – and Maria was a slave to flattery. Love, such

---

[1] The US–Canada tour included Philadelphia, Toronto, Washington DC, Boston, New York (twice), Detroit, Dallas, Miami Beach, Chicago, Columbus, Brookville, Long Island, Cincinnati, Seattle, Portland, Vancouver, Montreal, Los Angeles and San Francisco.

as she had for Onassis, was non-existent, but di Stefano, so strongly male, made her feel once again a desirable woman.

Also joining the tour was the young, talented pianist Robert Sutherland and the well-known octogenarian accompanist Ivor Newton. Di Stefano convinced Maria that they would be better served and tour costs lower not to use an orchestra. This way they would not be bound by a fixed programme, nor a fixed key. Two pianists were engaged as Newton (who had accompanied many of the great artists – Melba, Lehmann, Flagstad) had difficulty in obtaining insurance due to the delicate state of his health. Sutherland would work with Maria and di Stefano as a rehearsal pianist and satisfy the insurance agent by being capable of stepping in for Newton in performance if the old gentleman was unable to play.

A brutal August heatwave suffused Paris when Sutherland arrived from his home in London to begin work in the music room on avenue Georges Mandel. He was impressed with Maria's graciousness: 'Reviving drinks arrived almost immediately – fruit juices in cut crystal and my tea [a concession to his English tastes] in fine white porcelain, with linen napkins…When we had finished our refreshments, di Stefano stood up and announced *Faust*,' Sutherland recalled. 'Ivor indicated that I play – it was a tricky piano part. I knew that to some extent I was on trial…We played through a variety of operatic duets, all chosen by di Stefano. Callas let him dictate and seemed content to go along with his choice.'

'You are very sensitive to the voice,' Maria told Sutherland, who had noted that there were two photographs in silver frames on the piano – one of Serafin with a long, handwritten inscription, and the other of di Stefano, his dark eyes gazing penetratingly into the camera, his signature bold.

An hour or so later Maria excused herself and di Stefano announced, 'It's so hot in Paris we've decided to go for a holiday in San Remo [where he had a summer home].'

Ivor said, 'How nice, when will you go?'

Di Stefano answered, 'Now, right now. We're waiting for the car.'

Maria reappeared a few moments later wearing a hat. They drove off with di Stefano at the wheel of Maria's Mercedes. It was most unlikely that they were actually going to San Remo, which is on the Italian coast and would have been an overnight journey by car. Also no suitcases seemed to have been transferred to the car. But the announcement did establish two points: di Stefano obviously wanted the two men to know that he and Maria were 'an item' and it ended the rehearsals for the time being. The latter commenced in earnest about three weeks later, when the hot spell in Paris had dissipated and di Stefano became more enthusiastic about getting down to work.

'No two singers could have been further apart in their methods or attitudes to work,' Sutherland noted.

> She spent her career searching for perfection. He believed he was born with it…Some days his coaching would have good results, but not without much badgering and cajoling and, if he lost his temper, which was often, some verbal abuse. His persistent call was, *'Aperta la gola'* ('Open your throat')…which puzzled Maria. She was confused, not understanding what he meant. 'Look at her,' he said to me, 'the greatest singer in the world and she doesn't even know how to open her throat!'

After several like scenes Maria railed at him in a rage, operatic in its fury, and di Stefano backed down, for a time being 'carefully polite, deferential'. But she had felt belittled by him and it had deeply affected her. She developed a small, nervous laugh and was to suffer more arrows when she learned that a few days after she and di Stefano were to sing the opening concert of the tour at the Royal Festival Hall, Gorlinsky had booked Renata Tebaldi and Franco Corelli into the Albert Hall for a programme of similar solos and duets. There would be comparisons and the pressure was something that Maria did not think she could endure. She was furious with Gorlinsky, whom she was unable to even reach on the telephone. She told Sutherland the next morning that she had cried all night. She felt betrayed. She talked about getting another agent, but of course at this stage of the tour negotiations this was impossible. Finally, having reached Gorlinsky and spent her anger, the matter was ameliorated somewhat by a decision to postpone the Royal Festival Hall concert until *after* the German segment of the tour. This would put several months between the Tebaldi recital and hers, and also give her an extra month to work on her voice, which she did not think was ready yet for the task before it.

During the months of rehearsals she could be at various times 'the vulnerable little girl' and the great, haughty diva. She relied a lot on Sutherland, with his quiet ways, quasi-Mona Lisa smile and sympathetic manner, to help her get through the rough patches. There were afternoons when she would spend hours with him in her music room playing the pirated tapes of her greatest performances. 'Don't you think I sang well that night?' she would say, more the kitten than the renowned tigress.

Rehearsals progressed from Paris to di Stefano's home in Milan where an out-of-tune piano and a jealous wife filled the air with discord. 'Maria had spent two summers with the [di Stefanos] in Milan and at their apartment in San Remo,' Sutherland reports. 'When she was not with them in Italy, di Stefano was with her in Paris "working". Her presence in their lives meant that [his] family saw less and less of their father and, with Luisa [the daughter in a progressive state of cancer and undergoing radiation] in danger, resentment grew.'

The situation was not a good one and Maria's complicity is at best thoughtless, at worst cruel. No doubt Signora di Stefano had accepted her husband's infidelity and insensitivity to her feelings long ago. But with her daughter fighting what had been diagnosed as a terminal disease, a glamorous, famous diva becoming her husband's lover and brought into her home was more than she could abide. Maria was obsessively self-centred. Being a great artist is not a viable exemption. She had been at the core of her own universe her entire life. Litza had helped to create her self-absorption, the struggle for fame and then the fight to maintain it had honed her tunnel vision. She saw people in relation to herself and seldom the other way round. Onassis had been the exception.

Yet she possessed a winning vulnerability, a duality of character that surprised and puzzled people, took them unawares. She never looked down on her servants and demanded equal conditions for them when they travelled with her, and yet she gave little thought to her sister's well-being. Despite the sleek figure she had had for over fifteen years, she had never let go of that fat, awkward person she had been in her childhood and youth. 'Look at these legs!' she would say at times in despair. 'They are ugly, like piano legs!' She was her worst critic, a perfectionist, always having to prove that she could achieve what others might think was impossible. 'God gave me my voice,' she was often known to say. 'I must always remember that and never desecrate His faith.' She was religious, but in her own fashion. She did not adhere to formal or organized religion, but she prayed and believed in the tenets of the Greek Orthodox Church in which she had been raised and to which she had returned after she left Meneghini (for she had attended the Roman Catholic Church during the better years of their marriage).

She had repeatedly felt betrayed – by her mother, by her husband, by Onassis whom she still could not stop loving, by the world of opera, her agents, managers, and the crowds who cheered her one day and hissed her another. When bad things happened to her she would cry, 'Oh God, what have I done to deserve this?'[2] But she was unable to see that she was often the responsible person.

---

[2] This is what Tosca says in 'Vissi d'arte', *perche, perche, signor, perche remuneri così* (after all I've done for you, God, why, why, God, have you repaid me so badly)?

All interested parties converged on the Plaza Hotel in Hamburg on 24 October, the night before the opening concert of the tour. Maria and Elena (who would be in charge of Maria's jewel case when they travelled) shared with the di Stefanos the penthouse suite, which had two bedroom wings and a very grand connecting reception room. Gorlinsky, bringing with him a good supply of Havana cigars and Scotch whisky, had a much smaller suite on a lower floor. Newton and Sutherland were both on hand, as was Kurt Collien, Gorlinsky's delegate to travel with the four main players on the German arm of the tour. During the final rehearsal neither singer was sure of the programme. Nor was it set when the concert began. Di Stefano would often decide what they would sing next between arias and duets, which rattled Newton. (He could imagine the headline, he told Sutherland, who turned the pages for him during the ensuing European concerts, 'CALLAS IGNORES DYING PIANIST!').

Her favourite designer Madame Biki had created a marvellous wardrobe for her to wear during the tour – gem colours, jade, ruby, topaz, sapphire blue, pale peridot green – and fabrics that moved and seemed to make her float when she crossed the stage. She had chosen an ankle-length peridot gown of silk and chiffon for the première, which was a sell-out. Di Stefano led her on stage, the panels of the chiffon dress that were attached to the sleeves flying behind her to cheers of 'Maria! Brava! Diva!'. Her luxuriant chestnut hair was pulled back from her face in a chignon and around her neck and on her ears were the fabulous pearls that Onassis had given her for her forty-fifth birthday. Di Stefano beamed as he marched her from one side of the stage to the other before they settled centre-stage at the microphones and waited for the enthusiastic applause to die out. They presented about seventy minutes of solo and duet singing interspersed with a few piano selections, the entire pro-gramme lasting just under two hours.[3]

---

[3] The programmes in each city on the tour listed a possible selection of eleven arias for Callas, and eight arias and four songs for di Stefano, and seven duets. It was rather like the choice on a Chinese menu – two from column A, three from B and four from C. In almost every city they sang a different selection. The music listed for Callas was: 'Pleurez, mes yeux' from Le Cid, the Habanera from Carmen, 'Suicidio' from La Gioconda, 'L'altra notte in fondo al mare' from Mefistofele, 'Non Pianger' and 'Tu che le vanità' from Don Carlos, the Bolero from I vespri Siciliani, 'O mio bambino caro' from Gianni Schicchi, 'Quando m'en vo' from La Bohème, 'In quelle trine morbide' and 'Sola, perduta, abbandonata' from Manon Lescaut. On the United States–Canada section of the tour Callas added 'Voi lo sapete' from Cavalleria Rusticana, 'Vissi d'arte' from Tosca, the Letter Scene from Werther and 'Adieu, notre petite table' from Manon. She did not in the end sing all these arias. The audience was never sure which numbers she would choose to sing. If it was one of their favourites there would be gasps of delight and applause to greet the opening notes.

The audience seemed happy enough to just see and hear Callas. For the most part, during the European leg of the tour the critics were kind, dwelling on her great presence and her glorious past, but they let it be known that *this* Callas was not the same great Callas who once had graced the world's stages. Maria refused to let it depress her. She was alive again, on stage, listening to the applause of an audience, and di Stefano had become an ardent lover; he had even suggested that he was planning to leave his wife. He hoped to propose marriage some time in the future to Maria, but could not at present in view of his daughter's illness. Maria refused to commit herself, although she did glow with renewed, youthful pleasure. Then, to her surprise, Signora di Stefano travelled with them to the United States; once there, the situation was charged with electricity. Di Stefano rode in a limousine with Maria wherever they went, while his wife, her anger mounting, followed in a second, less comfortable car.

The first concert was in Philadelphia. 'Callas displayed all the qualities of the superstar,' wrote Louis Snyder in the *Christian Science Monitor*. 'A majestic figure, the impeccable taste of Callas's platform manner could, in itself, be an etiquette lesson for aspiring performers. This, unfortunately, was not the outstanding characteristic of Callas's singing partner Giuseppe di Stefano...he committed all the sins of vocal excess that self-confident favorites are heir to, and offered a strangely florid contrast to the dignified carriage and projection of Callas.' Such criticism only inflamed di Stefano's festering discontent.

In New York Maria and the di Stefanos had separate suites at the Stanhope Hotel on Fifth Avenue. The management had installed a piano in Maria's apartment, along with a handsome Persian rug to absorb the sound. Elena was also staying at the Stanhope, as was Robert Sutherland who had replaced Ivor Newton as accompanist for the remainder of the tour, the old gentleman having found great difficulty in Maria's and di Stefano's mode of working. Sol Hurok, of whom Maria was extremely fond, was handling the American wing of the tour. To welcome her back 'home' Hurok, always one for grand gestures, gave a gala dinner in her honour shortly after her arrival. Knowing that she would be on show to some of the most celebrated denizens of Manhattan, she went out and bought an emerald organza gown with an astronomical price tag of $4000 and sent the bill to Hurok's office. At dinner that night he told her how beautiful her gown was. 'Oh, I'm so glad you like it, Sol,' she said, smiling warmly, her hand on his. 'You paid for it.'

In New York also at this time, was a Greek pianist, Vasso Devetzi, a woman of about Maria's age, who had met Callas in Paris the previous year and insinuated herself into a friendship. Vasso's fortunes were decidedly shaky. Her pianistic talents had not generated much excitement in the music world and what concerts she gave, and tours she made, were on the school and club circuit where fees were minimal. She met Maria at a time when Callas was at an emotional low, after her return from the master classes and before di Stefano had reappeared in her life. Her dearest friend, Maggie van Zuylen, had died after a lingering illness and Bruna had taken a leave of absence to return to her Italian village where her mother was seriously ill.

Vasso was both Greek and a musician, and she appeared to be a reverential fan of Maria's, always flattering, always obliging. She was a fairly tall, attractive, dark-haired woman, with flashing eyes and a glib tongue, who carried herself well. Ferruccio took an immediate dislike to her. When out of Maria's sight Vasso was curt and bossy, an imperious woman who seemed to make herself too quickly at home at avenue Georges Mandel. Maria's staff were certain that Callas was helping her financially. She was in New York, presumably to sign with an American agent. Vasso had accompanied Maria on her shopping spree for the gown she wore to Hurok's gala, made sure she was on the guest list and had borrowed one of Maria's gowns to wear for the evening. Di Stefano resented Vasso's presence and they argued about it. Maria was irritated by his troublesome wife who she thought should return to Milan to tend to their sick daughter.

After the final rehearsal for the Carnegie Hall recital, a drive through Central Park was planned by Maria, di Stefano and Sutherland with the possibility of also doing some sightseeing. As they went to get into the limousine waiting for them outside the stage door on 56th Street, Signora di Stefano suddenly appeared and stepped into the rear seat of the vehicle with them. Di Stefano insisted the driver take them back to the Stanhope. Maria was furious when Sutherland visited her later. 'Can't she ever respect my privacy,' she shouted. She then rang him in the middle of the night to tell him she was worried about some parts of the concert the following day.

She was exceptionally distressed and Sutherland asked her whether she was alone.

'Yes, he's gone to the *other woman* [his wife],' she replied. 'Will I be all right tomorrow?' she asked Sutherland. Then, 'Will you pray for me Robert? Please pray for me,' she begged. She had taken a sleeping pill earlier, which had not worked, and now took several more. When she did not appear by midday, Elena was sent to her suite to see if she was all right. She found Maria unconscious. Terrified, she rang di Stefano and a doctor, Louis Parrish, was called. He managed to rouse her, but she was incoherent. She was given an emetic and walked around the two rooms of the suite and forced to drink black coffee. By 3 p.m., although weak, she was able to talk. In Sutherland's presence as well as the doctor's she told di Stefano, 'There's something I must tell you but can't say it. Elena will tell you.'

Di Stefano turned to the young Italian woman and waited. 'Madame can't have Mrs di Stefano around any longer,' she managed nervously, shifting her glance back and forth from Maria to di Stefano, who turned away and said nothing, leaving the room – obviously distressed – moments later.

The result of her overdose was an inflamed throat. Dr Parrish swabbed and sprayed it, to no avail. By now it was 6 p.m. Maria would never be able to sing. An announcement was posted an hour later in the box office that the concert was cancelled as Callas was suffering from 'an acute inflammation of the upper respiratory tract'. A spokeswoman made the same announcement to those already in the hall having drinks before the concert. Everyone was informed that the concert was rescheduled for 5 March. The majority of the ticket holders, although disappointed, were sympathetic to Maria's condition. No one assumed that she had taken an overdose of sleeping drugs because she was jealous of her lover's wife. But the next day the *New York Post* headlined CALLAS: THE FLU OR A CASE OF NERVES. One of the first persons to call her was Renata Tebaldi. They spoke for nearly two hours. It was the one good thing to come out of the whole unpleasant episode, because when they finally hung up, they did so as friends – not *best* friends but peace did reign from this time on between the two divas.

Boston was the next stop on the tour. Signora di Stefano was glaringly missing and her husband took to his bed almost immediately with what he called 'the imminent arrival of the flu'. He was running a high fever and unable to sing on the day of the performance. Another cancellation would be ruinous. Maria would have to carry the recital alone. But that was impossible as well. Then she suggested they call Vasso, who was still in New York, and ask her if, as a favour to her, she would play several piano solos to give Maria a respite between arias. Vasso arrived on the next scheduled flight.

That evening was a great test for Maria. She was on her own and, in fact, without di Stefano, sang (according to Sutherland) 'with greater technical control than in any other concert, high notes still giving trouble, but finding impromptu ways of disguising the weaknesses. This was a voice that was within reach of a return to the operatic stage … Vasso Devetzi played groups of Schumann and Chopin, but in her first spot was unkind enough to subject the audience to seventeen minutes of keyboard music by Handel [harpsichord music transposed to piano consisting of themes and endless variations].'

Richard Dyer, in the *Nation*, wrote: 'The evening…moved me mostly because it was such a human triumph of an artistic personality, the triumph of a will, still daring and risking much when it sets out to dominate ever more refractory means.'

Maria's relationship with di Stefano was now severely strained. 'He's let me down again,' she said before she stepped out on to the stage at Boston Symphony Hall, 'and just when I need him most – in Kennedy country.'

Signora di Stefano reappeared in Chicago. Di Stefano's voice was in decline and Maria was holding up the concerts. They headed back to New York where Sander Gorlinsky, having flown over from London, was waiting. Never a man known for his sensitivity, he came right out and told di Stefano, 'I can no longer offer you work. Nobody wants you,' which sent him into a very black mood. Later that day, after sending Maria a large bouquet of red roses, Sol Hurok was seized with a massive, fatal heart attack. Maria was visibly distressed. Hurok had always been a special favourite of hers, a generous man of great warmth and spirit.

It was turning out to be the tour from hell. Di Stefano was almost completely devastated by the sequence of events, the arguments, the pressures, Gorlinsky, the critics' jibes. But Maria seemed to gain strength with each new crisis and became di Stefano's comfort and support. Signora di Stefano finally did return to Italy as their daughter's health was deteriorating. Maria sang alone in three concerts due to di Stefano's indisposition, but her own health seemed to grow more robust. By the time they had reached Japan (there had been several return trips in between to Paris and well-deserved, if short, rests) the love affair was over and she vowed that after the tour she would never again sing with di Stefano.

She sang well and to a full house in the modest town of Sapporo, Hokkaido, on 11 November 1974; a notable occasion, for (though she was not aware of it) this would be the last time that Maria Callas would ever sing in public. The audience was unaccustomed to Western opera and the response was cool. Maria and di Stefano took only two bows. When Maria returned to their hotel there was a message to call Vasso in Paris right away, despite the hour. 'It's bad news. I know it. I *feel* it,' she said. Then, when Vasso answered, 'It's Onassis, isn't it?' she asked. Vasso said it was. He had been taken seriously ill and had been admitted to the American Hospital suffering from myasthenia gravis believed to be incurable and fatal.

Shortly after 10 February 1975, when Onassis was operated on for gall bladder at the American Hospital in Paris, a bizarre quirk of fate placed Vasso Devetzi's grievously ill mother on the same floor, a few doors down from his room.

Once back in Paris, Callas remained a prisoner in her apartment afraid to leave in case there was news about Onassis's condition. The ties that had drawn her closer to Vasso now tightened. Vasso would return each evening from visiting her mother with every detail she was able to glean about Onassis, the doctors who were seeing him, any words a nurse might have had to say, who his visitors were. Jackie (who was in the midst of hostile divorce proceedings) was at the hospital daily, as were Christina and Artemis. Jackie had left orders with Onassis's staff at the hospital that if Maria Callas turned up she was not to be admitted to see her husband.

Those who did visit reported he was a skeleton of his old self, grey and haggard, having lost over fifty pounds. For five weeks, following an operation, he drifted in and out of consciousness. Once he had told his physician Dr Jean Caroli, 'Do you know the meaning of the Greek word *thanatos* – death? You know I will never come out of the hospital alive. Well, you must practice *thanatos* on me. I do not want to suffer. I would rather be dead.'

Jackie remained in Paris, staying in the apartment on the avenue Foch, visiting her estranged husband daily, but in the evenings she dined out in style. Her attitude did not endear her to Christina and Artemis. 'Jackie is only here because the whole world is watching,' Maria said bitterly. Finally, after five weeks, the news was that Onassis had to remain in the hospital but he was getting better. 'He had tubes in his arms, and in his nose, and it looked like he had tubes in his head, too,' his old friend Johnny Meyer said. 'All he could do was give me a little wave with his hand. But the doctor said he was getting better.'

Jackie flew back to her children in New York. Later that week, after being told that his condition remained unchanged, she went skiing in New Hampshire. Onassis went into a rapid decline and Jackie could not be reached. Early on Sunday morning, 9 March, Artemis rang Maria and told her she should come to the hospital to say goodbye. Arrangements were made for her to use a service entrance at the rear so that she would not be seen. She was then taken up through a back elevator and led to his room. Christina and Artemis left them alone. Onassis was under an oxygen tent and appeared to be unconscious. She stood there for a while talking to him, bringing up happy times. There was a moment when he opened one eye and seemed to recognize her. She could not touch him and she did not want his last sight of her to be with tears. 'It is me,' she said, 'Maria – your canary.'

His eyelid lowered. She whispered that she loved him and would love him always. She said something to him in Greek, which later she could not recall. She had just wanted to establish their common heritage. Then she left by the same route she had come in. The next day she flew, with Elena, Bruna, Ferruccio and the two dogs, to Palm Beach, Florida where friends had offered her their home, so that she would be away from the paparazzi that were certain to descend upon the avenue Georges Mandel the moment Onassis closed his eyes for ever.

Christina sat vigil by her father's hospital bed for the last days of his life. He died on Saturday, 15 March. Vasso telephoned Maria in Palm Beach the moment she heard the news. 'I feel like a widow,' Maria would say. She was inconsolable for several days. Her loyal staff were fearful for her own life and they held back telling her that Visconti had died just two days later. This was followed by the expected, but sad, news that di Stefano's daughter had succumbed to her illness.

Maria did not return for Onassis's funeral held on the island of Skorpios, where he was buried in a tomb beside Alexander. 'How would it look – his two wives by the side of his coffin,' she told her staff.[3] She returned to Paris in May. The chestnut trees were in full bloom. It was the best time to be alive if you were in Paris. Vasso was there to greet her and from that time, seldom strayed too far away.

[4] Onassis left an estate well over a billion dollars, most of it to his daughter Christina, who had already inherited $270 million from her mother's estate when she died two years earlier under extremely suspicious circumstances of an overdose of barbiturates, but with bruises on her body, as had been the case with her sister Eugenie. Stavros Niarchos was held for investigation, but released soon after. Jackie and Christina were embroiled in a bitter eighteen-month legal dispute over the estate. Jackie finally received $125 million. Maria was left nothing but Artemis sent her several mementoes, including her letters to him, which his sister thought might be meaningful to her.

26

Machiavellian Influences

NIGHT HELD THE greatest terror for Maria. Sleep never came easily. The Mandrax that Jackie sent her from Greece no longer worked as a sleeping potion. Pixie and Djedda slept at her feet. Lights were kept lit in several rooms so that she would not have to face blackness if she chose, in her sleeplessness, to walk about. And in her bedroom the television set was never turned off. Sometimes, in the silent, gaping hours in the middle of the night, she would ring a friend. There weren't many left who welcomed such intrusions. Nureyev, although she seldom saw him, was a patient listener. Zeffirelli could be counted on, if one could locate him. And, of course, there was Vasso.

Vasso was living with a lawyer just a few blocks away. 'Take some of those new sleeping pills I got for you at the pharmacy,' she would suggest. 'I left them by your bed.'

She would do so, often waiting until dawn for them to take effect and while she waited she would turn off the sound on the television, images still moving on the screen, and play tapes on the machine she kept in her bedroom (and upon which she had formerly used to record her practice sessions); always of her performances, most them pirated, recorded by fans in the audience and sent or given to her. 'If I could live just three more years with my voice, I could die happy,' she repeated to the few visitors she had. But her voice would never return and she was only too painfully aware of the truth.

There were nights that were so bad that she would raise Bruna from her bed and ask her to sleep on the cot in her dressing room with the door opened between them. Loneliness was not her only demon. She genuinely feared the night. Vasso came in every morning at about 10 a.m. and gave her some amphetamines to awaken her. Neither Bruna nor Ferruccio knew exactly what Vasso's place was in Maria' current life. She was not exactly a secretary, nor was she merely a friend. She did not write her letters, nor did she answer the telephone unless Maria asked her to do so. She had her own key and came in and out during the day, and often in the evening, scolded the staff and issued curt orders in French; 'Madame Callas is not to be disturbed', 'Whatever telephone calls come in, direct them to me', 'Bring me a tray [for lunch] in the office'. *Please* and *thank you* were not a part of her vocabulary.

Rarely did her boyfriend, M. Jean Roire accompany her, when he did it was usually at a time when Maria had gone to the hairdresser's, one of the few outside excursions she made. Ferruccio claimed the man rifled through Maria's business papers. He was a quiet sort, a slight, balding man in horn-rimmed glasses, always nattily dressed, pocket handkerchief in place, ascot about his neck, in his late forties or early fifties.

Since Onassis's death, Maria had taken little interest in her business affairs. She was no longer singing, so had no need for an agent or manager. She had never liked the company of lawyers (which was, perhaps, why she never became friendly with Vasso's friend). An accounting firm paid her bills and took care of her taxes. She was by now an extremely wealthy woman with assets of over $15 million. Income from her recordings continued, but investments overseen by Onassis during their years together generated the greater part of her income. And then there was the multimillion-dollar collection of jewels he had given her, perhaps not as flashy as those owned by Elizabeth Taylor, but all of the finest quality, Cartier, Harry Winston, Asprey, Tiffany.

Every few months Madame Biki (her design label was 'Madame Biki, Milan'), travelled from Milan to Paris to Maria's apartment, with an assistant carrying bolts of fabric. Maria had developed a passion for caftans made of exotic embroidered brocades and silks, loose-fitting garments, to the floor, very dramatic, which she would wear to greet those guests who came – generally for tea in the afternoon or cocktails in the evening. She could no longer cope with dinner parties. Too many people she knew, she said, now either bored or irritated her. Hélène Rochas had enraged her by having an affair with Stavros Niarchos after Tina's tragic, and suspicious, death. Nadia Stancioff lived in London, but she spoke to her and saw her when she came to France. Di Stefano visited when he was in Paris. He had returned to Japan and sung three *Toscas* with Montserrat Caballé to more discouraging reviews. An old, vital photograph of Onassis had replaced his on the piano in the music room, but their affair had mellowed into what di Stefano called 'two soldiers who had fought a war together'.

Occasionally, someone arrived at her door with an offer. 'They want me to sing *The Merry Widow*,' she told Robert Sutherland who had continued their friendship and came to Paris from time to time to see her. 'It's all so undignified.'

'I began to fear what I would find each time I arrived in Paris,' he wrote in his memoir, *Maria Callas – Diaries of a Friendship*. 'Maria became very pessimistic, bitter even. She had run out of spiritual energy … Friends fell off, tired of last-minute changes, or the voice of Bruna on the telephone saying that Madame was unwell and must cancel the dinner appointment.' She had put on weight, indulging herself with chocolate and ice cream. 'As she walked she hunched her shoulders as though protecting herself. Her eyes, which I had seen so often blazing forth her feelings, had a faraway look, empty and unresponsive.'

Sleeping pills and amphetamines were greatly responsible. Ferruccio spoke to Vasso about this, concerned that she filled prescriptions and fed them to Maria indiscriminately. He received a curt look of annoyance. 'When she asks I give them to her,' was Vasso's reply.

'[Maria] was full of doubts,' Sutherland noted. 'She had no confidence in her own thoughts, any opinion she expressed was followed by, "Am I right?" We listened even more often to her recordings … "Now, let's hear some singing," she would say.'

Vasso managed always to arrive when Maria was having guests. From the hallway she would call, 'You're looking beautiful today, Maria,' in her stridently accented English; this was without truly looking at her – perhaps a glance as she walked past to busy herself in Maria's office. Vasso had long ago realized that flattery went a long way with Maria who, despite the dramatic woman the world saw, inside felt condemned to be the overweight young girl who had never been able to please even her mother.

There was something of Norma Desmond and *Sunset Boulevard* about Maria's life after Onassis and her voice died. What was missing was the one thing that had previously driven her on – the determination to survive. In the summer of 1976 she sent her sister a cheque and began to telephone her in Athens. Jackie said she didn't need to send her money. 'I wanted you to have a present,' she said. 'You're my only family now [not true, for Litza was still alive and living only a few streets from Jackie].' The now elderly Dr Lantzounis had visited Jackie in Athens before coming to Paris to see Maria. 'Godfather says you have a nice place, a beautiful garden on the terrace. Tell me about it,' she asked in another conversation. Jackie described 'the view from Mount Parnis and the big tubs of white and red roses and the real pine tree' that were the best features of a pleasant, modest apartment.

'And canaries?'

'Yes, just like the old days,' Jackie replied.

In September she made one of her middle-of-the-night calls to her sister and talked for over an hour. 'I don't go out much since...' Her voice faded for a moment. 'Aristo died. I want to die, too. Since I lost my voice I want to die.'

Jackie reprimanded her for talking that way and reminded her how much she had done for her art, that she had much she could still give the world...perhaps she needed to give another series of master classes. Maria just laughed.

Maria's fifty-third birthday had been on 2 December 1976. There was no celebration. She had always disdained such things. 'Mine, as a child, were never happy occasions,' she once said. 'Something would be promised, but it would never happen. I would rather have none than be disappointed.' She still nursed old wounds. Bruna surprised her with a beautiful cake and Ferruccio opened champagne. 'You are my family now,' she said as she kissed them both.

Nine months later, on the morning of 16 September, Bruna brought in a glass of orange juice and opened the curtains. A glittering streak of autumn sun sparked the room. Maria sat up as Pixie and Djedda jumped off the bed and followed Bruna out in expectation of their usual morning biscuits. About five minutes later Bruna returned with a pot of hot coffee, the dogs trotting after her, to find Maria collapsed on the floor at the entry to the bathroom. '*Mi sento male* [I feel unwell],' Maria said as Bruna rushed over to her. Maria attempted to get up, but slumped back on to the carpet. Bruna shouted for Ferruccio to come.

Between them, they lifted her and placed her on the bed. Her appearance alarmed them. Her face was pale white, her lips blue, her hands trembling and ice-cold, and she was having difficulty breathing. As Bruna fed her some coffee with a spoon, Ferruccio tried to get through to the American Hospital to ask for an ambulance. On several frantic tries the line remained busy and he finally rang his own physician whose office was only a few streets away. The doctor agreed to come over straight away, arrived perhaps fifteen minutes later and was greeted by a shaken Bruna. Maria was dead. Ferruccio took the dogs and closed them in the kitchen because they were wailing pitifully. Only moments passed after the doctor's arrival before Vasso appeared, called out 'Maria?' from the hallway and then entered the bedroom, believing at first that Maria had not awakened from a drugged sleep. Suddenly the truth sank in. She looked pale but contained as she walked over to the bed where Maria still reposed and stood there for a few moments before turning furiously and shouting at Bruna and Ferruccio that they should have telephoned her immediately.

'Who is the next of kin?' the doctor asked.

'There is no next of kin. I am Madame Callas's executor,' Vasso replied with great authority. Neither of these statements was the truth. Both Maria's mother and sister were still alive, and there was no legal proof that Vasso had ever been made her executor. Nonetheless, the doctor accepted Vasso's words. While they waited for the gendarmes (the death had to be reported to the police), Vasso took the doctor into Maria's office where they spoke for a time. No mention was made by Vasso of Maria's heavy dosages of sleeping pills and amphetamines. She picked up the death certificate later in the day. It stated that Maria had died of a heart attack, which is what the doctor stated to the investigating officer.

It was not until the following morning that Jackie received a call from a M. Jean Roire, informing her of her sister's death. She was too shocked and upset to enquire as to the caller's connection to Maria. She did ask how. *A heart attack*. And when and where was the funeral? *In three days in Paris*. Jackie dressed quickly and walked at a wild clip to her mother's apartment. Litza was inconsolable. She was also very frail and Jackie knew she could not have endured the journey nor the emotional trauma of attending Maria's funeral. She managed to pull together enough money for the trip to Paris and arrived the following day. When she reached Maria's apartment (the first time she had ever been there), she was met at the door by Vasso who led her into Maria's bedroom where she was laid out on her bed. Bruna had washed and dressed her in a grey chiffon gown and arranged her long hair elegantly. Her hands were crossed on her chest. She wore no make-up and her lips were pale.

'She was really lovely,' Jackie recalled. 'It made a deep impression on me. I don't understand it. She was never more beautiful than she was in death.' Shortly after Jackie's arrival di Stefano was announced. Vasso instantly issued orders that he was not to be allowed up to the apartment. She had completely taken over and her autocratic behaviour led Jackie to believe that she must have been Maria's agent or manager. Vasso suggested that Jackie return to her hotel to rest and that she would be picked up by a limousine an hour before the funeral, which was at four thirty the next afternoon. It was assumed that Maria would be buried.

The service was held in the Greek Orthodox Church in rue Bizet (composer of *Carmen* – an opera that Maria had never sung on stage). The church was filled with tributes of flowers – vases bursting with expensive bouquets from Christina and Artemis, enormous wreaths from Covent Garden, La Scala and the Metropolitan Opera House, more from the Churchill family, and the Presidents of Greece and France. A rectangular cushion of red, yellow and orange marigolds was inscribed 'Grace and

Rainier' (Princess Grace had become fairly friendly with Maria after Onassis left Monaco). On the top of the coffin was a simple bunch of garden flowers – white and red like those in Jackie's flower boxes in Greece – from her sister and her mother. No one had sent red roses. Vasso managed to place Jackie so far to one side that she had little or no contact with the rest of the mourners, who did not even know that Maria's sister was among them.

When the coffin slid into the hearse, believed to being taken for private burial, 'a lone man lifted his hands in the air, and began to clap, "Brava, Callas!" Within a moment his applause was taken up by the tense crowd...men and women were weeping as they cried "Brava, Diva!"' The hearse was actually carrying Maria's body to its cremation. The hastiness of this decision, the fact that Vasso had allowed no one to be consulted, brought about serious questions. Did Maria leave these instructions in her will? There was no will, Vasso asserted. Oh, there had been one drafted a while back, but Maria had never signed it and, she said, it contained no interment instructions. Maria had never spoken to Bruna or Ferruccio about a wish to be cremated and it was not a usual or accepted course in the Greek Orthodox Church. Rumours of suicide persisted, leading to the possibility – could it be? – of murder. And if so, who would have had a reason to kill Maria Callas?

One thing agreed to later by medical doctors was that Maria had not died of a heart attack. The symptoms described by Bruna of Maria's condition the previous day – breathlessness and back pain – and the account of the morning of her death, indicated an infarction of the lungs – a massive pulmonary infarction. 'A thrombo-embolism travelled from the legs up through the blood system and finally blocked the pulmonary artery,' was the doctor's analysis. '[Maria] was taking pills to sleep, pills to wake up, she was depressed, her circulation slow. All these circumstances – being inactive, lying in bed a lot, lack of exercise, the pills – are usual causes of pulmonary infarction.'[1]

That seems logical and possible, although the symptoms, according to other physicians, could still indicate a coronary thrombosis or heart seizure, caused by a blood clot travelling directly to the heart. Since Vasso took care to get the body to the crematorium quickly, without requesting an autopsy or an inquest, or announcing her intentions to anyone else including Jackie, no one will ever be likely to know. Why Vasso made this decision on her own is suspect, what the motive might have been a mystery.

[1] This diagnosis was made by Dr Andreas Stathopoulos who married Jackie Callas in 1984 and did some research on his wife's behalf.

Vasso Devetzi's intentions were, however, not a mystery. They were cunning and Machiavellian, certainly well planned. She was after Maria's money and she almost succeeded in taking it all. The will that could not be found – although said to be unsigned – had made Bruna and Ferruccio her principal beneficiaries. Vasso had been advised that in French law Maria's mother and sister could claim the inheritance if there was no will. Before Jackie returned to Athens, Vasso assured her that as Maria's 'closest and dearest' friend, she wanted to make sure that her family was compensated. Jackie, never the most clever of women, was told not to worry, she – Vasso – 'would guide her through the tedious intricacies of French law and business... You and your mother will be very rich,' she confided.

Before the funeral she had decided on a plan to create a trust in Maria's name with herself as director with sole authority to write cheques and disperse the money, and that she would convince Jackie and Mrs Callas to assign the largest part of their inheritance over to this 'foundation'. Whether she was alone in this enterprise is also a mystery. Vasso appeared confident that she could appease Jackie with a small slice of Maria's estate for her mother, which would eventually go to her. What she did not anticipate was the sudden appearance two days after the funeral of Meneghini and an Italian lawyer who had with him documents stating that, as in Italy their divorce had not been recognized, he was still Maria's husband and entitled to her entire estate.

Vasso had to do some fast talking. Maria had died in France and was a Greek citizen. For Meneghini to win his claim he would have to go to court in France where he did not speak the language and where his legal fees would be astronomical. This was also something that Vasso needed desperately to avoid as she then stood a strong chance of being exposed as not having any legal rights to become executor of Maria's estate. She offered Meneghini a settlement. He would receive half her holdings and the monies from the sale of the apartment, if he signed an agreement releasing any claim he might think he had. The rest, including Maria's copyrights and with the exception of 'some small personal bequests that she knew Maria would want', would go to the Maria Callas Foundation to encourage and give grants to worthy young singers and musicians. When Meneghini was told the size of the estate, he became malleable – *but* he wanted Maria's jewellery. Certain pieces, Vasso agreed, the others and the contents of the apartment would be placed at auction and the money derived from the sale would also go to the Foundation.

Meneghini (apparently advised to do so by his representative) signed the documents Vasso had had drawn up, which were duly filed with the court. By inheriting half of Maria's estate Meneghini would be rich beyond his grandest dreams and the much younger woman, Emma Roverselli-Brutti, with whom he now lived (he told people she was his housekeeper)[2] would be bedecked with jewels – parcelled out slowly and guaranteed to keep her by his side (Meneghini was now in his eighties).

Vasso was a clever crook and one who hid her deviousness behind an aristocratic front. From the time that she had insinuated herself into Maria's life, she had become a far more stylish and polished woman. She *looked* and had the demeanour of a woman whom Maria would have trusted to manage her affairs. Maria had, in fact, allowed Vasso to do banking for her and sign for shopping purchases in her name at her favourite shops. But there is good reason to believe that she was never completely taken in by Vasso, but with the falling away of her old friends, her growing neurosis and her accelerating isolation and loneliness, allowed herself to become dependent upon her.

Sutherland recalls that on one visit that he made to Maria in the last year of her life, when Vasso was out of hearing, she 'lifted her eyes to the ceiling and shrugged her shoulders, "She's company," she said.'

Still fearing Meneghini could cause trouble, Vasso turned her attention to Jackie and Litza, who was in deep mourning, rocking, sobbing. 'Why didn't I die first?' she kept repeating. She had written a poem in her grief. 'Little bird, you have flown away and left me lonesome in the dark nights,' it began. Vasso rang Jackie and offered to pay her expenses for her to return to Paris 'to fight for rights if Meneghini decided to go to court, after all'. The idea that Meneghini might try to claim all of her Maria's estate enraged Litza who insisted that Jackie do as Vasso had said.

Back in Paris, Jackie saw Meneghini for the first time in twenty-nine years and did not like him any better than she had at the outset. With Jackie represented by a lawyer of Vasso's choice and a notarized letter

---

[2] Meneghini claimed, in his memoir, that he had refused to take anything that had been given to Maria by Onassis. This was not true. Ms Roverselli-Brutti was seen to wear rings that Onassis had given to Callas. And, of course, the investments that generated the larger part of the money in her estate had been given to and made for her by Onassis. When Callas left Meneghini he had taken most of the money she had earned until that point. She had been left with under $75,000 and part of their possessions from the apartment in Milan.

Meneghini died in 1986 leaving his entire estate (mainly consisting of Callas's fortune and personal possessions) to Roverselli-Brutti. Shortly thereafter, she sold most of Callas's former personal possessions (including those Meneghini had retained before they separated) to a private collector, Ilario Thomassia, as well as to several private archives in Italy. On 2–3 December 2000 these items, plus some that Jackie Callas sold to a Greek journalist, Nicolas Petsalis-Diomidis (the author of the Greek book, *The Unknown Callas*), were put on auction in New York by Leftbid.com after an international tour.

giving her the authority to speak for her mother, she faced Meneghini across a negotiating table to get him to sign an agreement not to contest his former document (as signed under emotional stress) and to accept Evangelia Callas as the legal, half-owner of her daughter's estate.[3] The matter was not settled at this meeting, a second one being scheduled for the following day.

Later, Jackie and Vasso sat in Maria's kitchen drinking coffee which Bruna had served them. 'Does Bruna still get her salary?' she asked when Bruna had left the room.

Vasso ignored the question, but Jackie persisted. Vasso told her that Maria had never paid Bruna and Ferruccio a salary. She had fed and housed them for twenty-seven years, sent small sums to their families in Italy and given them gifts during the years. With a small sneer she said that Maria never liked to think of them as servants. Jackie then decided (without knowing the wishes of Maria in her unsigned will) that Maria would have wanted these two loyal retainers to be shown her gratitude. Vasso was much against this, but backed down in the face of Jackie's adamant attitude.

The next day the settlement between the two sides was agreed upon and included a substantial sum (said to be $100,000 each) to be paid equally from both shares to Bruna and Ferruccio (far from the millions they would have received if Maria had had her wishes granted). Bruna was also given the two small poodles, whom she took with her when she returned later to her village in Italy. When Jackie and Vasso were finally alone once more, Vasso informed her that 'just before Maria had died', she had told her that she wanted a scholarship trust to be established in her name to help young singers.

To Jackie this sounded reasonable.

'You won't live for ever,' Vasso pressed on, asserting that after both her mother and Jackie had died, their inheritance should be left to this same trust. 'Of course,' she went on, 'there was a problem as there was as yet no foundation, or other institution' for Jackie to leave the money to. But never mind, she had a solution; if Jackie made a will leaving everything to her, she would see that it went to the right source.

Once back in Athens, Litza, with Jackie's encouragement, agreed. They

---

[3] The irony of this is that had Jackie Callas had proper counsel in Greece, she would have discovered that Meneghini actually had no rights in her sister's estate. This was because Maria had denounced her American citizenship and taken Greek citizenship. Therefore, since she had not married Meneghini in the Greek Orthodox Church, she was never legally considered his wife. Had the estate been settled in a Greek court, without a signed will, Evangelia Callas would have inherited the entire proceeds.

would still be very rich and Maria's wishes would be carried out. It was also agreed that all monies as they came in from the estate would go directly to the foundation which, as its director, Vasso could draw cheques on and disburse to Litza in Athens. An agreement was also made that Jackie and Vasso would meet in Paris in four months' time to 'divide the more portable items in the apartment'. There would then be an auction for what remained, the revenues to be divided half to Meneghini, the other half to Mrs Callas. It seemed that the mother whom Maria had cut out of her life and who had given her such unhappiness would now benefit greatly from her daughter's death. It was only at this point that Vasso rented a small space next to a shoeshine parlour in Geneva (she had established a Swiss account) in the name of the Maria Callas Foundation.

Jackie returned to Paris on 6 January 1978 and Vasso took her to the apartment where Meneghini was already going through cupboards and drawers with Signora Roverselli-Brutti, and an officer of the court who had come to remove the seals on everything in the apartment.[4] It was nearly nightfall before the exhausted group, Jackie in an emotional state having gone through her sister's most personal things – lingerie, perfumes, clothing, letters – ended their mission. Signora Roverselli-Brutti had been packing up Meneghini's selections in the dozens of boxes that they had delivered, and these were now stacked neatly on one side of the grand salon and in the entrance hall. Jackie's selection was spread out on the dining-room table and in the kitchen, unpacked. Vasso had told her that she should take back to Athens the objects she felt most meaningful and she would arrange for the rest of them to be placed on exhibition.

That Jackie was so easily taken in is not so amazing. Here was a woman who had allowed her mother to rule over her for her entire life, and who had entered into a no-end, no-win situation with Milton Embiricos, a member of one of Greece's richest maritime families and after many years – most of them nursing a cancer-ridden, horribly deformed man – was left in penury, having been pushed out of any claim by his family. Jackie's self-confidence and will had long ago been lost. She was a good woman, of much better temperament than her sister. But her sense of

---

[4] Ferruccio was to say that in the short three-day span between Callas's death and her funeral, while he and Bruna were working to close the apartment, Vasso had appeared daily and left with numerous small items from Maria's various collections – her Limoges and Sèvres boxes, the enamelled Asian pieces, jewelled Cartier frames and small clocks. These items Ferruccio and Bruna could clearly see had gone missing. There could only be speculation on what else might have been taken. None of these valuable possessions ever reappeared.

self-worth was nil and she possessed no greed for what she had been
deprived of. Jackie was accustomed to living a humble life and felt comfortable with it. Vasso sensed her weakness immediately (and from discussions she had had with Maria about her family). Having been unable
to stand up to her mother, she could not muster the courage to do so to
Vasso. She had even made and signed a will at Vasso's urging, making the
Maria Callas Foundation her beneficiaries.

The following June an auction of Maria's remaining possessions was
held in the grand salon of the apartment. Jackie did not attend;
Meneghini did, buying what he claimed Maria had taken with her when
she left him. The profits from the auction were then divided (Meneghini
thus not really paying for what he purchased) between the two heirs.
Vasso had made an arrangement with Jackie (who handled Litza's affairs)
that cheques would be sent periodically to her as they came due from the
estate and she would then sign them and send them back to her, to be
deposited in the account of the Maria Callas Foundation. Vasso then sent
Jackie funds to Athens at various times, never grand amounts but more
money than either mother or daughter had ever seen at one time in their
lives. (Jackie writes in her memoir, *Sisters*, that the first cheque she sent
back to Vasso was for $300,000.)

Suddenly, to Vasso's horror, Litza decided – and Jackie could do
nothing but agree – to move from Athens to Paris where she could enjoy
her last years playing out the role of the great diva Maria Callas's mother.
When Jackie called Vasso to tell her of this decision she was appalled and
tried to convince her not to contemplate such a thing. After all, what
would Litza do in Paris? Jackie insisted it was her mother's wish and she
must abide by it. 'There was a pause while I heard her talking to
someone, presumably M. Roire, in French,' Jackie wrote. 'It was too rapid
for me to follow but I could guess that she was passing on the news to her
friend. I heard him speak and then Vasso came back to me: "When do
you want to come?" she asked.'

They decided to leave straight away. Vasso took over the details. A
comfortable apartment in Neuilly, out of the centre of Paris, was found
and they arrived during a cold snap in November 1978. Vasso had furnished the apartment with some of Maria's furniture, which had not
been included in the auction and which just seemed to appear. There was
one very beautiful chest and the piano, but the rest were odd pieces and
some that had come out of Bruna's and Ferruccio's quarters and the
kitchen. She also hired a Portuguese maid for them.

At Christmas the shocking news was heard that Maria's ashes had
been stolen from their resting place in the Père-Lachaise cemetery. 'It was

obviously her ex-husband Meneghini who has stolen my daughter's remains,' Litza told a reporter. '[He] seems to believe that everything that was hers must now be his – including her ashes.' Later the same day the ashes were found in another section of the cemetery, obviously as a ghoulish prank. Vasso immediately decided that a ceremony should be arranged and Maria's ashes scattered on the Aegean Sea, which she had sailed upon happily so often with Onassis on the *Christina*.

This was organized by Vasso with the co-operation of the Greek government, only too glad to bring their most famous diva back to her home in Greece. Litza was too ill to attend, but Jackie did, Vasso keeping her well in the background as she commanded the entire procedure. Bruna and Ferruccio were also on board the naval destroyer that had been lent for the occasion. A high wind rose just as the ashes were being offered to the blustery sea, and some of them flew back and landed on the clothes of the mourners. Jackie felt a smudge on her face. It was a horrifying moment, one she would never be able to erase from her mind.

Vasso now told Jackie that due to all her work for the Foundation she had had to desert her own 'international career as a concert pianist' and was nearly out of funds. She thought there could be some way for her to receive a comfortable enough stipend so that she could carry on with Maria's wishes. It seems incredible, but Jackie questioned none of this, feeling only compassion for this woman who had done so much for Maria and her family. Maria's jewel box was then taken from a vault and a goodly portion of the precious gifts given to her by Onassis handed over to Vasso, to sell on her own behalf.[5]

Evangelia Callas died in 1982, in Athens, to which she and Jackie had returned. Jackie, her mother's heir, was duped by Vasso for several more years – there was a huge tax bill on the Foundation that must be paid, always some excuse to get her to sign over another six-figure sum of money. Not until 1985 when Jackie, in her mid-sixties, married Dr Andreas Stathopoulos did she come to the full realization of the crime that had been perpetrated by Vasso. There was only a storefront and no real Maria Callas Foundation. No singers had been helped. Nor could any of the money that had been fraudulently taken be accounted for. But by the time legal action could be filed, Vasso had terminal cancer and died, taking her secret bag of tricks with her.

---

[5] $1,570,000 was turned over to Vasso Devetzi in her name and that of the bogus Foundation between 1978 and 1980. '...Such enormous sums of money were meaningless to someone like me who had always been used to scraping and saving,' Jackie Callas later wrote.

Callas was a phenomenon of her own making, a force in the world of opera. Her career was relatively brief but its impact was lasting. She was that rare opera singer who connects on an emotional level with an audience. She brought the women she portrayed alive – Norma, Tosca, Violetta. Although their voices might have been technically better, no other opera singer of the twentieth century spoke to people as she did. She changed opera, opened its heart, revealed its deepest meanings and her imprint will remain. Listening to Callas on any one of the many dozens of recordings she made is like opening a window and letting life enter your room. Life has many imperfections and so did Maria the woman. But life goes on, it survives, and so will Callas: unforgettable, distinctive – the prima donna assoluta for ever.

Bibliography

Allegri, Renzo & Roberto; *Callas by Callas*, Universe U.S., 1998

Ardoin, John; *Callas at Juillard: The Master Classes*, Robson Books, London, 1988

    The Callas Legacy, Duckworth, London, 1977

    (with Fitzgerald, Gerald): *Callas: The Great Years*, Holt, Rinehart and Winston, New York, 1974

Bing, Rudolph, Sir; *5000 Nights at the Opera*, Doubleday, N.Y., 1972

Brady, Frank; *Onassis – An Extravagant Life*, Prentice-Hall, N.J., 1977

Callas, Evangelina (with L. Blochman); *My Daughter, Maria Callas*, Fleet Pub., N.Y.

Callas, Jackie; *Sisters*, Pan Books, London, 1990

Capote, Truman; *A Capote Reader*, Random House, N.Y., 1987

Churchill, Winston S.; *The Second World War Vol I – VI*, Cassell, London, 1949

Clarke, Gerald; *Capote*, Random House, N.Y., 1988

Collier, Peter & Horowitz, David; *The Kennedys: An American Drama*, Summit, N.Y., 1984

Downes, Edward; *Bel Canto in 1956*, Opera Annual, Calder, London, 1956

DuBois, Diana; *In Her Sister's Shadow*, Little, Brown & Company, N.Y., 1995

Dufresne, Claude; *La Callas*, Perrin, Paris, 1990

Edwards, Anne; *The Grimaldis of Monaco*, Morrow, N.Y., 1992

Evans, Peter; *Ari: The Life and Times of Aristotle Socrates Onassis*, Jonathan Cape, Ltd., London, 1986

Fraser, Jacobson Ottoway & Chester; *Aristotle Onassis*, Lippincott, N.Y., 1977

Frischauer, Willi; *Onassis*, Meredith Press, N.Y., 1968

Galatopoulos, Stelios; *Callas, La Divina*, Dent, London, 1966

    Callas: Prima Donna Assoluta, W.H. Allen, London, 1976

    Callas: Sacred Monster, Simon & Schuster, N.Y., 1998

Gatti-Casazza, Giulio; *Memories of the Opera*, John Calder, London, 1977

Gobbi, Tito; *My Life*, Macdonald & Jane's, London, 1979

Grobel, Lawrence; *Conversations With Capote*, New American Library, N.Y., 1985

Haltrect, Montague; *The Quiet Showman*, Collins, London, 1975

Harewood, George, Earl; *The Tongs and the Bones: Autobiography*, Weidenfeld & Nicolson, London, 1981

Harvey, Jacques; *Mon Ami Onassis*, Editions Albin Michel, Paris, 1979

    (with Christian Cafarakis), *The Fabulous Onassis*, Morrow, N.Y., 1972

Heymann, C. David; *A Woman Named Jackie*, Lyle Stuart, N.Y., 1989

Jellinek, George; *Callas: Portrait of a Prima Donna*, Dover, N.Y., 1986

Kazanantzakis, Nikos; *Report to Greco*, Simon & Schuster, N.Y., 1965

Kesting, Jurgen; *Maria Callas*, Quartet, London, 1992

Klein, Edward; *Just Jackie: Her Private Years*, Ballantine Books, N.Y., 1998

La Rochelle, Real; *Callas: La Diva et le Vinyle*, Triptyque, Quebec, Canada, 1987

Lee, Arthur S. Gould; *The Royal House of Greece*, Ward, Lock, London, 1948

Lowe, David Allen, Editor; *Callas As They Saw Her* (criticism), Unger, N.Y., 1986

Maxwell, Elsa; *RSVP*, Little, Brown, Boston, 1954
   The Celebrity Circus, Appleton-Century, N.Y., 1963

Meneghini, Giovanni Battista; *My Wife Maria Callas*, Farrar, Straus, Giroux, N.Y., 1982

Merlin, Oliver; *Le Bel Canto*, René Julliard, Paris, 1961

Nicolas, HRH Prince of Greece; *My Fifty Years*, Hutchinson, London, 1953

Nowakowski, Tadeusz; *The Radziwills*, Delacorte, N.Y., 1974

Peyser, Joan; *Bernstein*, Beech Tree Books, Morrow, N.Y., 1987

Remy, Pierre-Jean; *Maria Callas: A Tribute*, Macdonald and Jane's, London, 1978

Rosenthal, Harold; *Great Singers of Today*, Calder and Boyars, London, 1966
   Two Centuries of Opera at Covent Garden, Putnam, London, 1958

Rushmore, Robert; *The Singing Voice*, Hamish Hamilton, London, 1971

Scott, Michael; *Maria Meneghini Callas*, Simon & Schuster, N.Y., 1991

Segalini, Sergio; *Callas: Portrait of a Diva*, Hutchinson, London, 1981

Serafin, Tullio; *A Triptych of Singers*, Opera Annual, John Calder, London, 1962

Seroff, Victor; *Renata Tebaldi*, Appleton, Century, Crofts, N.Y., 1961

Servadio, Gaia; *Luchino Visconti*, Franklin Watts, N.Y., 1983

Stancioff, Nadia; *Maria Callas Remembered*, Dutton, N.Y., 1987

Stassinopoulos, Arianna; *Maria Callas, the Woman Behind the Legend*, Simon & Schuster, N.Y., 1981

Stirling, Monica; *Visconti: A Screen of Time*, Harcourt Brace Jovanovich, N.Y., 1979

Sutherland, Joan; *A Prima Donna's Progress*, Weidenfeld & Nicolson, London, 1999

Sutherland, Robert; *Maria Callas: Diaries of a Friendship*, Constable, London, 1999

Wisneski, Henry; *Maria Callas: The Art Behind the Legend*, Doubleday, N.Y., 1975

Wright, William; *All the Pain that Money can Buy – Christina Onassis*, Victor Gollancz, London, 1991

Zeffirelli, Franco; *Autobiography*, Weidenfeld & Nicolson, London, 1986

Articles

After Dark – October 1969; February 1974

Arts – December 10, 1958

Atlantic Monthly – August 1981, 'The True Biography of Maria Callas.'

Chicago Tribune – November 21, 1954

Dallas Morning News – November 8, 1958

Fugue – 'Maria Callas' (John Ardoin), December 1978

Life – April 20, 1959; April 10, 1960; October 30, 1964

Look – February 17, 1959 ('Sacred Soprano.')

Newsweek – April 9, 1959; February 15, 1971

The New Yorker – February 7, 1959; March 26, 1965; April 27, 1981

New York Review of Books – April 2, 1981 (Joseph Kerman)

New York Times – March 21, 1965; November 30, 1970; November 26, 1978; March 1, 1981 ('Maria Callas Her Decline and Fall.')

Opera – 'Tullio Serafin' – March, 1968

Opera News – 'An Ancient Woman' – December 13, 1969
   'Callas Legacy Updated' – August 1978
   'Splendor in the Night' – November 1977
   'Chicago' – May, 1981
   'The Callas Class' – April 15, 1972

Saturday Review – Callas, Serafin, and the Art of Bel Canto,' March 30, 1968; January 31, 1959 (Teodoro Celli.)

Spectator – 'Fact and Fiction About Callas,' October 1, 1977

The Sunday Times – Interview with Derek Prouse, March 19, 1961

Time – (Cover Story) 'The Prima Donna,' October 29, 1956; March 26, 1965

The Times (London) – November 16, 1971

Vision – 'In Search of Callas,' December 1978

Woman's Wear Daily – November 23, 1970

(Sources of reviews are quoted in the text.)

Television and Radio Interviews

(Museum of Broadcasting – N.Y.)

Callas – South Bank Show, LWT, London, 1987

Callas – 'Life and Art', Kultur 1168 video cassette.

Edward R. Murrow – TV January 24, 1958

Callas – Radio interview with Harry Fleetwood, 1958 (school days)

David Frost – TV December 10, 1970

Mike Wallace – TV 'Sixty Minutes', February 3, 1974

Today – TV with Barbara Walters, April 15, 1974

National Public Radio – 'Callas in Her Own Words', 4 hour documentary, on Pale Music Cassettes, PM001-1-4 (1957–1972)

EBCA – radio, documentary on Callas, December 2, 1978

BBC – David Holmes TV interview, November 29, 1973

Archival Material

Museum of Broadcasting, New York

Museum of the City of New York

Metropolitan Opera New York

Covent Garden London

Astoria, L.I. Historical Society

British Library

Churchill Library

Index